The Collected Works of Edith Stein

V

EDITH STEIN

Sister Teresa Benedicta of the Cross
Discalced Carmelite

SELF-PORTRAIT IN LETTERS

1916-1942

Translated by Josephine Koeppel, O.C.D.

ICS Publications
Institute of Carmelite Studies
Washington, D.C.
1993

The Collected Works
of
EDITH STEIN

Sister Teresa Benedicta of the Cross
Discalced Carmelite
1891-1942

Edited by
Dr. L. Gelber
and
Romaeus Leuven, O.C.D.

Volume Five

ICS Publications
Institute of Carmelite Studies
Washington, D.C.
1993

The original of this work was published in German in two volumes by Archivum Carmelitanum Edith Stein under the titles of (Band VIII)
Selbstbildnis in Briefen: Erster Teil, 1916-1934
and (Band IX)
Selbstbildnis in Briefen: Zweiter Teil, 1934-1942
Translation authorized.

ICS Publications
2131 Lincoln Road NE
Washington, DC 20002-1199

Typeset and produced in the U.S.A.

Photos used with permission of Cologne Carmel and Archivum Carmelitanum Edith Stein

Library of Congress Cataloging-in-Publication Data

Stein, Edith, 1891-1942.
[Selbstbildnis in Briefen. English]
Self-Portrait in Letters, 1916-1942 / Edith Stein, Sister Teresa Benedicta of the Cross, Discalced Carmelite, translated by Josephine Koeppel.
p. cm. — (The collected works of Edith Stein, Sister Teresa Benedicta of the Cross, Discalced Carmelite, 1891-1942; ISSN v. 5)
Translation of : Selbstbildnis in Briefen.
Includes index.
ISBN: 0-935216-20-0
1. Stein, Edith, 1891-1942—Correspondence. 2. Carmelite nuns—Germany—Correspondence. 3. Philosophers—Germany—Correspondence. I. Koeppel, Josephine. II. Title. III. Series : Stein, Edith, 1891-1942. Works. English. 1986; v. 5.
B3332.S672E54 1986
[BS4705.S814A4]
193 s—dc20
[193] 93-18621
[B] CIP

Contents

Laetatus sum in his quae dicta sunt mihi: in domum Domini ibimus. – Ich freute mich, da mir gesagt wurde: wir wollen ins Haus des Herrn gehen.

In der Hoffnung, daß ich recht bald wieder aus dem gastlichen Haus an der Holzbrücke ins „Haus des Herrn" gehen darf, und in herzlicher Dankbarkeit

9. IV. 28.

Dr. Edith Stein
Speyer/Rh. Kloster St. Magdalena.

"I rejoiced when I heard them say, let us go to the House of the Lord."

Letter 46: Edith Stein's first entry in the guestbook of the Mayer family, with whom she often stayed during her visits to the Benedictine abbey in Beuron.

Translator's Preface

Translation, a craft that comes with tools and develops skills, is also a science and an art. I now have another perspective—it can be a school of fidelity. Conscience is the monitor; style, the tempter; dedication, the teacher. After 20 years of apprenticeship, it is still necessary to drill in fundamentals. One might call these ABCs, but always guided by the "law of laws" so clearly expressed by Edith Stein herself: that the translator must be and remain invisible. How, then, can a translator add a personal note? Through the very ABCs, perhaps?

Acknowledgments should come first. I am especially grateful to the late Father Romaeus Leuven, OCD, his successor Michael Linssen, OCD, and Dr. Lucy Gelber, for their years of painstaking effort as editors of *Edith Steins Werke* and curators of the *Archivum Carmelitanum Edith Stein.* Special thanks are due to many others who have assisted me over the years, including: Alphonse Kroese, OCD, provincial of the Dutch province; John Sullivan, OCD, Kieran Kavanaugh, OCD, and the late Adrian Cooney, OCD, of ICS Publications; Jude Langsam, OCDS, for her skillful editing; the Carmelite communities of Cologne, Germany, and Beek, The Netherlands[1] (as well as my own community of Elysburg, PA); and Edith Stein's natural family, especially Susanne Batzdorff (her niece) and Susanne's husband, Alfred.

Bonding with Edith and her world has followed from the years of work, and creates a blessing and a challenge. Having Edith's thoughts constantly in one's mind has been tremendously enriching. The translation of *Life in a Jewish Family* demanded a thorough knowledge of the contents of the entire book, because while Edith was writing any part, *she knew* everything else that would be written, even before she thought of expressing it. This holds, to a large extent, for the letters also. It proved necessary to keep in mind all the concrete details about her family, education, employment and vocation. The intangible details regarding the feelings and emotions expressed in her letters had to be discerned through what I term bonding—sensing along with her what was behind the words. Her thought had to be respected so thoroughly that nothing was taken for granted when choosing one English expression rather than another to convey her meaning.

And so, the **challenge:** to allow the individuality of her communication with each correspondent to stand out as clearly in English as it does in her excellent German. Edith was as warmly open to others in her letters as she was when meeting them in person, but there are degrees to that warmth. Her love, her solicitude, her humor, and, similarly, her determination and sense of justice come through in a great variety of ways, depending upon whom she is addressing. This challenges a translator to constant vigilance to express, without repetition *or* exaggeration, her gift for being "all things to all her correspondents," and especially a most faithful and honest friend.

Though more of Edith Stein's correspondence has come to light since the German edition of this collection first appeared, and will no doubt be published and translated in the future, even now these 349 letters, in whole or in excerpt, present a valuable portrait of this great woman.

Sr. Josephine Koeppel, OCD
Carmel, Elysburg, Pennsylvania

1. [The community of Discalced Carmelite nuns that received Edith Stein (Sister Teresa Benedicta of the Cross) in Echt, The Netherlands, when she had to leave Germany, has merged with the Carmel of Beek, The Netherlands, where they now reside. Several nuns who lived with Edith in 1942 shared their memories with me in 1975 and 1987.]

Editor's Preface

We could think of no more fitting words as Preface to Volumes VIII and IX of *Edith Steins Werke* than the introductory quotation of J. H. Cardinal Newman's *Letters and Diaries,* translated by Edith Stein[1]:

> It has ever been a hobby of mine (unless it be a truism, not a hobby) that a man's life lies in his letters.... So, not only for the interest of a biography, but for arriving at the inside of things, the publication of letters is the true method. Biographers varnish—assign motives, conjecture feelings—they interpret Lord Burleigh's nods, but contemporary letters are facts.[2]

This quotation reminds me of the answer my erstwhile teacher of mysticism gave when a classmate of mine asked a question during the explanation of the *Interior Castle* of our Holy Mother St. Teresa. "Does our Holy Mother always soar at such heights?" The answer was: "If you want to know St. Teresa, then begin by studying her letters."

Therefore the *Archivum Carmelitanum Edith Stein* publishes this collection of letters in order to give a sense of Edith Stein's creative ability, an ability by which Edith Stein grasps the appearances of things and persons in their spiritual, living context, draws them into her own life and, in doing so, portrays herself and the other persons.

Edith Stein's scholarly understanding broadens the horizon of her spiritual world, but at the same time sets in motion her will and her feelings all the more. She writes on this in *Act and Potency:*[3]

> A person's inner dispositions and emotions stand between her intellectual perception of the world and her construct of the world by the will. As a rule, meeting a spiritual subject is not merely an intellectual encounter; there is an inner contact and a challenge to take a stand. The contact is characterized in opposites: as pleasant or unpleasant, the corresponding attitude as acceptance or rejection, in its highest form as love or hatred. When the being one meets

is a person, then acceptance and rejection take the form of love and hatred.

When reading this collection of letters we meet many and very different persons, but the person of the letter-writer herself remains the same, and her essential quality manifests itself with steadily increasing clarity precisely through this multiplicity of persons and personal relationships. Therefore, the mind's eye of the reader will form a mental image of Edith Stein that, without doubt, will resemble my perception of her.

Edith Stein seemed to me the personification of truth as Kierkegaard presents it in existential thought: Her answer to questions and problems was open; her depiction of her own situation, straightforward. Edith Stein's tie with eternity was one of faith: There her love found its highest intensity in confidence in the providence of God, when the darkness in this world cast its shadow on life's earthly path. Thus she showed the truth of the words of Pope John XXIII: "The only way to be happy in this life is to be ready to accommodate oneself to the will of God."

Openness, simplicity, and confidence radiate from Edith Stein's letters, for these qualities undergird her own experience of life, and do so to the ultimate sacrifice of that life. May the reading of this self-portrait in letters help many also to meet their neighbor with the Yes of love, so that, in doing so, *we* experience that love is, simultaneously, grace.

P. Romaeus a S. Teresia, OCD

1. J. H. Newman, *Briefe und Tagebücher bis zum Übertritt zur Kirche,* translated by Edith Stein, was published in Munich, 1928.
2. [The quotation is given here in Newman's own words, not in a retranslation of Edith's German. Newman repeated these comments almost verbatim in a letter to his sister Jemima in May, 1863.]
3. An unpublished essay written in 1931. The manuscript is preserved in the *Archivum Carmelitanum Edith Stein.*

Editors' Foreword

Orientation and Compilation

The orientation of Volumes VIII and IX within the *Edith Steins Werke* is at once indicated by the joint title given to them: *Self-Portrait in Letters.* They constitute the transition, a meaningful bridge, between Volume VII, which brings the autobiography as far as [Edith's] professional maturity, and Volume X, which is to continue the story to her life's fulfillment and end.[1]

This, at the same time, determines the way the collection is compiled. It aims to reproduce, authentically, the material at hand, while excluding family letters and without expanding to include an exchange of correspondence between Edith and the circle of her friends. All letters, or in some cases cards or short messages, that private persons, archives and publishers have put at our disposition have been arranged according to a threefold evaluation to form a chronological as well as contextual whole.

In part, the value of the letters lies in their "self-evidence." They contain questions and answers, references and cross-references, situations and reactions. They present a soliloquy addressed to an imagined person whose outline is clearly recognizable or perceptible. They refer to events and dates that can be confirmed.

Part of the particular worth of the letters lies in their diversified as well as informative content. They bring together a variegated multiplicity of happenings and meetings; of the past, present and future; of what is easy or difficult, distressing or elevating, painful or joyful. In this way, figuratively speaking, a comprehensive look at the letters reveals Edith painting a colorful picture of a destiny experienced and endured.

Beyond that, dividing the letters according to content and to the phases of [her] life is very informative. Such a division sketches, through its variety of counterbalances, a portrait that is true to life with its emphasis, appropriately, at any given time on characteristic traits rather than on insignificant details. It also illustrates with fitting shading the decisive and the less important segments and stages of [her] life.

Thus the present collection comprises a series of 350 letters to approximately 100 persons, some of whom are important personalities in either the secular or religious sector. This gives the combined eighth and ninth volume[2] its particularly significant meaning in the framework of Edith Stein's writings: as a biography, a philosophical document, a pedagogical declaration, a religious testimony.

Documents and Documentation

The documents, for the most part, are letters with or without envelopes, and a small number of plain and picture postcards, as well as small notebook pages. They are all written by hand, mostly in ink. The script is clearly legible and easy to read for anyone familiar with Edith Stein's handwriting.

Only the letters to Professor Roman Ingarden are not known to us in their original, complete version.[3] We have all the rest of the documents either in the original, in photocopy, or in certified transcripts.

The handwriting of Edith Stein guarantees the authenticity of the documents. The persons and archives that put transcripts at our disposal are responsible for the exact wording of the texts. Thus we may assume that the authenticity of the material published in Volumes VIII and IX of *Edith Steins Werke* is secured.

The originals of the letters are at this time in the possession of their rightful owners, as indicated at the heading of each letter.

We sincerely thank all private persons, secular and religious institutions, archives, and publishers for the loan of the letters and the permission to publish them as part of *Edith Steins Werke.*

In a synthesis of their content the letters furnish a fundamental documentation of personal, professional, and religious relationships. The examples, in part, have the character of communications; again, they appear to be the result of a lively exchange of thoughts. In this singularly wide range of themes, questions arise from the hidden depths of the spiritual and emotional life. As most significant themes one might mention:

—discussions of philosophical problems and the issue of personal intellectual creativity;

—pedagogical tasks and the vocation to religious education and leadership;

—information on the professional life and reflections on a contemplative lifestyle;

—critique of others and of herself in various situations;

—religious self-reflection and surrender in religious life;

—tragic conflict between filial love and witness to God, but a non-conflictual blending of Jewish and Catholic love of God;

—bonds with home and loving concern for the family in the diaspora;

—varied, friendly relations and encounters with authorities;

—dispute with the shocking political situation of the 20th century and recognition of [her] own destiny;

—life's optimism and resignation.

Only letters that contain personal statements can contribute to [flesh] out such a cycle of themes, thereby creating a self-portrait. But again, only persons for whom an intellectual exchange with friends constitutes a vital need, and to whom a fluency and liking for writing letters has been given, will cultivate intimate human relationships through correspondence.

Edith Stein possessed a talent for letter-writing. Her letters reveal a particularly lively trait of her personality: while apparently secluded and reticent, she established a sympathetic, close, intellectual and spiritual relationship with like-minded friends.

Persons and Personalities

The following has to do with Edith Stein as author of the letters, with the addressees or those who received the letters, and with persons mentioned in the letters. To help the less knowledgeable reader refer to data more readily, there are two separate lists: one of addressees, the persons Edith wrote to; the other of the persons she mentioned in her letters. Accordingly, the names of addressees who are also among those mentioned appear in both lists.

EDITH STEIN (Sr. Teresa Benedicta of the Cross, OCD)
1891 Breslau — 1942 Auschwitz [death in gas chamber]

The letters are dated from 1916 to 1942. We give, in eight segments, the significant [biographical] dates for that span of time.

1916-1918	Doctorate in Philosophy at the University of Freiburg-im-Breisgau, and assistant to Prof. Edmund Husserl.
1918-1922	Independent intellectual work while staying in Breslau, Freiburg and Göttingen. Unsuccessful efforts to get an habilitation [appointment as a lecturer] at a German university. Conversion to Catholicism; 1922, Baptism and Confirmation.
1923-1932	Instructor at the Teachers College of the Dominican Sisters at St. Magdalena, Speyer. Lecturer in pedagogy; lecture tours in Germany, Austria, and Switzerland. Intellectual study and writing.
1932-1933	Docent at the German Institute for Scientific Pedagogy in Münster.
1933-1934	Entrance at the Carmel of Cologne (Postulancy and Reception of the Religious Habit [April 15, 1934]).
1934-1938	Monastic life in the Carmel of Cologne. Philosophical and hagiographical writings.
1938-1942	Flight to Holland.[4] Monastic life in the Carmel of Echt. Commissions to work in philosophy of religion.
1942	Arrest and Deportation [Death August 9, 1942].

These phases are divided to fill two [German] volumes. Volume VIII of *Edith Steins Werke* contains 170 letters from the first five segments of her life; Volume IX, an equal number from the subsequent three segments.

[Vol. VIII of the German *Edith Steins Werke* contains 170 letters from 1916 to 1934. Vol. IX contains 172 letters from 1934 to 1942, plus 7 letters that the *Archivum* received after Vol. VIII was in print. These seven have been inserted in chronological order. They are identified by an "a" after the number. All letters are numbered as they are in the German volumes, and information about a recipient is always given under the first letter addressed to that person. In 1991, the *Archivum* published Volume XIV of the *Werke,* the entire collection of Edith Stein's letters to Roman Ingarden.]

Recipients of the Letters

Persons Cited in Letters

Text and Text Structure

Whenever we have the letters in an unabridged text, they are reproduced without any abridgement of our own. Only from the letters directed to Erna and Hans Biberstein [Nos. 24, 176, 307] have we excerpted portions of interest for this collection.

Since the majority of the letters are available in the original or a photocopy, the reproduction of their content should be largely complete. Whenever we know of abbreviations, we have indicated them by periods.

Supplementary texts between angle brackets (< >) as well as all footnotes are elucidations of the [German][5] editors. These have been kept to a minimum; however, in conjunction with this restriction, we have made certain to give information necessary to any reader who has insufficiently comprehensive prior knowledge to understand the [letter's] context.

For this reason we have also preserved abbreviations of names or places where Edith Stein used these for political reasons, and have completed the abbreviations between angle brackets. However, when Edith Stein used abbreviations to save space or time we have given the full text in these instances.

To make the text generally understood we have given the vernacular translation of Latin quotations and idiomatic expressions.

With respect to structuring the text, Edith's own division into paragraphs was taken into consideration at all times. However, beyond that, we have undertaken a thoroughgoing revision of the textual form, aiming to give each letter a clearly arranged and uniform structure. In this sense, the salutations and conclusions of the letters have been revised as to content and form: uniformly shortened or completed.

The footnotes accompany each letter to enable the reader to use them immediately. Further data on recipients of the letters or persons mentioned may be located by referring to the lists of addressees and of cited persons that precede the letters in this volume.

Style and punctuation have been revised according to German grammatical rules valid today [1977].

Edith Stein belonged to the community of the Carmel *Maria vom Frieden* [Mary of Peace] of Cologne. We hereby express our gratitude to that community of nuns, above all to the [former]Mother Prioress

[Sr.]Maria Amata Neyer, OCD, to Sr. Teresa Margaret Drügemöller, OCD, and to Sr. Maria Johanna Hauke, OCD, for their untiring collaboration in the editing of the authentic edition of Edith Stein's letters herewith submitted.

Dr. L. Gelber

1. [Vol. X of *Edith Steins Werke* is entitled *Heil im Unheil (Blessedness Amid Peril).* It was not written by Edith but by Fr. Romaeus Leuven, OCD, who includes excerpts from her writings.]
2. [Vol. VIII of *Edith Steins Werke* contains letters 1 to 170, inclusive; Vol. IX, letters 171 to 342, with 7 additional letters in a supplement. In the English translation, the 349 letters are given in chronological order in a single volume, numbered as in the German volumes.]
3. [Vol. XIV of *Edith Steins Werke,* entitled *Briefe an Roman Ingarden (Letters to Roman Ingarden),* published in 1991 (Freiburg: Herder), contains 161 letters Edith Stein wrote to Ingarden between 1917 and 1938. An English translation will follow.]
4. [Edith went to Holland on December 31, 1938.]
5. [Throughout the book, square brackets ([ ]) identify information and notes supplied by the Discalced Carmelite Nuns' *Edith Stein Archiv* in the Carmels of Cologne, Germany, and Elysburg, Pennsylvania. Principally, these update the biographical information given in the 1977 German edition of the letters.]

Letters

1. Letter to Fritz Kaufmann[1] <at the Front>

Original in *Archivum Carmelitanum Edith Stein*

Breslau, August 16, 1916

Dear Herr Kaufmann,

Thank you very much for your kind letter. It does me so much good to have all of you rejoice with me this way [at having been awarded the doctorate "Summa Cum Laude"] since, actually, I have found it a bit troubling that just at this time fortune should be heaping so many gifts on me. Well, it did exact a small tribute from me: I have not been completely well for the past few days, and it is all I can manage to keep up with my official duties. I simply cannot miss school [as a teacher] such a short time before graduation, when there is no substitute to be had here.[2] Despite that, I hope that by October 1 when I go back to Freiburg (by then, I will not be needed here any longer) I will have sufficiently recovered so that I can put all my powers to work.

Yes, I must tell you more of the details about this wondrous development. When I was in Freiburg for about a fortnight and the Master [E. Husserl][3] was still sulking because I was so cruel, forcing him to read my thesis,[4] one evening I overheard him tell a lady he considered it necessary to have an assistant, just as Hilbert[5] does. Little Meyer[6] then told us that Husserl had been toying with this thought for a long time, certain that unless he had assistance he would never be able to get at his manuscripts again. Then, timidly, I began to weigh the proposition: should I offer my services to him? And I found the nerve to do so when, the next day, he confided that he was very satisfied with my thesis, and that, indeed, a good bit of it coincided with essential portions from Part II of *Ideen*.[7]

His delight at the thought of now having a person entirely at his disposal was apparent—although, obviously, he has no clear idea as yet how we will actually work together. In any case we are agreed that first of all we are going to get at the manuscripts of *Ideen*. In preparation for this, I have to learn Gabelsberger shorthand,[8] since that is the key to the holy of holies.[9]

1. Fritz Kaufmann (b. Leipzig, 1891; d. Zurich, Switzerland, August 9, 1959). Studied under Husserl with Edith in Göttingen. Privatdocent in Freiburg, emigrated to United States via England; professor of philosophy in Buffalo, New York, then in Zurich. [See *Life in a Jewish Family*—hereafter abbreviated *Life*— pp. 256-309, 492-3.]
2. At this time Edith Stein was teaching at the Viktoria School for Girls, Breslau.
3. Edmund Husserl (b. Prossnitz/Mähren, Austria, April 8, 1859; d. Freiburg-im-Breisgau, April 27, 1938). He was called "The Master" by his students. [He was professor of philosophy in Halle, then] in Göttingen [where] Edith studied under him from 1913 on, [and Freiburg where] she got her doctorate in 1916 and became his first assistant, 1916-1918. [See *Life*, pp. 249, 489, etc.]
4. Her dissertation *Zum Problem der Einfühlung*, (Halle, 1917). [English translation published as *On the Problem of Empathy* (Washington, DC: ICS Publications, 1989).]
5. David Hilbert (1862-1943). Professor of mathematics, Göttingen. [See *Life*, p. 85.]
6. Rudolf Meyer, known as "Little Meyer," a young Protestant theologian, studied under Husserl in Göttingen and followed him to Freiburg. [See *Life*, p. 403. He is also mentioned in the Ingarden letters, 14, 18.]
7. The full title of the work is *Ideen zu einer reinen Phänomenologie und phänomenologischen Philosophie* [available in English as *Ideas: General Introduction to Pure Phenomenology*, trans. W. R. Boyce Gibson, (New York: Collier Macmillan, 1962)]. This is frequently mentioned in the early letters. *Ideen* may, at times, be given as its title without adding the English equivalent. The reference in this letter is to Volume II of Husserl's work. [During her assistantship, Edith prepared two important works of Husserl's for publication. According to the European scholar Peter Schulz, Martin Heidegger published these writings of Husserl's, unchanged, in his own name, a few years later, but with no mention of Edith Stein at all.]
8. Edmund Husserl wrote all his notes and manuscripts in Gabelsberger shorthand.
9. The conclusion of the letter was lost.

2. Letter to Fritz Kaufmann <at the Front>
Original in *Archivum Carmelitanum Edith Stein*

Freiburg, December 13, 1916

Dear Herr Kaufmann,

First of all, best wishes for the new phase of the war, which one hopes (and that surely is a hope based on reason) will be very brief.

At the same time, this is a timid announcement of a Christmas package. Unfortunately, I got your address just at the time when acceptance of large packages expired so that, regrettably, the gift I really intended for you cannot be sent until after the holidays. It is Konrad Fiedler's work on art. If (as I hope) you aren't familiar with his writings yet, I believe you'll find in them much that is stimulating on the subject that has been occupying you lately. Today, my head is not fit for philosophizing.

If only one were a few days older and could know what the Entente[1] will say to the peace offer! Is your imagination *[phantasie]* keen enough to paint a picture of our having peace once more and how everything will turn out then? If it doesn't happen, then perhaps I will go—despite the *Ideen*—to work in a munitions factory or somewhere similar. But I just have to annoy you a bit more with my ghastly optimism and so I wish you a Merry Christmas accompanied by an armistice!

With best regards,
Edith Stein

1. [On December 12, 1916, the day before this letter, Germany made a peace initiative that the Entente, a British-French-Russian alliance against middle Europe in World War I, rejected.]

3. Letter to Roman Ingarden, Göttingen
First published in *Philosophy and Phenomenological Research,* Vol. 23, 1962

Freiburg, January 5[1], 1917

My dear Ingarden,

...Actually I should strike out the last paragraph[2] because of a discussion I had with the Master <E. Husserl> the day I returned. I begged him earnestly to read your work <the doctoral dissertation> and he was really convinced (since then it lies, together with mine, on his window sill); then, when I began to talk of eventually preparing a *Jahrbuch,* it became clear that he would like to get one out this summer and thought to use as much of your work as is finished, marking it "To be continued." What do you say to that? Come to think of it, it was an exciting discussion. I painted so drastic a picture of the trouble involved in processing the raw material of the *Ideen* that, as before, the result was that we totally agreed once again that I should be allowed to have all the pleasure. Then when I told about the difficulties I had encountered, the not-unjustified thought occurred that one should actually reconsider the entire doctrine of constitution and for that purpose take another look at the first part of the *Ideen <zu einer reinen Phänomenologie und phänomenologischen Philosophie>*. That was done for two days, then it again became too boring.

I am now determined that, independent of the dear Master's sudden and variable fancies and as speedily as other assignments will permit, I will put the material I have into a form in which it will be available to others also. When I have accomplished that, and if by then he is still not resolved to go through it systematically, then I will attempt on my own to clarify the cloudy points. Perhaps you find that a bit conceited, for it seems to me that you (and probably justifiably) do not have too high an opinion of my philosophical talent. But after seeing all that is already available, the task appears to be within even my modest ability. Time shall not matter to me. After I determined on this mode of operation, I explained to my mother that I had enough to occupy me forever and that all I lacked was a lifelong income. By return mail, I was informed not to worry on that point. Therefore, the specter of a return to teaching has been banished, and that is a great relief. I cannot tell you about anything outside of work, since I have been living like a hermit this week.

[End of excerpt.]

1. [The letter was begun on January 5, but the section given here was actually written on January 17.]
2. [This and 16 other excerpts from letters to Roman Ingarden were published by him in 1962 in defense of Edith Stein's work for Husserl. They appear in full among the 161 letters to Ingarden that constitute Vol. XIV of *Edith Steins Werke,* (Freiburg: Herder, 1991). The previous paragraph, to which Edith here refers, concerns Ingarden's own dissertation on the work of Henri Bergson; the closing paragraphs, also omitted, discuss a novel by the Polish author, Wladyslaw Reymont, who was awarded the Nobel Prize for Literature in 1924.]

4. Letter to Fritz Kaufmann <at the Front>
Original in *Archivum Carmelitanum Edith Stein*

Freiburg, January 12, 1917

Dear Herr Kaufmann,

I am rather upset when I see that I have owed you an answer for such a long time. But that happens to me now with everyone. The circle of people with whom I am in correspondence is so large that a long time expires before I get around to everyone. On top of that, I made a little excursion to Göttingen in order to talk to Reinach[1] on his Christmas furlough. He is in excellent health and continues to be in a very cheerful mood but, naturally, he would be happy if the whole game were over.

He claims to have discovered, at the front, that he has no talent for philosophy and he has never been seriously interested in it. That is the result of his having become totally engrossed in religious questions, and when the war ends he will surely work primarily in that field. Despite that, during the days we spent together his philosophical interest awoke again; we even got out his manuscript on movement again, and he is going to see whether, out there, he can add anything to it. That's wonderful. I had hardly dared to hope he would ever take it up again at all.

As far as my work is concerned, the difficulties are even greater than appeared at first. Essentially, there is a whole lot to be done yet, and in any case, collaboration with the dear Master is a highly complicated matter; there is a concern that it will never even come to an actual *collaboration.* He keeps occupying himself with individual questions about which he dutifully informs me, but he cannot be moved, even once, to look at the draft I am making for him out of his old material to enable him to regain the overview of the whole that he has lost. As long as that cannot be achieved it is obviously impossible to think of composing a definitive draft. But I have now set my mind at rest by deciding to bring the matter to a close with or without him, regardless of how long it will take to get everything into some generally accessible format. Every means must be taken to prevent its being lost. You can see by this resolve that I have given up all thought of a return to teaching (unless some unforeseen circumstance should force me to do so) and <I> hope to be able to remain at such scholarly work totally and forever.

Lipps[2] will soon be having a furlough again, and I am very hopeful of seeing him here.

With best regards,
Edith Stein

1. Adolf Reinach (b. Mainz, October 23, 1883; killed in battle Dixmuiden, Flanders, November 16, 1917) studied under Husserl, whose privatdocent he was when Edith went to Göttingen in 1913. Reinach and his wife, Anna, were close friends of Edith's. [See *Life*, pp. 247-300.]
2. Hans Lipps (b. Pirna, November 22, 1882; killed in action in Russia, September 10, 1941). Another close friend of Edith's from the time they met as members of the Philosophical Society of Husserl students in Göttingen. Lipps was professor of philosophy at the University of Frankfurt-am-Main. [See *Life*, pp. 253-307.]

5. Letter to Roman Ingarden, Göttingen

Excerpt first published in *Philosophy and Phenomenological Research*, Vol. 23, 1962

Freiburg, January 28, 1917

Dear Herr Ingarden,

...The Master's latest prognosis for the production of *Ideen:* first of all, I am to stay with him until I marry; then I may only accept a man who will also become his assistant, and the same holds for the children. Highly unpropitious! Even apart from time, the requisite preconditions are absent. For if, in the long run, it is not entirely beyond the realm of the possible that someone could be found who would not shy away from an alliance with me (and vice versa), I deem it essentially impossible that a man could be his assistant.

He is now busying himself with the constitution of nature (of course, without any review of the draft[1]). In the meantime, I have continued working on that draft on my own authority, without running into any opposition about that, and am as far as "Person."[2] The natural consequence of this is that we hardly talk together anymore. For me, this is very painful, for matters are very complicated and the material I have at hand is altogether incomplete. However, I am working pretty independently now, and that is, of course, very enjoyable, but some exchange of ideas could be highly beneficial. So I would have a great deal of use for you now, and in all likelihood you would get more from me on a philosophical plane than in the terrible time during which I had become a semi-imbecile from getting the manuscript notes in order.

...A piece of news that will make you happy: Elsenhans wrote a reply to Linke, and Frischeisen-Köhler sent it to Husserl, urging him to prepare a rejoinder, and he has pledged himself to do so.[3]

[End of excerpt.]

1. Edith prepared Part I of *Ideen* for publication. [Her work on the manuscript resulted in the second revised edition, published in 1922, although she is not given credit.]
2. ["Person" is examined in Chapter 3, No. 54 of *Ideen.* This section is designated as Part II, Chapter 5, No. 54, in W. R. Boyce Gibson's translation, *Ideas* (see Letter 1, n. 7).]
3. This rejoinder is found in the Husserl Archive, Leuven, Belgium. [Linke's article on *Bewegungsauffassung* appeared in Husserl's *Jahrbuch* 1916, Vol. II.]

6. Letter to Roman Ingarden, Göttingen

First published in *Philosophy and Phenomenological Research,* Vol. 23, 1962

Freiburg, February 3, 1917

Dear Herr Ingarden,

So the connection works![1] That is a great consolation. You took the theme of "my philosophical talent" too seriously. That belonged to the crazy part of my letter—at least as far as you yourself are concerned. I have already told myself that you gave me very little cause for my surmise (really, it never occurred to me that you would have to read my work). The conjecture, I suppose, is founded on my "projecting" my self-appraisal on others. But precisely at the time when we were most frequently together I was suffering because of the highly depressing nature of my occupation.

One thing more, in conclusion, so I can make you understand the significance of the whole problem: I keep asking myself the question whether, if I lack an aptitude for productive scientific work [in philosophy], I have the right to renounce another career in which I would be capable of some accomplishment. And apropos of my bad habit of seeing ethical conflicts everywhere: you probably know that I have been depressed for a long time because, currently, I'm doing nothing "for the fatherland." After my last postcard, you can easily imagine that this feeling has only been intensified in the last few days.

Now the women students have organized themselves by department to report for auxiliary service where they can best be utilized. I, too, have resolved to get involved if I can find employment in Freiburg—for, after all, I should not want to separate myself from the *Ideen.*[2] In any case, (after being disconcerted at first) the Master expressed his opinion that, as I have prepared work for him that would last a long while, it would be possible for me to go somewhere else; he would consider himself espec-ially fortunate if I were to remain here. However, I am still afraid that the matter would come to a standstill were he to be left to himself, and so I feel co-responsible, after all, even if that sounds funny.

It seems you still have no clear understanding about the nature of my work on the *Ideen:* I am now seeking to establish from the material at hand a unified draft[3] of the entire thought process (of which I have a pretty clear view even though nothing is fixed or even carried to a conclusion). That is to become the basis of the Master's work, so I would like to finish it because I believe he would never be able to find his way through the material and would forever remain hung up on particulars. Only if worst came to worst, and he were never to rework it himself, had I considered doing it myself. Naturally, that would mean years of work for me. But I do hope that will not become necessary. A philosophical walk we took together to Haslach[4] recently has made me feel fairly confident again.

Besides, as a consequence [of the discussion] I have experienced a breakthrough. Now I imagine I know pretty well what "constitution" is—but with a break from Idealism. An absolutely existing physical nature on the one hand, a distinctly structured subjectivity on the other, seem to me to be prerequisites before an intuiting nature can constitute itself. I have not yet had the chance to confess my heresy to the Master....

1. [In an earlier letter, Edith told Ingarden that if he expected "many letters" from her he would have to write many in return.]
2. See Letter 5.
3. This manuscript is in the Husserl Archive, Leuven, Belgium.
4. [Haslach is a district in the southwestern section of Freiburg. Husserl had a habit of discussing philosophy on such walks. Winthrop Bell described them in *Life*, p. 292.]

7. Letter to Roman Ingarden, Göttingen

First published in *Philosophy and Phenomenological Research,* Vol. 23, 1962

Freiburg, February 9, 1917

Dear Herr Ingarden,

Thank you very much for your letter. I am very happy that your understanding of "German-ness" is progressing. You are "in love with the Polish soul"—that was the precise phrase that occurred to me also, as I sought recently to clarify what is essentially different in our approach to the State and to the People. You see, I can no more be in love with Germany than with myself for, after all, I am myself it, that is, a part of it. Peoples are "persons" who have life, who are born, who grow, and who pass away. It is a life beyond our own, although it includes ours. Therefore, one cannot reasonably inquire whether they "should" be great or small; i.e., whether we ought to do something about it, for we have as little power within that sphere as cells have in deciding whether the organism they constitute should grow or decrease.

However, we are not merely used up as cells are, but we can become aware of our relationship with the wholes to which we belong (I even believe one can experience the operative developmental tendencies) and can voluntarily submit to them. The more lively and powerful such a consciousness becomes in a people, the more it forms itself into a "state" and this formation is its organization. The state is a self-confident people that disciplines its functions.

Since, for me, the increase of such self-assurance appears to be bound up with an increased developmental tendency, organization appears to be a sign of interior strength and that people is most perfect (according to its development as a people, not, of course, according to its "character traits") which is most a state. And I believe I can assert objectively that since Sparta and Rome there has never been as strong a consciousness of being a state as there is in Prussia and the new German Reich.[1] That is why I consider it out of the question that we will now be defeated.

Perhaps all this appears to you to be wild speculation. But it is not that. Pretty unclear, I know, but based throughout on phenomena. One experience impressed itself on me particularly: on mobilization day, when I arrived at home after a 24-hour train ride and withdrew from the family circle because I could not bear to listen to talk of indifferent (i.e., personal) matters, it was suddenly crystal clear and evident to me: today my individual life has ceased, and all that I am belongs to the state. If I survive the war, then I will resume it <my life> as newly granted to me. That was not the product of overstimulated nerves, but it has remained vital in me to this day, and I suffer continually because I have not found the right place in which I can live up to this conviction. And that is the spirit most alive in us, even though the majority may think otherwise and although, assuredly, a lot of foolish stuff is being said.

There has been no further development concerning my auxiliary service. Only that the Master soon began to worry what he would do in the summer without me, and so decided to talk to the school directors himself to find out whether there is a shortage of teachers here. I shall probably hear tomorrow whether he has already done so....

1. [This "new" Reich is the second, federal German state, i.e., neither the imperial First Reich of 1871, nor the infamous Third Reich of 1933.]

8. Letter to Roman Ingarden, Göttingen
First published in *Philosophy and Phenomenological Research,* Vol. 23, 1962

Freiburg, February 20, 1917

Dear Herr Ingarden,

...You may be at peace regarding my auxiliary service for the time being. The Department [of Education] has sent us a commendatory reply advising us to wait until we can be given assignments in our specialties, which will hardly be the case before late spring. So quite "sensibly" I signed up for a teaching position on the proffered lists for Freiburg, and now the matter will probably rest in the files. If I did not consider my activity here important enough, of course, I would not be content with this development.

...Recently I laid before the Master, most solemnly, my reservations against idealism. It was not at all (as you had feared) a "painful situation." I was deposited in a corner of the dear old leather sofa, and then for two hours there was a heated debate—naturally without either side persuading the other. The Master is of the opinion that he is not at all disinclined to change his viewpoint if one demonstrates to him such a necessity. I have, however, never yet managed to do that. In any case, he is now aware that he has to think this point through once more, thoroughly, even though, for the moment, he has postponed that. I will write you the details separately some other time; today I am too tired to do so. I've just come from a prolonged evening visit at Husserl's; it was in a way a semi-farewell, for on Saturday we have the final lecture, and I depart that afternoon....

...Now I am occupied with putting my [literary] remains[1] in order. The expositions on *Natur und Geist [Nature and Spirit]*[2] have fused into a unified whole. I have not yet added the epistemological arguments that belong with it; that is to be a second part. But I believe that what is finished (on my part) could be published by itself had the Master revised it. When I read it over I made a list of the "cloudy points" to take with me to Breslau so I can deal with them as soon as I have recovered somewhat from *Natur und Geist.* (I've been at it exclusively for five months.) The Master had the good idea that rest was a must for me. At first he thought that for the month I intend to be away I should not work at all but simply "play the young lady"; then he offered to let me take along, for my amusement, the draft of a new revision of the Sixth Study.[3] That was not "asking too much, surely."

At the present, a great deal is being made of my "teaching activities" and there is consideration of assigning some beginners' exercises to me officially for the next semester and letting me use the lecture hall for that purpose. I am to become here—this was expressed to me with touching naïveté—what Reinach was in Göttingen. Only habilitation is out of reach for me (though Elly[4] pleaded my case in that regard), for that is opposed "on principle"....

1. [Here "my remains" probably refers to the loose ends of "her" work, the pages left over from her organization of Husserl's notes.]
2. Husserl gave this lecture in the summer semester of 1913.
3. This Sixth Study in Volume II of Husserl's *Logische Untersuchungen [Logical Studies]* was not contained in the second edition (1913). The original text was published with only minor alterations in the third edition (1923).
4. Elisabeth Husserl, daughter of Edmund Husserl (b. Halle, June 2, 1892; d. Boston, Massachusetts, 1982).

9. Letter to Roman Ingarden, Göttingen
First published in *Philosophy and Phenomenological Research,* Vol. 23, 1962

Breslau, March 7, 1917

Dear Herr Ingarden,

...I have been here about ten days and on the 24th will go back via Berlin in order to spend a few days with my sister. I believe I wrote to you that I brought along the Sixth Study. The most I can do, though, is to get the pages in order for future work on them. They were in such a state that it seemed as though the good Master had enough of them one day and shoved them all, just as they were, into a drawer—where they stayed until the day before my departure. In any case, I cannot do any real work here....

10. Letter to Roman Ingarden, Göttingen
First published in *Philosophy and Phenomenological Research,* Vol. 23, 1962

Breslau, March 17, 1917

Dear Herr Ingarden,

...It is high time for me to get back to work. I have done nothing serious here and seem to have become utterly stupid. The Master writes, too, that his thoughts have become frozen, but added the consoling assurance that he is doing his utmost despite it. If only he were available now for some collaboration. Pray for me regarding the *Ideen*....

11. Letter to Roman Ingarden, Göttingen.
First published in *Philosophy and Phenomenological Research,* Vol. 23, 1962

Breslau, March 20, 1917

Dear Herr Ingarden,

...I have done almost nothing here. I have looked through what I brought along of the Sixth Study[1] and have put that into such order that it will be easy for me, sometime, to get to it seriously. There are some really beautiful things in it, but it seems even farther from a conclusion than the *Ideen.* I don't know yet what will happen on my return. I have a burning desire for a thorough discussion with the Master about the work I have accomplished so far before I take up something else. I simply have no will at all to amass a new stack of papers he won't even look at. Besides, I should then be more free to begin to do something of my own once again.

For the past two days, just to see if I can actually still do something on my own, I have begun to examine more closely one of the points on which the Master and I differ (the necessity of a body for empathy). In doing so, I at once came up with some historical-philosophical questions again. It would be wonderful if I had time for that. But surely that, too, will come sometime.

On the 24th I am going as far as Berlin, and on the 27th I will go on [to Freiburg]. Most probably I shall meet Fräulein Gothe[2] in Frankfurt in order to take her with me for two weeks. Doesn't that tempt you also to come to Freiburg? *Tymczasem do widzenia panu* <Farewell for today, sir>.

Edith Stein

1. Cf. Letter 8, n. 2
2. Erika Gothe (b. Darmstadt, January 23, 1887; d. Schwerin, August 31, 1966). Educator, Ph.D.; she had already taught school for several years before she went to Göttingen to study under Husserl. She was Edith's friend throughout the Göttingen years. [See *Life*, pp. 255, 405.]

12. Letter to Roman Ingarden, Göttingen

First published in *Philosophy and Phenomenological Research,* Vol. 23, 1962

Freiburg, April 9, 1917

Dear Herr Ingarden,

I already owe you a reply to two letters but during the fortnight Fräulein Gothe spent here I needed all of my free time for her. Together we read my draft of the *Ideen* and I was happy to have an opportunity to discuss it with someone at last. My own impression was confirmed. The two first sections (on the constitution of material and animal nature) have a unified continuity and could be printed after some insignificant changes. The third part (on the intellect), which is absolutely necessary to complete the others, must be gone over anew, by all means, since at present it is merely an orderly arrangement of the available material. Therefore it would please me very much to have the first two parts appear in the next *Jahrbuch.* If only the Master could finally be brought to read them over!

But imagine what he surprised me with! During the vacation, the ominous inaugural lecture was to have been composed. Instead, what developed was an *Einleitung in die Phänomenologie [Introduction to Phenomenology]* separated into the sections *Phänomenologie und Psychologie [Phenomenology and Psychology]* and *Phänomenologie und Erkenntnistheorie [Phenomenology and the Theory of Knowledge].* Whatever happens, this is to be completed and published now. Yesterday, Fräulein Gothe and I had the pleasant mission (and on his birthday, to boot) of making him aware that this is not suitable for the *Jahrbuch,* that one now expects from him some new concrete expositions such as the *Ideen* abundantly provides, not just old material presented from other perspectives.

I will do my best to get him to dress up that product into an answer to Elsenhans and then have him submit it for inclusion in the *Kantstudien [Kant Studies].*[1] At present, he is not yet convinced and is thinking of specially preparing the response he has pledged himself to. All this means wasting a lot of precious time.

I am now thinking of realizing a good idea he has suddenly had: to restyle into short articles for the *Jahrbuch* the parts from the Sixth Study that are complete in context. There remains so much to do on the Study as a whole that I hardly dare think of its being concluded in this life. At the same time I will write out in neat format my reservations about certain points of the *Ideen* in preparation for a common discussion. I began today with "Idealism." Besides, Fräulein Gothe showed me some notes of Frau Martius[2] on the question of Idealism. They were, however, not a refutation of Husserl; the main argument seems to me to be based on a misunderstanding of his expositions....

1. [See Letter 5. The *Kantstudien* referred to is a philosophical journal initiated and published by Hans Vaihinger since 1896.]
2. See Letter 23.

13. Letter to Roman Ingarden, Göttingen

First published in *Philosophy and Phenomenological Research,* Vol. 23, 1962

Freiburg, April 27, 1917

[Dear Herr Ingarden,]

...Thank you for the first critical appraisal on my thesis.[1] It is really too bad that no one could give me an opinion on it before it was printed. I never had as much as a comment on it from the Master himself. As for your objections, I can agree with almost all of them. I knew that the first chapter was not worth much and it was, perhaps, thoughtless to publish it. Moreover, there are some very fine things in Husserl's [writings on that subject] and I do not know whether I will really do more work on this point later.

I, too, am aware that the concept of the psyche is not yet clearly developed. That will be possible only when the concept of the intellect has been completely clarified. There, too, a whole lot is missing (although the Fourth Part is the only thing I produced "con amore"); however, I believe that the direction I have been heading in is correct. It is just that it all does not go far enough.

Moreover if the psyche [concept] has not been clearly explained in my work so far, it is by no means clearer in Scheler's,[2] and I am convinced the statements I have made in opposition to him will prove valid. Perhaps he will soon express his opinion about it. I had not sent him my thesis since I did not know his address before this. In the meantime he happened to see it in Berlin (I do not know who had it) and he asked Cohn[3] for it. Naturally, I sent him a copy immediately with a few words of explanation. It appears almost as though he suspects us of some deception.

In view of this potential quarrel, I was very gratified to hear from Bell[4] that my dispute with Scheler pleased him. Beyond that, all he was able to write to me was that he had made hundreds of marginal comments that he would like to talk to me about, which is obviously impossible on a postcard. So much for phenomenology in wartime!

I have long been aware that I must learn to go into greater depth. In any case, I believe that is the weak spot of my talent. Basically, I work more with my poor understanding than with intuitive gifts; perhaps that is why I am especially suited to be the Master's assistant. But, obviously,

I too saw the whole thing merely as a plan I would fulfill in the course of my lifetime. Since I have come here, I sometimes have the scary feeling that I no longer have my life as firmly in hand as I used to. For one thing, the problems that lie close to my heart are dependent on the conclusion of the *Ideen*. Then, my duties as assistant make such demands on me that it is impossible to think of doing any intensive and undisturbed work on the side. At the same time, I cannot possibly think of giving up [those duties] in the foreseeable future, for I am certain that, left alone, the Master simply would not publish anything more. I consider the publication of his work more important than any possible products I might eventually present to the world.

If the new treatises have alarmed me somewhat, then, of course, that was partly because I told myself how much time would be lost because the Master tires so easily and is so slow (once more this is an "impertinence" on my part; oh yes, I know well enough I have this fault and despise it sufficiently). I have the highest appreciation of their [the new treatises] pedagogical value. But four months have already been spent on them, and it will take another month. My regrets about this situation have at least brought me the promise (and I had him shake hands on that) that we will begin on the *Ideen* immediately after Pentecost. On Pentecost, the Master is going to his mother's in Vienna. Today I urged him to take your paper[5] along to read during the trip. Will it be allowed to cross the border?

The Sixth Study[6] contains some expositions that are complete in themselves and can be lifted out of the context. Since the main problem is still far from a satisfactory solution, I thought it an excellent idea to publish as much as is finished now. Of course, the thought of a *Festschrift* occurred to me at times, but there are still two more years left, and I continue to hope the war will have ended by then. During this endless winter, summer and peace blended for me into a single goal. After all, since the laws of nature are not likely to have changed, summer has to come some time and it seems to want to come now. Maybe peace will come too?

Cordially, your
Edith Stein

1. Her dissertation *Zum Problem der Einfühlung* (Halle, 1917), available in English as *On the Problem of Empathy*, trans. Waltraut Stein (Washington, DC: ICS Publications, 1989).

2. Max Scheler (b. Munich, August 22, 1874; d. Frankfurt-am-Main, May 19, 1928), professor of philosophy in Munich; when teaching faculties were denied him [cf. *Life*, p. 258] he became a freelance author and scholar. Edith Stein met him in Göttingen.
3. [Jonas Cohn was a professor of philosophy at Freiburg-im-Breisgau.]
4. Winthrop Pickard Bell, Ph.D., (b. Halifax, Canada, May 12, 1885; d. Chester, Canada, April 4, 1965). A colleague of Edith Stein in Göttingen, he studied under Husserl and Reinach. He belonged to the circle of Edith's closest friends, took his degree under Husserl in the early days of World War I, and was subsequently interned as an enemy alien in the prisoner-of-war camp at Döberitz near Berlin until 1918. Later he had a professorship in Toronto, Canada.
5. [Husserl had the manuscript of Ingarden's doctoral thesis on intuition and intellect in Henri Bergson.]
6. See Letter 8.

14. Letter to Roman Ingarden, Göttingen

First published in *Philosophy and Phenomenological Research,* Vol. 23, 1962

Freiburg, May 31, 1917

Dear Herr Ingarden,

...The Master has not yet recovered from his trip to Vienna;[1] all work is at a standstill. On Pentecost I did my utmost to lure him into the Black Forest, but, stiff-necked, he persisted in saying he had to work. So I went up to Fräulein Busse's[2] for two days and, as it turned out, when I got back I learned he had been unable to accomplish anything. Now we have put him up in Bärental for the rest of the vacation.

At present I am occupying myself somewhat with physics and mathematics (in the interest of natural philosophy). A good bit of time is wasted because of that, since I have to attend the lectures regularly. It is absolutely necessary, however; otherwise the continuity would be at risk.

The Master has come to me more than once to find out what was to happen in the afternoon. I am now holding my kindergarten in the lecture hall. Its composition is remarkable: three women students and two men; [plus] a Benedictine priest and a Protestant minister.[3] Of course, no trace of philosophical companionship, rather strictly ABC-instruction. But it is fun nevertheless. Please write soon.

Best regards,
Edith Stein

1. To his home in Austria. See Letter 13. [Husserl's mother was born Julie Selinger, in Prossnitz/Mähren, Austria, in 1834. She died in Vienna in 1917.]
2. [Ilse Busse (m. Proesler), a student in Edith's beginners' course in Freiburg, owned a small chalet in Saig above the Titisee, a mountain lake in Bavaria close to the Swiss border.]
3. [Probably these were, in the order in which she enumerates them: Ilse Busse, Amalie Jaegerschmid, Gerda Walther; Ludwig Ferdinand Clauss, Otto Gründler; Nikolaus Thiel OSB, and Rudolf Meyer (known as "little Meyer," cf. *Life*, p. 403).]

15. Letter to Roman Ingarden, Göttingen

First published in *Philosophy and Phenomenological Research,* Vol. 23, 1962

Freiburg, July 6, 1917

Dear Herr Ingarden,

...Now about my other problem child: the *Ideen* lies as untouched as ever in my desk. The "good work period" began only after Pentecost and was used for an intensive preoccupation with Kant.[1] I would be happy if the treatises for the *Kantstudien* were finished before vacation and we could get at the *Ideen* in September. But here, too, when it comes to expectation I have about reached the point of full stop, period *[Epoché]*!

Recently I have been putting more and more stacks of manuscripts in order; I have just come upon the bundle on *Zeitbewusstsein* [time-consciousness]. You know best how important these matters are: for the theory on "Constitution" and for the dispute with Bergson[2] and, it seems to me, with others as well, e.g. with Natorp.[3] What I have is rather a sorry mess: scraps of paper from as far back as 1903. Still I am very eager to see whether it can be made into some kind of monograph. After all, that would represent a step toward print-readiness, even though there is no knowing whether and when publication will follow.

Before the discovery of this material restored my taste for the work, I had about decided to lay down my portfolio in October. Now it seems to me, once more, that what I am doing here is not entirely without sense.

Fond regards,
Edith Stein

1. [Immanuel Kant (b. Königsberg, April 22, 1724; d. Königsberg, February 22, 1804.)]

2. Henri Bergson (b. Paris, October 18, 1859; d. Paris, January 4, 1941). French philosopher and winner of Nobel Prize for Literature, 1928.
3. Paul Natorp (b. Düsseldorf, January 24, 1854; d. Marburg, August 17, 1924). Professor of philosophy in Marburg, and cofounder of the so-called Marburg School.

16. Letter to Roman Ingarden, Göttingen

First published in *Philosophy and Phenomenological Research,* Vol. 23, 1962

Herzogenhorn,[1] August [7], 1917

Dear Herr Ingarden,

I have been up here since yesterday; it is just beautiful, 1400 meters altitude, very quiet, solitary; and there is a gorgeous view toward the Belchen [Mountain]. This afternoon I want to go down to see Husserl who has been at Bernau for the past eight days. He will surely be delighted when you come here in autumn.

Do you know by now that the semester has been rescheduled? It will start on October 1 and will end on February 1. Therefore, if you plan to attend, you have very little time left for travel arrangements. I am not much edified by having the vacation cut short because that puts the work planned for vacation time in jeopardy. The final days in Freiburg were very good ones for me; Fräulein Gothe was with me again for ten days and during that time Lipps visited one day and Hering[2] three. I had the joy of seeing that the phenomenologists are beginning to feel at home in Freiburg.

Fräulein Gothe went home by way of Bergzabern[3] laden with good wishes from Lorettostrasse,[4] and I am hoping she will persuade Frau Martius to pay us a visit sometime after the fruit harvest. Frau Martius has written *Gespräch über die Seele [A Discourse on the Soul]*[5] that is to appear in the next issue of the *Summa* (have you already discovered what a lovely creation that is?). I am most eager to see it [the discourse]. Hering was really enchanted by it.

Reinach has come to Germany now for a six-week course for Battery Commanders. Unfortunately I will probably be unable to see him this time, for in this brief vacation period I cannot get in a trip to Northern Germany as well.

You asked recently, I believe, about the results of my "pedagogical" efforts. There are some very promising people there, especially Herr

Clauss,[6] from whom I eventually expect something on linguistic philosophy, and Fräulein Walther,[7] who comes from Munich and who wants to work, in connection with studying Pfänder[8] on the phenomenology of social communities....

Last month I worked over Husserl's *Zeitnotizen [Notes on Time],* beautiful things but not yet completely matured.

Let us hear from you soon. Hopefully, your hand has completely healed.

Best regards,
Edith Stein

1. [This is a mountain in the southern Black Forest. Edith was there for a fortnight beginning August 6. The Belchen she mentions is the third-highest peak in the Black Forest, and Bernau a health spa not far away.]
2. Jean Hering (b. Ribeauville, Alsace-Lorraine, September 12, 1890; d. Strasbourg, France, March 23, 1966). Full professor for Protestant theology, Strasbourg. He was one of the older Göttingen students of Husserl and met Edith when both belonged to the Philosophical Circle there. [See *Life,* p. 253, etc.]
3. Dr. Theodore Conrad and his wife, Hedwig Conrad-Martius, both philosophers, lived on a fruit farm in Bergzabern, in the Palatinate. [See *Life,* p. 218, etc.]
4. Prof. Edmund Husserl and his wife, Frau Malvine Husserl-Steinschneider, lived on Lorettostrasse [Loretto Street], Freiburg.
5. Published in 1921 in the book *Metaphysische Gespräche [Metaphysical Discourses].*
6. Ludwig Ferdinand Clauss (b. Offenburg, February 8, 1892; d. Ruppertshain/Taunus, January 13, 1974). One of the students in Edith Stein's beginners' class. He got his doctorate under Husserl; later became a professor in Frankfurt-am-Main, with an international reputation in ethnopsychology.
7. Gerda Walther, Ph.D. (b. Nordrach/Black Forest, March 18, 1897; d. Weilheim, January 6, 1977). She was one of Husserl's students for a while in Freiburg where she, too, attended Edith Stein's "philosophical kindergarten." She earned her degree in Munich; her later work was principally concentrated on the study of mysticism and parapsychology.
8. Alexander Pfänder (b. Iserlohn, February 7, 1870; d. Munich, March 18, 1941). He was the center of the Munich circle of phenomenologists and co-editor of Husserl's *Jahrbuch [Yearbook].*

17. Letter to Roman Ingarden, Göttingen

First published in *Philosophy and Phenomenological Research,* Vol. 23, 1962

<Freiburg>, August 28, 1917

Dear Herr Ingarden,

...The Master is still in Bernau and is thinking of remaining there until the middle of September. So nothing will come of the longed-for joint work. I have now taken up his notes on the constitution of space and will see what can be done with them. In between, I am occupying myself somewhat with my own work and am supplementing it by writing down what has occurred to me, partially in connection with the *Ideen.*

Best regards,
Edith Stein

18. Letter to Roman Ingarden, Göttingen
First published in *Philosophy and Phenomenological Research,* Vol. 23, 1962

Bernau, September 8, 1917

Dear Herr Ingarden,

I am here with the Master for three days; assiduous work is being applied on *Zeit [Time].*[1]

We would like to send some manuscripts to Bell, who is pining for philosophical stimulation. Since we cannot take anything if only one copy of it is available—apparently, he is not permitted to return anything—we thought of a copy of your work. Please write to let us know whether you will be kind enough to spare one.

Best regards,
Edith Stein

1. See Letter 15.

19. Letter to Roman Ingarden, Göttingen
First published in *Philosophy and Phenomenological Research,* Vol. 23, 1962

Breslau, February 19, 1918

Dear Herr Ingarden,

...As "work," I still have before me the analysis of the person. Quantitatively, I have done more than a little at it, but how much of it will prove tenable is something beyond my judgment at present. When the Master recently favored me with a whole set of directions regarding the handling of his manuscripts (in a most friendly manner, but I simply cannot bear that kind of thing), I explained to him (also, of course, in a most friendly manner) that such a procedure (1) is impossible, in principle; (2) if at all valid, could be set up that way for his own use only by himself; and that (3) I am especially unsuited for it, and can only continue with this occupation if I do something original on the side. I am curious what he will have to say to that. I offered to remain on in Freiburg and to help him with the editing of the *Jahrbuch* and similar things, only not as his assistant in works for which I am unable to find meaning.

Basically, it is the thought of being at someone's disposition that I cannot bear. I can place myself at the service of something, and I can do all manner of things for the love of someone, but to be at the service of a person, in short—to obey, is something I cannot do. And if Husserl will not accustom himself once more to treat me as a collaborator in the work—as I have always considered our situation to be and he, in theory, did likewise—then we shall have to part company. I would regret that, for I believe there would then be even less hope of a connection between himself and "youth."

Lipps urgently directed me to send you his regards. He is once more at the Western Front (at his own request).

Best regards,
Edith Stein

[P.S.] I do not know yet what I should do were Husserl to take offense at my letter and if I were then, like Conrad, to fall into disfavor. Perhaps I would go for a while to Göttingen where—if, indeed, anywhere—I would feel somewhat at home. But I believe my staunch patron, Frau Malvine <Husserl>,[1] will see to it that it will not come to that....

1. Malvine Charlotte Husserl, née Steinschneider (b. Klausenburg/Siebenburgen, March 7, 1860; d. Freiburg, November 21, 1950) wife of Edmund Husserl. They had three children: Gerhart and Elisabeth [Elly], who both emigrated later to the United States, and Wolfgang, who was a casualty in WWII. In 1940, two years after her husband's death and shortly after WW II began, Franciscan Father H. L. Van Breda helped bring her and her husband's entire literary legacy safely to Belgium. The writings were safe in the *Institut Supérieur de Philosophie Cardinal Mercier* [Catholic University, Leuven, Belgium] but Frau Husserl was unable to save herself as planned by journeying on to the United States. In Belgium, courageous religious Brothers and Sisters saved her from the Nazis as well as from bombing attacks that destroyed part of the convent where she was being hidden. In 1945, she was able to join her son's family in New York. Frau Husserl kept up a secret correspondence with Edith Stein until Edith's deportation. See Volumes VII and X of *Edith Steins Werke* [See *Life*, p. 249, etc.]

20. Letter to Roman Ingarden, Göttingen
First published in *Philosophy and Phenomenological Research,* Vol. 23, 1962

Breslau, February 28, 1918

Dear Herr Ingarden,

...The Master has graciously accepted my resignation. His letter was most friendly—though not without a somewhat reproachful undertone. So now I am free, and I believe it is good that I am, even if, for the moment, I am not exactly happy....

Best regards,
Edith Stein

21. Letter to Fritz Kaufmann <Barracks in Romania>
Original in *Archivum Carmelitanum Edith Stein*

Breslau, March 10, 1918

Dear Herr Kaufmann,

Now perhaps your "barracks service" in Romania will also not last much longer. I hope you will be able to complete the preparations for your exams, undisturbed, while you are still there. Since when have you ventured among the Germanists? If you are looking for *easy* texts, I recommend to you *Meier Helmbrecht* (the Panzer edition), perhaps some selections from *Minnesangs Frühling* (Lachmann-Haupt), or Konrad von Würzburg's *Engelhart* (Haupt). Hartmann, too, is not difficult.[1]

Ingarden wants me to send you his very best regards; he is very happy about the forthcoming promotion and wishes you the best of luck with it.

As far as my activity as assistant is concerned I must inform you that I have asked Husserl to dispense me from it for the time being. Putting manuscripts in order, which was all my work consisted of for months, was gradually getting to be unbearable for me, nor does it seem to me to be so necessary that, for its sake, I should have to renounce doing anything on my own. So, as I told you, I am working at present on the analysis of the person. I want to be in Göttingen for Easter. Whether I will stay there for a longer period or go on to Freiburg (in order to be available if I should be needed), or whether I will come back here is something I just do not know at this time. In any case, I am thinking of starting on the treatise on Movement.[2] A while ago, I believe only after your visit, I received a transcript of Reinach's notes of the last two years on the philosophy of religion, very beautiful things. A few pages of expositions are so beautiful that they might be printed as a fragment. I must see what Frau Reinach[3] thinks about that.

You will recall, occasionally, that I am happy to hear from you, won't you?

With best regards,
Edith Stein

1. [The works and the "Germanists" mentioned here are not included in the index. The references, however, show Edith's familiarity with these "old masters" from her study of philology.]
2. This is Adolf Reinach's manuscript *Über das Wesen der Bewegung [The Essence of Movement]*, also mentioned in Letters 4 and 22.
3. Anna Reinach, née Stettenheimer (b. Stuttgart, June 21, 1884; d. Munich, December 29, 1953). Widow of Adolf Reinach, Anna had asked Edith Stein to organize her husband's literary legacy. [See *Life*, p. 248, etc.]

22. Letter to Fritz Kaufmann <Barracks in Romania>

Original in *Archivum Carmelitanum Edith Stein*

Freiburg, May 20, 1918

Dear Herr Kaufmann,

Finally, another sign of life! I wanted to get in touch with you for some time but just could not get to it lately. I have only been back here for three weeks. Before that, I spent a full month in Göttingen and looked over the entire literary legacy with Frau Reinach. The essay on Movement[1] has progressed fairly well. The constancy of movement seems to me to be clarified sufficiently. But on the problem of the differential and the mathematical determination there is so little material that it is hardly possible to get more out of it than a footnote.

Unfortunately the essay and the whole volume in which it is to appear will not come out so soon, since—and, in fact, partially through my fault—a rival undertaking threatens to develop. Husserl's 60th birthday will be in April of next year; I pointed that out in Munich and it has been decided that a *Festschrift* is indispensable. Luckily Pfänder[2] has allowed himself to be persuaded to take over its publication, provided he is assured of enough contributions, so that I will not have to solicit[3] for both undertakings simultaneously (and at this [war] time!) He himself [Pfänder] and Frau Conrad will probably provide something. How about a contribution from you for one or the other of these volumes? The rank of a noncommissioned officer is no prerequisite for collaboration. I am having some copies made of Reinach's notes on philosophy of religion and will send you one as soon as possible.

Ingarden (Krakow, Krupnicza 28) is at present applying for a position at the State *Gymnasium* in Warsaw. I am very unhappy about that, for with the limited resistance he has, eventually [his job there] will engage all of his energy.

Lipps (100th *Leibgrenadier* Regiment, 1st Battalion) was slightly wounded a while ago and, on his return trip to the front, came through Göttingen on the very day I left. Since he knew nothing of my impending departure and I nothing of his presence, he slept through the few hours we might have spent together!

The book you are searching for is *Der Wille zur Ewigkeit [The Will to Eternity]* by D. Mahnke,[4] published by Niemeyer.

Best regards,
Edith Stein

1. This essay, mentioned in Letter 21, was published in *Adolf Reinachs Gesammelte Schriften [Collected Works of Adolf Reinach]*, published first in Halle, 1921. [A new edition of his works was published by Karl Schuhmann and Barry Smith in Mu-nich, 1989].
2. Cf. Letter 16, n. 8.
3. [The contributions to be solicited can refer to articles and money—either or both. At first Reinach's students had intended to put out a memorial volume with essays they were to write in his memory. This plan was cancelled, and Reinach's collected works were published instead as a joint project by his students.]
4. [Dietrich Mahnke (b. 1884, d. 1939) was one of Husserl's earliest students. He later influenced Husserl to investigate monadology.]

23. Letter to Hedwig Conrad-Martius[1] <presumably in Bergzabern>
Original in the S*taatsbibliothek* [State Library], Munich <Literary Legacy H. Conrad-M.>

Freiburg, <presumably May 25, 1918>[2]

Dear Frau Dr. Conrad,

I am in agreement with the above-mentioned assessment. By the way, I had thought that was clear after your, and my, last letter. I have had no direct information from Rosenblum[3]; but I have heard that he will do something. If it is the essay on numbers then it can be considered *only* for the Reinach volume, and Rosenblum may not then be imposed upon for the *Festschrift.* Aside from that, I am in complete agreement that the *Festschrift*—timewise, above all—should have priority. There will be opportunity in future to discuss a collection of Reinach's writings with Frau Reinach. To incorporate the scattered works in the planned volume, as Hering proposes, would not, I believe, be according to her wishes. That requires more reflection. I had word from Pfänder today and will reply to him directly.

Best regards,
Edith Stein

1. Hedwig Conrad, née Martius (b. Berlin, February 27, 1888; d. Starnberg, February 15, 1966); married Theodor Conrad, philosopher and Husserl scholar, in 1912; she was a philosophy professor at the University of Munich. One of the earlier students of Husserl, she had great influence on his later ones. [Edith corresponded with Hedwig for two years before actually meeting her in the summer of 1920. From then on they were lifelong friends.]
2. This letter is written on notification of a decision made by Hedwig Conrad-Martius and Jean Hering that no memorial edition for Reinach is to be published, but that a collection of Reinach's writings including his lectures will be brought out. This paper bears the date May 25, 1918.
3. [Alexander Rosenblum—who later used his mother's surname, Augustowski—was one of Husserl's pre-WWI students. He became a teacher in Warsaw, where he died in the 1950s.]

24. Letter to Erna Stein, Breslau[1]
Original in private possession of family.

Freiburg, July 6, 1918

My dear Erna,

It is very painful for me to find such decidedly pessimistic leanings in you and Rosa <Stein[2]>. I would like so much to instill in both of you some of what, after every new blow, gives me fresh strength. I can only say that after everything I went through in the past year, I affirm life more than ever. I am sending an article by Rathenau[3] so you can see that other people have the same opinion about the outcome of the war as I have.

I really believe, at times, that one has to get accustomed to the idea of possibly not living to see the end of this war. Even then, one may not despair. One should not restrict one's view merely to the particle of life that is within one's ken, much less to what lies clearly apparent on the surface. After all, it is quite certain that we are at a turning point in the evolution of the intellectual life of humankind; and one may not complain if the crisis lasts longer than is acceptable to the individual. Everything that is now so terrible, and that I have no intention of glossing over, is precisely the spirit that must be surmounted. But the new spirit already exists and will prevail beyond all doubt. It may be clearly seen in philosophy and in the beginning of the new art form of expressionism. As surely as materialism and naturalism have become outmoded here, just as surely will they become obsolete in all the other spheres of life, even though slowly and amid painful struggles. One senses the will for this also in the political and social struggles that are driven by motives that differ totally from the hackneyed slogans people are wont to ascribe to them. Good and evil, knowledge and ignorance are mixed on *all* sides, and each one sees only the positive of his own side and the negative of the others'. That holds for peoples as well as parties. All this, intertwined, is spinning madly so no one can tell when some calm and clarity will set in again. In any case, life is much too complex for anyone to impose on it even the most clever plan for bettering the world, nor can one prescribe finally and unequivocally how it should proceed. Surely you will realize this is not directed against you. You will, after all, agree with me for the most part. I would only like to infuse in you a belief that the development, the direction of which we anticipate only within narrow limits, and in which we could have a voice within even narrower borders, will come to a good end.

Tomorrow I am going to pick up Martha in order to make a tour with her of Blauen, Belchen, Todtnau, Herzogenhorn, Feldberg and Titisee.

Love and kisses, your
Edith

1. Erna Biberstein, M.D., née Stein (b. Lublinitz/Upper Silesia, February 11, 1890; d. Davis, California, January 15, 1978). Married Hans Biberstein, a dermatologist, on December 5, 1920. They and their children, Susanne (later m. Batzdorff) and Ernst Ludwig, emigrated to New York in 1939. [See *Life*, pp. 14, 40, etc.]
2. Rosa Adelheid Stein (b. Lublinitz/Upper Silesia, December 13, 1883; d. with Edith in Auschwitz, August 9, 1942). [Rosa became a Catholic in 1936, and in 1939 she joined Edith in Echt, Holland; both were deported to Auschwitz from there. See *Life*, p. 40, etc.]
3. [Walter Rathenau was a German politician (1867-1922). A member of the Democratic party, he served May to October 1921 as Minister for Reconstruction; in 1922, as Foreign Minister, he sought to show the Versailles Treaty as impossible. He was murdered in 1922 by antisemitic Nationalists.]

25. Letter to Fritz Kaufmann <presumably in Romania>

Original in *Archivum Carmelitanum Edith Stein*

Freiburg, August 25, 1918

Dear Herr Kaufmann,

Sincerest thanks for your letter. Its lively descriptions gave me much pleasure (certainly more through the liveliness than through what you had to describe). It reached me in Göttingen where I spent three weeks with Fräulein Gothe. Hering joined us also at the beginning of August. I read them the essay on Movement[1] as I had formulated it and, to my joy, received their full agreement.

The plan to put out a memorial volume has been struck down as a result of certain difficulties. Instead, we have now decided, with Frau Reinach, to publish an assortment of Reinach's writings in one volume; the work on Movement will be included.

A Husserl *Festschrift* promises to materialize under Pfänder's leadership. I have agreed to contribute an essay on psychic causality. I have completed the basic outline for it but must rework it thoroughly.[2]

Lipps, who took part in the Battle of the Marne, recently announced he would be visiting me. Hering and I, however, have been waiting for him in vain for all of ten days.

Husserl is spending the vacation in Bernau again and is—as always happens in the Black Forest—diligently at work, while during the semester nothing got done at all.

Probably I will be here only for the winter and then will move permanently to Breslau, since that is my Mother's ardent wish. Naturally I will visit here often and will look for some way in which I can collaborate with Husserl on an ongoing basis.

Best regards,
Edith Stein

1. See Letter 22.
2. See Letter 28.

26. Letter to Fritz Kaufmann <presumably in Leipzig>
Original in *Archivum Carmelitanum Edith Stein*

Göttingen, June 9, 1919

Dear Herr Kaufmann,

I received your postcard today and I hasten to answer it. Of course, today—Pentecost Monday [a legal holiday]—I cannot do a thing about an apartment, but I can give you information about all the other matters.

Lipps and I shall, in any case, be here for several more weeks; neither of us knows for certain whether that will be until the end of the semester. Still, it will probably become clear during that time how the situation in Freiburg will shape up and whether one can consider going on from there. Besides, I consider the Freiburg nervousness[1] wholly unjustified. It does not seem to have penetrated at Husserl's [home], although one has been hearing such rumors for a long time among the students. It seems as though the students in all of South and West Germany are a little beside themselves; even in Göttingen there are people who dream of occupation by English forces. Since it is quite impossible to judge where one is going to be able to work peacefully in the coming months, in my opinion one should entirely exclude such considerations from the realm of factors to be considered. Of course, one must always be ready for surprises.

To make a long story short, I believe you should come here first, then make further decisions. If that makes sense to you, then please let me know soon, and give both information on time plus authorization to rent an apartment. Even though I intend to inquire at *Theaterplatz* even before I hear, such noncommittal inquiries are no more binding on the opposite side and would assure you of nothing, especially now when lodgings in Göttingen are so scarce.

Well, I hope to hear from you soon.

With best regards, I am your
Edith Stein

1. [There were persistent fears that Freiburg would be bombed.]

27. Postcard to Fritz Kaufmann, Göttingen
Original in *Archivum Carmelitanum Edith Stein*

Göttingen, July 17 <Stamped:1919>

Dear Herr Kaufmann,

It seems forever since I've seen you. I just wanted to tell you that I no longer live up there at the Reinachs' but down here with Fräulein Gothe. Perhaps sometime soon you'll find your way here? Gauss Street crosses the Reinhäuser Chaussee directly behind the Geismar gate.

With friendliest greetings,
Edith Stein

[P.S.] On Friday, before supper (after approximately 6 o'clock) we are sure to be at home.

28. Postcard to Fritz Kaufmann, Göttingen
Original in *Archivum Carmelitanum Edith Stein*

Breslau, August 15 <Stamped:1919>

Dear Herr Kaufmann,

Thank you for sending on my paper[1] and your notes on it. As soon as I can take a closer look at them I will write about them in detail. For the present I am too engrossed in Part II. I am touched by the thoroughness with which you have gone into the matter and I am very happy that you feel you have gained something from it. That it is not brought to a conclusion anywhere, I know very well.

Your [book of Hans Christian] Andersen has been an excellent companion meanwhile. I am very satisfied with the discussions I had with Niemeyer. They are really the ideal publisher and belong right in the family of the phenomenologists.

With best regards, your
Edith Stein

1. *Beiträge zur philosophischen Begründung der Psychologie und der Geisteswissenschaft [On the Philosophical Foundation of Psychology and the Humanities]* published in *Jahrbuch für Philosophie und Phänomenologische Forschung [Yearbook for Philosophy and Phenomenological Research]*, Vol. V, 1922.

29. Letter to Fritz Kaufmann <presumably in Göttingen>
Original in *Archivum Carmelitanum Edith Stein*

Breslau, September 16, 1919

Dear Herr Kaufmann,

Now at last you are to have the promised reply to your marginal comments on my paper. Perhaps it will be too late since, presumably, after such a long time you may no longer really recall the content. However, it was impossible for me to get to reviewing Part I sooner since Part II completely occupied my attention.

1. You cannot really reconcile yourself to the concept of expired experience. This is how that is meant: Whatever is actual—the *Now* phase—is always something momentary, and as such has no chance for

existence; rather it must become embedded in an experience that in its totality will have some duration. That from which this reality has sprung is—insofar as it no longer belongs in the Now—expired. However, insofar as it necessarily belongs to the unity of the experience and makes possible the ever present Now, it is still alive, not extinguished.

2. The position of the "foreign-to-the-I" data caused even me a great deal of headache, and I freely admit that on that question much is still needed for final clarity. That there is in it a contrast between experience and content, I expressed by the designation "foreign-to-the-I" *[ichfremd]*. On the other hand, it seems to me to be impossible to separate it from experience and show it as transcendental being. A datum foreign-to-the-I cannot be thought of other than as embedded in an experience; it has absolutely no independent being: therefore—despite its being foreign-to-the-I—*content.*

3. I do not believe I have cut the knot concerning the problem of the free will. I have only emphasized the negative—at least, what seems to me to be certain—that the spontaneity of the will cannot be deduced from the individual strengths and natural tendencies. Then, I have opened the door to the philosophy of religion in whose domain further investigations must take place.

4. I never claimed that the strength of a feeling is unequivocally determined by the level of the respective value. Of course, a value can be grasped fully as what it is, without its being felt with the appropriate strength. But there *is* an *appropriate* strength (perhaps not to be staked out by a fixed point, but within vaguely defined boundaries) and a Beyond and Beneath that is unreasonable *[Unvernünftig]*.

5. It is a misunderstanding when you think that I wish to speak of free action only where no position is taken. I speak of it most of all, wherever intention can take hold (positive or inhibiting), as well as in cases where intervention is not necessary, as it were, because a position has been taken.

6. You are not incorrect when you cast up to me my inability to handle the section reason-motivation-stimulus. Under the title *stimuli* I have combined [two] motivations: those only comprehensible but not rational motivations in the intentional sphere, and the *lower* motivations. I prefer not to say anything more here on the theme of association, since at that stage of the essay I have now inserted a few supplementary expositions.

Besides, this probably covers what is most important. Again, many thanks for your thorough study and for all the critical annotations.

I want to let you in on something else: I always have to laugh when anyone praises the *outline* of my work. That is always done retrospectively, when the work is all done.

How are you, and when will you go to Freiburg? With best regards, your

Edith Stein

29a.[1] Letter to Fritz Kaufmann, Freiburg
Original in *Archivum Carmelitanum Edith Stein*

Breslau, October 3, 1919

Dear Herr Kaufmann,

If this letter reaches you after you get to Freiburg, then you need not read any further. Otherwise, I would like you calmly to weigh the following concern with me. It had already occurred to me on former occasions, but more intensely in connection with your last letter.

I am worried at seeing how, for months, you have avoided doing purely philosophical work, and am gradually beginning to wonder whether your "profession" should not lie in a different direction. Please do not take this as a vote of "no confidence" or as doubting your ability. I only mean that one should not use force to make the center of one's life anything that fails to give one the right kind of satisfaction.

If you are convinced you have not set out on a wrong path but this is only a depressive phase that temporarily makes any strenuous effort impossible, then do not let my question divert you but rather, wait patiently—without violent exertion, which would only aggravate the situation—until the mood to work returns. But should you have had reflections similar to those I have had, then probably it would be time to face them seriously.

If you find discussion on this point disagreeable, then leave this letter unanswered and forgive me for writing it. I merely thought that, in general, four eyes see better than two, and only wanted to let you know that I am ready and willing to consider the matter with you, should no better counselor be available to you.

About October 15, I will go to Göttingen with my opus.[2] It is just now being typed—a highly unpleasant phase.

With best regards, your
Edith Stein

1. [This is the first of seven letters that form an appendix to Vol. II of the Letters in German. In the translated edition, they are inserted in chronological order, identified by the "a" following the number.]
2. See Letters 29 and 31.

30. Letter to Fritz Kaufmann, Freiburg
Original in *Archivum Carmelitanum Edith Stein*

<Breslau,> October 14, 1919

Dear Herr Kaufmann,

I am very glad at the way you accepted my last letter, and I thank you for that as well as for your good wishes [presumably for her birthday on the 12th] and the [book by] Rilke, which I did not yet have and like very much.

For the present I am satisfied that you are in Freiburg at this time and hope that, now, all will go well. After all, one need not make further plans for the future before they are necessary. I never had a doubt about Husserl's accepting you. According to your letter, everything seems to be going exceptionally well for him. Give the good Master my very fond regards. I will write to him myself, soon. If he inquired so lovingly about me, he must have a very guilty conscience, to be sure.

I am going to Göttingen in two days. I have no apartment at the present. Letters will reach me at Reinachs' or in care of Professor Courant,[1] Am Weissen Stein 5. Best regards to as many as I know in the Philosophical Society, of course, especially to you and Lipps.

Your,
Edith Stein

1. Richard Courant (b. Lublinitz, January 8, 1888; d. New Rochelle, NY, January 27, 1972). Maternal first cousin of Edith. Professor of Mathematics in Göttingen. [Cf. *Life,* p. 148 etc.] His first marriage, to Nelli Neumann in 1912, ended after three years. In January 1919 he married Nerina, called Nina, daughter of Prof. Carl Runge of Göttingen. Edith refers to Richard and Nina's home here.]

31. Letter to Fritz Kaufmann, Freiburg
Original in *Archivum Carmelitanum Edith Stein*

Göttingen, November 8, 1919

Dear Herr Kaufmann,

Thank you very much for your letter. Actually, I wanted to write for a long while to tell you that what was *impossible* according to your conviction, became possible. For all of ten days, the rejection[1], in black and white, has been in my pocket, or, more exactly, the document is in our files, closing the matter. [The application] was not even taken up by the faculty, but was quietly dispatched.

I received a letter from Hermann, the department head, that was meant to appear as an official notification, for a *pre-commission* had decided not even to judge my thesis since the habilitation of women continues to create many difficulties. The following day, evidently after the irregularity of this procedure had been explained to him, he told me orally that the danger had existed of having the thesis rejected because Müller[2] had asserted that it "would unseat psychology, as it is pursued here" (which is a slight error), and they had wished to spare me that [rejection].

I still see Misch[3] as the moving spirit behind it all; by any and all means he wanted to get himself out of the predicament of antagonizing either Müller or Husserl by his decision. You may tell that to Husserl, and add furthermore that I am not *crushed*. I only regret that now I am again faced with a decision about what to do in the future. There is a whisper of hope in Kiel. Heinrich Scholz,[4] whom I know personally, has been there since the beginning of this semester as successor to Deussen[5]. He wrote me today that for the time being he could really do nothing there, since there are already three privatdozents [outside lecturers] and three additional applications for habilitation have been received. But toward these applicants he intends to be very critical, because he would prefer to have me. But, of course, he can only turn them away if their theses are not useful and that has to be determined first. So I shall have to wait until spring for the final decision.

From here, I am going to go on to Hamburg to my eldest sister <Else>[6] and there, I will consult my old friend William Stern[7] once more.

I have not the heart to ask him to use his influence on my behalf since philosophy in Hamburg is already represented by two Jewish professors. Were he, contrary to my expectations, to consider it possible, then probably he would offer it to me himself. I am taking no further steps. Wherever I cannot count on personal goodwill, I will be given—as happened here and in Breslau—good advice: why don't you go to Freiburg! I do not care if you tell that to Husserl also, but I emphatically warn you of the debate that will ensue.

I am so glad that Freiburg agrees with you so well. I had already heard about it from Lipps. You see, a fortnight ago he appeared here "like a streak of lightning" (as Lachmann usually puts it). By the way, it was not nervousness that drove him away from Freiburg. Nor mania, of course. I knew very well that he would not have enough emotional resistance to endure the skirmishes in *Lorettostrasse.* After all, he suffers unspeakably whenever confronted with *injustice* and there [at Husserl's home in Lorettostrasse] you run into that at every step. That is why I was so determined to prevent his going to Freiburg until his habilitation dissertation was finished. Now, I fear he will never go back there, even though he is still determined to return. Will our good Lipps ever find rest at all, I wonder? One sees so clearly what he lacks and, at the same time, that one does not have the chance to help him. And one is so terribly eager to do so.

With best regards, I am your
Edith Stein

1. Her application for habilitation at the University of Göttingen was rejected.
2. Georg Elias Müller (b. Grimma/Sachsen, 1859; d. Göttingen, 1934), Ordinary Professor of Philosophy and Psychology at Göttingen.
3. Georg Misch (b. Berlin, 1878; d. Göttingen, 1965), Professor of Philosophy, Göttingen.
4. Heinrich Scholz (b. Berlin 1884; d. Münster, 1956), Professor of Philosophy, Kiel and Münster.
5. [Paul Deussen (b. Oberdreis/Westerwald, January 7, 1845; d. Kiel, July 6, 1919) Professor of Philosophy in Kiel.]
6. Else Gordon, née Stein (b. Gleiwitz/Upper Silesia, June 29, 1876; d. Bogota, Colombia, November 23, 1954), Edith's eldest sister, wife of Max Gordon, M.D., and mother of Ilse, Werner, and Anni Gordon. The Gordons lived in Hamburg, Germany until they emigrated to South America. [Cf. *Life*, p. 42, etc.]
7. Louis William Stern (b. Berlin, April 29, 1871; d. Durham, England, March 27, 1954) Professor of Philosophy and Psychology in Breslau and Hamburg. [Cf. *Life*, p. 185 etc.]

32. Letter to Fritz Kaufmann, Freiburg
Original in *Archivum Carmelitanum Edith Stein*

Göttingen, November 22, 1919

Dear Herr Kaufmann,

I have just received your dear letter of the 14th (service was faster from the Front) and must hurry and sit down to dampen somewhat your fury against this wicked world, in case it has not evaporated in the meantime. Yes, it was terribly dear of you to be so zealous on my behalf, but I must still tell you that things have gone very well here for me in the past weeks and that I am no longer the least bit furious or sad. Instead I find the whole matter very funny. After all, I do not consider life on the whole to carry so much weight that it would matter a great deal what position I occupy. And I would like you to make that attitude your own. So much for the world in general. And now, in particular:

First, re: Lipps. Here you misunderstood a small detail. On his way to Hamburg, he stopped here for a few hours. Since the direct routing includes Göttingen, he considered [stopping] as a matter of course and probably did not find it necessary to make special mention of it. And he did not have anything *to confide* concerning Husserl, either. Nothing in the least *happened* of which Husserl would have any knowledge. The whole thing concerns some minor personal matters that are best brought up in Göttingen, because there they will be appreciated as *hard-luck stories.* And should he, perhaps, express himself more freely to us, you may not see that as a bad intention. One cannot expect confessions from Lipps. But in the particular atmosphere one finds here, it is, on occasion, easy to speak about things that are ordinarily not mentioned. I, too, am much less reserved here than even with my nearest relatives.

Secondly, the Master. Dear Herr Kaufmann, that at times it is not easy to maintain the right attitude is something I have experienced to the full in the two years of my personal relationship [with him]. But one must keep reminding oneself that he himself suffers most because he has sacrificed his humanity to his science. That [work] is so overpowering and the amount of gratitude we owe him for it is so incalculable that, in view of that, any kind of personal resentment should not even arise. For me, he will always remain the Master, whose image cannot be blurred by any human weakness. Hering, for instance, is of the very same opinion, and were things not quite so bad for Lipps, surely he too would be able to accept that.

On Monday, I am going to Hamburg <to my eldest sister, Else> (19, Ottersbeckallee 6) and probably will go home at the beginning of December. Heartfelt thanks for taking my part in such friendly fashion, and best regards, your

Edith Stein

[P.S.] Greetings to all my Freiburg acquaintances. I am only assuming that he (Husserl) would explain to you in a long-winded way why he is unable to do anything, and I think I would find that highly disagreeable. I have never been afraid that it could lead to an *argument* with Husserl.

32a. Letter to Fritz Kaufmann, Freiburg
Original in *Archivum Carmelitanum Edith Stein*

Breslau, January 25, 1920

Dear Herr Kaufmann,

I received your letter today and was not a little horrified—for one thing, because, without my knowing or willing it, I offended you so much, for another, at the dreadful image of me that you create there. Do not think that I now want to take a turn at being oversensitive. I take it that, being in a depressed mood, you read all kinds of things into my letter that were neither in nor between the lines, and I hope intensely that you have already practiced some self-correction on your impression. Otherwise, I should despair of being able to persuade you to any other perception. For I cannot *prove* to you that such sentiments as you attribute to me in your letter are totally foreign to me.

I have neither passed a "verdict" on Husserl nor have I had a patronizing attitude toward you. As far as the former is concerned, I was completely in agreement with your viewpoint (perhaps I did not expressly emphasize that); I only meant that I was not inclined to warm to the positive aspect on that side, while such words still rang in my ears as "*You* may not pass any value judgments. You have forfeited that right." That to our Hans Lipps! And no one in the Husserl home would extend a hand to him any longer.

Dear Herr Kaufmann—as I already wrote to you a few months ago—I will never stop having a boundless veneration for the philosopher Husserl and will always concede any human weakness as his fate. And I would feel ridiculous to count as my merit that I am a bit closer to life than he. But you will surely understand *that* an insuperable barrier has been raised here when it comes to purely human relations and that I now feel this more strongly than ever. It is a fact that, today, I still cannot imagine how I could ever again face him person-to-person.

And now about [my] being patronizing! I do not know what would wound me most about this idea, had I to accord it a serious and lasting meaning: the arrogance you attribute to me; the exaggerated esteem of the intellectual (in case you indeed assume I fancy myself particularly competent in the scholarly domain); or, finally, that you are able to believe that I could feign a friendship for five years while relishing only my own superiority. But enough of that.

Now, I would only like to say something on the points on which serious self-examination gives me cause for self-reproach.

First, it is an old failing of mine that—professionally as well as personally— I tend to criticize without reflecting at length whether I have a right to do so. Many a time, I have thought (in retrospect) that people (not exactly my closest friends, of course) might easily take me for a megalomaniac.

Secondly, I must concede you are right—and about it I really cannot blame myself—that I probably like Lipps somewhat more than you and therefore have identified myself with him so intensely that I could thank you for "also" troubling yourself for him. (That "also," by the way, was occasioned by my just having heard of little Emmerich's efforts and of Frau Reinach's participation, etc.—Therefore it was meant as purely enumerating the people without giving them rank.) After all, it has nothing to do with either a human or even a scholarly evaluation. And it is true, isn't it, that you cannot be angry with me about that?

Thirdly, you must consider that, for at least three weeks, I had lived in complete ignorance [of the situation].[1] A few intimations from Lipps which allowed my fantasy the widest range of speculation—otherwise nothing. Several times I wanted to write to you for clarification. But I had no way of knowing that the news need not be treated as confidential and therefore did not want to discuss it with anyone. Immediately prior to your communication, I received word from Frau Reinach and felt so relieved at her confidence that Lipps would get over the catastrophe, that I treated the obvious facts with a kind of flippancy which, naturally, you could not understand. And one always ought to consider whom one is addressing and what an effect it might have. The only excuse I can offer is that, at present, so very many things burden me. Therefore, one of them is forever encroaching on the others so that none can really work itself out.

I would be very sad were this to be more than a passing mood on your part. In any case, I do want to tell you yet that I was very glad you told me everything right away. I know from personal experience—for I am much better acquainted with depressions than you perhaps surmise—what happens when one allows something like this to fester and tortures oneself with it in silence, whereby it takes on more and more monstrous dimensions.

Farewell and do please write soon to your old "patroness"!

Edith Stein

Incorrigible person!

P.S. At present I am not living at home, but with an elderly aunt who suddenly lost her daughter and who should not be left alone.

1. [This and the earlier comments about Lipps must certainly refer to a highly unpleasant lawsuit that involved Lipps. Edith makes some reference to it in *Life*. All the references in this letter are vague and can be understood only when the background is taken into consideration. Kaufmann did much to help Lipps in this difficult situation and his misunderstanding of Edith did not prevent his being a faithful friend to Lipps. This letter and the following one are important for understanding some of the references in Edith's letters to Ingarden. She noted uncanny analogies between her experiences in December 1917 and those of 1919-20. Cf. *Life*, Chapter VI, etc.]

33. Letter to Fritz Kaufmann, Freiburg

Original in *Archivum Carmelitanum Edith Stein*

Breslau, February 2, 1920

Dear Herr Kaufmann,

Only one thing in answer by return mail to your letter: I wrote to Clauss *only* on your and Frau Reinach's suggestion, for since [I left]

Freiburg I have not had a line from Lipps, and so am not in any way at all commissioned by him. I hope you will not make him pay for something I have incurred. Besides, it was not my intention to exclude you or anyone else in Freiburg, I only wanted Lipps to be excluded.

I neither wish nor am I able to say any more today. I am now downright afraid to use language.

With best regards, your
Edith Stein

34. Letter to Fritz Kaufmann, Freiburg
Original in *Archivum Carmelitanum Edith Stein*

Breslau, February 12, 1920

Dear Herr Kaufmann,

Thank you for your kind lines. Please don't plague yourself now with self-reproach. I can readily understand that my clumsy way of crossing your self-sacrificing efforts exasperated you thoroughly, and I have not[1] been angry with you for a moment. I think we will let this matter be buried now, and consider our old trusting relationship as the immovable foundation which underlies all words and dealings. Right?

And now I wish you and all the others much joy as you carry our cause, at which we will not disturb you anymore.

Best regards, your
Edith Stein

[P.S.] At your convenience, I would like to hear just *how* badly Husserl thinks of me.

1. [Considering the emotional importance of the situation this letter refers to, it may be of interest to note that, on rereading what she had written, Edith used a caret and inserted *not* at this point.]

35. Letter to Fritz Kaufmann, Freiburg
Original in *Archivum Carmelitanum Edith Stein*

Breslau, April 30, 1920

Dear Herr Kaufmann,

A small eternity has passed since I heard from you, and I am not even sure that I should still look for you in Freiburg. My formal reason for writing is that I have two pleas to put to you.

One of them is a concern of Ingarden's. He writes to me today that, some time ago, he requested Herr Clauss to return a copy of his [Ingarden's] work on Bergson and has had no reply. He had left it with Herr Clauss, in Freiburg, and now needs it to make some changes before he hands it over to Husserl for the yearbook.

Would you be so kind as to inquire whether it has been dispatched and, in the event this is necessary, send it off yourself? (Address: Dr. R. Ingarden, Warsaw, Zlota 41, No. 4) Perhaps you can keep from mentioning my mediation in this matter in order not to awaken painful memories? And should, for any reason, the whole matter be unpleasant, please do not hesitate to decline. It was just an inspiration of mine that perhaps I might help Ingarden in this way.

The second request is more harmless. A young man from here has gone to Freiburg in order to attend Husserl's lectures, and I promised him an introduction to you that, actually, I should have sent long ago. His name is Norbert Elias (recognizable by a blue-white [lapel] pin!) Medicine is his main occupation—or sideline; he has been drilled philosophically by Hönigswald,[1] but was instructed by me that he has to curb his criticism if he is to get the gist of some phenomenology. I also gave him a card for Herr Thust, but I do not know whether he is back in Freiburg.

I must inform you about myself that *faute de mieux* [for want of anything better] I have awarded myself the *venia* [license to lecture] and am holding lectures with exercises in my home (Introduction to Philosophy on a Phenomenological Basis) at which more than 30[2] people take part. Besides that I will soon begin [to teach] a course in the public high school on basic questions in ethics.

What are you doing? With best regards, your

Edith Stein

1. Richard Hönigswald (b. Altenburg, Hungary, 1875: d. 1947, New York) was Professor of Philosophy in Breslau, Munich and the United States. [Cf. *Life,* p.185, etc.]
2. [A typographical error in the German edition of the letters gives this number as "50," The original letter shows a distinct "30." In a letter to Roman Ingarden written on the same day, she again gives the number as "30." (Cf. Ingarden Letter 68).]

36. Letter to Fritz Kaufmann, Freiburg

Original in *Archivum Carmelitanum Edith Stein*

Breslau, May 31, 1920

Dear Herr Kaufmann,

When I returned home from my Pentecost [holiday] trip to the *Riesengebirge* [mountains], I found your letter and, at the same time, a postcard from Ingarden with a renewed plea for his Bergson essay. I am very glad that has now been taken care of. There is no need to apologize about Herr Elias. I believe it would do him a great deal of good if he were to come into the "kiddies' circle"[1]. For, as you obviously have already observed, he has the usual critic's arrogance. However, I do believe that, if he could be shorn of that, something useful would surface. I would be sorry, too, if he were not satisfied in Freiburg for he went there with the best intention of learning something.

I find it difficult to orient myself in the Freiburg you describe to me. It would make me so happy sometime to hear all about it in detail, in person, when one could really discuss what is to come from it all. For in no way do I consider myself as no longer belonging there, as disenfranchised, and that is how I feel about the others who, in Husserl's view, have faded away. As far as one can foresee, I will be meeting with Erika Gothe and Hans Lipps in Göttingen in August. Perhaps you, too, will pop up there sometime? I find your suggestion about Lipps' habilitation very worthy of consideration, and I would rather talk to him about it in person.

Right now, I would like to engage your services as an agent once more. At the suggestion of Pfänder, who dealt with me originally about my contribution to the *Jahrbuch,* I recently wrote to Husserl and asked him to put my *whole* "Habilitation thesis" (Parts I and II)[2] into Volume V. Since you are of the opinion that he is not holding anything in particular against me, it might not be uncomfortable for you to feel him out whether he will answer me by letter or whether he would give you the answer. Were he to want Part II to look over, it would, at the same time, be an opportunity for you to get to know the work yourself.

So far, my lectures have not hindered me completely from continuing my writing, but since it all has to be done in the evening, after a full day's work, it causes considerable overexertion and has somewhat undermined my health. In the mountains I gathered some reserve energy that hopefully will last until the end of the semester. I am not thinking of trying again for habilitation. That circular to the universities regarding the habilitation of women was due to my request, certainly, but I promise myself very little by way of results. It was only a rap on the knuckles for the gentlemen in Göttingen.

I do not know where things stand regarding the litigation; Lipps has not written anything about it to me for a long time. Has Herr Clauss really pulled himself together to some extent, and is he able to work? And what happened to Frau Clauss?

I ask these questions because of purely personal interest, but I ask only you, for obvious reasons. I would not want this expression of interest to go any further.

With best regards, your
Edith Stein

[P.S.] A very warm greeting to your energetic little brother. I am happy that you have someone like him there, for it surely must be awfully good for you.

1. See Letters 14 and 16.
2. See Letter 28.

37. Letter to Dean Eugen Breitling,[1] Bergzabern
Original in Convent Archive of Cologne Carmel

Breslau, October 10, 1922

Most Reverend Dean,

I have been at home, now, for a week. Today I found some time to look in the library for literature on aesthetics in music. Whatever I considered important for the special theme I marked with a "+." Apparently very little has been published on the subject.

Everything is going well for me here. In the coming weeks I will have considerable time for myself and will be able to do some scholarly work again. At present I have an older manuscript that's ready to be printed.

I hope all is well with you and your housemates.

With most respectful greetings, your ever grateful

Edith Stein

<Father Breitling added a postscript to this:>

Bergzabern, October 20, 1922

Honorable Herr Expositus![2]

I am sending you some literary references for your topic that Frl. Stein put together *for you* at the library of the University of Breslau. Fraulein Stein is a convert *ex Judaismo* and was baptized here on January 1, 1922—a highly talented, very learned Fräulein Doctor of Philosophy.

Wishing you the best success, greetings from your most humble,

Breitling, g.R.

1. Eugen Breitling (b. Böhl in the Pfalz, 1851; d. Bergzabern, 1939) priest, pastor, and Dean. He baptized Edith Stein in the parish church of St. Martin, Bergzabern. [The initials after his signature designate his role as *geistlicher Rat,* that is, spiritual Councillor, advisor to the priest to whom his note is written.]
2. [A cleric who had sole spiritual charge of a portion *(Expositur)* of a parish.]

38. Letter to Fritz Kaufmann, Freiburg

Original in *Archivum Carmelitanum Edith Stein*

Breslau, July 28, <19>25

Dear Herr Kaufmann,

A few weeks ago I heard that you almost came to Conrads' in Bergzabern, and yesterday, while putting old letters in order, I came across several of yours. These—I cannot say "reminded me of you" since forgetting has never been my thing where human relations are concerned—but [the letters] moved you out from the fog-shrouded distance into palpable nearness again, and I wanted to tell you that.

I was sorry to hear that your mother's illness kept you bound to Leipzig; and throughout the years, whenever anyone came from Freiburg, I asked about you, but they were always the most meager accounts and usually from people who did not know you well. Of course, I would be interested in all you would have to tell me about yourself. But if you prefer not to do so, then just let it be, please. I have always readily understood why you no longer wrote, and have never been cross about it.[1]

Right now I am at home for vacation. Otherwise I live, as you probably know, in Speyer at St. Magdalena's convent.

With best regards, your
Edith Stein

1. He was estranged by her becoming a Catholic on January 1, 1922.

38a. Letter to Fritz Kaufmann, Freiburg
Original in *Archivum Carmelitanum Edith Stein*

St. Magdalena <Speyer>, September 13, 1925

Dear Herr Kaufmann,

I was very happy to have your letter. Mainly because of the fact that...[1] For after the long interval I had strong reservations about possibly having committed another inappropriate intrusion. Surely, when I heard a fortnight ago in Bergzabern that you lost your mother I was very glad indeed that I had sent you regards. It seemed almost strange to me that I never saw your mother. You, of course, told me hardly anything about her, but I always had a very strong sense of the maternal care that supported you. That, indeed, is something no one can replace. But perhaps it will lessen the feeling of loneliness somewhat if you know that there is someone who thinks of you constantly. The formation of an unshakable bond with all whom life brings in my way, a bond in no way dependent on day-to-day contact, is a significant element in my life. And you can depend on that [tie] even when I do not always reply as promptly as this time.

In my experience, it is beneficial to have a fixed round of duties, whatever they may be; for that reason, I welcome your habilitation and wish, with all my heart, that it will fulfill all your expectations, and even more. Has not your doctoral thesis been printed even as a dissertation? I was always somewhat surprised that I never received a copy.

Now, I am to tell you something about myself. Where shall I begin, Herr Kaufmann, after 5 years? There is something I would like to comment on about the time just prior to those years. If I failed you, humanly speaking—and it was only much later that I realized fully just how much I did so, although even that summer of 1919 in Göttingen I was painfully and oppressively aware of it—then it was probably at least partially due to my being in such a pitiable state myself, almost as deplorable as yours. It occurred to me only a few days ago that, most likely, you never really knew about that and that it can explain a great deal to you. That [condition] began even earlier and, through many changes, lasted for years longer, until I found the place where there is rest and peace for all restless hearts. How that happened is something you will allow me to be silent about today. I am not reluctant to speak about it and, at the right time, will surely do so with you also, but it has to "come about"; it is not something about which I can "report".

For all of three years now I have been living behind the sheltering walls of a convent, at heart—and this I may surely say without any presumption—like a real nun, even though I wear no veil and am not bound by vows or enclosure. Nor, for the present, may I think of contracting such a bond. That I am teaching at a college [belonging to Dominican nuns] you will probably have heard. Let me divulge something to you: I do not take myself too seriously as a teacher, and still have to smile when I have to put it down anywhere as my profession. But that does not hinder me from taking my responsibilities seriously, and so, in spirit and soul, I am deeply absorbed by them. That is why the opportunity to do any scholarly work is still a problem. During the first two years, I only did a bit of translation besides my school work; that was as far as it went. Then I wanted to get at something bigger, namely a critical examination of St. Thomas [Aquinas]. I did make a start with the study of the *Quaestiones Disputatae* but so far the necessary continuity has not been established, and I have to wait to see what comes of it.

And now, something entirely different: have you completely given up the plan to go to Bergzabern to gather strength for your career as a *privatdozent*? I would be very happy if that were to happen. First of all, and I say this quite frankly, in the interest of the Conrads' finances.[2]

Then, there would be an opportunity to make a side trip to Speyer, and a few hours spent together would surely do much more than many letters.

Will you kindly give my best regards to your sister, and tell me sometime, what has become of her?

Most cordially, your
Edith Stein

1. [The dots here are in Edith's original letter. The context must have been evident to Fritz Kaufmann without words.]
2. [The Conrads, Hans Theodor and Hedwig, had an orchard at Bergzabern and counted on the help of friends from Göttingen and Freiburg to harvest the fruit, in return for room and board.]

39. Postcard to Fritz Kaufmann, Freiburg
Original in *Archivum Carmelitanum Edith Stein*

St. Magdalena <Speyer>, November 14, 1925

Dear Herr Kaufmann,

I hope, by now, you will have reached your goal.[1]

Bergzabern is finished insofar as the Conrads have rented two rooms to the new district councilman and will in future be unable to accommodate even their oldest regular guests at their house. I was still able to meet Hering and Lipps there, on a Saturday shortly before.

Of course, you can just as easily see me without that arrangement [going to Bergzabern]. All you have to do is get on a train to Heidelberg some Saturday morning and, in Heidelberg, take the little Rhine train that will get you to Speyer in an hour and a half. It will take you but two minutes from the Rhine station in Speyer to the convent, where everyone who comes to visit me finds the friendliest reception.

Best regards to the Husserls, also, from your
Edith Stein

1. His habilitation in Freiburg-am-Breisgau.

Edith Stein in 1925, as an Instructor at St. Magdalena's, a training institute for women teachers run by the Dominican Sisters at Speyer.

40. Holy card [picture of St. Agnes by Ribera] to Sr. Agnella Stadtmüller, OP[1] <Speyer>
Original in Convent Archive of the Dominican Nuns, St. Magdalena, Speyer

January 19, 1926

Best Wishes for your *Name Day* and many greetings from your
Edith Stein

[P.S.] A second answer has arrived from Regensburg. The first one got lost.

1. Maria Stadtmüller (Sr. Agnella, OP) (b. Landstuhl, 1898; d. St. Magdalena, Speyer, 1965). Ph.D., taught in the Dominican Sisters' colleges in Speyer and Ludwigshafen. [No explanation is given for the P.S. about Regensburg.]

41. Letter to the General Vicariate, Speyer on the Rhine
Original in *Archivum Carmelitanum Edith Stein*

Speyer (St. Magdalena), February 21, 1926

Most Reverend Bishop! [Dr. Ludwig Sebastian[1]]
Your Excellency!

Respectfully, I ask your Grace kindly to permit me to keep in my possession the following books that are on the Index; and may I use them when needed?

1. Henri Bergson, *Les Données Immédiates de la Conscience [Time and Free Will]*
2. Henri Bergson, *L'Évolution Créatrice [Creative Evolution]*
3. Henri Bergson, *Matière et Mémoire [Matter and Memory]*
4. David Hume, *Treatise on Human Nature* (2 Vols)
5. Immanuel Kant, *Critique of Pure Reason*
6. John Locke, *Essay Concerning Human Understanding* (2 Vols)
7. Baruch Spinoza, *Opera omnia.* [complete works]

All of them are writings that I formerly used in the study of modern philosophy. Currently I am principally occupied with the works of

St. Thomas. Since it is important to me to attain clarity regarding the connection between Thomistic and modern philosophy, it will scarcely be possible to avoid the occasional use of the above-named writings for comparison. For that reason, I would be most grateful for your Excellency's kind permission.

Respectfully yours, Your Grace,
Dr. Edith Stein

Returned to: Fräulein Dr. Edith Stein at the direction of his Excellency with the response that the desired permission is granted for the duration of the circumstances as described.

Speyer, February 26, 1926

(Signed) Vicar General Schwind[2]

1. [Most Rev. Dr. Ludwig Sebastian (b. Franken, 1862; d. 1943, Speyer) is the prelate who confirmed Edith Stein in the private chapel of the Bishop's house in Speyer on February 2, 1922.]
2. [Mons.] Joseph Schwind (b. Schifferstadt, November 28, 1851; died Speyer, September 17, 1927) was Vicar General of the Diocese of Speyer on the Rhine.

42. Art[1] postcard to Fritz Kaufmann (Freiburg)
Original in *Archivum Carmelitanum Edith Stein*

St. Magdalena <Speyer>, December 21, 1926

Most cordial Christmas greetings to you, dear Herr Kaufmann, from your

Edith Stein

1. [The postcard carries no address nor postal cancellation. The portrait is a madonna from an exhibition of art of the Middle Ages presented by the Silesian Museum in Breslau in autumn, 1926.]

42a. Letter to Fritz Kaufmann <presumably Freiburg>
Original in *Archivum Carmelitanum Edith Stein*

St. Magdalena <Speyer>, January 6, 1927

Dear Herr Kaufmann,

This letter [of yours] was an unexpected major achievement. I know how difficult it is for you to write, and therefore I thank you doubly for it.

Why do you regret that you spoke openly with me then? You must have realized that all your misgivings could not touch me in the least. And if you gave me a glimpse of your innermost thoughts, then I was only grateful for it. I always appreciate being able to see a person's distress at close range and very clearly, because then I am better able to know what I must ask on his behalf. I believe there is hardly anything else I can do for you right now. Arguments will be of no help to you. Were one able to free you from all argumentation, then you would be helped.

And advice? I have given you my advice: Become like a child and lay your life *with* all the searching and ruminating into the Father's hand. If that cannot yet be achieved, then plead; plead with the unknown and doubted God for help in reaching it. Now you look at me in amazement that I do not hesitate to come to you with wisdom as simple as that of a child. It *is* wisdom *because* it is simple, and all mysteries are concealed in it. And it is a way that most certainly leads to the goal.

I thank you too for your report on the Pater. But I beg you to spare me the need to reply to it. I noticed that I must, perhaps, have followed a misguided approach when I spoke to you on this matter (but even so you must not conclude that I am sorry I confided in you) and I would prefer not to compound my guilt by continuing the discussion.

This Christmas Eve I spent, as in the past few years, here in the convent. It cannot be more lovely anywhere else. Then for a few days I was in Bergzabern and returned on New Year's Eve. Frau Conrad told me you are planning to go there some time.

Now, what about the *Jahrbuch?* Is its publication still held up?

Best regards and most cordial wishes, your

Edith Stein

43. Letter to Fritz Kaufmann, Freiburg
Original in *Archivum Carmelitanum Edith Stein*

St. Magdalena <Speyer>, September 13, 1927

Dear Herr Kaufmann,

Your announcement [of his forthcoming wedding to Alice Lieberg] reached me today. In the meantime you have probably left Freiburg, and I do not have your address in Kassel. But I want to try, at least, to reach you before the 18th [September 18, 1927, a Sunday].

No doubt Ingarden has delivered my best regards; but even without them you would be in no doubt as to how I received the news. Of course, I would be even happier if I knew your bride.[1] As it is, I have the highest expectations [of happiness] for you. That you were able to arrive at this decision is in itself sufficient proof.

When Sunday morning dawns, remember that, in Speyer, someone with a happy and confident heart is getting ready to go to the Cathedral to join in your celebration in her own way.

With heartfelt greetings, your
Edith Stein

1. [Kaufmann's first wife was Alice Dorothee Lieberg. Her birthdate is not recorded; she died in Buffalo, NY, in 1953. Cf. *Life,* p. 492.]

44. Letter to Sr. Callista Kopf, OP[1] [presumably sent to Munich]
Original in Convent Archive of the Dominican Sisters in Speyer

St. Magdalena <Speyer>, October 12, 1927

Dear Sister Callista,

Your farewell note is still in my purse. I wanted so much to answer it at once, but did not get around to it. I wanted to tell you that no words at all were necessary. There are matters that are best understood without words. [On September 17, Canon Schwind had died suddenly.] I know there is no one in St. Magdalena who more truly shares my joys and sorrows than you. Only, do not think of the sorrow as too great and the joys too meager. Heaven never takes anything from us without making it up to us beyond measure.

Now let us celebrate our Name Days together [October 14, St. Callistus; October 15, St. Teresa, one of Edith's baptismal names]. When you return, we will have to look back and seek out from the treasures in my library (to which, by today, several volumes have been added) something that you will be able to use in Munich.[2]

But let me tell you something encouraging now that the new semester is beginning. Sr. Agnella <Stadtmüller> visited me several times even after the Newman manuscript was completed.[3] I believe we need not really worry about her so much. She bears a cross like everyone else, but it has borne fruit for her, and she knows that and so would not wish to give it up. We too, dear Sister, have to learn to see that others have a cross to carry and to realize we cannot take it from them. It is harder than carrying one's own, but it cannot be avoided.

I believe you can be of the greatest help to others when you trouble yourself least about how you are to accomplish that, and remain, instead, as unconcerned and cheerful as possible. And when you yourself get to have the difficulties of a religious who is also a student, then tell yourself that this is the very way you are to serve. I expect great benefits for the entire house from Sisters who are pursuing studies: not merely for the schools (obviously, for them they are a necessity) but also for the religious life. Even though you may think, at this moment, that you do not know what I mean by that, you will surely know it after a few semesters.

Many good wishes and best regards, and these for Srs. Immolata and Theophana, as well, from your

Edith Stein

1. Elisabeth Kopf (Sr. M. Callista, OP) (b. Speyer on the Rhine, 1903; d. Dannenfels, 1970) assistant teacher of Germanistics [i.e., German language and literature], taught at the girls' high school at St. Magdalena's. Later she was prioress at the Convent of St. Magdalena, Speyer.

2. Sr. Callista was studying German, history, and English at the Universities of Munich and Würzburg.

3. Edith Stein's translation *J. H. Newman, Briefe und Tagebücher bis zum Übertritt zur Kirche [John Henry Newman's Letters and Diaries to His Conversion]*, Munich, 1928.

45. Letter to Sr. Callista Kopf, OP <presumably sent to Munich>
Original in Convent Archive of the Dominican Sisters in Speyer

St. Magdalena <Speyer>, February 12, 1928

Dear Sister Callista,

I would have liked to answer the kind greetings you sent for the Feast of the Purification [the anniversary of Edith's Confirmation] much sooner, but it was impossible. And since I know I shall soon be interrupted, I will get at once to the heart of your letter and answer your principal question.

Of course, religion is not something to be relegated to a quiet corner or for a few festive hours, but rather, as you yourself perceive, it must be the root and basis of all life: and that, not merely for a few chosen ones, but for every true Christian (though of these there is still but a "little flock"). That it is possible to worship God by doing scholarly research is something I learned, actually, only when I was busy with [the translation of] St. Thomas [Aquinas' *Quaestiones de Veritate* from Latin into German]. (In the little booklet that the Sisters here use for the Thomas Sundays, there is a beautiful meditation about that.) Only thereafter could I decide to resume serious scholarly research.

Immediately before, and for a good while after my conversion, I was of the opinion that to lead a religious life meant one had to give up all that was secular and to live totally immersed in thoughts of the Divine. But gradually I realized that something else is asked of us in this world and that, even in the contemplative life, one may not sever the connection with the world. I even believe that the deeper one is drawn into God, the more one must "go out of oneself"; that is, one must go to the world in order to carry the divine life into it.

The only essential is that one finds, first of all, a quiet corner in which one can communicate with God as though there were nothing else, and that must be done daily. It seems to me the best time is in the early morning hours before we begin our daily work; furthermore, [it is also essential] that one accepts one's particular mission there, preferably for each day, and does not make one's own choice. Finally, one is to consider oneself totally as an instrument, especially with regard to the abilities one uses to perform one's special tasks, in our case, e.g., intellectual ones. We are to see them as something used, not by us, but by God in us.

This, then, is my recipe, and I presume that Sr. Dolorosa's will not be very different; so far, I have never talked to her about it. My life begins anew each morning, and ends every evening; I have neither plans nor prospects beyond it; i.e., to plan ahead could obviously be part of one's daily duties—teaching school, for example, could be impossible without that—but it must never turn into a "worry" about the coming day.

After all that, you will understand why I cannot agree when you say I have "become" someone. It does appear as though the orbit of my daily duties is to expand. But that, in my opinion, does not change anything about me. It has been demanded of me, and I have undertaken it, although I am still in the dark about what it will comprise, and what the routine will consist of. I shall be thinking of you on the 15th.

I would appreciate your allowing Sr. Agnella <Stadtmüller> to read this letter, for I cannot write another one to her now. But do so only if you like the idea. Otherwise just give both of the Sisters my warmest regards and au revoir. After all, they will be coming here soon.

Most cordially, your
Edith Stein

46. Entry in Guest Book of the Mayer Family, Beuron[1]

Original in Convent Archive of Cologne Carmel

<Beuron> April 9, 1928

Laetatus sum in his quae dicta sunt mihi: in domum Domini ibimus. I rejoiced when I heard them say: let us go to the House of the Lord.

In the hope that very soon I shall again be able to go from the hospitable home at the Holzbrücke [the wooden bridge] to the "House of the Lord," and with sincere gratitude

Dr. Edith Stein
Speyer on the Rhine, Convent St. Magdalena

1. On her visits to Beuron, Edith Stein usually stayed with the Mayers, parents and daughters, in this "hospitable home next to the wooden bridge." The Mayers' guest book contains many entries in Edith Stein's handwriting. The one cited here is the first.

47. Postcard to Fritz Kaufmann, Freiburg
Original in *Archivum Carmelitanum Edith Stein*

St. Magdalena, Speyer, October 5–7, <1928>

Dear Herr Kaufmann,

You are not to wait a year for an answer, even though there is no time for a long letter. So thank you very much for your kind lines and for the *separatum* [off-print]. Of course, I have not yet been able to read it.

(N.B. Could you perhaps find out diplomatically whether Husserl has any intention of sending me a *separatum* of [his] article on time? Then, you see, I would return the *Jahrbuch* volume that Niemeyer sent me.)

Perhaps during the Easter vacation I will have an opportunity to get to know your wife and daughter. That would make me very happy.

I hope to conclude my work on the *Quaestiones de veritate* before the end of this year and, in the new one, to be able to give it to the printer. But, in my case, one cannot foretell anything definitely because so much always interferes. My translation [from English into German] of New-man's *Letters and Diaries,* which lay for years <in manuscript form> at the *Theatiner-Verlag*,[1] has just been published. Unfortunately, I did not receive enough copies to be able to send you one.

With all best wishes for you and yours, I am your

Edith Stein

1. [*Theatiner-Verlag,* the publishing firm of the Theatine order, in Munich, had Dietrich von Hildebrand as one of its founders. When Edith's translation of St. Thomas Aquinas was ready in 1930 the firm had gone out of business.]

48. Letter to Frau Adelheid Noack, Heidelberg
Original in private possession of Frau Adelheid Noack, née Hester-Cramer

St. Magdalena <Speyer> December 22, 1928

My dear Frau Noack,

You will allow me a few words, won't you? If you should now cancel your trip, or postpone it, and if you thought that being with me would do you good, then I ask you sincerely to make use of me—until the 28th, for then I must go away for a bit (until January 7).

In any case, I think most warmly of you and your little one,[1] and I will do so especially on Christmas Eve, at the creche which I would love to show to your children. There one is united with all who are scattered throughout the world, and also beyond the world. That is such a consoling mystery.

Lovingly, your
Edith Stein

1. Frau Noack's small daughter had died shortly before that.

49. Letter to Frau Callista Brenzing,[1] OCist, Seligenthal
Original in Convent Archive of Cologne Carmel

St. Magdalena <Speyer>, April 29, 1929

Dear Reverend [Mother] Frau Callista,

Since Sr. Agnella <Stadtmüller> has suddenly been summoned[2] and will be coming to you, I am able to give her a brief greeting to bring to you. You will surely notice that Sr. Agnella still has the afterglow of Beuron about her. What one takes away from there is lasting. And in the space of twelve days there, one can gather a treasure that will keep for a very long time and will help to digest everything that comes from outside. That will answer the question about my condition. I, too, would be very happy to meet you again. For the time being there are no definite prospects of a trip to Munich in sight. But you already know that such things can come up suddenly.

Otherwise, I wish you would make an educational tour of the Cistercian abbeys in Silesia[3] in August, and I offer my services as your guide. All the best for the coming semester. I am sending along the Companion for that [semester]. [She enclosed a Beuron holy picture of the Child Jesus.]

With best regards, respectfully yours *in Christo,*
Edith Stein

1. Maria Brenzing (Frau [Mother] Callista, OCist) (b. Landshut, Bavaria, 1896; d.

Seligenthal, 1975) taught in the public schools, and studied Germanistics in the university. In 1917, she entered the monastery of the Cistercian nuns at Seligenthal Abbey above Landshut. Through some Dominican Sisters from Speyer, with whom she studied, she became acquainted with Edith Stein.
2. For a year of practice teaching in Munich.
3. These abbeys were founded from the abbey of Cistercian nuns in Trebnitz, Silesia.

50. Postcard to Katharina Schreier,[1] Munich
Original in Convent Archive of Cologne Carmel

St. Magdalena <Speyer>, May 20, 1929 Pentecost Monday
Dear Fräulein Schreier,

The greater part of the Munich group is together and sends you many thanks and best regards,

Edith Stein

<In another's handwriting:> Sincere greetings from the Rhine: Anna Liebel, Susi Wannemacher, Marianne Schneider, Paula Westerdorf.

1. Katharina Schreier (b. Munich, 1900; died there in 1954), a teacher, was active in the [German] Catholic Youth Movement as leader and educator.

51. Letter to Sr. Adelgundis Jaegerschmid,[1] OSB, Freiburg-Günterstal
Original in Convent Archive of Benedictine Sisters, St. Lioba, Freiburg-Günterstal

Pax! St. Magdalena <Speyer>, January 26, 1930
Dear Sister Adelgundis,

Thank you very much for your kind, detailed letter. I am not only willing to agree to what you say in criticism of my lecture, I would augment it: not only was church history treated very briefly, actually it was not treated at all. A reference was simply made to point out that it should also be dealt with. Therefore, a lecture from you, or an article, would be a welcome complement.

My inability to treat everything on an equal basis was due, for one thing, to [the lack of] time: given the framework of the meeting, the lecture was already long enough. Then, of course, there was also my position: if you look up what I wrote to Sr. Placida <Laubhardt> about my preparation, you will understand why I dealt predominantly with liturgy. Far be it from me to underrate church history. For years I have had a keen desire to take it up, but so far I have been able to do so only sporadically and unsystematically. In the present circumstances of my life, I can do no more than wait patiently until heaven presents me with this opportunity some day. Everything comes in its own time.

I have had the thought privately: How good it would be for St. Magdalena if you could give a course in choral [singing and recitation] here sometime. But I have not mentioned it to anyone yet. I do well to speak only when I am asked—in such matters at least.

The old Pastor <Breitling> at Bergzabern who baptized me sent me a touching letter about the article, giving me some practical tips on the education of our children. For many years he was the Diocesan Moderator of the Caecilian Societies and he is an enthusiastic admirer of choral music. Therefore, in Bergzabern, every child in school has learned choral singing, and coming from there, I know of scarcely anything for Sundays but a choral Mass.

Now, my congratulations on having been granted the privilege of studying theology; and with best wishes and *in desiderio vitae monasticae* <in longing for monastic life> I remain united to you as your

Edith Stein

1. Amelie Jaegerschmid (Sr. Adelgundis, OSB) (b. Berlin, 1895) studied philosophy and history in Freiburg; earned her Ph.D., majored in history. She attended Edith Stein's "philosophical kindergarten" in Freiburg, and belonged to the younger of Husserl's students. In 1921, she became a Catholic and later entered the convent of the Benedictines of St. Lioba in Freiburg-Günterstal. Here she met Edith Stein again, forming a friendship that lasted many years.

52. Letter to Sr. Adelgundis Jaegerschmid, OSB, Freiburg-Günterstal

Original in Convent Archive of Benedictine Sisters, St. Lioba, Freiburg-Günterstal

Pax! St. Magdalena <Speyer>, February 16, 1930
Dominica Septuagesima

Dear Sister Adelgundis,

Thank you so much for your kind, detailed letter. The coincidence of events, as well as of the letters on my desk, would almost be sufficient basis for a teleological proof of God's existence. I have had Husserl's *Formale und transzendentale Logik [Formal and Transcendental Logic]* (at his direction, the publisher sent it to me) since the summer vacation. I started reading it on Thursday, because of its connection to my work precisely now, and on Friday I got your letter. I had an analogous conversation with Husserl when I saw him for the first time after my conversion; I had not seen him for an interval of eight years.

His wife was present, and every time she made a remark that was totally lacking in understanding, he responded with such depth and beauty that I scarcely needed to add anything at all. And I was able to be totally frank. But I believe one must be on one's guard against illusions. It is good to be able to speak to him so freely about the last things.[1] But doing so heightens his responsibility as well as *our* responsibility for him. Prayer and sacrifice are surely more important than anything we can say to him, and therefore—I have no doubt about this—they are very necessary.

There is a real difference between being a chosen instrument and being in the state of grace. It is not up to us to pass judgment, and we may confidently leave all to God's unfathomable mercy. But we may not becloud the importance of these last things. After every encounter in which I am made aware how powerless we are to exercise direct influence, I have a deeper sense of the urgency of my own *holocaustum.* And this awareness culminates increasingly in a: *Hic Rhodus, hic salta.*[2]

However much our present mode of living may appear inadequate to us—what do we really know about it? But there can be no doubt that we are in the here-and-now to work out our salvation and that of those who have been entrusted to our souls. Let us help one another to learn more and more how to make every day and every hour part of the structure for eternity—shall we, by our mutual prayers during this holy season?

In caritate Christi <in Christ's love>, your
Edith Stein

1. [These so-called four "last things" in Catholic doctrine are death, judgment, heaven, and hell.]
2. "Rhodes is right here, perform your phenomenal leap here!" [Aesop's fable.]

53. Postcard to Erna Hermann,[1] Bamberg
Original in Convent Archive of Cologne Carmel

<Speyer>, St. Magdalena, March 7, 1930

Dear Fräulein Hermann,

This is your official notification by the government of the *Pfalz* [Palatinate] of admission to the entrance examination that will begin on Thursday, March 13, at 7:30 A.M., in the Women's Vocational School, Karmeliterstrasse 3, Speyer.[2] Please submit your application as soon as possible to the Government of the *Pfalz,* Department of the Interior, giving [your] exact address and enclosing the following papers:

1. Curriculum Vitae (time and place of birth, religion, latest domicile, status and domicile of your parents, a record of your education).
2. The final report from school.
3. Official medical certificate of fitness for the teaching profession.
4. Dispensation from the age requirement.

With best wishes,
Dr. Edith Stein

1. Erna Haven, née Hermann (b. Schesslitz, Bavaria, 1902) was a cousin of Bruno Rothschild, D. Pharm., who, having become a Catholic and a priest, put her in touch with Edith Stein through correspondence. In 1930, they met in person. In 1931, Erna received Baptism and Confirmation; she applied for admission to the teachers college of the Dominican Sisters in Speyer (St. Magdalena) where she was helped a great deal by Edith Stein.
2. The examination was required for acceptance at the Dominican Sisters' teachers college in Speyer.

54. Letter to Sr. Adelgundis Jaegerschmid, OSB, Freiburg-Günterstal
Original in Convent Archive of Benedictine Sisters, St. Lioba, Freiburg-Günterstal

St. Magdalena <Speyer>, March 28, 1930

Dear Sister Adelgundis,

During the past weeks I have been very busy and have not even gotten around to packing the little Schott [the German translation of the *Missale Romanum]* for Sr. Placida <Laubhardt>. In all this diversity the longing to rest in the liturgy naturally becomes very strong, and therefore I thought I would go to Beuron as soon and as directly as possible. Then, yesterday, a matter was put into my hands that makes a personal discussion with Professor Krebs[1] urgently desirable. That is why I am writing to you. Would you be so kind as to see whether he will be in Freiburg on Friday, April 11, and whether he could give me an appointment? I do not know him at all personally and would be very happy if my visit could be arranged through you. Should he not be there, you might perhaps get his address. Then I would have to attempt to take care of the matter through correspondence. In any case, I would appreciate hearing from you promptly, since all my traveling plans have to be made. Were I able to talk to Prof. Krebs, I should probably arrive on Thursday evening (the 10th) and would go on to Beuron early Saturday. It would be very practical if I could stay with you, for then we would have the two evenings [together]. If that is not possible, then I would stay at the Hohenzollern [a small hotel].

For today, only this hurried request and best regards to you and Sr. Placida, your

Edith Stein

1. Engelbert Krebs (b. Freiburg, 1881; d. Freiburg, 1950) was Professor of Catholic Dogma in Freiburg.

55. Letter to Sr. Adelgundis Jaegerschmid, OSB, Freiburg-Günterstal
Original in Convent Archive of Benedictine Sisters, St. Lioba, Freiburg-Günterstal

Pax! Beuron, Easter Sunday <April 20>, 1930
Dear Sister Adelgundis,

Holy Saturday ended too quickly to send you Easter greetings. To make up for it, I can say a bit more now. Of course, I don't know where to begin nor where to stop. And what is best about these most blessed days cannot be expressed in speech, much less in writing. *"Praestolari in silentio salutare Dei"* [Lam 3: 26][1] was the text of the sermon on Good Friday that Father Archabbot <Raphael Walzer[2]> again delivered himself. The silence of mobilization on Holy Thursday, the silence of battle on Good Friday, the silence of victory—the mute jubilation of Eas-ter joy. We will let it go at that.

But I would like to tell you something about what happened earlier. Almost the first topic that came up on the day I arrived—and I was not the one who raised it—was Irmgard Koch and her problematic future. Thus I gained a thorough insight into her situation without having to ask for it. I was advised against paying her a visit. My motto "Hic Rhodus, hic salta" was thoroughly sanctioned. I was able to present everything else freely and all of it was accepted with benevolence. Here, as you know, no "diplomacy" of any kind is necessary, and there are no ulterior motives.

His Excellency <Archabbot Walzer> has several travel plans for the summer: 12th and 13th of July—hear ye and be amazed—in Speyer for the main celebration of the Cathedral's 900th Jubilee; during the second half of August, the Emmerich Jubilee in Hungary and the Neuburg Jubilee. It is anticipated that the first half of August will be free. But you would do well, in any case, to check once more, later.

Today P. Ambrosius <Würth, OSB>[3] gave the feast-day sermon ("Christ lives"), and I also heard the Holy Week liturgical talks of P. Damasus <Zähringer, OSB>.[4] Now, I shall have to leave on Wednesday. I ask you and Sr. Placida <Laubhardt> to give me the strong support of your prayers for my lecture on Thursday. I thank you both again for all the love you showed during my visit. Please thank Reverend Mother Prioress once more for allowing me to stay with you, and express my cordial wishes for many blessings for her entire house. Sr. Placida is not to be cross with me for not writing to her especially. There is still too much else to do.

In caritate Christi, your
Edith Stein

1. "It is good that one should wait quietly for the salvation of the Lord."
2. Archabbot Raphael Walzer, OSB (b. Ravensburg, 1888; d. Neuburg Abbey near Heidelberg, 1966), Doctor of Philosophy and Theology, fourth Archabbot of Beuron. He and Edith Stein first met in Beuron at the beginning of her teaching career at St. Magdalena's, Speyer. The Archabbot became and remained Edith Stein's spiritual advisor and trusted spiritual friend before and after her entrance into Carmel.
3. P. Ambrosius Würth, OSB (b. Stühlingen, Baden, 1889; d. Weiler, Allgau, 1972) monk at Beuron Abbey.
4. P. Damasus Zähringer, OSB (b. Ibach near St. Blasien, 1899) was the seventh Archabbot of Beuron. He resigned from that office in 1967, and went to live in Kressbonn on Lake Constance.

56. Letter to Erna Hermann, Bamberg
Original in Convent Archive of Cologne Carmel

<Speyer>, St. Magdalena, June 26, 1930

Dear Fräulein Hermann,

The Mother Superior of St. Dominic's, Ludwigshafen, (who is at the same time the Principal of the school there) is expected to attend a meeting here in the near future. I have something I must discuss with her then, and it would be possible to bring up your concern also, even perhaps, if Mother Superior has enough time, to summon you by telephone. So, I believe, you can save yourself a trip to Ludwigshafen for the time being.

I would be very happy to be your Confirmation sponsor. Unfortunately, I will have to forego attendance at the festivities at your baptism since, in the meanwhile, other pressing engagements have been made for the last part of my vacation.

I wish you great joy for the Hour of Adoration this evening. Your
Edith Stein

57. Letter to Sr. Adelgundis Jaegerschmid, OSB, Freiburg-Günterstal
Original in Convent Archive of Benedictine Sisters, St. Lioba, Freiburg-Günterstal

Pax! Breslau, <presumably July, 1930>

Dear Sister Adelgundis,

Tomorrow I shall probably see Sr. Placida <Laubhardt> for the last time; so it is high time to get my return letter ready. You can well imagine how happy I was to see the "consultation chair"[1] beside my desk occupied by a black habit. I just saw another one at the railway station—a very young Pater [i.e., religious priest] was wearing it—and I found it peculiar not to be able to go over and say hello.

My presentation [in Salzburg, Austria] will treat of *Das Ethos der Frauenberüfe [The Ethos of Women's Professions]*.[2] Originally I was scheduled to present the basic theme [of the conference], "The Ethos of Christian

Professions," and actually I had accepted only because, at the time, that topic particularly attracted me. But then the people in Salzburg decided it was essential to address the women's theme separately, so I consented to change: [Dietrich von] Hildebrand[3] has taken over the other topic. Sr. Placida will have much to tell you about; after all, we were together every other day.

The second half of September or the beginning of October would be feasible for Beuron; for the time before or after, there are a lot of travel plans. Countess Bissingen is, I believe, a cousin of my dear room-and-board companion, Baroness Uta von Bodman.[4] It sounds that way, according to what I heard.

St. Peter in Chains[5] is also a feast I particularly like, not as honoring him, but as a commemoration of being freed from fetters through the ministry of the angels. How many chains have already been removed in this fashion, and how blessed it will be when the last of them falls away. Until then, one must continue bearing quietly those [chains] that are still one's portion—the more quietly we do so, the less we feel them. And, after all, one must not meddle in the angels' business.

In caritate Christi, your
Edith

1. [This chair was so named by Trude Kuznitsky Koebner as Edith explains in *Life in a Jewish Family*. See *Life,* p. 235.]
2. See *Essays on Woman* [Washington, DC: ICS Publications, 1987].
3. Dietrich von Hildebrand (b. Florence, Italy, October 12, 1889; d. New Rochelle, NY, January 26, 1977.) Professor of philosophy in Munich until 1933; in Vienna, until 1938; from 1940 to 1960, full professor at Fordham University, New York. He belonged to the older of Edmund Husserl's students in Göttingen. He became a Catholic in 1914 and was a friend of Edith Stein, with whom he shared religious and spiritual interests. See *Life,* p. 253, etc.
4. Countess Maria Theresia Bissingen (b. Schramberg, 1888; d. Vallendar, 1954). [Baroness von Bodman also taught at St. Magdalena's and, like Edith, lived in the Dominican Sisters' convent in Speyer. See Letter 142.]
5. Before the reform of the liturgy in the wake of Vatican II, the Feast of St. Peter in Chains was kept on August 1. Twelve years after Edith wrote this letter, August 1 was the last full day she spent in Carmel, since she and her sister Rosa were arrested on the afternoon of the following day. The reference in this letter is to the first reading at the feast's liturgy, taken from Chapter 12 of the Acts of the Apostles.

58. Letter to Erna Hermann, Bamberg
Original in Convent Archive of Cologne Carmel

Pax! Breslau, July 23, 1930
Dear Erna,

Last evening I received your card. I want you to have a short note right away. I am so sorry that the operation had such bad aftereffects. It seems as though your patience has to undergo a profound trial in order to become ready for your acceptance into the Church. If you will see and utilize the whole experience in this light, it will surely be a blessed time. Can you still keep it all from your mother? I think that will hardly be possible much longer.

After my last visit to you, I actually was allowed to be the sponsor at the baptism of a seven-year-old girl and a nine-year-old boy. There was so little that was festive about it—five minutes in our sacristy—that it pained me greatly. I recalled with what holy seriousness and with what rich liturgy my own was carried out. That is what I wish for you and very soon!

With fond thoughts, your
Edith Stein

59. Postcard to Frau Callista Brenzing, OCist, Seligenthal
Original in Convent Archive of Cologne Carmel

Pax! Breslau, July 26, 1930
Dear Reverend Mother Callista,

Only now that I am at home have I found a moment to look at the map and confirm that from here it is much closer to Salzburg via Vienna or Prague than through Munich. Therefore I will be passing through Munich only on my return trip on September 1st, and then probably I will have a layover only from 8 to 10 P.M. I hope we will be able to meet then. Surely P.P.[1] will be glad to function as your protector for that.

Best regards from your
Edith Stein

1. Presumably, Edith refers here to Erich Przywara, SJ, who had commissioned her to translate *John Henry Newman: Letters and Diaries until his Conversion* into German. Later, he urged her to translate St. Thomas Aquinas' *Quaestiones Disputatae* into German. [Father Przywara was stationed in Munich and would be able to accompany Mother Callista to the station at such a late hour.]

60. Letter to Erna Hermann, Bamberg

Original in Convent Archive of Cologne Carmel

Breslau, August 20, 1930

Dear Erna,

Right now you are probably getting ready for your departure. I hope you have made a complete recovery in the meantime, so that you can get to work with fresh energy. If you were not already provided with admonitions from various other sources, I should have presented you with some of my own: that a reasonable measure is better than blind zeal, and obedience better than sacrifice. But as it is, I will do no more than send you most cordial wishes for the new trimester.

I will arrive in Speyer only on September 2nd, since I must still go to Salzburg. For September 1st, I beg you for a special memento.[1]

Looking forward with pleasure to seeing you again, your

Edith Stein

1. That day she gave her lecture on "Das Ethos der Frauenberüfe" ["The Ethos of Women's Professions," in *Woman,* pp. 41ff.]

61. Letter to Emilie Bechtold,[1] Wettenhausen

Original in private possession of Emilie Bechtold

<St. Magdalena, Speyer> September 9, 1930

Dear Fräulein Bechtold,

It was a very great surprise for me to find you gone upon my return; I knew nothing about your decision. With all my heart, I wish you the best of luck on your way and will be happy to hear from you some time.

With cordial best wishes, from Fräulein von Bodman as well, your
Edith Stein

1. Emilie Bechtold, b. Saargemünd, lived in Edesheim in the Pfalz [Palatinate]. This former colleague of Edith's at St. Magdalena's transferred to another educational institution of the Dominican Sisters in Wettenhausen.

62. Letter to Erna Hermann, Speyer
Original in private possession of Erna Haven, née Hermann

Pax! St. Magdalena <Speyer> Sept. 16, 1930
Dear Erna,

It will be easier to answer your question in person than in writing. Perhaps you could stop by on Sunday; there will probably be some kind of devotions here and you will certainly be able to meet me afterward, though I might possibly not be alone.

With best regards, your
Edith Stein

63. Letter to Erna Hermann, Speyer
Original in Convent Archive of Cologne Carmel

Pax! St. Magdalena <Speyer> Sept. 16, 1930
Dear Erna,

Thank you very much for the invitation, and please thank Sr. Alexandra also. I shall pass it on to the children. I do not know yet whether they will be able to come. You will excuse me, please, in any case, since I have to budget my time so carefully and cannot allow myself such undertakings. For the same reason, dear Erna, I cannot visit you. During all these years in Speyer, I have never fostered any social life involving mutual visits. Anyone familiar with my commitments will not hold this against me. Many people come to me and everyone who comes, hoping to find some help from me, is heartily welcome. Obviously, that also holds for you, and I should no longer need to assure you of this.

Since you could not come for that reply recently, I would like to give it in writing after all. The young teachers who meet with me every other Saturday for continuing education would have no objection to your participation. But, taking into account your time and your energy, I can only advise you urgently to postpone such things that are, after all, not that essential at this time.

Our academy students cannot manage it, either. I should probably speak to Sr. Ernestine personally sometime to see whether it would be right for you.

Always, with best regards, your
Edith Stein

64. Postcard to Emilie Bechtold, Wettenhausen
Original in private possession of Emilie Bechtold

[The card has no form of address. It was mailed presumably in the autumn of 1930 and is postmarked "Maikammer." The stamped date is indecipherable. There is a brief message:]

Cordial greetings from our autumn excursion.
Edith Stein
[Fifteen other signatures are added.]

65. Letter to Theodora Aberle,[1] Heidelberg
Original in private possession of Maria, Countess Graimberg

St. Magdalena, <Speyer> October 9, 1930

Dear Fräulein Aberle,

Unfortunately my program is already so overloaded until Easter that I no longer dare to promise anything beyond what is already scheduled, since I would, in all probability, be unable to fulfill it. However, my schedule does include a lecture[2] in Heidelberg to the Society of Catholic Academicians at the beginning of December. It will be open to the public, so the Catholic Women's Society could participate although, of course, the topic is not [specifically] one for women.

The Salzburg lecture is being printed and will therefore be available to everyone. Time permitting, I will be very happy to take the opportunity for a visit to the *Soziale Frauenschule* [Social School for Women]. Would you please convey to Countess Graimberg my sincere thanks for her invitation?

With best regards, yours sincerely,
Edith Stein

1. Theodora Aberle (b. Leutkirch, 1887; d. Heidelberg, 1963) lecturer in social and political sciences at the *Soziale Frauenschule* in Heidelberg.
2. Edith's lecture was given December 2, 1930, and was entitled *Der Intellekt und die Intellektuellen [The Intellect and the Intellectuals]*. It was published the following year in two installments in the periodical *Das heilige Feuer [The Sacred Fire]*, Vol. 18, May-June and July-August numbers.

66. Letter to Emil Vierneisel,[1] Heidelberg
Original in Convent Archive of Cologne Carmel

Pax! St. Magdalena <Speyer>, October 9, 1930
Dear Professor,

This is the first moment I have to answer you. Recently a topic occurred to me but I mention it to you only tentatively since I will definitely have no time until mid-November to reflect on it and to decide whether I can lecture on "The Intellect and the Intellectuals." It would derive from [my work on St.] Thomas and would then be most practical. Would it be possible to have the lecture in the afternoon so that I could return at 7:30 P.M.? A Tuesday, possibly December 9, would do. If it is a question of an evening only, then it would probably have to be a Saturday, that is, the 6th.

Could you postpone your visit until after October 19? On the 18th, I have to deliver an important lecture[2] to teachers [male and female] that demands thorough preparation and is not at all ready yet. And for the 19th, another visitor from out of town made arrangements a long time ago.

With best regards, your
Edith Stein

1. Emil Vierneisel (b. Lauda, 1890; d. Heidelberg, 1973) was professor of philosophy in Heidelberg.
2. [This lecture "On the Idea of Education" appears in Vol. XII of *Edith Steins Werke* and awaits translation.]

67. Letter to Peter Wust,[1] Münster

Original in Convent Archive of the Franciscans, Münster

Pax! St. Magdalena <Speyer>, October 31, 1930

Dear Professor,

My very best wishes as you assume your new position. I will be happy to remember [to pray for] you particularly on Tuesday. On my departure from Salzburg, I felt I owed you something, since we did not get to have the discussion you wanted. I am glad that you are so understanding of my situation. Please do continue in the same vein in future. It's [a] chronic [occurrence] for me that more [work] accumulates here than I can manage.

Therefore, no more than this brief note, your

Edith Stein

1. Peter Wust (b. Riesenthal, Saar Region, 1884 ; d. Münster, 1940) was Professor of Philosophy in Münster; became acquainted with Edith Stein in Salzburg.

68. Letter to Emilie Bechtold, Wettenhausen

Original in private possession of Emilie Bechtold

Pax! St. Magdalena, <Speyer>, November 5, 1930

Dear Fraulein Bechtold,

Sincere thanks to you and to Liesel Huber for your kind name day greetings. You know that my time is always fully taken up. That is why I do not get around to answering promptly. Our children had a retreat over All Saints Day and they all emerged from it full of joy and peace. We do not forget you here. It still seems unbelievable to me that you have left for good.

With best regards, your

Edith Stein

69. Letter to Sr. Callista Kopf, OP <presumably in Würzburg>
Original in Convent Archive of the Dominican Sisters in Speyer

Pax! St. Magdalena <Speyer>, November 13, 1930
Dear Sister Callista,

I will answer your questions briefly. I do not use extraordinary means to prolong my workday. I do as much as I can. The ability to accomplish increases noticeably in proportion to the number of things that must be done. When there's nothing urgent at hand, it ceases much sooner. Heaven is expert at economy. Therefore, whatever comes your way after nine o'clock is evidently no longer essential. That, in practice, things do not proceed smoothly according to reason is due to our not being pure spirits.[1] There's no sense in rebelling against that.

O Lord God, will to give me
All that leads me to you.
O Lord God, take away from me
All that diverts me from you.
O Lord God, take me, also, from myself
And give me completely to yourself.[2]

These are three graces; the last is the greatest and includes the others; but, take note: one must pray for it....

1. [This observation that we are "not pure spirits" is often made in spiritual direction, as a way of acknowledging that the body, too, has an influence in our daily life.]
2. [This is not a poem of Edith Stein's, but rather a widely known prayer composed by St. Nicholas of Flüe, a Swiss hermit-saint who lived in the 15th century. It is translated in prayer form, rather than as a poem, although in German the construction rhymes readily.]

70. Letter to Emil Vierneisel, Heidelberg
Original in Convent Archive of Cologne Carmel

<St. Magdalena, Speyer>, November 22, 1930
Dear Doctor Vierneisel,

Yesterday, for the first time, the "little train that could" went across the bridge again. Let's hope it will remain in good health over the 2nd of December.

I cannot prophesy for certain, but it will probably take a little more than an hour and a quarter. In any case, it is not good to have to reckon to the minute.

If it's a beautiful day, I would come as early as two o'clock. I have not been in Neuburg [a Benedictine Abbey at Heidelberg] since January and could, perhaps, "meditate" better there than here.

In the meantime, best regards,
Edith Stein

71. Postcard to Emil Vierneisel, Heidelberg
Original in Convent Archive of Cologne Carmel

Pax! <St. Magdalena, Speyer>, November 28, 1930
Dear Doctor Vierneisel,

It will suit my schedule better, after all, if I come later, at 4:20 P.M. Furthermore, may I give you notice that I would like to bring another guest along: Baroness Bodman, our art teacher? I doubt that you will have any objection, nor will your car. If we leave [as soon as our train arrives], we will most likely still be in time for Vespers at Neuburg. Fully confident, I leave the rest to your provision.

Yours,
Edith Stein

72. Letter to Emil Vierneisel, Heidelberg
Original in Convent Archive of Cologne Carmel

Pax! <St. Magdalena, Speyer>, St. Nicholas, <December 6>, 1930
Dear Doctor Vierneisel,

I am delighted that St. Thomas[1] awakened so much joy in you. We had a very pleasant trip home and were dropped off at the convent gate after a mere half-hour. Thank you and your wife most sincerely for all your kindness and care.

Would you, please, tell Professor Lossen that I have spoken to the Prefect of the school and she is very much inclined to fulfill his wish, even if it is hardly possible this Easter. She will be able to give definite advice only after she speaks to the Reverend Mother who is out of town right now.

Best regards to you both and to the three towheads[2] from Uta von Bodman and

Edith Stein

1. [Her lecture at Heidelberg four days earlier, "The Intellect and the Intellectuals," was based on St. Thomas Aquinas. Cf. Letter 66.]
2. The three eldest children of the Vierneisel family.

73. Letter to Ottilie Küchenhoff,[1] Coesfeld

Original in Convent Archive of the Benedictine Sisters, Burg Dinklage

Pax! St. Magdalena <Speyer> December 7, 1930

Dear *Frau Studienrat,*[2]

Thank you very much for your kind, gracious letter. Time would not permit me to write sooner. Truly, one is happy anytime one finds a person who works by the same philosophy. I was prepared for resistance in Bendorf.[3] I only wish it had been expressed more clearly and less convolutedly. For no one said a word about its being "too pious," that is, that they took exception to the radical orientation to the supernatural. But, probably, that was in the background for several [of the participants], although the discussion was directed to completely different matters. Don't you agree?

Besides, I also heard some very warm and heartfelt expressions of agreement there (in private). Because of the weeks of total silence since then, I perceived that the rejection was probably stronger [than I had thought], and your kind words confirm it for me. However it may be, it must not lead us to stray from our path. There will, no doubt, be many a tougher battle to fight in Christ's militia. Please give me, once in a while, a memento to reinforce my arsenal.

Wishing you the fullness of grace in Advent and at Christmas, your

Edith Stein

1. Ottilie Küchenhoff (b. Neheim-Husten, 1887; d. Schmallenberg/Sauerland, 1971)

taught at a *Gymnasium.* [The German educational system is described in *Life,* p. 471.]
2. This title is given to a teacher at a Gymnasium. No proper English equivalent exists; an English correspondent would use "Dear Madam."
3. The lecture Edith Stein delivered at Bendorf on the Rhine on November 8, 1930 was entitled *Grundlagen der Frauenbildung.* [It may be found in *Woman,* pp. 115ff., "Fundamental Principles of Women's Education."]

74. Letter to Sr. Adelgundis Jaegerschmid, OSB[1] and Sr. Placida Laubhardt, OSB,[2] Freiburg-Günterstal

Original in Convent Archive of Benedictine Sisters, St. Lioba, Freiburg-Günterstal

Pax! St. Magdalena <Speyer> December 10, 1930

Dear Sisters,

For a good while it has been clear to me that I have not even replied to the name day greetings. And the pre-Advent letter has become a mid-Advent letter and will, in the end, have to count as a Christmas letter. You can well imagine why. Salzburg has drawn astonishing ripples. I have to show up as speaker here, there, and everywhere. In between, there are mountains of essays [to be corrected]. Probably, I will chuck school at Easter (please, don't mention that for the present); and after that, I don't know yet. I have put aside—as useless and a waste of time—all reflection about it until after the Christmas vacation. But now it will have to be considered thoroughly in Beuron. For that reason I don't want to make any detours on the way there. I think it will be possible to return by way of Freiburg. I will write to you about that from Beuron. If you have no room for me, I could always stay at the *Hohenzollern.*

I have a very big favor to ask today: that, in the coming days, you help me to pray very specially for my sister Rosa[3] and for my mother.[4] It does seem there's a very critical situation there right now. For some months my sister <Rosa> has been suffering a great deal; Erika <Tworoger>'s[5] increasingly pronounced Jewish leaning and her interference in running the household are becoming almost unbearable for Rosa. So far she has avoided any argument in order to spare my mother. Now she has entrusted her secret to Erika herself, and it is not apparent yet what consequences that will have. For the moment, I can see hardly any (other) possibility than to help by prayer, and so I want to call upon all my auxiliary troops.

I would have so much to tell you, but for the present I have to postpone that until the planned visit. However, one more prayer-intention. In Beuron I look forward with particular joy to the prospective baptism of a Jewess (please, don't mention this, either) regarding which I had a small share as *causa secunda*. For the present, everything promises to go smoothly. But you know well how much tends to happen before the decisive moment.

On Gaudete Sunday there's to be a radio broadcast from Beuron; I presume that Father Archabbot <Raphael Walzer> will speak about the Holy Land. And I hope to be there by the last Sunday of Advent.

Wishing you, with all my heart, all the graces and blessings of Advent, your

Edith Stein

1. Amelie Jaegerschmid (Sr. Adelgundis, OSB); see Letter 51.
2. Eva Laubhardt (Sr. Placida, OSB) (b. Berlin, 1904; lives in the Convent of St. Lioba, Freiburg-Günterstal). She, too, carried on a regular correspondence with Edith Stein; the letters have been lost.
3. Rosa Stein, Edith's sister; see Letter 24.
4. Augusta Stein, née Courant (b. Lublinitz, Silesia, 1849; d. Breslau, September 14, 1936) Edith Stein's mother.
5. Erika Tworoger (b. Breslau, 1911; died in Israel, 1961) niece of Edith Stein, daughter of Elfrieda Tworoger-Stein. Erika was a Jewish theologian who emigrated to Palestine. In Jerusalem, she married an orthodox Rabbi. Edith corresponded with her frequently regarding translation and commentary on Old Testament Hebrew texts. [For more on these family members see *Life*.]

75. Letter to Erna Hermann, Speyer
Original in Convent Archive of Cologne Carmel

Pax! St. Magdalena <Speyer> December 11, 1930
Dear Erna,

I have no books on that topic here. Perhaps my old lecture will be of some use to you. The other essay is enclosed because of the literary references it gives. Perhaps you can find something from that list in the public library.

Hopefully, you will hold up well until the vacation.—Will you return the things when you have finished with them, please?
Cordial Advent wishes from your

Edith Stein

76. Letter to Erna Hermann, (Bamberg)
Original in Convent Archive of Cologne Carmel

Pax! St. Magdalena <Speyer> December 19, 1930
Dear Erna,

Of course, I cannot compete with your beautiful handiwork, but I would also like to send you a small decoration for your room as a Christmas greeting. Of course, were it in my power, I would much rather give you something else, something far more beautiful: the true childlike spirit that opens the door to the approaching Savior, that can say from the heart—not theoretically but practically in each and every case—"Lord, not mine, but thy will be done." I am telling you this because I would like to help you attain the one thing necessary. In the past months I have often been concerned because, repeatedly, I had the impression that there is still something lacking on this most important point, that an obstinate self-will is present, a tenacious clinging to desires once conceived. And if I have seemed to you, perhaps, hard and relentless because I would not give in to your wishes, then believe me, that was not due to coldness or a lack of love, but because of a firm conviction that I should harm you by acting otherwise. I am only a tool of the Lord. I would like to lead to him anyone who comes to me. And when I notice that this is not the case, but that the interest is invested in my person, then I cannot serve as a tool and must beg the Lord to help in other ways. After all, he is never dependent on only one individual.

Won't you make use of these last days of Advent for an honest self-examination, so that you will be granted a truly grace-filled Christmas? I think Resl[1] will also be happy to assist. When you get to Konnersreuth, tell her I, too, ask her most cordially to help you.

Now my first wish for you is that you recuperate thoroughly at home, and that you will then be able to return here, strengthened, and with a heart filled with Christmas peace.

I will remember you at Beuron. Most sincerely, your

Edith Stein

1. Resl is the familiar name of Theresa Neumann, baptismal sponsor for Erna Hermann.

77. Greeting to Sr. Agnella Stadtmüller, OP <Speyer>
Original in Convent Archive of the Dominican Sisters in Speyer
<Beuron, Christmas> 1930

A Beuron Christmas-filled-with-grace for time and eternity!
Edith Stein

78. Letter to Rev. Ludwig Husse, <Ludwigshafen>
Original in private possession of Father Husse

Pax! Beuron, January 2, 1931
Dear Reverend Father,

My conscience stirred several times during my Christmas stay in Beuron to point out to me that a lecture is facing me on January 13.[1] You will surely understand that here no other theme would come to me but that of the mystery of Christmas itself. Do you think it will suffice to say simply: The Mystery of Christmas? Please send your reply to me in Speyer; I shall be back there again by the 5th as I am leaving here early tomorrow morning and will stop over in Freiburg.

Now, I send belated wishes that the holy season will have brought you rich graces, a good provision for the New Year.

Respectfully yours,
Edith Stein

1. This lecture, "The Mystery of Christmas: Incarnation and Humanity" was given to the local Society of Catholic Academicians in Ludwigshafen on the Rhine, January 13, 1931. [It is printed in Vol. XII of *Edith Steins Werke.*]

79. Letter to Anneliese Lichtenberger,[1] Ludwigshafen
Original in Convent Archive of Cologne Carmel

Pax! St. Magdalena <Speyer> January 6, 1931
Dear Anneliese,

Your New Year's wishes are reciprocated most cordially. I thought about you and your big [prayer] intention very often while I was at Beuron. At St. Lioba's I verified again that you cannot be admitted to the *Sozialen Frauenschule* [Social School for Women] before you are 21 and unless, as a prerequisite, you have completed practical training in nursing, care of infants, kindergarten or homemaking. Housekeeping skills are required under all circumstances, for a social worker may, at any time, be put in a position of having to run an unfamiliar household. I hope you have already begun to give your mother some help.

I will be glad to pass on your farewell greetings to your companions at school. Surely you can come to be our guest sometime.

With sincere greetings and best wishes, your

Edith Stein

1. Anneliese Lichtenberger (b. Schwarzenacker near Saarbrücken, 1912; d. Ludwigshafen, 1935) was a student of Edith Stein's at the teachers college of the Dominican Sisters, St. Magdalena, Speyer.

80. Letter to Anneliese Lichtenberger, Ludwigshafen

Original in Convent Archive of Cologne Carmel

Pax! St. Magdalena <Speyer> January 8, 1931

Dear Anneliese,

Of course, your new decision surprises me even more than the previous one. It *is* a good thing not to shut out advice from knowledgeable persons and your parents' wishes. But I have serious doubts whether it is wise to change schools. Were you to enter Wettenhausen now in the fifth class, intending to take the examination at Easter, one has to assume that the result would most probably be even worse than here. In that short time you would have to accustom yourself to new teachers and a new school situation. Would you succeed in that? Fraulein Bechtold has often written how difficult the adjustment has been for her. If it is a matter of repeating the fifth class, then, of course, I could understand it being easier for you somewhere other than here.

So give the matter a thorough consideration once more; examine, too, whether it was not a certain pride that contributed to your decision, and whether that deserves to be given priority over common sense. But whatever you decide, I wish with all my heart that it will lead only to good results for you.

With best wishes and greetings, your
Edith Stein

81. Letter to Anneliese Lichtenberger, Ludwigshafen
Original in Convent Archive of Cologne Carmel

Pax! St. Magdalena <Speyer> January 15, 1931
Dear Anneliese,

When your letter arrived I immediately had the thought: If you want to conclude your college training, why would you want to lose a year? So why don't you come back to us and try the examination at Easter? Of course, you would have to be prepared for everyone's surprise. But that would soon be over. For the time being, I'm not telling anyone anything. But if you can decide to do so, then I advise you to just come at once. They will not send you away again. And if you write to me beforehand, I will prepare the Prefect and the Principal.

Most cordially, your
Edith Stein

82. Letter to Frau Callista Brenzing, OCist (Munich)
Original in Convent Archive of Cologne Carmel

Pax! St. Magdalena <Speyer>, January 18, 1931
Dear Reverend Mother Callista,

I have just finished writing a little cheer-up note to your "name-sister" in Wurzburg.[1] Now it is your turn. I received your kind letter while I was still in my beloved Beuron. My heart is still there and only comes here when I need it; otherwise it waits there until I return, that is, probably for Holy Week. Easter week I am supposed to be in Munich. By that time you will no longer be there.

You must not think that Sr. Agnella <Stadtmüller>'s lot is too sad. Of course, her father's prolonged suffering was hard; his death was a release. She need not fear becoming Principal for some time. Already last spring, in Gemund, she was assured by Reverend Mother that she certainly would not have this burden imposed at once. When it happens, she will accommodate herself to it, and it will also be a healthier state of affairs—for the entire institution—than the provisional one that began a long time ago. Her situation is not an easy one, but she has the inner strength needed and is strongly supported by the certainty that Reverend Mother is of one spirit with us and that she will find, near to her, future allies in Srs. Callista and Reinhildis.

Because of her delicate health, Sr. Reinhildis was always a worry for her father, as she will always be for the convent as well. But I hope that her unusually swift and competent intelligence will compensate for the deficient physical strength. I am glad you were able to have her in Mu-nich for a few more months. Perhaps later I, too, may visit you some time. Certainly, if Newman[2] is officially approved, it will be much better for you than Hume. So it was a lucky misunderstanding.

Many good wishes for the close [of your studies] and cordial greetings, your

Edith Stein

[P.S.] If you see Sr. Reinhildis or P.P. <presumably Pater E. Przywara> in the next few days, please extend my best regards and pass on the message to Father that quarters for him have been prepared at St. Magdalena's.

1. Sr. Callista Kopf, OP.
2. Mother Callista had asked Edith which philosopher she should choose for specialization for the 2nd State Boards. Though Edith named Hume, Mother Callista understood her to mean Newman, and the latter was approved [by the University].

83. Letter to Sr. Adelgundis Jaegerschmid, OSB, Freiburg-Günterstal

Original in Convent Archive of Benedictine Sisters, St. Lioba, Freiburg-Günterstal

Pax! St. Magdalena <Speyer> January 19, 1931

Dear Sister Adelgundis,

You are surely wondering why there has been no word from me. It is because I myself have not yet heard anything. Immediately after my return I wrote to Finke,[1] [asking] whether I might come on January 24-25. There has been no answer to that yet. Perhaps it would be possible for you to go to him after all? Not on my behalf; but the conversation would probably lead to it effortlessly, and you could find out whether he intends to talk to me. (Without word from him, of course, I would not come.) If the situation is completely without any prospect—and expert opinion assures me of this—he would surely prefer not to have to tell me so in person. You could also make him understand that the whole thing does not affect me inwardly, and that, if nothing comes of it, I shall be neither disappointed nor saddened.

If I could have an answer by Friday at the latest, I should be most grateful, for practical reasons. Otherwise, I could scarcely come to stay with you again. Besides, if I do not have to make the trip I would plan something else for Sunday, that is, I would have the convert from Darmstadt <Alice Reis>[2] come for a visit. What's more, she would like very much to accompany me on the trip to Freiburg; but I believe it is better not to plan it for this time, since I would have no time to take care of her there. I have had my Christmas lecture typed. If I came, I would bring it along. I do not have enough copies at present to mail one. Today I got the proofs of the Salzburg lecture.

Please give my greetings to Sr. Placida and the tenants of St. Placid's. A respectful greeting to Reverend Mother Prioress.

Best regards, your
Edith Stein

1. [Heinrich Finke (not to be confused with Eugen Fink, cf. Letter 262), Professor of Philosophy in Freiburg, signed Edith's doctoral certification, adding *"pro decano"* [for the Dean, a proxy signature. She required it to apply for habilitation in Freiburg. In 1931, Finke was president of the Görres Society.]

2. Maria Alice Reis (b. Berlin, 1903; killed in Auschwitz, August 9, 1942) was Jewish. Edith Stein was her baptismal sponsor in 1930. [Later, Alice fled to Holland; in 1942, she met Edith Stein again at Westerbork, after both had been arrested by the Nazis, and they were on the same transport to the death camp at Auschwitz.]

84. Letter to Erna Hermann, Speyer
Original in Convent Archive of Cologne Carmel

Pax! St. Magdalena <Speyer> January 11, 1931
Dear Erna,

I am very sorry that after such a good beginning in the New Year a setback should have occurred so quickly. If I thought it would do you any good, I would have put everything else aside, today or already last Sunday, in order to see how you were doing. But I am as convinced as ever that in doing so, I would do you more harm than good. If you are really seeking help with your spiritual life, you will learn—as do all others who come to me for that purpose—to take my personal situation into consideration.

Speedy recovery! Your
Edith Stein

85. Letter to Sr. Adelgundis Jaegerschmid, OSB, and Sr. Placida Laubhardt, OSB, Freiburg-Günterstal
Original in Convent Archive of Benedictine Sisters, St. Lioba, Freiburg-Günterstal

Pax! St. Magdalena <Speyer> January 26, 1931
Dear Sisters,

Sr. Adelgundis will probably have given a report as far as Rötebuckweg 47.[1] When I rang, a creature who had evidently been waiting for that signal leaped down the stairs to the door. It was the eldest boy, who had obviously been instructed to receive me, and did so faultlessly. It was a very friendly beginning. Heidegger was not at all astonished by my question; he said that he had no objections at all, either professionally or personally. But he would only be able to give an endorsement when he had learned from the governing board whether he could get a *stipendium* [grant][2] for me. From that I perceived he thought I intended to get it in his department. I considered how I might begin to dissuade him. But he came to my aid: Were I thinking of a Catholic appointment, it would be very impractical for me to seek it through him. And a grant would be obtained much more easily by other means. The governing board would hardly be able to refuse Honecker,[3] just on the basis of parity, for he did not have anyone [as assistant] so far. I was very amazed to find myself back on the street [in so short a time?]. Honecker was much more reluctant in the beginning. But in the end he, too, declared himself willing to present the matter to the faculty, making only a stipulation that his own candidate be not eliminated. On his next trip to Karlsruhe he would talk to them there about a grant.

There was great surprise and joy at the Husserls' over the outcome. What's more, I only left at 5:30 P.M. If need be, I could still have made the earlier train; that, however, would have meant dashing away as soon as we got up from dinner and, after all, I could not do that to the old folks. This way they could have their afternoon nap—I, too, was made to lie down on a sofa—and then we could talk at leisure for a while longer. Frau Husserl took me to the train.

Now I thank you for your prayers, and Sr. Placida for swallowing her disappointment at my "lodger's behavior."[4] But it did me so much good to be able to stay at St. Lioba's overnight and to be allowed to hear the *Alma redemptoris mater*.[5] The other world would, otherwise, be too hard to endure.

Please, continue your prayers. I will be very much in need of them in the time ahead. Most cordially, your

Edith

1. Martin Heidegger, Professor of Philosophy in Freiburg, successor of Edmund Husserl, lived at this address. [Edith Stein had an appointment to consult with him about habilitation in Freiburg.]
2. [Habilitation conferred the license to deliver lectures but without remuneration. Professors had assistants—usually two—who received, as this so-called *stipendium* or grant, fifty marks a month from the university.]
3. See Letter 119.
4. [Edith here no doubt refers to some "inside joke" on Sr. Placida.]
5. [Seasonal hymn to the Virgin Mary at night prayers.]

86. Letter to Sr. Callista Kopf, OP, Würzburg
Original in Convent Archive of the Dominican Sisters, St. Magdalena, Speyer

Pax! St. Magdalena <Speyer>, February 8, 1931
Dear Sister Callista,

A brief but cordial greeting to express joy at the road you have put behind you and encouragement for that still ahead from your faithful
Edith Stein

87. Letter to Sr. Callista Kopf, OP, Würzburg
Original in Convent Archive of the Dominican Sisters in Speyer

Pax! Beuron, March 28, 1931
My dear Sister Callista,

By the time you get this letter all the agony will, hopefully, be past. I am writing this in advance because tomorrow, Palm Sunday, I want to begin the silence [of Holy Week]. I've been here since Thursday evening so, from these first two days alone, I already enclose for you an abundance of peace, rest and love. And when you are filled with that, then I may surely give you the news that I wanted to spare you before your examinations: on Thursday I took leave of St. Magdalena's. St. Thomas [her translation] is no longer satisfied with my spare time, he demands all of me.

On the Tuesday after Easter, I have to go to a conference in Munich (teachers, young women, from all of Bavaria and some fifteen from the Palatinate will be coming).[1] From there, I will go to Breslau for a while, in order to have the quiet in which to carry on with a big project I have begun.[2] Several prospects are at hand for later. Sr. Agnella <Stadtmüller> is fully informed about it all and can give you a verbal account. That this will enable me, once more, to be at home for a longer period is surely very good. My sister <Rosa> seems to be especially in need of my presence now.

Now I wish you, after this difficult Lent, a very grace-filled Holy

Week and Eastertime, and the same to Sr. Immolata. Best regards to you and all the dear Sisters in Speyer, from your

Edith Stein

1. Lecture of April 8, 1931 on "Woman's Vocation." [Published in Vol. XII of *Edith Steins Werke.*]
2. "Potency and Act," studies she wrote on the philosophy of being.

88. Postcard to Anneliese Lichtenberger, Speyer
Original in Convent Archive of Cologne Carmel

<presumably Breslau> April 14, 1931

Dear Anneliese,

I just received your dear note of welcome. Cordial thanks and all the best, your

Edith Stein

89. Letter to Sr. Adelgundis Jaegerschmid, OSB, Freiburg-Günterstal
Original in Convent Archive of Benedictine Sisters, St. Lioba, Freiburg-Günterstal

Breslau, April 28, 1931

Dear Sister Adelgundis,

You ask whether I have already begun my work.[1] That happened at the end of January, two days after I returned from Freiburg, and in the six weeks in which I was still able to work in Speyer, a rather bulky manuscript materialized. At the same time it became clear that combining it with school and everything else was no longer possible. So, two and a half weeks before school ended, I arranged for another consultation with our Reverend Mother, and in full understanding of my situation, she released me. For the others it caused great consternation when, suddenly, on the last day of school, I said farewell. The children and most of the Sisters had had no inkling beforehand. The few initiates helped me, with touching sisterly love, to complete the whole of my packing in the short time there was outside of school, so that I could escape to Beuron as soon as school closed.

I would prefer to come to Freiburg only when my work is finished. When that will be, I do not know. And were I to receive my appointment to the P.A. (Pedagogical Academy) before [it is finished], I might forego the habilitation completely. Once I had begun the work, it immediately became more important to me than any other purpose that it might perhaps serve. God knows what he has in store for me. I do not need to concern myself about it.

So far, I have been unable to send you the Salzburg booklet[2] because the ten free copies I recently received are far from enough to meet my needs. I have just ordered more of them.

Your criticism is not quite clear. It is, of course, true that the third part is not detailed enough. (The entire religious formation should have been included, as I once treated the matter in Munich.) But then, it appears that you did not want the supernatural to be brought up at all. But, if I could not speak about that, I would probably not mount a lecturer's platform at all. Basically, it is always a small, simple truth that I have to express: *How to go about living at the Lord's hand.* Then when people demand something else from me and propose very clever themes which are very foreign to me, I can take them only as an introduction in order to arrive eventually at my *Ceterum censeo.*[3] Perhaps that is a very reprehensible method. But my entire activity as lecturer has hit me like an avalanche, so that I have been unable as yet to reflect on it in principle. Most likely, I will have to do that some time.

In Beuron, I learned that a liturgical consultation is in the offing. I am glad that your way will now become clearer. With most cordial wishes for you and your work I am your

Edith

1. See Letter 87.
2. Printed text of her lecture "The Ethos of Women's Professions". [See *Woman,* pp. 41ff.]
3. [An orator's distinctive, familiar phrase, habitually used to close every talk.]

90. Letter to Anneliese Lichtenberger, Ludwigshafen
Original in Convent Archive of Cologne Carmel

Pax! Breslau, April 29, 1931
Dear Anneliese,

You studied the pictures in the church at Beuron [Abbey] with greater observation than I. The painting on the ceiling is said to tell the legend of the foundation: how the Mother of God appeared to Duke Rupert and showed him where the monastery was to be erected. I don't know which birds you refer to on the altar paintings. As far as I recall, St. Scholastica and St. Gertrude are holding doves. You know what they symbolize, don't you? On the picture of the Good Shepherd, there's a bird of prey ready to swoop on a lamb. You will also understand that one. I cannot recall any others.

Did the practice teaching go well? Of course, it had to include math so you would add to your knowledge right away! All the best for the future! Your

Edith Stein

91. Letter to Erna Hermann, Speyer
Original in Convent Archive of Cologne Carmel

Pax! Breslau, May 11, 1931
Dear Fräulein Hermann,

Again, it has taken me longer to reply than I would have wished. In the meantime the 8th of May has passed, and with it your first practice teaching stint, which I hope went well.

You did not let me know the date of your baptism. I would like to celebrate it with you at a distance. Naturally, I am very happy that the time is coming so close now. With all my heart, I wish the day to be one of a truly new birth. Then the grace of your baptism and the ever new reinforcement through the holy sacraments will give you the strength to bear with the difficulties, the arguments with your relatives, and your final year in college with its small and trivial daily cares.

For the present I am staying in Breslau, but at times I shall be going away for brief lecture trips, for example, soon one to Vienna.[1] I don't know who your friend is who has an aunt in Bamberg.

Many things have happened at the convent [in Speyer] since I left. I have faithful reporters. So far, I have not heard from Sr. Raymunda. Give her my regards if you happen to talk to her.

With best wishes and warm greetings, your

Edith Stein

1. Edith Stein gave a lecture during a meeting of the Reich's Organization of Catholic Women of Austria, on May 30, 1931, on the topic *Die hl. Elisabeth, Natur und Übernatur in der Formung einer Heiligen-Gestalt [St. Elizabeth: Nature and Supernature in the Formation of a Saint].* The text is included in Vol. XII of *Edith Steins Werke,* published in 1990 by the *Archivum Carmelitanum Edith Stein.*

92. Letter to Anna Bosslet,[1] Höchen

Original in private possession of Anna Bosslet

Pax! Mödling, near Vienna, May 11, 1931

Vigil of Pentecost

Dear Ännchen [diminutive of Anne],

I received your dear letter shortly before my departure from Breslau, otherwise I should have answered you sooner. I had thought of you often and was very happy to hear from you. I, too, hope very much that we will meet again sometime, and I feel you will have no reason to be embarrassed when we do so. When two people have been together in the presence of the Savior as often as we, it should be easy for them to talk about it to each other at some time. If only there were many persons with whom one could do that without having to fear profaning something that is sacred! Go right ahead and allow yourself as much time in church as you need in order to find rest and peace. That will not only benefit you, but also your work and all the people with whom you deal.

For the time of Pentecost, I have fled into solitude. In a foreign land, as you can see. On the 30th, I must give a talk in Vienna in honor of St. Elizabeth (help me with a memento, won't you!). I came here ahead of time because, at home, on [Catholic] feasts it is particularly difficult for me. (Surely you know that my relatives are not of our faith.)...[2]

But I am not...in Vienna...Steyler Missionaries...boarding with the guests of the monastery, I have a room with some Sisters of the Holy Cross who live nearby.[3]

On Monday, May 25, I will go back to Vienna; then I shall have to meet with lots of people. Everywhere I am handed difficult problems and am always glad when I think that many of you still remember me and help me.

Your
Edith Stein

1. Anna Bosslet was a former student of Edith Stein.
2. [The letter is damaged at this point and could not be reconstructed in full.]
3. During these days, Edith Stein was a guest of the Steyler Missionaries of St. Gabriel's in Mödling, Austria. At night she stayed in the nursing home run by the Sisters of the Holy Cross in Weyprechtgasse, Mödling.

93. Postcard to Anneliese Lichtenberger, Speyer
Original in Convent Archive of Cologne Carmel

Breslau, June 9, 1931

Dear Anneliese,

Only a short note. The Sisters on the fourth floor will surely be glad to accept your help. "Common human traits" are such that all people have in common, as opposed to those that are individual or belong to a particular category (e.g., the feminine category).

Don't lose courage, even when outwardly everything goes amiss.

Most cordially,
Edith Stein

93a. Letter to Fritz Kaufmann, (presumably Freiburg)
Original in *Archivum Carmelitanum Edith Stein*

Breslau, June 14, 1931

Dear Herr Kaufmann,

At last I get around to redeeming a long-accrued debt of gratitude to you. I never thanked you for your articles, never wrote any commentary about them (because I never found time to read them although they lay waiting on my desk in Speyer for many months).

Since I found it impossible to keep up with all the urgent duties, I finally felt compelled to leave St. Magdalena. (N.B. The financial catastrophe did not affect St. Magdalena; another convent in Speyer was involved.) The good sisters were very loath to let me go, and did so only because they saw the *vis major.*[1]

I thought you were informed; Husserl promised me he would tell you all about it when, at the end of January, I was in Freiburg one Sunday and bemoaned my inability to talk to you. At the time I spoke with Honecker and Heidegger about the possibility of habilitation, and found them both cordially forthcoming.

I have been at home since Easter, busy with a large project[2] that mushrooms unpredictably under my hands because I have so many years to work through. I might possibly come to Freiburg in autumn; it is not a certainty yet because other possibilities are still in the wind.

It was not my fault that Thomas[3] took so long. First of all it was difficult to find a publisher for the lengthy work. Then the printing of Volume I dragged on from June of last year until the beginning of [this] May. I had them send you review copies because I received too few free ones to take care of my old friends. I would be satisfied (for the publisher's sake) if you put a brief notice about it in *Logos.* If you could write in greater detail, I would gratefully accept that as a free gift from you. The publisher was to send announcements to the journals but I do not know whether that happened. Besides, I would be glad if you spoke to Krener yourself.

Should I really come to Freiburg, we would have an opportunity to catch up on everything that has been lacking for years in personal and written contact. For my part this lack has changed very little of the actuality of our relationship.

The circle of persons whom I consider as connected with me has increased so much in the course of the years that it is entirely impossible to keep in touch by the usual means. But I have other ways and means of keeping the bonds alive.

Best regards to you and yours, your
Edith Stein

1. [Pater Erich Przywara encouraged Edith to make this change, and the Sisters would have recognized his advice as a "*higher force.*"]
2. See Letter 87.
3. See Letter 47.

94. Letter to Rose Magold,[1] Landau
Original in Convent Archive of Cologne Carmel

Pax! Breslau, June 16, 1931
Dear Rose,

I know you are aware that you may write me anything you wish. That I will not reply when I cannot find time to do so, I have shown you by this long delay.

You wanted to know about books for your study group. Had I stayed with you another year I should have thought of Siegfried Behn's *Philosophie der Werte [Philosophy of Values]* or Rudolf Allers' *Das Werden der sittlichen Persönlichkeit [The Development of the Moral Personality]*. Now, of course, books from your new syllabus should be considered.

When we were in Munich, we saw that difficulties will arise in some [subject] areas because of problems in communicating between the older and younger generations. Despite that, one ought to make an effort to maintain good relations. There is always something to be learned from the opinions of our elders if one only listens without prejudice and reflects on it; and there is even more to be learned from their experience. To test the necessity of a parochial school, and not simply to defend it blindly, is, of course, entirely permissible. Otherwise one will never be able to convince people who have a different viewpoint. Perhaps by autumn you will be able to save up some questions that you can present to me in a study group, preferably in Speyer.

The problem of keeping company with the young teachers is not such a simple one. It is very natural for young people to enjoy the company of other young people. And it is also very natural to find particular enjoyment in being together with people of the opposite sex. I believe both of these experiences were true in your case, and simply admitting it to yourself was all you had to do—after all, there's nothing whatever wrong with it—nor should you have felt it was permissible for you only because of the others. If one is intent on having all of one's life consist exclusively of sacrifices, the danger of pharisaism is around the corner. Of course, when one becomes aware that there is a personal risk in matters that are innocent in themselves, then one must be on guard against them. When one has a clear call to the religious life and is determined to follow it, it is surely advisable not to establish too close a relationship with any man, nor should one encourage a mutual attraction since it cannot attain its natural fulfillment. In most cases that would jeopardize the religious vocation. And it has often concerned me that you have burdened *yours* in ways that did not serve it well.

The cultural levels of the *Nibelungenlied:* 1. Germanic-pagan (migration of peoples), for the time of origin of the saga; 2. chivalry in the 13th century, the time in which the poem was composed; 3. the Christian component. (Possibly, read up on this in *Mimirs Quell [Mimir's Sources]*.)

Best regards to you and to all acquaintances whom you run into, from your

Edith Stein

1. Rose Magold (b. Spiesen, Saar Region, 1908) was a student of Edith Stein's at the Dominican Sisters' teachers college, St. Magdalena, Speyer.

95. Letter to Sr. Adelgundis Jaegerschmid, OSB, Freiburg-Günterstal
Original in Convent Archive of Benedictine Sisters, St. Lioba, Freiburg-Günterstal

Pax! Breslau, June 28, 1931
Dear Sister Adelgundis,

Because we are celebrating here the feast of John the Baptist (patron of the cathedral, of the city and of the diocese, whose head is pictured in the city's coat of arms, and whose finger is kept as a sacred relic in the cathedral) and because you have him as your special patron for the year, you are to have Feast Day greetings.

Yesterday I tried to catch some festive liturgy; but at the Pontifical Vespers the psalms were sung in polyphony by the cathedral choir with orchestral accompaniment. So it was not so difficult for me, today, to return to the silent liturgy that is my portion here. Even this way one can be richly supplied with what one needs. I experience that daily. But only when, once again, I am able to live in fullness, do I realize how I thirsted for it. When I decided to leave Speyer, I knew it would be very difficult not to be living in a convent any longer. But I would never have imagined that it would be as difficult as it has proved to be in these first months. For all that, as I cannot doubt that things are as they should be, I have never for a moment regretted making the move.

On my return from Vienna, I was very happy to find [a picture postcard of] your convent's gate as a greeting from Sr. Placida <Laubhardt>. It consoled me to look at it and to think that in a few months it would open to offer me asylum. In the meantime, though, an entirely new possibility has surfaced here. For the present, the following is in confidence for you and Sr. Placida.

My brother-in-law <Hans Biberstein> has a regular social get-together with other professors [at the University of Breslau], including several Catholic theologians. One of these (Koch[1]) has inquired repeatedly about his sister-in-law (especially since Salzburg). Recently he said that, in Rome, he had heard some very favorable comments about me (i.e., about my "Thomas") and would be very happy to make my acquaintance: he asked whether I would not like a habilitation here [in Breslau].

Thereupon I asked my mother, first of all, whether it would be all right with her if I were to engage, publicly, in a Catholic enterprise here in town. To my great surprise, it developed that she would make allowance for anything that would keep me in the area. On Tuesday, my relatives [Hans and Erna] invited Professor Koch and me [for dinner]. He would welcome it greatly if I could teach phenomenology (with my modification) here, and has, meanwhile, begun to work along those lines on Professor Baur, the Catholic head of faculty for philosophy. Tomorrow, I'm to come with Baur to Professor Koch for coffee. I am going to just let the matter run its course, waiting to see what will come of it.

My work[2] cares little about where it can be used. It has already grown into a monster and gives no sign of coming to an end. I want to keep at it until autumn, without interruption if possible. For the month of October, the Academic Society has concocted a lecture circuit for me throughout the Rhein-Westphalian industrial belt. So far, fourteen chapters have signed up for it.

On November 22, I'm to give the principal address to Heidelberg's Catholic community, meeting in the large town hall for the Jubilee of St. Elisabeth [of Thuringia]. (Did you see the lecture in the *Neues Reich* [magazine] of June 13 and 20?) And for the second half of January, I've been engaged [in Switzerland] to give four lectures, twice,[4] to the Catholic women in Zurich.[5] I do not know yet where I shall spend the time in between. That will depend on what happens in the matter of the habilitation.

Sr. Placida wrote to me about her concern over her father. Naturally, I share it with both of you.

Give my regards to Reverend Mother Prioress and specially warm greetings to you and Sr. Placida from your

E. St.

1. Joseph Koch (b. Münstereifel, 1885; d. Cologne, 1967) was professor of Catholic theology in Breslau and Cologne.
2. See Letters 87 and 89.
3. See Letter 106.
4. [She was to give four lectures, then repeat them at a second location in the city, thus enabling a large number of enthusiastic hearers to be accommodated.]
5. See "Spirituality of the Christian Woman" in *Woman,* pp. 86ff.

96. Letter to Erna Hermann, Speyer
Original in Convent Archive of Cologne Carmel

Pax! Breslau, July 1, 1931
Dear Fräulein Hermann,

This time the answer could not come as promptly. Although I do not have to teach any longer, my time is as fully occupied as it was in Speyer, and there is no clock that can lengthen the days. (I had no doubt about identifying the "Nicholas.")[1]

I was very happy to see from the letter you wrote on Ascension Day how things have brightened up for you. I hope your spirits have been raised even more by the beautiful feasts that have just passed and by the prospect of having your wishes fulfilled. I doubt very much that you can count on me to be your Confirmation sponsor. Actually, I plan to visit Speyer in connection with a lengthy lecture tour.[2] But that will hardly happen before the beginning of November. And you will not want to wait that long. Fräulein von Bodman would surely be glad to perform that service of love. I think your association with her brings you much joy and benefit. Please give my warmest regards to her and do that to all of my acquaintances whom you get to see at the convent. Should your cousin[3] be ordained in the meantime, I would like to ask you to give him my congratulations.

Wishing you all the best and thinking of you faithfully, I am your
Edith Stein

1. [Evidently Edith had received a clock from an anonymous donor. St. Nicholas is credited with that manner of giving gifts, and Edith realizes Frl. Hermann sent the gift.]
2. See Letter 95.
3. Bruno Rothschild; see Letter 53.

97. Letter to Anneliese Lichtenberger, Ludwigshafen
Original in Convent Archive of Cologne Carmel

Pax! Breslau, July 4, 1931
My dear Anneliese,

Your question deserves a prompt answer. It would indeed be good to give your parents a clear picture of the situation by letter, even now. But it would have been wiser to keep them currently informed about everything. Don't you want to ask your parents at the same time to consider whether you should stay on or whether they will permit you to stop now? Perhaps then your father would come to Speyer to consult with the Principal before school closes. It might occur to your parents that you should go back to the fifth class. However, I believe that the Principal would tell them that repeating the fifth would not make any difference in the poor results in the sixth. Don't you agree?

If your parents decide to let you quit, then you should express the wish that you be given some kind of regular work, possibly one that will lead to vocational activity and independence. You won't be able to bring up the Social School for Women again this soon. It would be best to allow your parents to suggest what you should begin to do. Almost anything that could be considered—homemaking, business, nursing, kindergarten—would be a step closer to the goal. But if not, I believe you are in real need of some kind of work. And your parents will surely understand that you need some kind of support.

When I hear of your failures, I always have to think of a verse in Psalm 118. *Bonum mihi quia humiliasti me.* (It is good for me that you have humbled me.) The Lord must have something special in store for you since he has put you through such a difficult course. Won't you place yourself under the particular protection of your patroness, St. Elizabeth? The lecture I gave in Vienna[1] about her was published in the June 13th and 20th issues of *Neues Reich.* Sr. Agnella <Stadtmüller> can probably get them for you. Please give the note to Sr. Agnella.

With loving remembrance, your
Edith Stein

1. See Letter 91.

98. Letter to Erna Hermann, Speyer
Original in Convent Archive of Cologne Carmel

Pax! Breslau, July 6, 1931
Dear Fräulein Hermann,

You will receive as printed matter—but only on loan since it is my last copy—the lecture I gave last year in Speyer. If you use any of it, it would be good to mention its source (Herr F. <?> heard my lecture that time). If you want a bibliography, you can get it from Sr. Bonaventura or from one of the young women who taught in the continuing education program last year. It lists the books recommended by the Department of Education.

Have a good vacation and best wishes, your

Edith Stein

99. Postcard to Frau Callista Brenzing, OCist, Seligenthal
Original in Convent Archive of Cologne Carmel

Pax! Breslau, July 9, 1931

Dear Mother Callista,

Finally, most cordial greetings with best wishes for your vacation, in response to your welcome card of May 10. I surely believe that you would understand my Thomas, but it would not be suitable vacation reading.

Recently I got to know E. Promnitz, a biographer of [St.] Hedwig. Most probably she could give you a good deal of information.[1]

Most cordially,

Edith Stein

1. Mother Callista was working on a commemorative booklet to mark the seventh centenary of her monastery and was seeking more information about its foundation. Edith Stein later made her a gift of the biography of St. Hedwig.

100. Letter to Sr. Callista Kopf, OP, Speyer
Original in Convent Archive of the Dominican Sisters in Speyer

Pax! Breslau, August 8, 1931

Dear Sister Callista,

We will have to discuss the women's question in person and in greater detail. Have you read the lecture I gave in Salzburg, and my article in *Stimmen der Zeit?*[1] (You can probably dig out both[2] in Speyer.) They contain quite a bit. But I do believe that in the meantime I've added to my knowledge but still have much more to learn on the subject.

During my years in the *Gymnasium* and as a young student [at the university], I was a radical feminist. Then I lost interest in the whole question. Now, because I am obliged to do so, I seek purely objective solutions.

The priest [identity unknown] is probably too one-sidedly set on fighting abuses that do exist and are perhaps much stronger today in the Catholic women's movement than elsewhere, because it is still going through "teething problems" that the others experienced 20 or 30 years ago. Much more can be accomplished with a *genuinely* catholic, that is, free and wide, viewpoint than is commonly supposed.

I consider Vérèna Borsinger's dissertation valuable for uncovering long-buried facts and I would welcome it if she could continue working in that direction. I did tell her, personally, that it would be more effective if she allowed the facts to speak for themselves and were to forego the subjective, belligerent tone she uses.

The insistence that the sexual differences are "stipulated by the body alone" is questionable from various points of view. 1) If *anima = forma corporis,* then bodily differentiation constitutes an index of differentiation in the spirit. 2) Matter serves form, not the reverse. That strongly suggests that the difference in the psyche is the primary one. Thorough consideration must be given, of course, to the question: To what extent can and should growth into the supernatural be a growing beyond the differences endowed by nature?

Best regards to all the Sisters up there, especially Sr. Canisia, Chrysostoma, Domitilla. Sincerely, your

Edith Stein

1. [The article "Fundamental Principles of Women's Education" appeared in the March, 1931 issue of the periodical *Stimmen der Zeit (Voices of the Times).*]
2. [Both essays, "Ethos of Women's Professions" and "Fundamental Principles of Women's Education," may be found in *Woman,* pp. 41ff. and 115ff., respectively. Letter 73 gives more indication of controversy at the time.]

101. Letter to Erna Hermann, Speyer
Original in Convent Archive of Cologne Carmel

Pax! Breslau, August 15, 1931
Dear Fräulein Hermann,

I guess you are back in Speyer, and perhaps a bit lonely until the trimester begins. Therefore, you are at last receiving thanks for all the vacation and pre-vacation greetings, and for the beautiful needlework as well. It did not distress me as much since it was probably not very taxing and your schedule not as terribly overcrowded as last year. But, please, no more such handiwork during the school term.

And now the long-awaited day of Baptism is not far away. I shall be sincerely happy with you when you have finally arrived at the goal. It certainly is difficult when one has to wait at the gate for such a long time. On that day of grace, may I ask you to remember my sister <Rosa> who has longed for years to enter the Church and who is still prevented from doing so by the unfavorable circumstances of her life?

If it is impossible for me to come for your Confirmation, you may ask Fräulein von Bodman without hesitation. I am convinced she would be glad to do it. Besides, if you prefer, I could also be your sponsor and Fräulein von Bodman could be proxy for me at the ceremony. That is permitted. According to my plans, the best time would be between the first and the tenth of November. So far, I have no commitments for that time. Should it become necessary for me to schedule anything else for that period, I would let you know.

With the most cordial wishes for the next few weeks and many greetings, your

Edith Stein

102. Letter to Anneliese Lichtenberger, Schwarzenacker
Original in Convent Archive of Cologne Carmel

Pax! Breslau, August 17, 1931
Dear Anneliese,

God leads each of us on an individual way; one reaches the goal more easily and more quickly than another. We can do very little ourselves, compared to what is done to us. But that little bit we must do. Primarily, this consists before all else of persevering in prayer to find the right way, and of following without resistance the attraction of grace when we feel it. Whoever acts in this way and perseveres patiently will not be able to say that his efforts were in vain. But one may not set a deadline for the Lord.

Is there an Old Testament or at least a translation of the Psalms available either in your home, or somewhere in the vicinity? The Psalms appeared in Latin and German in the collection *Ecclesia orans.* But I believe you can get the psalms in any Catholic book store (e.g., in Homburg). If not, Sr. Agnella <Stadtmüller> in Speyer would surely be glad to get you a German breviary from one of the Sisters sometime. Psalm 118 is recited every Sunday in the Little Hours (Prime to None). It is the longest one, but very rich and beautiful.

Obviously it is no small matter for you to return to Speyer. But that's what has been decided for you, and you have no responsibility for it. Do as much as you can, and give your parents a regular account of your standing so there will be no surprise if things go badly at Easter.[1] Then we will see about the future. Among the books you got as a child, do you have Andersen's Fairy Tales? If so, read the story of the ugly duckling. I believe in your swan-destiny. Just don't hold it against others if they haven't discovered this yet, and don't let yourself become bitter. You are not the only one to make mistakes day after day—we all do it. But the Lord is patient and full of mercy. In his household of grace he can use our faults, too, if we lay them on the altar for him. "*Cor contritum et humiliatum Deus non despicies* (A contrite and humbled heart, O God, you will not scorn)" (Ps. 50). That, too, is one of my favorite verses.

With best regards and remembering you faithfully, your

Edith Stein

1. [In many German schools Easter was the time for final reports and promotions.]

103. Letter to Rose Magold, Landau
Original in Convent Archive of Cologne Carmel

Pax! Breslau, August 20, 1931
Dear Rose,

If I don't write soon, your letter will disappear under a pile of other papers, and it is best that you receive a prompt reply. If all is as you portray it, I cannot see any problems. To contend for souls and to love them in the Lord is the Christian's duty and, actually, a special goal of the Dominican Order. But if that is your goal and if the thought of marriage is farthest from your mind, then it will be good if you soon begin to wear appropriate dress. That will make it clear to people who it is they are dealing with. Otherwise there will be the danger of your misleading others, of your behavior being misinterpreted (I would be surprised if, without your being aware of it, that has not already happened at times), and of your achieving exactly the opposite of what you desire. Whether one ought to tell people what one is doing for them cannot be decided in general. Sometimes it is appropriate, but sometimes definitely not. So I believe you should arrive at a decision soon after the examinations. After that, if you hesitate much longer before entering, I would be seriously worried about your vocation. Surely, Sigrid Undset[1] will ruthlessly remove all kinds of scales from your eyes. That won't harm you; rather, it will be useful in many respects. But as for what God wants of you, that you will have to seek to learn from him, eye to eye.

I expect to be in Speyer at the beginning of November. I will be in the Rhineland until October 30 (in Aachen last). If nothing comes up that would immediately follow that trip, I could probably come as soon as All Saints and stay for several days. If anything in this plan changes, I will let you know.

Regards to all you see, from me. Faithfully remembering you, your

Edith Stein

1. Sigrid Undset (b. Kalundborg, Denmark, 1882; d. Lillehammer, Norway, 1949) Norwegian author; converted in 1925; won the Nobel Prize for Literature in 1928. [Edith suggests Undset's portrayal of life's reality will free Rose from illusions.]

104. Letter to Rose Magold, Landau
Original in Convent Archive of Cologne Carmel

Pax! Breslau, August 30, 1931
Dear Rose,

Your table of organization is good; I hope it will not stay on paper only.

It is not so easy to answer your personal questions. As far as associating with people is concerned, it seems to me you have become too anxious (about the past). I don't believe you have harmed anyone. I only believe that in many cases you did not have the desired result since—with the best intentions—you took the wrong turn because of your great naïveté as well as, probably, an inflated self-esteem. In some cases you will have damaged your image in the eyes of others. You will have to accept that as a small penance. In my opinion, there is no use trying to explain matters to all the people concerned. It will be best for you to exercise as much restraint as you can (I mean especially with regard to talking about yourself with persons from whom you cannot expect any help). Only when you are asked for an explanation, then give it as best you can.

You ask whether you are so "pitiable that only through your clothing can you convince people of your intention." Of course I don't mean that. But if you don't wear that kind of clothing, anyone is entitled to think they are dealing with a girl like any other (that does not necessarily have to be bad), and that, e.g, you may be courted. That, naturally, is not sufficient reason for wearing religious dress if one has no vocation. That is now the great question. When I look at your behavior in the last year and a half, I see only two possibilities. Either you *have* a vocation for the Order, for St. Dominic and St. Magdalena, but you are making every effort to free yourself from it (even in this letter with the many questions about a guarantee that it is the right thing for you)—or you don't have a vocation but are unable to decide to bring to an end a plan that's been harbored for a long time. I do not dare to decide with absolute certainty, but I have the impression that the first is the more likely alternative.

There is no general solution to the question of how to choose between entering a religious order, or [joining] a pious union, or leading, on the other hand, a solitary life in the service of God. The decision has to be made for each individual case. The multiplicity of religious orders, congregations, and associations is not an accident, nor a mistake; rather, it reflects the multiplicity of purposes and of people. No individual is suitable for everything; nor is there any form of union or other organization that can accomplish everything. *One* body—but many members. *One* Spirit—but many gifts. Where the individual belongs is a vocational question, and so it is *your* most important question now that the examinations are over. The question of vocation cannot be solved merely through self-examination plus a scrutiny of the available possibilities. One must pray for the answer—you know that—and, in many cases, it must be sought by way of obedience. I have given this same advice several times, and those involved have arrived at peace and clarity by following it.

I think the very best thing for you would be to get yourself some firm guidance. I do not know whether you have a confessor at this time to whom you could entrust yourself completely. If not, I know of two confessors near you in whose ability to help you I have complete confidence: Vice-Rector Dr. Lutz[1] and Pater Petrus <Jans, OSB>[2] in Neuburg. The one has the advantage of knowing St. Magdalena's thoroughly, the other of being a religious priest. Of course I do not advise going to both, but rather, that you decide on one of them. Finally, I recommend, urgently, that you make use of the time remaining of Sr. Reinhildis' stay in Speyer for a thorough discussion with her. She is most capable of telling you what you will and what you won't find in St. Magdalena.

Most cordially,
Edith Stein

1. Otto Lutz (b. Linden/Palatinate, 1881; d. Speyer, 1952) Vice-Rector, later Rector at the [diocesan] seminary in Speyer. He was confessor at St. Magdalena's for many years.
2. Anton Jans (P. Petrus, OSB) (b. Kressbach near Tübingen, 1887; d. Neersdomer Mühle, 1970) was a monk at Neuburg Abbey near Heidelberg.

105. Letter to Erna Hermann, Speyer
Original in Convent Archive of Cologne Carmel

Pax! Breslau, September 8, 1931
Dear Fräulein Hermann,

Today Fräulein von Bodman wrote that you are somewhat upset and would like me to tell you more about the ceremony at Baptism. Of course, the water was poured on my head (after all, that's not so bad and it is dried with a towel right away), nor have I heard of its ever being done in any other way. Certainly you have no need to worry that anything may be done incorrectly. Everything is outlined very clearly in the ritual. At the time, I asked the priest who baptized me to lend me the book and I looked at the rite very carefully. I wore a black dress and had a white mantle put around me. At the Baptism[1] I attended in Beuron at Christmas, a white veil was used.

I am sorry that, just at this time, you are being burdened by so many other things. One should be able to prepare oneself in peace. I was lucky in that way. It is in the nature of such an event that before the decisive step is taken, you see before you once more all you will be renouncing and risking. That is how it ought to be: that, without any kind of human assurance, you place yourself totally in God's hands, then all the deeper and more beautiful will be the security attained. My wish for your Baptismal Day and for all of your future life is that you may find the fullness of God's peace. I would like to make you happy with a small gift on your special day. Since you are already richly provided with all that belongs to the life of a Catholic Christian, I could think of nothing better than my little book. I am convinced you have known and owned it for a long time; however, it may please you to receive it once more from my hands.

If you will ask Resl <Theresa Neumann> for her prayers for my sister Rosa, we will, of course, be most grateful. Please give my best regards to Resl and to your cousin <Rothschild>.

In the meantime, I trust all will have gone well with your lecture. I felt the time after your next to last letter was too short to send it back and forth. That's why I did not offer to read it any more.

With best regards, and a faithful remembrance, your
Edith Stein

1. [In December, 1930, Edith Stein was the sponsor at the baptism of Alice Reis who, twelve years later, was arrested in Holland on the same day as Edith. Both were killed in Auschwitz on August 9, 1942.]

106. Postcard to Emil Vierneisel, Heidelberg
Original in Convent Archive of Cologne Carmel

Pax! <St. Magdalena, Speyer> November 1, 1931
Dear Professor,

Does it surprise you to get my reply from here? Yesterday I found your letter awaiting me upon my arrival after my lecture tour. I will stay about ten days. I am very glad to forgo the talk in Heidelberg after having already helped to celebrate St. Elizabeth eleven times.

On the 12th I must return to Bonn, then I want to go directly to Freiburg (possibly for the winter), and will be glad to return to my work peacefully without having to interrupt it almost immediately.

With best regards, your
Edith Stein

107. Postcard to Anneliese Lichtenberger, Speyer
Original in Convent Archive of Cologne Carmel

Pax! (Beuron), November 18, 1931
Dear Anneliese,

Cordial greetings for your name day. Please extend some to Sr. Elizabeth, also! I am so sorry I was unable to talk to you anymore. I am here for two days only; from tomorrow on [I will be] in Freiburg/Breisgau-Günterstal, St. Placidus.

Best wishes to all the children. Your
Edith Stein

108. Letter to Mother Callista Brenzing, OCist, Seligenthal
Original in Convent Archive of Cologne Carmel

Pax! Beuron, December 23, 1931
Dear Mother Callista,

How good that you have adjusted to the invisible correspondence! Then you will in no way take offense with a gyrovague[1] when she returns your Name Day wishes [for October 15] only at Christmas with cordial wishes sent from her beloved home. That is the greatest plus to this wanderer's life, that it led me to St. Lioba-Freiburg for Advent and here [to Beuron] for a *plenitudo* [to top it off].

You must have been told that I did not get to Speyer until the beginning of November; and immediately thereafter to Ludwigshafen; and to Munich, not at all. I found Sr. Agnella <Stadtmüller> very well settled and not at all dissatisfied with the transfer. With Sr. Reinhildis, I was able to have a good talk in Speyer.

Because of the economic crisis, none of those prospects of a permanent position that I had at Easter, or that arose subsequently, have materialized. In the middle of January, I will leave Freiburg for two weeks of lectures in Zurich.[2] Beyond that, all is shrouded in darkness. Will you help me to implore the Christ Child to let me know what he intends to do with me?

Respectful greetings to Mother Abbess and I wish you all the blessings of the Feast, your faithful

Edith Stein

1. ["Gyrovague" *(Gyrovagen)* is an archaic term for a medieval wandering (vagus) monk or scholar who makes a circuit (gyro) of places of learning.]
2. See Letter 95.

109. Letter to Emilie Bechtold, Wettenhausen
Original in private possession of Emilie Bechtold

Pax![1] St. Lioba, Freiburg-Günterstal, January 3, 1932

At last, my sincere thanks to you and Liesel Huber for your kind

Name Day wishes, which arrived safely in Breslau and were forwarded to me to Westphalia.

At the same time, my very best wishes for the New Year, especially for the difficult beginning [in a new school]. Your

Edith Stein

1. [No salutation is given.]

110. Letter to Sr. Callista Kopf, OP, Speyer

Original in Convent Archive of the Dominican Sisters in Speyer

Pax! St. Lioba, Freiburg-Günterstal, January 14, 1932

Dear Sister Callista,

Greetings, before I go to Switzerland. (Not until Sunday. The lectures will be held January 18 to 28.[1] On Septuagesima, another big Cantonal celebration to honor St. Elizabeth.[2])

When I received your letter recently, I knew as soon as I saw the outside that it contained a death notice.[3] The last news I had from Sr. Edeltraud was in Breslau. There was no follow-up to my reply. So, unfortunately, I did not write to her for Christmas. I believe she was well prepared through her own suffering and her mother's.

Do not let yourself worry uselessly that the results of your years of study will be lost. [What you learned] is a habit [*habitus*], that is, a firm possession, which is not readily lost. There is much more to oneself than one realizes. And that is a wise arrangement. When one needs [something], it comes to hand.

I have had no word from Rose <Magold> since Speyer. It would be high time for her to make a decision, and high time, too, for her to join a congregation.

Sincere greetings to all your Sisters. I beg all of you for your prayers. Sincerely, your

Edith Stein

1. See Letter 95.
2. See Letter 97.
3. [In Germany and other European countries, letters containing death notices are mailed in envelopes edged in black.]

111. Letter to Erna Hermann, Speyer
Original in Convent Archive of Cologne Carmel

Pax! Zurich, January 27, 1932
Dear Fräulein Hermann,

It is very kind of you to wish to do something for my sister <Rosa>; I thank you most sincerely for it. The one who requested it is without doubt Sr. Raymunda. After what you went through during the past few weeks, you will understand that I want to spare my mother and sister a similar experience. For the time being, my mother knows nothing of my sister's intentions. So I beg you, earnestly, to treat the matter most confidentially. I will give my sister your address so she can establish contact with you herself. If you want to do anything before she does, then please do so at first without giving her name. For the time being, I would think of no more than an inquiry in Nürnberg. Nothing can be considered for Rosa other than working in a household. She is already 48 years old and has been running my mother's household for decades. She is also very good at caring for and rearing young children.

Will you please tell Sr. Raymunda, also, that I am very grateful to her for her good intention to be of help, but I beg her most earnestly to be very discreet about it, for the reasons already mentioned.

I shall probably remain here until Saturday; January 31–February 3, I will be in Beuron, then stop in St. Lioba-Freiburg, but probably not for long. Moving around so much is very tiring, of course, but after all, my health is not bad. Here I get most solicitous care.

All the best for the examinations and all your other concerns. Best regards, please, to Fräulein von Bodman, also. Your

Edith Stein

112. Letter to Elly Dursy (Sr. Mary Elizabeth of Divine Providence, OCD), Auderath

Original in Convent Archive of Carmel of Auderath

Pax! [March 20] Beuron, Palm Sunday, 1932

Dear Elly,

I received your letter in Münster, but since I did not want to answer it immediately, my trip intervened (lectures that I have to give in Munich, April 1 and 4 on the Bavarian Radio,[1] make it possible for me to spend Holy Week and Easter in Beuron once more). Now, unfortunately, I don't have your letter at hand—I "forwarded" it in a small package that has not yet arrived—so I can only answer as much as I remember: first of all, of course, you may go to <the Benedictine Abbey at> Neuburg on Good Friday. Also of course, I have often reflected whether my coming here so frequently is justifiable. But after all, one has to provide one's inner life with the nourishment it needs, especially when at other times we are required to give a great deal to others. Obviously, one cannot discuss this with persons who are oriented purely to material matters, and who have no sense for the values of spirit or soul.

Couldn't you arrange to go to Speyer for Confession once a month? I do believe it would be good to go regularly to someone who knows you and your situation.

Could you please write to me in Munich, giving me, once more, as accurate an account as possible of your present situation: that, according to all human reckoning, permission from your parents is not to be expected; and what considerations still keep you at home; and then, asking whether *despite that* it is recommended that you enter.

Of course, you must try to help P.'s sister.[2] It does not matter that she is older. Maturity is not always a function of age. Obviously, you must take care to help her according to *her* nature, not yours, and if she needs to express her attachment, don't reject it—surely there's nothing wrong in that connection? Have patience with yourself; God also has it.

I would rather not recount anything further about myself, for, actually, I am already in silence today.

Best wishes for Holy Week and the Easter days, your

Edith Stein

1. Edith Stein spoke on the program *Stunde der Frau [The Woman's Hour]* on "Fragen mütterlicher Erziehungskunst" [literally, "Questions Regarding the Maternal Art of Rearing (Children)"].
2. [Sister Elizabeth gave the names of P. (Pauline) and her sister (Elizabeth) to Sr. Maria Amata Neyer, OCD, at the Cologne Carmel, who supplied most of the clarifying notes shown in [ ] in this volume.]

113. Letter to P. Petrus Wintrath,[1] OSB, Maria Laach
Original in Archive of the Benedictine Abbey Maria Laach

Pax! <College Marianum> Münster, April 22, 1932
Dear Reverend Father,

Thank you so much for your kind letter. I will forward the inquiry to my publisher; perhaps he can accomplish something with the editorial staff. Sincere thanks for the trouble you have taken, as well as for your kindness in sending on your off-prints. Please forgive me for not acknowledging their receipt before this. I am busy getting acquainted with an entirely new sphere of endeavor *(Deutsches Institut fur Wissenschaftliche Pädagogik)* [the German Institute for Scientific Pedagogy]; in addition to that the second volume of the Thomas[2] set is being printed in a big rush.

With respectful greetings, sincerely in Christ,
Edith Stein

1. Johannes Baptist Wintrath (P. Petrus, OSB) (b. Bernkastel, Mosel, 1876; d. Abbey of Maria Laach, 1962), Ph.D., was a philosopher at the Benedictine Abbey of Maria Laach.
2. See Letter 116.

114. Letter to Anneliese Lichtenberger, Ludwigshafen
Original in Convent Archive of Cologne Carmel

Pax! College Marianum, Münster, May 2, 1932
Dear Anneliese,

Letters do reach me now with no more than "Münster i. W."[1] as an address. But at that time I had been here for too short a time. I learned the result of the tests from Speyer. But I waited eagerly for your own report. I am glad that you have the right attitude toward it.

Now you will have to help your parents with moving. And then, if they can use your help in Ludwigshafen, perhaps in the [family] business, it will surely be the best thing you can do. It is so difficult to find any other employment at this time. Should your time not be fully occupied at home, then, of course, it would be necessary to look around for something else. If earning something were not the question, but simply making a good use of time, surely there is plenty of opportunity in Ludwigshafen for volunteer social work. All you would have to do is go to see Fräulein Husse at the Sacred Heart Rectory (and give her and the pastor, Father Husse, my cordial greetings) and ask her to let you help her. Do you know that I am to give a lecture to the Catholic women teachers in Ludwigshafen[2] on June 26 (at St. Dominic's)? I will be there only over Sunday but perhaps we could still meet.

Besides, if you do not yet have a confessor in Ludwigshafen, perhaps you want to consider Father Husse. Surely, you will be visiting Sr. Agnella sometimes. That is very close to Sacred Heart [Parish].

Don't take your departure [from Speyer] too hard. All the best and my regards to your parents also, your

Edith Stein

1. [The "i.W." is the abbreviation for "in Westphalia," which identifies the Münster in Germany to which the letter is addressed.]
2. On June 26, 1932, Edith spoke at a commemoration of the First Centenary of Goethe's death.

115. Letter to Mother Callista Brenzing, OCist, Seligenthal
Original in Convent Archive of Cologne Carmel

Pax! College Marianum, Münster, May 5, 1932
Dear Mother Callista,

Your kind Easter letter caught up with me in Beuron. The *Bayrische Rundfunk* [Bavarian Radio Network] had made it possible for me to travel through all of Germany, and thus I had another chance to spend almost two weeks as a "happy monk" [in Beuron]! I might call myself one here also, but with a different distribution of the *Ora et Labora* [pray and work, a Benedictine motto]. I am very grateful to all those whose prayers have obtained this new sphere of work for me [at the Pedagogic Institute in Münster]. But now they have to help me further by asking with me for the energy and enlightenment to carry out all the tasks. On the 18th, I am to speak in Essen at the meeting of the Society of German Catholic Women Teachers; on June 26th, in St. Dominic's, Ludwigshafen [the Goethe Address].

You probably know that my three grown-up children[1] are all in leadership positions, now, in Speyer.

Best regards, your
Edith Stein

[P.S.] I think Sr. A. <Agnella Stadtmüller> is silent because she is not allowed to write uncensored letters.

1. [The three Dominican Sisters whom she taught when she first came to St. Magdalena's: Sr. Agnella Stadtmüller, Sr. Callista Kopf and Sr. Reinhildis Ferber.]

116. Letter to Sr. Adelgundis Jaegerschmid, OSB, Freiburg-Günterstal
Original in Convent Archive of Benedictine Sisters, St. Lioba, Frei-burg-Günterstal

Pax! College Marianum, Münster, June 9, 1932
Dear Sister Adelgundis,

I want you to have a note of greeting as the Octave of the Sacred Heart closes. Certainly you had occasion to celebrate the feast in an entirely new fashion this year. I am very happy about your prison ministry, even though I foresee you will have many difficult experiences in the future.

I sent on your article, which I received but a short time ago, to my sister <Rosa> because I believe it will be very valuable to her. If you want to have it back or if you want me to return it to the lady in Dortmund, please let me know. Things seem to be somewhat better for my sister now. She laments a good deal over the difficulties of living together with relatives whose thinking differs so much from hers (surely you can readily understand her feelings). And obviously I cannot even think of having her join me at any foreseeable time. As things are now, one has to be glad just to have the Institute continue in existence.

I have to put up quite a struggle to justify my scholarly existence—not with any of the people, since they do all they possibly can to help me—but with the situation created by my ten-year exclusion from the continuity of [academic] work and the lack, rooted so deeply within me, of contact with the contemporary scene. What is good is that gradually I am establishing rapport with the faculty members as well as with the [women] students. (That it is gradual is my doing, since I am still unable to devote more time to it.)

Two Catholic student societies and the academic Conference on Elizabeth had their emissaries visit me to ask me to visit them. With the first of these I recently held an evening discussion program on the status of women—it became very lively. I believe this is a way in which the female students at the university could be attracted to audit courses at the Institute (at future lectures). That would be a gain for both sides.

My second volume on Thomas has been published. As soon as the bound volumes are available, you will receive yours.

On Corpus Christi, Koyré[1] visited me. He had been in Cologne for three days for a consultation on the literary legacy of [Max] Scheler. One volume is to come out pretty soon. Some beautiful sketches on death and on suffering are said to be among the papers.

In caritate sacratissimi Cordis, your
Edith Stein

1. Alexander Koyré, Professor of Philosophy at the École des Hautes-Études, Paris; he was one of the first students of Edmund Husserl in Göttingen. Edith met him there when he was one of the leaders in the group of phenomenologists. His opinion was important to her for the rest of her life. [Cf. *Life,* p. 253 etc.]

117. Letter to P. Petrus Wintrath, OSB, Maria Laach
Original in Archive of the Benedictine Abbey Maria Laach

Pax! College Marianum, Münster, June 12, 1932
Dear Reverend Father,

Thank you very much for occupying yourself so thoroughly with my translation of Thomas, and for your corrections of which some—especially those on the first pages—are very substantial.

I sent your card to the publisher at the time; he believed it would be easy to arrange for a consultation because he had a good relationship with the publishers of *Theologie und Glaube* [Theology and Faith]. That, so far, it has not taken place, I only learned from your letter. I pointed it out once more to Herr Borgmeyer <the publisher>, primarily so he would send you the second volume, which has come out in the meantime.[1] You see, he is not at all generous with review copies. If you do not receive it, please let me know so that I can order it for you.

No one could be more convinced than I am that others would have been better qualified for this work. Perhaps I would have been unable to summon the courage for it had I been aware about all the difficulties beforehand. After all, I approached it as a neophyte in scholasticism (though not in philosophy) for the very purpose of becoming acquainted with Thomas. I consider it almost a miracle that the work was finished and that, in spite of all deficiencies, it turned out as it did. For it was produced, without guidance and without resource material, in hours pared from a full teaching schedule and various other duties. I would have lacked competence to give more extensive explanatory notes than I provided. Perhaps just such an unsuspecting little David had to attack Goliath in order to give stimulus to the heavily armored knights. Were I 15 or 20 years younger and free to do what seems best to me, I would start all over again with the study of philosophy and theology. But I am of an age when what one has [learned] must bear fruit, and only in between can one try to the best of one's ability to make up for deficiencies. Perhaps I may call on you occasionally for advice. Besides that, I beg you very much for a memento [in your prayers] for my work.

Once more, I thank you sincerely and send respectful greetings.

Yours, in Christ,
Edith Stein

1. See Letter 116.

118. Letter to Erna Hermann, Speyer
Original in Convent Archive of Cologne Carmel

Pax![1] College Marianum, Münster, June 19, 1932

At last a greeting in return for your many kind notes. Please excuse me, but on account of the demands of my new sphere of activity, I did not get around to it before, nor even to expressing my congratulations on the examination.

Always with the best regards, your
Edith Stein

1. [This letter carries no salutation.]

119. Letter to Martin Honecker,[1] <presumably in Freiburg im Breisgau>
Original in Convent Archive of Cologne Carmel

College Marianum, Münster, July 8, 1932

Dear Herr Professor,

Thank you very much for your friendly letter of June 20. I was very happy about your favorable judgment on my translation of Thomas, as I am about every indication that the countless hours I gave to it were not spent in vain. Because of it, there was so much else that I was unable to get done, that I now miss and will gradually have to make up. For the passage on [Q.] 21 a 1, it seems to me that your version deserves preference. No matter how often one reworks the material, one always finds something else to change.

I have friendly relations with the philosophers (Scholz, Wust, Rosenmöller)[2] but for the present have not raised the question of habilitation. I believe even here difficulties would arise—especially now—and, as it is, I have so much to do to get a firm foothold at the Institute <German Institute for Scientific Pedagogy in Münster> that I would not like to start immediately with something else besides. The Catholic women students have already found the way to me privately, and I hope that by such means I will be able to attract an appropriate audience to the Institute. You can imagine that the "leadership course" has shrunk to a minimum. Those who come to the lectures are, preponderantly, teachers [male and female] and it would, of course, be difficult to draw from them a proper circle of students. For that reason, I feel that a closer bond to the university is very desirable. Professor Steffes[3] promised to do his utmost in this direction.

I have agreed to a course in Aachen on the anthropology of St. Thomas Aquinas for September and October. But I still have a hope that it will not become a reality, for there are few people, today, who can afford the price. I would be glad if I could spend my vacation quietly at work. For the 12th of September, I also have an invitation from the *Société Thomiste* to go to Juvisy in the vicinity of Paris for a conference on phenomenology and its relationship to Thomism.[4] I promise myself a lot of stimulus for my work.

For the present, things are still very peaceful. One will have to wait to see what the coming weeks will bring.

With best regards, your grateful
Edith Stein

1. Martin Honecker (b. Bonn, 1888; d. Freiburg, 1941) was professor of philosophy in Bonn and Freiburg.
2. Heinrich Scholz (b. Berlin, 1884; d. Münster, 1956) professor of the philosophy of mathematics and natural sciences in Münster; director of the Department of Logistics in the Philosophy Seminar. For Peter Wust, see Letter 67. Bernhard Rosenmöller (b. Hamburg, 1883; d. Münster, 1974) was a professor of philosophy in Münster.
3. Johann Peter Steffes (b. Utscheid-Neuerburg near Trier, 1883; d. Münster, 1955) was professor of theology in Münster; at the time of this letter, he was the Director of the Institute that employed Edith Stein.
4. See *Journées d'études de la Société Thomiste; Tome 1: La Phénoménologie,* Juvisy, September 12, 1932.

120. Letter to Sr. Adelgundis Jaegerschmid, OSB, Freiburg-Günterstal
Original in Convent Archive of Benedictine Sisters, St. Lioba, Freiburg-Günterstal

Pax! Breslau, August 28, 1932
Dear Sister Adelgundis,

For more than two months I've owed you thanks for your last kind letter. Since then you have had to travel a great deal, and hopefully everything has been weathered successfully. For me the final weeks of the semester were very fruitful. First of all, I have already won amazingly good rapport with the women students (not only those who attend my lectures but those from the university), and also with the Sisters from the Marianum who are students. I expect that in winter the best part of my audience will come from these two groups, and so will no longer consist principally of women teachers and candidates for school administration.

On July 24 and 25 I attended a very enjoyable convention for young girls in Augsburg. At the leadership meeting I had to give a talk on "The Task of Woman as Leader of Youth to the Church."[1] From there I came to Breslau still under the impression that I would have to give the course in Aachen in September-October. Fortunately for me, though, that did not materialize.

Vacation projects: 1. The Thomas Index. 2. Study of the psychological Questions of the Summa and of several [items] of Thomas literature. 3. Various new philosophical matters that I have to discuss or to review. 4. Family and other things of human interest.

I shall be setting out next Saturday on a trip, including several stopovers,[2] to Paris where the Société Thomiste will have a workshop on phenomenology and Thomism. Before the meeting, which will be held on September 12 [at Juvisy near Paris], I would like to spend about a week with Koyré, getting to know a bit of Paris and gaining much profit for my scholastic studies.

I intend to go to Münster by mid-September to prepare my lectures for this winter and to get as many of the other things done that are now my responsibility.

How is everything with you? I have not heard from Sr. Placida <Laubhardt> since time immemorial. Might the little Countess still be in St. Placid? Have you heard any more from Marianne? Alice writes often from Constance [Switzerland], and seems to keep up her courage despite all the difficulties.

My mother is in good spirits most of the time, but some effects of old age can no longer be denied. The business situation is most distressing. I would like to have my sister <Rosa> along with me right now, but we must not rush into such things [impulsively]. Although my other siblings already take it for granted that she will join me some day, we do our utmost to keep from upsetting Mother.

I ask for a special remembrance in your prayers for a protégé of mine who is in an alarming condition.

With best regards, your
Edith Stein

[P.S.] The cards are for the photographer-priest.

1. [This lecture has been translated as "The Church, Woman and Youth" and appears as Chapter 6 in *Woman*, pp. 230ff.]
2. Enroute to Paris, Edith Stein made stops at Heidelberg to visit Hedwig Conrad-Martius in the hospital and at Neuburg to stop at the Benedictine Abbey, according to a report by P. Daniel Feuling, OSB, Neuburg.

121. Letter to Sr. Callista Kopf, OP, Speyer
Original in Convent Archive of the Dominican Sisters in Speyer

Pax! College Marianum, Münster, October 11, 1932
Dear Sister Callista,

Just now, when I rummaged through my bookcase to find something for your name day, this copy of a letter I wrote in St. Lioba at the request of Maria Buczkowska[1] came to hand. The *Societas Religiosa* is a congregation of professional women who live according to a rule. The "Monthly Letter"[2] is to be a stimulus to strive for self-improvement in certain specific areas. The topic was determined by Maria Buczkowska in consequence of my lecture at Bendorf on November 30.

I believe this inner silence is the best thing I can wish for you. You surely must have many questions on your mind that I am unable to answer because they will be mentioned only in your letter for my name day, or may not be there at all.

I assume you will have read my detailed letter to Sr. Agnella <Stadtmüller>. Therefore I have scarcely anything to recount about myself anymore. About actual happenings I need only tell you that last Saturday and Sunday I was in Aachen. The Educational Council of the Catholic Women's Society had a public discussion on "The Spiritual Character of the Young Generation," with its keynote address a lecture by Prof. [Aloys] Dempf,[3] from Bonn, on Saturday evening. He's a superb person, an Upper Bavarian, blunt, and thoroughly honest. He himself was in the first wave of the Youth Movement before the war, and belonged with Professor Platz of Bonn and with Brüning to the first Liturgical Circle in Germany. All this contributed to making things very lively.

Of the leading women of the Rhineland who were present, there are, of course, many known to me from earlier events. With some others I have strong bonds merely through common interests, not through close personal relationships. One of these, above all, is Annie Bender.[4] She and Sr. Agnella know one another from Belgium. A friendly relationship has now been established with several others who showed me such strong opposition that time in Bendorf,[5] although the differences of opinions keep turning up repeatedly in such discussions. They are after all persons with very serious intentions who invest their entire personalities in their positions, and one has to respect that. Besides, I understand very well now how much, at that time, I must have displeased people who live very much in the midst of things. For I notice only now since I, too, am in that situation, how completely estranged from the world I had become and what a struggle it is for me to get back into the stream. I doubt that I shall ever succeed entirely.

Please extend my greetings to your Reverend Mother Prioress and to Sr. Agnella. With best regards, your

Edith Stein

1. Maria Buczkowska (b. Vienna, 1884; d. Munich, 1958) was foundress and director of the *Societas Religiosa.*
2. Edith Stein wrote "Ways of Inner Silence" for this "Monthly Letter." [The text has been published in *Woman,* pp. 130ff.]
3. Aloys Dempf (b. Altomünster, Bavaria, 1891). He was professor of philosophy in Bonn. In Munich, he had the same position from 1947 to 1959.
4. Annie Bender (b. Rhineland, 1890; d. Cologne, 1973) Ph.D., headmistress of a secondary school in Cologne, member of the League of Catholic Women.
5. See Letter 73.

122. Letter to Mother Callista Brenzing, OCist, Seligenthal
Original in Convent Archive of Cologne Carmel

Pax! College Marianum, <Münster> October 18, 1932
Dear Mother Callista,

In the past few days I have thought of you often, but to my great shame not early enough to write to you in time for your name day. Now it is a small consolation that your dear letter also arrived a bit late, and that I can now combine my belated wishes with those for your Jubilee [of the Foundation of the Abbey] (which I beg you to share with your Rev. Mother Abbess). I also want to answer your questions.

I would recommend neither Handel-Mazzetti nor Stockhausen (there is a mixture of Catholicism and erotica in them that I find especially painful), and I find the war [WW I] is not [a] suitable [theme] for young people. You will be amazed at what I want to suggest: as an historical novel, *Der Papst aus dem Ghetto,* and as an educational novel *Das Schweisstuch der Veronika.*[1] Probably you will have to choose only one or the other, and so you will have to decide which of them you feel more confident to make accessible to your youngsters. In no way does it seem to me to be impossible; however, it will be a big piece of work for you. Here, such attempts are made without giving it a second thought and they succeed. Of course, as far as I can tell, the educational system in Rhineland/Westphalia is decades ahead of the Bavarian one and, on the average, the children bring more along from home.

As an educational novel, something by Hermann Hesse [1877-1962] might be considered since the younger generation still acknowledges him as someone who inspires or, at least, understands them. For the fifth and sixth classes, I always used some carefully chosen samples from the three great novels of adolescence—*Wilhelm Meister [W.M.'s Apprenticeship,* by Goethe, published in 1795], *Der Grüne Heinrich [Green Henry,* by Gottfried Keller, published in 1880], and *Maler Nolten [Painter Nolten,* by Eduard Mörike, published in 1832]. To read any of them in their entirety in class is hardly possible. Beyond that, I find it an excellent idea to include vital contemporary writings. But they must be truly first-rate fiction.

I would not dodge the questions on sex—on the contrary, one ought to be glad when a spontaneous opportunity arises to speak honestly and clearly on the subject, since it simply will no longer do to send the girls out into the world without having taught them about sex. But one must choose [the topics] carefully, avoiding sultry eroticism. However, teaching the elementary facts of life and their meaning, honestly as well as realistically, is far from dangerous. Of course, should you have totally ignorant children among your students, even this may precipitate a crisis; you have to know your class and treat them accordingly.

Sr. Agnella <Stadtmüller> and Sr. Callista <Kopf> both have great difficulties. It has to do with matters they cannot write about. You will have heard that I was in Ludwigshafen at the end of June and that I was able to speak to both those Sisters, with Sr. Agnella in great detail. She keeps taking up her cross with great courage. Since they are very close and can meet sometimes, they are able to support each other. About Sr. Reinhildis I know scarcely more than you, i.e., about her health. She keeps that veiled somewhat, even from me.

With my best regards, your
Edith Stein

1. Both novels are by Gertrud von le Fort: *Der Papst aus dem Ghetto [The Pope from the Ghetto]*, published in 1929, and *Das Schweisstuch der Veronika [The Veil of Veronica]*, in 1927.

123. Letter to Sr. Callista Kopf, OP, Speyer
Original in Convent Archive of the Dominican Sisters in Speyer

Pax! College Marianum, Münster, October 20, 1932
Dear Sister Callista,

A distressing mound of letters has piled up for me in the last week —distressing, when one thinks of answering them. One wishes so much to send a word of thanks immediately, and yet I can only accomplish it very, very slowly. Now I am operating according to priority: Answer first those with urgent questions. Therefore you will receive a few lines so promptly.

Surely the children who attend convent schools should gain there the strength to form their lives in the spirit of Christ. Surely it is most important that the teachers truly have this spirit themselves and vividly exemplify it. At the same time they also need to know life as the children will find it. Otherwise there will be a great danger that the girls will tell themselves: "The Sisters have no notion about the world"; "They were unable to prepare us for the questions we now have to answer"; and the [danger] that then everything might be thrown overboard as useless.

I have the impression that the Rhineland-Westphalian convents are more advanced in this (altogether the educational system here is decades ahead of the Bavarian one). You personally, though, have the advantage of not having entered too soon and of having belonged to the youth movement. That gives you access to much that others lack. However, it is necessary to keep up contacts. Today's young generation has passed through so many crises—it can no longer understand us, but we must make the effort to understand them; then perhaps we may yet be able to be of some help to them. There is not much use in recommending books to you since you do not have time. But it seems to me you should be able to gain many an insight through your sister. Besides that, you probably have people come to consult you in the speakroom[1] who sees more of life than you do. And, of course, the children themselves bring in all sorts of things. All this has to be utilized.

As far as the faculty is concerned: I am convinced that it should be predominantly feminine. But *only* feminine? That I would not consider the ideal situation. In a family, it is also preferable if both father and mother are present and, together, bring up their children. There are paternal tasks a teacher has toward the girl students. Of course, it is preferable to have no male teachers than unsuitable ones. The same applies to the director. I consider a woman quite acceptable, but would not turn down a male just on principle. And if he were a skilled educator of girls—that is, one who at the same time is aware of the limits of his influence—then, where there is a *mixed* faculty it might be preferable.

Naturally I am also for a subject-oriented school system. I believe the weakness regarding education could be compensated if one had truly responsible "homeroom teachers" who gave as many courses as possible to their classes. If you teach German, history, and English to a class, you have enough opportunity to exercise an educational influence.

From the end of July to the beginning of September, I was in Breslau. The day before yesterday my mother had her 83rd birthday; things are still going well with her. My sister <Rosa> will have to continue to be patient. Please, return Irmgard's letter at your convenience. I know nothing about an invitation to Mannheim.

Heartfelt thanks and best regards to your Mother Prioress.

All the best, your
Edith Stein

1. The room in which visitors were received in semi-cloistered and cloistered convents was called the "speakroom" in English.

124. Letter to Anneliese Lichtenberger, Ludwigshafen
Original in Convent Archive of Cologne Carmel

Pax! Gerleve b. Coesfeld <Postmarked: Oct. 31, 1932>
St. Joseph's Abbey

Dear Anneliese,

Heartfelt thanks for your dear wishes for my name day. I would be happy to hear more details from you, how you came to join the *Freiwilliger Arbeitsdienst* [Volunteer Corps][1] and what your duties are there. In the last two issues of the *Christliche Frau [Christian Woman]* (September/October) there were articles on the Volunteer Corps that interested me very much. The organization is very much in its initial stages, and I readily believe that there is much that has not yet been perfected.

I remember you always in my prayers and would be grateful if you would do the same for me, for, of course, I too have difficulties. I have just been able to arrange to spend the Feast of Christ the King and All Saints with the Benedictines. That will feel good again.

With best regards,
Edith Stein

1. [This is a government-sponsored organization for young unemployed people. Its American equivalent is the CCC (Civilian Conservation Corps).]

125. Letter to Jacques Maritain,[1] Meudon <Paris>
Original in *J. Maritain Archiv,* Molsheim/Strasbourg

Pax! College Marianum, Münster, November 6, 1932
Dear Herr Professor,

My heartfelt thanks for your kindness in sending me your important new work.[2] To study it will be a great gain for me. Unfortunately, my immediate duties make such demands on my time at the Pedagogic Institute that I can devote all too little of it to principally philosophical questions and to the study of scholastic philosophy which would be so necessary for me.

I recall with great pleasure the wonderful day in Juvisy and the hours spent in your home. With grateful and most cordial greetings to you, your dear wife and your sister-in-law, I am, respectfully yours

Edith Stein

1. Jacques Maritain (b. Paris, 1882; d. Toulouse, 1973) was professor of philosophy at College Stanislaus, Versailles; at l'Institut Catholique, Paris; then in Canada at the Pontifical Institute of Mediaeval Studies, Toronto; and in the United States at Princeton and Columbia Universities. He was the first post-war French ambassador to the Vatican (1945-1948).

2. Prof. Maritain sent Edith Stein his work *Distinguer pour unir, ou les degrés du savoir* with a personal inscription (in French): "To Mademoiselle Edith Stein in token of respectful friendship, Jacques Maritain." [For an English translation of this work, see Jacques Maritain, *Distinguish to Unite, or The Degrees of Knowledge,* newly translated from the fourth French edition under the supervision of Gerald B. Phelan (New York, NY: Charles Scribner's Sons, 1959).]

126. Letter to Hedwig Conrad-Martius, Bergzabern

Original in Convent Archive of Cologne Carmel; first published, *Kösel Verlag,* Munich, 1960

Pax! College Marianum, Münster, November 13, 1932

My dear Hatti,

For a long time now, I have been waiting again for the decision from England.[1] When I read your metaphysical article I felt it would result in something positive. For there one can see how a complete philosophy—I prefer to call it an "organon" rather than a system—is mature and only waits to be put in order with care. On the other hand, of course, I would wish for you and all the others at "Eisbrünnelhaus"[2] with all my heart, that you will not have to go away. Deus providebit! <God will provide!>

I am very grateful for your essay; not only because, technically, it was very enlightening for me, but because I saw in it once more, very clearly, what authentic philosophizing is and where my limits lie. This recognition of my own limits has rapidly progressed in me during the last few months. I do not know whether you remember that once, years ago, you said something about it to me—that is, about my lacking such recognition and [having] an all-too-naive self-confidence. At that time, I did not understand much about it. One usually understands such criticism only when the truth dawns from within. Now that I am in constant contact with people who are totally caught up in their life's work, who have been educated for it with technical thoroughness and have grown up in it, I notice that, actually, I have lost connection with it on all sides, and am generally incompetent for this world.

Of itself, this recognition does not depress me. Only it is not altogether easy to remain in a responsible position for which one lacks so much that is essential and when one has so little prospect of being able to make up for it all. But as long as the indications are that the Lord wants me in this position, I may not desert. I am sending you a little sample to show how I extricated myself from the difficulty last semester. This time it seems to me even more difficult, despite, or perhaps precisely because of my going back to tackle questions that I have always been working on.

In the meantime, did you receive the little Heidegger-introduction from Koyré? I am very eager to know what you will have to say about the *Questio de veritate* and about the positive definition of metaphysics. In the demarcation [of metaphysics] from ontology I am, of course, of one opinion with you. I believe I can also follow along on the going beyond experience. But I have another idea about metaphysics: as a grasp of the whole of reality through an inclusion of revealed truth, therefore grounded on philosophy *and* theology. When you occupy yourself with Thomas [Aquinas] you will, of course, also have to deal with this.

Do you know the dates of your radio lectures?[3]

Sincere congratulations to Fräulein Käthi[4] on her birthday, which is coming soon. If you knew of something that would have as much meaning for Autós[5] <Theodor Conrad> as the purse had for you, it would please me very much to give him a belated fiftieth birthday present, this year.

Most cordially, your
Edith

1. Hedwig Conrad-Martius applied for a fellowship in England.
2. The Conrad-Martius couple lived on the "Eisbrünnelweg" in Bergzabern.
3. On the theme: "Do plants have a feeling soul?" Later it appeared in book form: *Die Seele der Pflanze [The Plant's Soul]*, Breslau, 1934.

4. Katharine von Graffen (b. Kaulbach/Rheinpfalz, 1894; d. Munich, 1938), for many years companion and friend of Hedwig Conrad-Martius. She lived with the Conrads.
5. Prof. Conrad had his 50th birthday in the preceding year. [His nickname Autós is a Greek word implying "self-confident."]

127. Letter to Sr. Adelgundis Jaegerschmid, OSB, and Sr. Placida Laubhardt, OSB

Original in Convent Archive of Benedictine Nuns, St. Lioba, Freiburg-Günterstal

Pax! College Marianum, Münster, December 12, 1932

Dear Sisters,

This is only a short but heartfelt greeting for Christmas. I wish you both the deepest peace. Surely you, too, Sr. Adelgundis, may be at home for the feast days, and that will do you good. And for Sr. Placida the Christ Child will have to make up for everything that has been in turmoil lately.

I am sending both of you only something that is very prosaic. Please share it with your protégées. Something for the spirit will go to Mother Prioress and you will probably benefit from that also.

Probably I will keep working here until the 23rd [of December] (for a course that we have to give in Berlin from January 2nd to the 5th),[1] and after the feast [Christmas] again until New Year's.

For the holidays I want to flee into the isolation of the cloister with a beautiful liturgy. Not to Gerleve because I am afraid of the overflow of people in the church and even more on the convent grounds: rather, very near here with the Ursulines in Dorsten who invited me a long time ago.

Think of me! Most cordially, your

Edith

1. [The lecture "Jugendbildung im Lichte des Katholischen Glaubens" ["Education of Youth in the Light of the Catholic Faith"] given as a course at the German Institute for Scientific Pedagogy, Berlin, Jan. 5, 1933, is included in Vol. XII of *Edith Steins Werke.*]

128. Postcard to Mother Callista Brenzing, OCist, Seligenthal
Original in Convent Archive of Cologne Carmel

Pax! <College Marianum> Münster, Gaudete Sunday (1932)
Dear Mother Callista,

My heartfelt greetings for Christmas. At the same time many thanks for your beautiful *Festschrift* [for the Abbey's Jubilee]. I would love to give you a detailed account about myself, but I really cannot take time to do so. And so I will only tell you that I believe the difference between ability and task is much greater for me than for you and it is to be borne only with confidence in God's assistance. Therefore I continue to beg for your faithful prayer, just as I never forget [to pray for] you. We will all meet one another at the [Christmas] Crib. *Prope est jam Dominus—Deo Gratias!* <The Lord is near—Thanks be to God!>

Most cordially, your
Edith Stein

129. Letter to Anneliese Lichtenberger, Ludwigshaven
Original in Convent Archive of Cologne Carmel

Pax! Dorsten, the second day of Christmas,[1] 1932
Dear Anneliese,

From the cloistered solitude (at the Ursulines' in Westphalia, with whom I have been allowed to celebrate Christmas) I return your good wishes most cordially. Before all else, I would like to answer your question. There is a vocation to suffer with Christ and thereby to cooperate with him in his work of salvation. When we are united with the Lord, we are members of the mystical body of Christ: Christ lives on in his members and continues to suffer in them. And the suffering borne in union with the Lord is his suffering, incorporated in the great work of salvation and fruitful therein. That is a fundamental premise of all religious life, above all of the life of Carmel, to stand proxy for sinners through voluntary and joyous suffering, and to cooperate in the salvation of humankind.

With cordial wishes and greeting, your
Edith Stein

[P.S.] Naturally I will still be glad to hear from you something about the *Volunteer Corps.* Tomorrow I must return to Münster, and from Jan. 2-5, participate in a vacation-course to be given in Berlin.[2] Pray for its success, please!

1. [In Europe, December 26 is a holiday and is called "second Christmas Day".]
2. See Letter 127.

130. Letter to Mother Petra Brüning OSU,[1] Dorsten
Original in Convent Archive of the Ursulines, Dorsten

Pax! College Marianum, Münster, January 15, 1933
Dear Reverend Mother,

For a long while, I have had it in view to write to you this Sunday. I did not dare allow myself time earlier.

I would like to thank you again most cordially for the beneficial and quiet Christmas days and for the hours you devoted to me. I want to admit to you that I wished to spend the holidays in Dorsten not only because I longed for the cloistered solitude but also because I had an inkling that an inner bond already existed between you and me, and that our meeting in person would be of special significance. Perhaps you know even more about that than I do.

The days in Berlin[2] are now over. Judged on mere externals they were a success for me, and I am heartily grateful to all who helped me achieve it by their prayers. Whether anything fruitful will result from it is, of course, hidden from our knowledge. They were very wearying days and they showed me again, very clearly, how great and responsible is the task we have before us.

Then I spent two days in Breslau and found my dear mother very alert and cheerful. I am back in the Marianum since Monday evening and at my normal work, as far as one can speak of "normal work" in my situation. I am very grateful that I am over the hump for this winter.

In the meantime you, too, have taken up your burden anew.[3] I wish you God's blessing for it. May I ask you to pass on a most cordial greeting to Mother M. Regina? Yesterday Mother Johanna from Erfurt completed her examination.

With respectful greetings, your grateful
Edith Stein

1. Agnes Brüning (Mother Petra of the Love of Christ, OSU) (b. Osterwick, Coesfeld Circle, 1879; d. Dorsten, 1955). She was superior at the convent of the Ursulines in Dorsten, and prefect of the school operated by the Order. Through Mother Regina and Mother Bernhardine, who were studying at College Marianum in Münster at that time, Mother Petra invited Edith Stein to spend the Christmas holidays in 1932 at the Ursuline nuns' convent in Dorsten. Their meeting blossomed into a deep friendship, which is chronicled in their correspondence.
2. See Letter 129.
3. Mother Petra was reelected as superior of the convent.

131. Letter to P. Petrus Wintrath, OSB, Abbey of St. Hildegard, Rüdesheim
Original in Archive of the Benedictine Abbey Maria Laach

Pax! College Marianum, Münster, January 29, 1933
Dear Reverend Father,

Please, by all means, keep Volume II.[1] If Rev. P. Graf (or the editors of *Divus Thomas)* will send author's copies of the review of Volume I to the publisher and request Volume II, he will most likely receive it. Should there be difficulties, I will take care that the matter is settled there.

Obviously I will be very sorry if no review from you appears anywhere. But I have learned from this publication that one cannot detour around editorial boards if the matter is to succeed.

With respectful greetings, yours in Christ,
Edith Stein

1. See Letter 117.

132. Letter to Emmy Lüke (Düsseldorf)
Original in Convent Archive of Cologne Carmel

Pax! College Marianum, Münster, February 6, 1933
Dear Fräulein Lüke,

Cordial thanks for your kind invitation, which reached me only at noon today (the German Institute for Scientific Pedagogy is now at Engelstrasse 25). Unfortunately, I cannot come tomorrow, no matter how important participation in the first discussion would be to me. First, I would have to miss a working session with our lecturers, and second, I would have to spend eight hours on the train in order to be in Düsseldorf for a scant two hours. Both [situations] are hard to reconcile with my professional duties.

If, in response to your request, I make some suggestions, this is in no way intended to anticipate your own proposals. After all, for the present I have only sketchy information about the whole matter.

Possibly, the subject: "The Value of Individuality Based on the Catholic Perception of Man [*Menschen*]"[1] might be taken up. I would consider it important to portray the difficulties encountered in today's school praxis that interfere with the formation of personality. Furthermore, a critical consideration of the collectivist ideas of the present should ensue. But what seems to me to be most important as a foundation for critique and practical work is to clearly establish the value of personal individuality from dogma and Scripture.

As far as readings are concerned, I would suggest first: Rudolf Allers, *Das Werden der sittlichen Person [Development of the Moral Person];* Rudolf Peil, *Konkrete Mädchenpädagogik [Concrete Pedagogy for Girls];* Ernst Knick, *Menschenformung [Formation of the Human Being]* (this to be given critical study). Then, an older work of mine can be considered: *Individuum und Gemeinschaft [The Individual and Community]* (from Volume V of Husserl's *Jahrbuch für Philosophie und phänomenologische Forschung*). Unfortunately, the new material I have produced in recent years is not yet in print. All of this, of course, is of heavy caliber. I am afraid that brief and easily grasped presentations, such as Fräulein Schmitz[2] would like to have for later participants, will be hard to find—at least such as would go into depth sufficiently at the same time. I would be very grateful if I might have the minutes of your meeting.

With best regards, your
Edith Stein

1. [Here, as elsewhere in these letters, although stylistic considerations seem to require the English "man," the German "Mensch" should be understood in the inclusive sense, as encompassing both men and women.]
2. Maria Schmitz (b. Aachen, 1875; d. Essen, 1962) a teacher, was the first president of the League of Catholic Women Teachers. She was a cofounder of the German Institute for Scientific Pedagogy and had a decisive role in bringing Edith Stein to work at the Institute in Münster.

133. Letter to Mother Petra Brüning, OSU, Dorsten
Original in Convent Archive of the Ursulines, Dorsten

Pax! College Marianum, Münster, February 12, 1933
Dear Reverend Mother,

Thank you with all my heart for your kind letter. It did me a great deal of good. But I had not been waiting for it at all, since I can imagine what a workload you must be burdened with, and since I myself have long ago lost control over my own correspondence. Hopefully, you have now recovered completely from your illness.

Of course, it would give me great joy to be able to welcome you here. I expect to be in Münster for all of March. It means so much to me that you can sense in me an identification with the "corpus monasticum" <the religious life> and that you see [wearing] a habit as unessential. That is already a little bit of a cloister-home.

God's guidance through [His] grace has been particularly clear to me again in the past few weeks. I believe I see my task more clearly and more definitely. Of course, that also means seeing my complete inadequacy more deeply as well, but at the same time I see the possibility of being an instrument despite the inadequacy.

I have only been to Gerleve three times this year and have not spoken much with P. Prior.[1] But I know that I have someone in the vicinity in whom I could confide without reservation, and that is something that gives rest and strength.

In *caritate Christi*, your grateful
Edith Stein

1. Alois Rebstock (P. Bonaventura, OSB) (b. Stuttgart, 1876; d. Abbey of Gerleve, 1958) was Prior and Novice Master in the Abbey at Gerleve.

134. Letter to Emmy Lüke (Düsseldorf)
Original in Convent Archive of Cologne Carmel

Pax! College Marianum, Münster, February 13, 1933
Dear Fräulein Lüke,

I received news of this severe blow with heartfelt sympathy. I will gladly remember your dear mother in my prayer.

Unfortunately I am again unable to come on Saturday. I have my lecture to give in the Institute from 5 to 6:30. Will the meetings be in Düsseldorf? Hopefully I will be able to arrange it during vacation. But during the semester, because of the poor connections, it is hardly possible.

With best regards, your
Edith Stein

135. Letter to Hedwig Conrad-Martius, <Bergzabern>
Original in Convent Archive of Cologne Carmel; first published, *Kösel Verlag,* Munich, 1960

Pax! College Marianum, Münster, February 24, 1933
My dear Hatti,

Today, my sincere wishes for your birthday. The little book I'm having sent to you from Breslau will not find a gracious [reception] from Autós <Theodor Conrad>. But I thought that if you have to have people like Klages[1] around you, then it will be good for you in the interim to be in touch with a kindred spirit.

I have already gotten Klages' four volumes <*Der Geist als Widersacher der Seele [The Mind as Opponent of the Soul]*> but have postponed reading them until vacation time. Besides I have many other and more necessary tasks planned for that time.

A few weeks ago R. Grosche[2] was here to give a lecture on Christian art and history (it was very good). He mentioned, after his lecture, that you have not yet been able to submit your contribution[3] about my Thomas [translation].

At the time I wondered whether, in connection with that, it might be possible for you to look through my other writings. Not in order to write about them, but because I believe you would be able to discern the immanent teleology in my writings much better than I could myself, just as you could when you wrote about Heidegger[4] and Hartmann.[5] And that could mean a great deal for me.

You are, of course, familiar with my earlier writings. We could also consider including the small *Festschrift* article[6] and, possibly, the paper on *Act and Potency*[7] that I wrote in the summer of 1931. True, it is in no way in a condition ready for publication and I believe I've advanced in many points this winter, but at least you would see in it the attempt to come from scholasticism to phenomenology, and vice versa. (You might also be moved through the impossible analysis of the *Metaphysical Discourses* to make available to me as soon as possible your work on matter and mind and the one on substance and soul.[8])

This semester I have held lectures on philosophical anthropology (as far as that is possible in one-and-a-half hours a week before a largely unschooled audience). During the summer I want to attempt to tackle the problems from [the viewpoint of] theology.[9] These are all attempts at joining on to my earlier work and progressing toward a foundation for pedagogy.

For weeks I have been carrying on an intense battle on principles with the other lecturers here. For ever so long they have had a contract from a publisher to develop an outline of pedagogy—in fact, it should have been completed last autumn. Then it was decided that our Berlin courses[10] in January should be a small dress rehearsal for it. But in our preparatory discussions for this [Berlin] course, I undermined their basic assumptions so passionately that they have now resolved not to go into publication until we, as a group, have succeeded in clarifying all the issues. That is no small matter.

Have you ever given thought to the question: What is pedagogy? Unless one clarifies all the principles involved, it is impossible to arrive at a clear solution. And all of us are people with entirely different backgrounds in philosophy (the psychologist, in fact, is totally without one); that will enable you to imagine how difficult it is for us to understand each other. The only unanimity we have is in our goal to develop a Catholic pedagogy and in the honest willingness to find common ground. This, of course, is excellent, and I am heartily grateful for it. I am also learning a great deal in all this and am handicapped only by my crass ignorance (especially in pedagogy and in the history of philosophy), as well as by the impossibility ever to make it up. My only consolation lies in the fact that since I have this group as co-workers, I can offer stimuli that others will then be able to bring to fruition, even if my own work should always fall short of the mark.

Now you have a little insight into the situation. How it affects me inwardly can hardly be expressed in a letter. I have perceived the weeks since Christmas (even more since my return from Berlin) as a time of great grace for me.

Yes, if you will undertake to mediate for your godchild <Edith herself> the meaning of her life's task, I shall be very glad to send you this monstrous opus, obviously so you may criticize it severely; a *radical* critique for I have often asked myself whether, in fact, I am not overreaching my own capabilities in the philosophical work I have undertaken. I believe this doubt haunts me ever since Lipps on one occasion (before my first visit to you) criticized my long article in the fifth *Jahrbuch* so radically: and at that same time, Frau Reinach attempted to show me that the shortcomings in my work (which, in themselves, she said she was unable to judge) lay in the fact of my having far deeper personal shortcomings. All of that depressed me a great deal at that time, perhaps precisely because I did not understand it at all.

Of course, in the intervening years when I had no thought of doing philosophical work, it obviously did not bother me much. And, really, now it does not disturb me anymore. However, since I am confronted with such large tasks, it is important for me to get a clear picture of how much I can reasonably undertake with confidence. But, of course, you must not do it [this critique] if it takes too much of your time, which you need for more important things.

With best regards to all of you from your

Edith

1. Ludwig Klages (b. Hanover, 1872; d. Kilchberg/Zurich, 1956) psychologist and philosopher. Founder of scientific graphology and of *Ausdruckpsychologie* [characterology].
2. Robert Grosche (b. Duren, 1888; d. Cologne, 1967.) monsignor, doctor of theology, dean of the city, at St. Gereon Church, Cologne. Publisher of *Catholica,* quarterly on controversies in theology.
3. The article Hedwig Conrad-Martius [cf. Letter 23] wrote on "Nature and Grace according to St. Thomas Aquinas' Questions on Truth" appeared in the periodical *Catholica,* April 1934.
4. Martin Heidegger, cf. Letter 85.
5. Nicolai Hartmann (b. Riga, 1882; d. Göttingen, 1950) was professor of philosophy in Marburg, Cologne, Berlin, and Göttingen.
6. *Husserl's Phänomenologie und die Philosophie des hl. Tomas von Aquino [Husserl's Phenomenology and St. Thomas Aquinas' Philosophy]* published in *Festschrift Edmund Husserl,* 1929.
7. See Vol. II, *Edith Steins Werke.*
8. Two manuscripts that Hedwig Conrad-Martius finished at this time. The first appeared later in a reworked version as Part 2 of the book *Das Sein [Being],* Munich, 1957; the second was published as an article entitled "L'existence, la substantialité et l'âme" in *Recherches Philosophiques,* Paris, 1932-33.
9. These manuscripts are in the *Archivum Carmelitanum Edith Stein.*
10. See Letter 129.

136. Plain postcard to Hans Brunnengräber,[1] Münster

Original in Archive of the Franciscan Fathers, Münster

Pax! College Marianum, Münster, March 3, 1933

Dear Dr. Brunnengräber!

Fräulein Bergmann asked me today to give a lecture to the teachers' society on Tuesday afternoon. Could we possibly postpone the study group until Wednesday, and would you have it at your place, so we could hear the lecture on "Plants and Animals" at the same time?

With cordial greeting, your

Edith Stein

1. Hans Brunnengräber, M.D., Ph.D. (b. Lorsch, Hessen, 1902) was director of the German Institute for Scientific Pedagogy from 1934 to 1937.

137. Postcard: Sr. Adelgundis Jaegerschmid OSB, Freiburg-Günterstal
Original in Convent Archive of Benedictine Nuns, St. Lioba, Freiburg-Günterstal

Pax! College Marianum, Münster, March 17, 1933
Dear Sr. Adelgundis,

Recently I recalled that you have use for picture postcards and so I am sending you a small collection. I can only lend you *Mädchenbildung [Education for Girls]* [1] because it is the only copy I have left.

What you wrote about the little Thérèse <of Lisieux> amazed me. For the first time, I saw how one *can* look at it from that point of view. My impression was simply that there the life of a human being has been formed entirely, from first to last, only and exclusively, by the love of God. I know of nothing more sublime, and I would wish to have as much of that as possible in my own life and in the lives of all who are near to me.

Most cordially, your
Edith

1. [In March-April 1932, this periodical carried as an article the lecture Edith Stein gave that January in Zurich. Cf. *Woman,* pp. 86 ff.]

138. Letter to Hedwig Conrad-Martius, <Bergzabern>
Original in Convent Archive of Cologne Carmel; first published, *Kösel Verlag,* Munich, 1960

Pax! College Marianum, Münster, March 23, 1933
My dear Hatti,

I was very happy to have your dear letter. Before I send a package of collected works, I would like to ask whether you really do not have all of them. For, except for the doctoral dissertation, everything has appeared in the *Jahrbuch:* in Vol. V, the work on psychology and the social sciences; in VII the one (dedicated to Autós) on the state (without doubt you received separate reprints of them both, for the first one came out while I was with you); the short one about Thomas and Husserl was in the *Festschrift.*[1] Besides I would certainly not expect you to read through all that again. The manuscript and the *Festschrift* article are perhaps not entirely useless for you because they lead somewhat into the problems of scholasticism. But again, this only if you have no urgent work of your own planned.

I heard three of your lectures with great joy; I found no announcement so far of the fourth.[2] Did I send you my Salzburg lecture two years ago? A neat blue little pamphlet: *Das Ethos der Frauenberufe*[3] *[The Ethos of Women's Professions].*

Most cordially, your
Edith

1. See Letter 135.
2. See Letter 126.
3. [See *Woman,* pp. 41 ff.]

139. Letter to Hedwig Conrad-Martius, <Bergzabern>
Original in Convent Archive of Cologne Carmel; first published, *Kösel Verlag,* Munich, 1960

Pax! College Marianum, Münster, April 5, 1933
Dear Hatti,

Since I am packing just now, I will send you the paper, after all. But you are to be free to put it aside until you really have time for it, and can promise yourself some gain from it for your own use. I am not in a hurry about Thomas either. There have been enough reviews about him. And Grosche[1] is not interested in any kind of review but rather a thoroughly scientific discussion of it precisely from you.

My relatives in Breslau are obviously very upset and depressed.[2] Sad to say, as far as the family business is concerned, it has not mattered for a long time now whether it is open or not. Also, my brother-in-law <Hans Biberstein> expects his dismissal any day (from his position as senior physician at the department of dermatology at the University of Breslau). Kuznitsky[3] has just lost his post as chief of dermatology at a municipal hospital. Every letter [from home] contains more bad news. My relatives in Hamburg <the Gordon family> do not seem to have been affected so far. I, personally, have been assured by everyone that I need not fear for my position. And just in these recent times I have experienced much kindness, which, of course, gives me a very good feeling.

Tomorrow I will travel to Beuron and will remain over Easter, returning here again about the 19th. I will not be able to hear the last lecture[4] because the matins of Holy Week will be held at that time. But if it is to be published, that will not be so bad.

You wrote recently that my memory must be a great help in mastering the factual material. But I have none at all anymore to assimilate new material. I can still remember only personal matters, often better than I would like. In addition, I find it difficult to understand material that I have not worked through myself, and therefore I cannot read [such material] quickly. Long ago, I resigned myself to remaining very ignorant, and also that everything I can still accomplish will be far more fragmentary than human achievement is bound to be anyway. I only hope to be able to give an impetus in a direction in which one has to go and that others can then improve on it. Just now, when I can look back over a year here at the Institute, and when I believe I can see the way ahead, I have a strong impression that it is necessary to go forward step by step and that I may continue calmly to allow providence to guide me.

I hope you will soon be restored to good health. If Autós' <Theodor Conrad's> plans are furthered by "The Great Time," I will be very happy.[5]

I wish you all beautiful Easter days. Your

Edith

1. Msgr. Robert Grosche, see Letter 135.
2. The persecution of non-Aryans by the National Socialists [Nazis] was becoming more and more blatant.
3. This was the first husband of Gertrude Koebner; he belonged to the circle of friends of the youthful Stein siblings.
4. See Letter 126.
5. [This ambiguous sentence could mean that the political situation might precipitate a decision on his part.]

140. Letter to Sr. Agnella Stadtmüller, OP, <Ludwigshafen>
Original in Convent Archive of the Dominican Sisters, St. Magdalena's, Speyer

Beuron, Easter Monday, 1933

Dear Sister Agnella,

You know how busy our days here are. Therefore you will accept my heartfelt Easter wish, even a belated one. I arrived here on Friday of Passion week; Father Archabbot <Walzer> had returned that morning from Japan, as I learned in Immendingen from Pater Aloys Mager.[1]

I would certainly have much to tell you. But when will it be possible? Tomorrow I am returning via Speyer in order to pay Sr. Reinhildis a little visit on [the occasion of] her profession. But then I have to go directly to Münster on Wednesday since I have a return ticket and can only stop over once. You don't happen to have business at the Motherhouse on Tuesday, do you?

I wish Rev. Mother Prioress and all the dear Sisters a most blessed Eastertime. Your

Edith Stein

1. Augustin Mager (P. Aloys, OSB) (b. Zimmern, Rottweil, 1883; d. Salzburg, 1946), a monk of Beuron Abbey, was professor of theology in Salzburg. [He and Edith met when they changed trains for Beuron.]

141. Letter to Elly Dursy (Sr. Maria Elisabeth of Divine Providence, OCD), Auderath
Original in Convent Archive of Auderath Carmel

Pax! College Marianum, Münster, May 7, 1933

Dear Elly,

As I have just come up from the Chapel where the Most Blessed Sacrament is exposed (and where *coram Sanctissimo* [before the Most Holy] a choral High Mass was sung—a horrendous thing for an ultraliturgist!) I would like to bring you greetings from our Eucharistic Savior, and at the same time, an affectionate reproach for letting yourself be led astray by a few printed words about something you have experienced before the tabernacle for so many years. Dogmatically, I believe the matter is very clear: the Lord is present in the tabernacle in his divinity and in his humanity. He is not present for his own sake but for ours: it is his delight to be with the "children of men." He knows, too, that, being what we are, we need his personal nearness. In consequence, every thoughtful and sensitive person will feel attracted and will be there as often and as long as possible. And the practice of the church, which has instituted perpetual adoration, is just as clear.

Furthermore, let me bring in a crown witness about whose liturgical expertise you can have no doubt: Father Archabbot <Raphael Walzer of Beuron>. Some years ago, he said to me: "It's a fact, isn't it, that you are not *liturgical,* you're Catholic!" (You see, he was so fed up with having people come to him to tattle about the liturgy.) Besides, remember that we are not meant to have heaven on earth. I believe if you were more aware how many thousands are now driven to despair, you would yearn to relieve them of some of that surfeit of need and of pain.

Which brings me to your first question: the meeting in Karlsruhe cannot be held because of the great crisis now engulfing all of the Catholic educational system. Therefore I will not go either. Our Institute has been drawn into this crisis. I am not permitted to give any lectures this semester (because of my Jewish descent). Provision has been made for me for the time being, because there is still some hope that my academic research activity may in some way continue to benefit the Catholic cause. I do not believe, however, in any return to the Institute nor, for that matter, in any possibility of a teaching career in Germany. I will stay here for the time being until the situation is clearer. Don't worry about me. The Lord knows what he has in mind for me.

Most cordially, your
Edith Stein

142. Letter to Uta von Bodman,[1] Speyer
Original in Convent Archive of Cologne Carmel

Pax! <College Marianum, Münster>, Pentecost Sunday, 1933
Dear Fräulein von Bodman,

At last my heartfelt thanks for the two certificates[2] and with these come my warmest wishes for Pentecost! Please tell the principal (Sr. Scholastica) how very grateful I am for the fine reference she sent me.[3] I was very happy to insert [your] two papers into a new folder along with the birth and baptismal certificates that came from Breslau and Bergzabern. It is good to be able to give official proof of having been born and reborn! At the same time I am adding Name Day greetings for Sr. Amata for June 9th. You will surely be so kind as to take them with you when you yourself congratulate her.

This is the first time (except for Corpus Christi) that I have remained in Münster for one of the solemn feasts. It is beautiful when one participates in the whole celebration at the Cathedral. I looked forward with particular joy to Pentecost this year; the novena already did me a great deal of good. Today I also received greetings from the Cathedral in Speyer where the academic meeting was held. From Münster, Professor Rosenmöller[4] and his wife attended it. If you were in Speyer, you probably participated in much of it.

To me it seems so long, long ago that we met in Karlsruhe. So much has happened since then, out in the world and in the interior of the soul. In times like these one learns a great deal. But it is hard to write about it. Please convey my greetings to Fräulein Hermann and my thanks for her letter.

If I add one more greeting to the dear Sister Portresses [at the Dominican convent] with an added request that they pray for me particularly in the coming weeks and months, then I shall have given you a great deal to do for me again. My heartfelt thanks for everything and always my most faithful best wishes for you, your

Edith Stein

[P.S.] At long last, a few beautiful stamps that I had been saving for you for some time.

1. Baroness Uta von Bodman (b. Baden/Lahr, 1896) taught aesthetics and drawing at the teachers college of St. Magdalena, Speyer, conducted by the Dominican nuns. She and Edith were friends.
2. [One was a reference from Baroness von Bodman, the other most probably a Confirmation certificate she obtained for Edith, who had been confirmed by the Bishop of Speyer in 1922.]
3. Edith Stein requested all these for her intended entrance into the Cologne Carmel.
4. Prof. Bernhard Rosenmöller (cf. Letter 119) and his wife, Hedwig.

142a. Letter to Georg Kifinger,[1] Munich
Original in Archive of the Heliand League

Collegium Marianum, Münster, May 17, 1933

Dear Reverend Father,

Even a few months ago I should have acceded to your request without further ado. Today—as on every similar occasion—I must ask a question in turn: Do you know that I am a convert from Judaism? And do you dare to go against the prevailing trend by putting a Jewess into a position of influence on German youth? If, after this, you repeat your request, I will consider whether I can still accept such an obligation by August. As a lecturer, I am on "status of availability"[2] but I do not count on a return to the Institute. I have no idea as yet what and where I will be in August.

If, after this information, you would rather turn to someone else, I could recommend Dr. Maria Bienias[3] (Waldenburg i. Schlesien, Freiburger St. 13). She would surely speak completely in accord with my sentiments and she is a Catholic from birth.

With respectful greetings, yours *in Christo,*
Edith Stein

1. Kifinger, Georg (b. Ebing/Bavaria, 1889; d. Munich, 1976) a clerical high school teacher, parish priest in Munich, leader of the "Heliand League," a society of Catholic schoolgirls in Munich.
2. [Having formerly assured her they would not dismiss her, Edith's employers at the Pedagogical Institute told her after Easter, 1933, that she would continue in their employ but would have no regularly scheduled lectures; she was to be at their disposal.]
3. Maria Bienias (b. Silesia, 1897; d. Straelen am Niederrhein, 1971) Ph.D., teacher, a friend of Edith Stein's since their youth in Breslau. Through her association in the League of Catholic Women Teachers she was constantly in touch with Edith Stein. Dr. Bienias, however, did not give the lecture that Edith had originally been invited to give at the convention of the Heliand League in Ettal in 1933, since the meeting was cancelled because of political upheaval. Dr. Bienias, among other things, wrote two valuable articles about Edith Stein: Edith Stein, in *Katholische Frauenbildung,* Vol. 53 (1952), No. 11; and *Das Lebensopfer der Karmelitin Edith Stein, [The Carmelite, Edith Stein, Makes a Sacrifice of Her Life]* (Stuttgart: Brentanoverlag, 1961). [She also wrote a book: *Maria Bienias: Begegnung mit Edith Stein [Maria Bienias: Encounter with Edith Stein]* (Leipzig: St. Benno Verlag, 1965).]

143. Letter to Hedwig Conrad-Martius, Bergzabern
Original in Convent Archive of Cologne Carmel; first published, *Kösel Verlag,* Munich, 1960

Pax! <College> Marianum, Münster, Pentecost Monday, 1933
My dear Hatti,

On this glorious Pentecost day I want to send you a cordial greeting and, finally, thanks for the baptismal certificate that made me very happy. It was put at once into a new folder with my birth and confirmation certificates, and with a letter of recommendation for the eight years at St. Magdalena's—all documents that I have only now obtained.[1]

Father Habermehl[2] sent me his dissertation in March when he was still vicar of the Cathedral of Speyer; I never imagined he would be the one whom my request would reach. His touching gratitude has disconcerted me a great deal, for the review [of his dissertation] caused me a lot of difficulty; hopefully it will not disappoint him too much when it comes into his hands.[3] His work was surely achieved with enormous diligence, but obviously without actual philosophical training.

I do not regret that I no longer give lectures. I believe that a great and merciful Providence is behind all of it. I am not yet able to tell you today where I can clearly see a solution [to my problems]. I shall probably not be in Münster much longer. I expect a final clarification this month, and then I intend to go to my mother for a lengthy visit. I beg you, sincerely, to pray intently for your godchild during these months. I also ask Fräulein Kathi to help with these prayers.

What you write about the separation of people at the end of time is totally Augustinian. My mother is admirably brave, but, naturally, she suffers very much.

Cordial greeting to all! In *Spiritu Caritatis* <the Spirit of Love>, your
Edith

[P.S.] If you read anything between the lines, then please keep it very confidential.[4]

1. See Letter 142.
2. Michael Habermehl (b. Edesheim/Pfalz, 1896; d. Ludwigshafen, 1964), Ph.D.; for many years he was spiritual counsel to the Federation of New Germany.

3. Edith Stein's critique of Dr. L. M. Habermehl's work, "The Abstract Teaching of St. Thomas of Aquinas," appeared in *Philosophisches Jahrbuch* 46 (1933): 502-503.
4. [Hedwig Conrad-Martius made a note here: "Refers to her entering Carmel."]

144. Letter to Sr. Callista Kopf, OP (Speyer)
Original in Convent Archive of Dominican Sisters, St. Magdalena's, Speyer

Pax! <College> Marianum, Münster, June 11, 1933
Dear Sister Callista,

Your greeting for Pentecost made me very happy. Now you receive the thanks of the *Beata Trinitas* <Blessed Trinity> for it.

It is hardly possible to think of an oral reply to your question. Just recently I wrote to Sr. Agnella <Stadtmüller> regarding similar problems. In any case, I consider it an educator's duty to live through these times with the children. This includes making the effort to form one's own judgment, measuring the "movement" <National Socialist [Nazi]> against our own standards, and speaking to the children in this vein. After all, the Bishops' Pentecost message gives you a good guideline.

An Ursuline from Fritzlar told me recently how much her girls participate in the *Kreuzfahrerbund* [Crusader Society]. She said they are completely captivated by the thought of Christ and, on their own, shape their lives from that viewpoint.

Since Sr. Agnella is now coming to terms with these questions in Ludwigshafen, you will surely be hearing about her experiences soon. I believe that a greater task devolves on the Catholic Youth Groups today than ever before. But I have little confidence if such an organization is imposed from the top. It has to come out of youth itself. Perhaps it is therefore best to pay particular attention to the children who are already enthusiastically following a cause, and to encourage them to have the self-confidence to win the others for it.

It might be very good for you if you could get a glimpse into one of the Ursuline schools run on wholly modern principles. There are a good number of them in the Rhineland and in Westphalia; [and these] convents are [accomplishing] much more than those in Bavaria because, for decades, they have had [as staff] women religious with full academic training. Reverend Mother in Dorsten would surely welcome you with joy as a guest sometime. I know nothing about the periodical *Das Innere Leben [The Interior Life]*.

I celebrated Pentecost beautifully in Münster, part of the time in the cathedral and part in the Marianum. Perhaps, in the meantime, you have heard from Sr. Agnella that my lecturing activity was terminated at Easter. Do not be sad about that. Something much more beautiful will be replacing it. What that is I am still unable to tell you today. But I do beg you to pray especially for me and for my relatives, particularly for my mother, in the next weeks and months. In a few weeks I will probably be going home for a while and will not be returning to Münster anymore.

I spoke to Rose <Magold> in Speyer; she is dearer than ever, has a heavy burden to bear with her family, and does it courageously. You will see from the letter how Sr. Irmengard is doing.[1] Sr. Reinhildis will perhaps write to tell you that recently she found the Latin model of her ill-starred poem in two manuscripts in the state library. So, after all, there will be a glorious conclusion.

From the deepest security in *tabernaculo Domini* <the Lord's tent>, your

Edith Stein

[P.S.] To Sr. Agnella, please, for the present, thanks and greetings!

1. [Presumably Edith enclosed a letter from a mutual friend that refers to Sr. Irmengard. This is Irmgard Koch, mentioned in Letter 55. She entered the Abbey of Kellenried and was given the name Sr. Irmengard.]

145. Letter to Jacques and Raissa Maritain, Meudon, near Paris
Original written in French: in *J. Maritain–Archiv,* Molsheim/Strasbourg

Pax! Collegium Marianum, Münster, June 21, 1933
Madame, Monsieur le Professeur,

You have given me great joy with your beautiful book; I thank you very much for your goodness and for your faithful remembrance. I, too, cherish a grateful memory of the beautiful hours in Juvisy[1] and Meudon.

Above all, during the past month I have been greatly consoled by the thought of having such good friends united to us by the bond of faith. I no longer have my position with the Pedagogical Institute and I will be leaving Münster in a few weeks. But do not be concerned about me: *diligentibus Deum omnia cooperantur in bonum.*[2] However, I will be very grateful for the help of your prayers.

With cordial greetings, your very devoted
Edith Stein

1. See Letter 119.
2. "All things work together for the good of those who love God." (Rom 8:28)

146. Letter(s) to Hedwig Conrad-Martius[1] and Theodor Conrad,[2] Bergzabern

Original in Convent Archive of Cologne Carmel; first published, *Kösel Verlag,* Munich, 1960

Pax! Collegium Marianum, Münster, <End of June, 1933>
My dear Hatti,

Thank God that Fräulein Käthi is somewhat better. I have been waiting so eagerly for that report.

Now I'll tell you what is going to become of your godchild. However, I do ask you to keep it confidential until further notice. You may tell only Autós <Theodor Conrad>. I ask him, also, to keep it to himself. On July 14 I will go from here to Cologne, at first as guest of the Carmelite Nuns in Cologne-Lindenthal (Dürener Street 89). From mid-August until mid-October I want to go to my mother's, to prepare her gradually. She already knows I will be going to the nuns in Cologne. When I wrote to her, I did not mention that I intend to enter there. I am going to enter as a postulant on October 15. I will tell you how all this came about when you visit me at my "grille"[3] sometime. It is quite marvelous. As it is, I may not be in Cologne very long. There are plans to make a foundation from there in Breslau and I have asked that my transfer on this foundation be considered right from the start.

Therefore you can understand that I am no longer that interested in my manuscript.[4] Keep it for yourself (I have two more copies). Were it to be of use to you sometime, I would be very happy—you will help me to give thanks for the great grace of this extraordinary vocation. And you will help me, won't you, with your prayers during the difficult months in Breslau?

With most cordial greetings, your
Edith

Letter 146-b [Edith wrote separately to Theodor.]

Dear Autós,

Cordial thanks for your dear letter. I am very happy that all is going better than the miserable pessimists feared. You should never have felt burdened by your debt to me. After all, I have always been well provided for. It is true that things in Breslau and in Hamburg have been going poorly for years, but I have seldom been allowed to be of help there. You know that I never wanted the sum I sent you that time to be looked upon as a loan. If I hesitated somewhat before giving it to you, it was in consideration of the plan for my future, which is now reaching fulfillment: I knew that Carmel asks for a dowry, because these monasteries have no means of earning an income.[5] Now the Sisters in Cologne have asked the religious superiors for a dispensation in order to receive me without the dowry. If you find yourself able to send monthly payments, without being burdened, I would now accept them with gratitude, on behalf of the monastery. I would ask you to transfer them directly into the bank account of the Monastery of the Carmelite Nuns of Cologne-Lindenthal (Deutsche Bank, Nr. 36 598, Cologne).

But if you cannot do so easily, it is not really necessary. The good Sisters, too, are unwilling that I make demands on anyone who is in need himself. In that case, we can calmly take for granted that heaven will give me back, with interest, whatever I have given to you and others.

Were the times not so sad, I personally could only be grateful to them because they have finally opened this way for me. To my great joy, my relatives are patient and brave, especially my dear mother; after all, she has such a firm belief in God, which has guided her throughout her long and difficult life.

Once I belong to this silent community of nuns I hope to be of better help to you than heretofore. Carmelite nuns are here only to pray, and they are not readily denied anything [they ask]. A visit to Bergzabern will probably no longer be possible. But you will surely find the way to me sometime.

Always your faithful
Edith Stein

1. Hedwig Conrad, née Martius, see Letter 23.
2. Hans Theodor Conrad (b. Beurig bei Salzburg, 1881; d. Starnberg, 1969) Professor of philosophy in Munich. He belonged to the older Göttingen students of Edmund Husserl. With his wife, Hedwig Conrad-Martius, he lived on Eisbrünnelweg, in Bergzabern (in the Palatinate) where, besides his scholarly occupation as a philosopher, he operated a large orchard. In the intimate circle of phenomenologists, he was familiarly called "Autós," [the Greek word for "self." The affectionate nickname was inspired by his self-assurance, as Edith wrote to Ingarden, December 13, 1921.]
3. [In this letter Edith begins using terminology proper to the Carmelite life, at times unfamiliar to the reader. For example, the *gitter* Edith refers to is a grille or, in Carmelite language, a grate, made of iron or wood, a separation in the "speakroom" or visitors' room.]
4. *Act and Potency*. See Letter 135.
5. As St. Teresa legislated from the beginning, the sisters engage in manual labor to earn their living, as much as is possible. [To supplement these earnings, a "dowry" is still highly recommended today, but the lack of one is never an insuperable hindrance to the admission of a postulant. A dispensation may be obtained, as in Edith's case. The community may never spend a dowry during a sister's lifetime; it must be invested. Should the sister leave the community at any time, the dowry is returned to her in full. This contingency is one reason for requiring a dowry. When Hedwig Conrad-Martius published this letter in her own book she omitted all mention of the dowry.]

147. Letter to Mother Petra Brüning, OSU, Dorsten

Original in Convent Archive of Ursuline Sisters, Dorsten

Pax! Cologne-Lindenthal, St. Joseph, July 26, 1933

Dear Reverend Mother,

Today I would like to express double and most cordial thanks to you: for the wonderful gift you intended for me, the most essential requisite for a choir nun, and for the loving reception afforded to the poor protégé <Ruth Kantorowitz>[1] whom I entrusted to your goodness.

The breviary has not yet been ordered. Our Reverend Mother Prioress wishes to wait a bit until she can order several sets at once, because that will mean a larger discount. You need not fear that I am in straits. I have an old breviary, with a Proper,[2] and am well able to follow everything. You see, I am already permitted participation in all of the spiritual exercises in the daily schedule, with my prie-dieu in the sanctuary set right next to the grille [in the choir]. Of course, it will be even nicer once I may stand on the other side of the grate, in the choir. But even now, it is a superabundant grace. The first Mass I attended here was for the Vigil of the Feast of Carmel. The Introit begins: *Induxi te in terram Carmeli, ut comederes fructum ejus et optima ejus.*[3] And every day supplies me with a generous portion. But the best part is that the spirit of Carmel is love, and that this spirit is very much alive in this house.

A breviary is not necessary to commend your intentions to me daily. But it will always remind me how many there are who would love to stand in my place, who would be more worthy of it than I am, and how much I must try to learn to respond adequately to such a high vocation.

You will surely have seen from the first visit how greatly Frl. Dr. K.[4] is in need of help. I know I have laid a heavy burden on you. You cannot do more than open your hospitable house to her, and you have made her that offer. I intend to encourage her to accept the invitation when her time permits.

My mother is now beginning to suspect and to fear. I commend this most urgent intention to your prayers again.

In sincere gratitude and reverent love, your

Edith Stein

1. Ruth Renate Friederike Kantorowicz (b. Hamburg, 1901; gassed in Auschwitz, 1942) Ph.D. in economics; friend of Edith Stein and her sister Else Gordon, Hamburg. Ruth became a Catholic in 1934.

2. [The breviary did not contain offices used exclusively in the Order of Carmel; these were printed in a supplement called a "proper."]

3. "I led you into the land of Carmel, that you might eat of its fruits and produce" (Jer 2:7), the entrance song for the Liturgy on the Feast of the Virgin Mary of Mount Carmel, July 16.

4. This is a repeated reference to Fräulein Dr. Kantorowicz. Edith used only initials.

148. Letter to Anneliese Lichtenberger, Ludwigshafen
Original in Convent Archive of Cologne Carmel

Pax! Cologne-Lindenthal, July 26, 1933
Dear Anneliese,

Unfortunately, I learned only yesterday from Sr. Agnella that you have been ill for several weeks. Therefore I could not write to you sooner. It would please me so much more if I were able to visit you, but that is impossible now. Therefore all I can do is think of you most cordially and send the good angels to you. May they bring you a great deal of the deep peace of the cloister here in which I now live.[1] Actually I am in my second week as guest of the very dear Carmelite nuns, and I am allowed to stay here until the feast of Mary's Assumption. Then I will go to Breslau to spend some time with my mother. Probably you are unable to write now. Perhaps your dear father would be kind enough to send me a few lines sometime to tell me how you are doing. Do any of your former classmates visit you once in a while?

Perhaps Sr. Agnella <Stadtmüller> will stop by to see me on her return trip from Gemund. If so, I will surely be able to learn more about you. For now, I want to wish you very much patience in your suffering, and the ultimate consolation that I have often had to point out to you: that the way of suffering is the surest road to union with the Lord. The saving power of joyfully borne suffering is particularly necessary in our time. I beg you especially for your prayer for my relatives.

With most cordial greetings and wishes, your
Edith Stein

1. Enclosed in the letter was a holy card made in Beuron, depicting a guardian angel. On the back of the picture Edith had written: "He has commanded his angels.... E. St. 26.7.33."

149. Letter to Maria Bruck[1]
Original in private possession of Dr. Maria Schweitzer, née Bruck

Cologne-Lindenthal, July 31, 1933

Dear Fräulein Dr. Bruck,

Only today am I able to thank you sincerely for your kindness in forwarding your dissertation. I am very happy that your opus has been brought to a successful conclusion. I did not want to reply before I had read it, which I did as soon as it was possible.

Undoubtedly this work demanded a great deal of effort from you. It is very neat and conscientious and will surely be of lasting use for anyone who will study the relationship of Husserl to Brentano.[2]

Of course, according to the concept of philosophy I learned from Husserl, I would classify [your work] as philological rather than philosophical. And I am convinced that if you have an opportunity to work for a few years longer at systematic philosophy, you will yourself experience the need to go beyond it; not merely to take an independent position on the problems you have touched but, above all, to tackle the interpretation from the basis of clearly established final principles. Without that no actual comparison of what is meant as systematic is possible. From the start, I missed a sharp delineation of what Brentano and Husserl understood as the *real* and as *essence*, and several other matters.

Only from that point could one really understand your position on the problems you handled, and one could see what to make, objectively, of the opposing polemic. At the conclusion you make an attempt to clarify the *real*. But to me it does not seem radical enough; and besides, it ought to be at the beginning in order to serve as a basis for the entire discussion.

You will understand these candid remarks correctly: when someone sends me their paper, I assume that they want to hear a judgment that will spur them on to further work.

With most cordial greetings and wishes for your future way, your

Edith Stein

1. Maria Schweitzer, née Bruck, Ph.D., a representative in the provincial diet of the Saar, with residence in Saarbrucken.
2. Franz Brentano (b. Boppard/Rhein, 1838; d. Zurich, 1917), professor of philosophy in Wurzburg and Vienna. Edmund Husserl was his student in Vienna.

150. Letter to Elisabeth Nicola,[1] Düsseldorf
Original in Convent Archive of the Cologne Carmel

Pax! Cologne-Lindenthal, August 6, 1933
Dear Fräulein Nicola,

Thank you so much for your kind letter. I may surely tell you that I have observed with great joy the transformation that has taken place in you during this past year. For there is nothing more beautiful on earth than the work of grace in a soul. If I am supposed to have cooperated therein as a *causa secunda* <secondary cause> it was totally without my knowledge and wholly unintentional on my part. But even if without one's own action one is able to be an instrument [of grace], it creates a very strong bond. And so I believe our common path has not come to an end, even though a lively correspondence and frequent meetings will not be possible. On August 16, I intend to go to Breslau (X Michaelisstr. 38) Then, as I foresee, two very difficult months lie ahead for me, and I beg you especially for your prayers for this time.

I rejoice with you over the preservation of your society; for your work I wish you much success and for vacation time, a very real relaxation for you and Fräulein Lieb.[2]

With best regards, your
Edith Stein

1. Elisabeth Nicola (b. Düsseldorf, 1908) teacher in Siegburg. As a student, she resided in the Collegium Marianum in Münster and became acquainted with Edith Stein there.
2. Helene Lieb (b. Düsseldorf, 1909; d. Carmel of Cologne, 1991) teacher; as a student she lived at the Collegium Marianum in Münster and met Edith Stein there. She entered the Cologne Carmel soon after Edith went to Holland; her name in religion was Sr. Maria Carmela of the Blessed Trinity.

151. Letter to Sr. Agnella Stadtmüller, OP, Gemund
Original in Convent Archive of Dominican Sisters, St. Magdalena, Speyer

Pax! <Maria Laach> Assumption Day <August 15>, 1933
Dear Sister,

My godchild[1] has given me this glorious feast in Aachen.[2] Tonight I am going on to Breslau.

Could you get me an address in England, through Sr. Callista, for a 17-year-old girl (niece of our Mother Prioress, and a graduate of the girls' high school) who wishes a position as an au pair?

Our next get-together is only postponed.

Best regards to you and all the dear Sisters, your

Edith Stein

1. Hedwig Spiegel, née Hess (b. Walldorf/Heidelberg, 1900), convert from Judaism. Edith Stein was her baptismal sponsor.
2. Sr. Agnella and Frau Hedwig Spiegel say Edith wrote Aachen by mistake, for she was at Maria Laach with Frau Spiegel on August 14 and 15.

152. Letter to Sr. Adelgundis Jaegerschmidt, OSB, Freiburg-Günterstal
Original in Convent Archive of Benedictine Sisters, St. Lioba, Freiburg-Günterstal

Pax! Breslau, August 27, 1933
Dear Sister Adelgundis,

Thank you so much for sharing my joy. Sr. Placida <Laubhardt> can give you an account of what I told her about my first Carmelite joys. We too are *in via* <on the way>, for Carmel is a high mountain that one must climb from its very base. But it is a tremendous grace to go this way. And, believe me, in the hours of prayer I always remember especially those who would like to be in my position. Please help me that I may become worthy to live in the inner sanctum of the church and to represent those who must labor outside.

In *caritate Christi,* your

Edith

153. Letter to Sr. Agnella Stadtmüller, OP, Speyer
Original in Archive of Dominican Sisters, St. Magdalena's, Speyer

Pax! Breslau, August 27, 1933
Dear Sister Agnella,

A cordial welcome to you on your coming out of retreat. Thank you for Sr. Roswitha's address; I forwarded it to Cologne.

The explanation of the frustrated rendezvous did not surprise me, and I find it so much better than if it had been something else. This way, one may always ask for it again later when an opportunity presents itself. Of course, you may also write to me later, but whether I may reply will depend on my superiors. I am convinced the permission will always be given when a labor of love for a [needy] soul is involved. After all, for us, *"maior horum caritas"* <"and the greatest is love" [1 Cor 13:13]> supersedes all other rules.

For the time being, my mother is happy just to have me home and in these first ten days has not raised any questions. I am waiting patiently till she is ready to listen. In a few days the Biberstein family will move from our house to the other end of the city because my sister <Erna> is taking over the practice of a woman friend who is going to Palestine. It will be very hard on my mother to be deprived of the daily association with my sister and the children.

I am very happy that heaven has sent you a Paraclete. I believe that one can only be thankful for that. It is God's will that one person should carry another's burden. It is a long time since I wrote to Mother Prioress in Speyer. I want to do so only after the discussion with my mother is past and I can speak freely. Please tell Mother Prioress I remember the deceased of St. Magdalena's daily; but [tell her] that I did not get to write because the past few weeks have been so eventful. For the same reason, I was unable to write to Mother Hyacintha for her name day. You will give her my regards, too, won't you? And particularly cordial ones to Reverend Mother, to the portresses, and Sr. Callista.

Today is the feast of the Transverberation of the Heart of St. Teresa. In *caritate Christi,* your

Edith Stein

154. Letter to Sr. Callista Kopf, OP <Speyer>
Original in Convent Archive of Dominican Sisters, Speyer

Pax! Breslau, September 13, 1933
Dear Sister Callista,

Thank you so much for your dear letter with the addresses. Please pray especially for me now and have Sr. Agnella do likewise when you see her. The first two-and-a-half weeks here were very peaceful, until my mother asked about my plans. I mean to say it is peaceful now, also; a second discussion on this theme has not followed upon the first.[1] But I know that my mother is only somewhat pacified because, inwardly, she still hopes I will not be able to manage to carry out what for her is the worst thing imaginable.

Help me [to pray] that I can leave as it was intended: my excursion ticket expires on October 13, and I should already be within the enclosure to celebrate the feast of our Holy Mother <Teresa of Avila>. If this tremendous grace falls to me, you may be certain that you and all your intentions will be included in all my prayers and sacrifices. I think that you will be allowed to come from Gemund to visit me sometime. And, of course, you may also write.

Many thanks, also, for the letter for the feast of Carmel that I was already allowed to celebrate in Cologne. With best regards, your

Edith Stein

1. Her decision to enter Carmel.

155. Letter to Mother Petra Brüning, OSU, Dorsten
Original in Convent Archive of Ursuline Sisters, Dorsten

Pax Christi! Breslau, September 17, 1933
Dear Reverend Mother,

Please forgive me for letting your loving, kind letter of August 19 go unanswered until today. It reached me when I was already in Breslau (I have been here since August 16) and in the stress and strain of the past weeks it has been difficult to write. After all, one wants to involve others as little as possible.

For more than two weeks, my mother did not ask at all about my future plans, since she did not want to disturb the joy of our being together. Two weeks ago the question came, and then, obviously, desperate resistance. No second discussion followed that one, and my relatives are just as loving toward me as before. But I am certain that my mother is holding up merely because she still hopes that I will not do this to her, and the farewell is going to be very hard.

In the meantime, two dear Sisters are diligently working at the founding of a Carmel at the gates of Breslau,[1] and I have every expectation of being transferred here from Cologne as early as next year. So there is hope that in the coming years, which promise to be even more difficult, I will be able to support my family by being as near them as possible. Our two Sisters are staying at the Ursuline convent here, so I can visit them often at their house.

Mother Subprioress[2] wrote to tell me that the breviary has been ordered. I hope the autumn volume will reach me while I am still here, and I will already be able to use it to celebrate the feast of little Thérèse <of Lisieux>. Otherwise, in any case, that of our Holy Mother <Teresa of Avila>, which I am to celebrate within the enclosure. My excursion rail-ticket expires on October 13. The proper Masses for the Discalced Carmelite Order have been published as an appendix to the missal by *Scapulier* Publishers, Linz on the Danube, Landstrasse 33.

If I could see you soon in Cologne, you would make me and my dear Sisters very happy. Surely we may hope that you will attend my clothing ceremony—*Deo volente* <God willing>—in April or May.

I have heard nothing more from Fräulein Dr. K. <Ruth Kantorowicz> since [I left] Cologne. I hope she will pay another visit to you and that you, in agreement with the Very Rev. Father Prior [presumably P. Bonaventure, OSB, of Gerleve], will be able to help her see things clearly. I know that this will be a difficult task.

With a most cordial wish that your retreat will have brought rich blessings to your house, I greet you with sincere gratitude.

In the love of Christ, your
Edith Stein

1. Mother Marianne (Countess Praschma) and Mother Elisabeth (Countess Stolberg-Stolberg) founded the Carmel of Pawelwitz-Wendelborn near Breslau. Edith referred to this foundation in Letter 146. The monastery was closed by the Nazis. After WW II, the Sisters attempted to rebuild the badly damaged monastery, but after some time they were expelled as Germans. These Sisters are now in the Monastery of Witten, Germany. The convent in Pawelwitz-Wendelborn is now occupied by Polish Benedictine nuns. The Carmelites in Breslau [now Wroclaw, Poland] today live in the inner city.
2. Resi Posselt (Mother Teresa Renata de Spiritu Sancto, OCD) (b. Neuss in 1891; d. Cologne, 1961). She was elected Prioress of the Carmel in 1936. She was close to Edith Stein as her spiritual mother. Soon after the collapse of the Nazi regime, Mother Teresa Renata wrote the first biography of Edith Stein. The first edition was published in 1948.

156. Letter to Gertrud von le Fort,[1] Baierbrunn im Isartal
Original in the manuscript section of the German Literature Archive, Schiller-National Museum, Marbach a. N.

Pax Christi! Cologne-Lindenthal, October 9, 1933
Dear Gertrud von le Fort,

Your dear letter made me very happy. It is so good for me during these very difficult last days [at home] to receive something from people who understand my path—in contrast to the great pain I must be causing here and have before my eyes daily. You will help me, won't you, to beg that my mother will be given the strength to bear the leave-taking, and the light to understand it? I have often thought it would mean a great deal to you to know my mother. She has a certain resemblance to Veronica's grandmother,[2] only she is not a person of culture, but rather of a very simple and strong nature.

Of course I have been thinking very often of you, too, these past months since I've found my way; [I have thought] that you will now truly get to know Carmel once you visit me in Cologne. And that will probably be better than Münster was, and perhaps even than Beuron. You must not believe that you will lose anything at all. Everyone who has a place in my heart and in my prayers can only gain. My dear Sisters in Cologne will be very happy when you come and you will quickly notice that the grate [in the speakroom] is no barrier at all. After all, [Cologne] is only an hour away from Aachen. Only you must not wait too long [before you visit]. You have perhaps heard that a Carmel is coming to Breslau and I will probably be transferred here then. In any case, you would be as welcome here as there, but for you it would probably be more difficult [to come here].

I heard of something very beautiful you have written about the nature of woman.[3] May I get to see that sometime? Once I have arrived in that deep peace—now there still lies a deep abyss before I reach it—then I will surely know that I have a holy duty toward those who must remain outside.

Until we meet again! In *caritate Christi,* your
Edith Stein

[P.S.] From October 13 on, [my address will be] Dürenerstr. 89, Cologne-Lindenthal.

1. Gertrud, Baroness von le Fort (b. Minden, October 11, 1876; d. Oberstdorf, Allgau, November 1, 1971), poet and novelist of worldwide repute. She became a Catholic in Rome in 1926. Her home was in Baierbrunn in the Isar Valley but she was forced to emigrate to Switzerland when the Nazis confiscated her property. Later she moved to Oberstdorf for the rest of her life.
2. One of the characters in Gertrud von le Fort's novel, *Das Schweisstuch der Veronika [Veronica's Veil]*.
3. Her later book *Die Ewige Frau [The Eternal Woman]*.

157. Plain postcard to Mother Callista Brenzing, OCist, Seligenthal
Original in Convent Archive of Cologne Carmel

Pax Christi! Cologne-Lindenthal, October 13, 1933
Dear Mother Callista,

I am writing to you on the express-train from Breslau to Cologne to send you my cordial wishes for your name day. I will now be allowed to spend the feast of St. Teresa as her child. Tomorrow morning I enter the Carmel of Cologne-Lindenthal. I beg you from my heart for your prayers for my dear mother.

In faithful remembrance, your
Edith Stein

158. Letter to Gertrud von le Fort, Baierbrunn im Isartal
Original in the manuscript section of the German Literature Archive, Schiller-National Museum, Marbach a. N.

J.M.J.T.[1]
Pax Christi! Cologne-Lindenthal, October 17, 1933
Dear Gertrud von le Fort,

In my quiet cell, I have just finished reading your beautiful "Praise of Mary." It is in its proper place in Carmel. Thank you with all my heart. I am even more grateful for your loving readiness to bring my mother some consolation. If you were able to visit her personally, I do not doubt at all that you would quickly establish close contact with her. To do so by writing will be a difficult task. If you wish to try it, I would be most grateful to you, of course, and will therefore give you some details to go on.

I have never told my mother about you. It was not possible to give any of your writings to her because she declines anything that is beyond her Jewish faith. For that reason, too, it was impossible at this time to say anything to her that might have somewhat explained the step I have taken. She particularly rejects conversions. Everyone ought to live and die in the faith in which they were born. She imagines atrocious things about Catholicism and life in a convent. At the moment it is difficult to know what is causing her more pain: whether it is the separation from her youngest child to whom she has ever been attached with a particular love, or her horror of the completely foreign and inaccessible world into which that child is disappearing, or the qualms of conscience that she herself is at fault because she was not strict enough in raising me as a Jew. The only point at which I believe you might make contact with her is in the very strong and genuine love for God that my mother has, and her love for me that nothing can shake. I am now going to leave it entirely up to you whether you want to venture on such a difficult task.

I arrived in Cologne late on the night of the 13th and stayed overnight with a friend of mine.[2] On the 14th, we both attended the First Vespers of the Feast of our holy Mother [Teresa of Jesus] and then had a farewell cup of tea outside the cloister. A little after 4 P.M. I was allowed to step over the threshold of the holy place. At Matins of the feast, I was already permitted to sing along in the choir.

In the love of Christ, your grateful
Edith Stein

1. [Many Catholics of Edith's time, particularly members of religious communities, followed the custom of writing the initials "J.M." (for Jesus and Mary) or "J.M.J." (for Jesus, Mary and Joseph) at the beginning of their letters, sometimes accompanied by a small cross. Carmelites often add a final "T" for St. Teresa of Avila. Here and in many subsequent letters, Edith adopts this custom.]
2. She stayed with Hedwig Spiegel; see Letter 151.

158a. Letter to Fritz Kaufmann, Freiburg
Original in *Archivum Carmelitanum Edith Stein*

Pax Christi! Cologne-Lindenthal, October 17, 1933
Dear Herr Kaufmann,

Your kind Christmas letter has accompanied me on many paths and is the oldest debt I have still to pay. Naturally, since Easter I have often wondered what may have happened to you. But it was impossible to write to all those about whom I had certain concerns.[1]

Perhaps you heard from our dear Master <E. Husserl> that I, too, had to give up my lectures in Münster. The *umsturz* was for me a sign from heaven that I might now go the way that I had long considered as mine. After a final visit with my relatives in Breslau and a difficult farewell from my dear Mother, I entered the monastery of the [Discalced]Carmelite nuns here last Saturday and thus became a daughter of St. Teresa, who earlier inspired me to conversion.

During the past months I have had news from Husserl on several occasions, but he never mentioned you. I wonder whether you are still able to work in Freiburg? Obviously I found much that had changed in Breslau too; some acquaintances had left already, others were preparing to leave. Almost all my relatives seem inclined to remain in Germany as long as things are in any way bearable.

I have prospects of being transferred from here, later, to a new foundation in Breslau. If you are not too far away, you will perhaps visit me sometime, either here or there. I would very much like to share some of the peace that is granted to us with all those I know outside.

With best wishes and regards for you and yours, your

Edith Stein

1. [In January 1933, Hitler came into power by an *umsturz* [coup]. Soon thereafter he forbade all Jews the right to hold office, to teach or to publish their work. Edith was told about her cancelled lectures when she returned after the Easter school vacation. Kaufmann was Jewish, and Edith here refers to all their mutual Jewish acquaintances about whom she was concerned.]

159. Letter to Mother Petra Brüning, OSU, Dorsten
Original in Convent Archive of Ursuline Sisters, Dorsten

J.M.+J.T.

Pax Christi! Cologne-Lindenthal, October 18, 1933

Very Reverend and dear Mother,

Our Reverend Mother Subprioress[1] has commissioned me to thank you most sincerely for the donation you so kindly sent us. At the same time, I can now combine with this my own thanks for the gracious letter you sent me while I was still in Breslau. It has given me consolation and strength in the past weeks and days when someone has assured me of her firm belief in my vocation, for in my immediate surroundings I saw only very great pain, in the face of which my leaving appeared to be an inconceivable cruelty.

I arrived here late on the 13th and stayed overnight with a friend. Together we then attended the First Vespers of our holy Mother in church [the public chapel of the monastery]. Between 4 and 5 o'clock the door of the cloister was opened for me. Compline was the first hour in which I was allowed to participate in Choir, and it was followed by Matins of the feast. So your precious gift is already in use, and I am better off than many others of the Sisters [in whose breviaries] everything is not yet so conveniently arranged. This gives me many an opportunity, daily, to remember your great kindness with gratitude. But I must still tell myself for the time being that you would have little satisfaction from the way I am praying the Office. In other ways, too, I am a very awkward child in the novitiate, for whom the superiors and my fellow sisters must show great love and patience. It will surely be a good while before I become a nun who is useful in any way. Will you help me to pray, please, that I can prove to be equal to the great grace of this calling?

By now, probably, your daughters also know what road I have taken. May I send greetings through you to Rev. Mother M. Regina, and to the young Sisters who are still studying in Münster?

In deep gratitude and with respectful greetings, I am, in Christ, your

Edith Stein

1. Sr. Teresa Renata Posselt who was also the Mistress of Novices, and was therefore Edith's immediate superior.

160. Letter to Hedwig Conrad-Martius, Bergzabern
Original in Convent Archive of Cologne Carmel; first published, *Kösel Verlag,* Munich, 1960

Pax Christi! Cologne-Lindenthal, October 31, 1933
My dear Hatti,

Sincere thanks for your dear letter. The bank account name is Carmelite Nuns, Cologne (address as above) Deutsche Bank No. 36598. But please send something only if it is possible without causing difficulties.

I am so sorry that you have to endure so much pain again. Hopefully, now that Fräulein Käthi will again relieve you somewhat, it will improve. My heartfelt wish for her is for an enduring improvement.

Naturally, the final weeks at home and the farewell were very difficult. It was totally impossible to make my mother understand anything. Everything remained in all its starkness and incomprehensibility, and I was able to leave only by placing a firm confidence in God's grace and by the strength of our prayer. That my mother, too, has faith, and finally, that she still has great inner strength made it a little bit easier. I am permitted, as was my custom in all previous years, to write home every week, and I also receive punctually a weekly letter from the family. The goodness and love from all my siblings was touching. Rosa is with me inwardly, all the way. She may well have the quiet conviction that this is also somehow for her benefit. We did not even need to speak about this.

For the time being I still have my civil name. Only at the time of my clothing (which has to be preceded by six months of postulancy) will I receive my religious name. The Clothing ceremony is very festive. My baptismal sponsor <Hedwig Conrad-Martius> really ought to be present at it! In any case, I will be allowed to inform you beforehand. Then you can see whether it is possible to arrange it. Actually, during the postulancy one ought not to have visitors. But a few have been here just the same. The first one was Pater Petrus from Neuburg Abbey,[1] whom we visited together last year (the painter, not the philosopher); the second [visitor] was Frau Reinach, who just came from seeing Pauline <Reinach>.[2] You can imagine that it was a particular delight for me to spend a very beautiful hour with her.

Dear Hatti, it is quite natural that you think with longing of the deep peace that is given us here. But then one has to have a calling for it. And for those who have their place outside, there is also a way outside. It goes without saying that I think constantly of all of you. I have no desire for anything that you might be able to fulfill for me. If you still had the orchard, I would ask for apples since in our meatless diet we use a lot of fruit. But I imagine that you scarcely have enough for your own use.[3]

In the love of Christ, your
Edith

1. See Letter 104.
2. Pauline Reinach, sister of Adolph Reinach. She became a Catholic and joined the Benedictines at Ermeton (Belgium). Pauline was a close friend of Edith Stein. [See *Life*, p. 291, etc.]
3. See Letter 146.

161. Letter to Hans Brunnengräber (Münster)
Original in private possession of Hans Brunnengräber, Münster

Cologne-Lindenthal, November 20, 1933

Dear Dr. Brunnengräber,

Of course I agree to the slight change in my review.[1]

Now I am at the place where for the longest time I felt I belonged. Far be it from me to reproach those who have opened the way for me—even though that was not at all their intention. I remember you with sincere sympathy for, presumably, you are still hemmed in under very unpleasant working conditions. With all my heart, I wish you many blessings in your work and all the best for your family. If you come here sometime, I hope I will get to see your youngster, or at least some recent photos of him.

Best regards to you and your dear wife, your
Edith Stein

1. This review of a book by Werner Dackweiler, D.Jur.: *Katholische Kirche und Schule [Catholic Church and School]* (Paderborn, 1933) was written for *Vierteljahrschrift für wissenschaftliche Pädagogik [Quarterly for Scientific Pedagogy]*, Münster, 1933.

162. Letter to Sr. Adelgundis Jaegerschmid OSB, Freiburg-Günterstal
Original in Convent Archive of Benedictine Sisters, St. Lioba, Freiburg-Günterstal

Pax Christi! Cologne-Lindenthal, November 29, 1933
Dear Sister Adelgundis,

The Carmelite Nuns of Cologne-Lindenthal, especially the Novitiate, thank the Sisters of St. Lioba sincerely for the generous offering, which arrived in such good time for Advent. On the First Sunday of Advent we will have a farewell celebration for our Sisters who will leave, finally, for Breslau on Monday.[1]

Sincerely, your
Edith

1. See Letter 155.

163. Postcard to Elizabeth Nicola, Düsseldorf
Original in Convent Archive of Cologne Carmel

Cologne-Lindenthal, December 29, 1933

[Has no formal salutation.]

A Blessed Christmas full of graces and a New Year of joy in Christ to you[1] and Fräulein Lieb, together with sincere thanks. I will be very happy about a visit from you. However, because of our change in the horarium on the Feast of the Three Kings, the afternoon would not do, only the morning between 9 and 11. Otherwise, perhaps, on a workday between 3:00 and 4:45 PM.

In the meantime, best regards, your
Edith Stein

1. This greeting was printed on the card.

164. Letter to Sr. Adelgundis Jaegerschmid, OSB, Freiburg-Günterstal
Original in Convent Archive of Benedictine Sisters, St. Lioba, Freiburg-Günterstal

J.M.+J.T.

Pax Christi! Cologne-Lindenthal, January 11, 1934

Dear Sister Adelgundis,

I always remembered your request that I write often, but surely you did not expect anything during Advent and I am able only now to gradually send out Christmas greetings. Actual acts of kindness must now be carried out in a different, quiet way. I believe, also, that I will be able to help you more by them than with words. Of course, it is hardly possible to think individually of every intention that is commended to me from so many different sides. All one can do is to try to live the life one has chosen with ever greater fidelity and purity in order to offer it up as an acceptable sacrifice for all one is connected with. The confidence placed in us, the almost frightening importance placed on our life by so many, outside, is a constant stimulus [to do better]. I imagine your present activity is extremely difficult and a big responsibility. Recently I was made to think of you vividly when a Jesuit priest who is a prison chaplain here told us about the execution of six prisoners.[1]

Yesterday I had a very surprising visit. A "Fräulein Marianne" was announced, and I could not imagine who it might be. There at the grate [in the monastery speakroom] was your erstwhile postulant. Her parents live in Lindenthal, and she often comes to our chapel. She learned the day before yesterday that I was here, and so came at once. Probably for both of us it was a peculiar experience, exchanging roles like that. A remarkable human being! I got no clearer picture yesterday than I did two years ago. Apparently she thinks of St. Lioba's with great gratitude but with the conviction that her path is a different one.

All kinds of people have been in our speakroom since I've been here. On Epiphany, it was good Pater Petrus Jans from Neuburg; he even stayed overnight because I needed his help in a pastoral matter. Most of the sisters consider it a penance to be called to the speakroom. It is, after all, like a transition into a strange world, and we are happy to flee once more into the silence of the choir and, before the tabernacle, to ponder over those matters that have been entrusted to us. But I still regard this peace, daily, as an immense gift of grace that has not been given for one's own exclusive benefit. And when someone comes to us worn out and crushed and then takes away a bit of rest and comfort, that makes me very happy.

I hope the grace of Christmas will be a means of strength for you in your work for a long while, and already I send you my sincere best wishes for your name day.

In *caritate Christi,* your
Edith

1. At that time Sr. Adelgundis had assumed the religious care of convicts. See Letter 116.

165. Letter to Mother Petra Brüning, OSU, Dorsten
Original in Convent Archive of Ursuline Sisters, Dorsten

J.M.+J.T.

Pax Christi! Cologne-Lindenthal, January 26, 1934

Very Reverend and dear Mother,

Many sincere thanks for your new gifts of love. Our dear Mother <Maria Josefa of the Blessed Sacrament> had to spend a long time yesterday going through all these treasures with me. They will be shown to the [sisters in the] novitiate—who are currently living in joyful anticipation—on Sunday, since at recreation on weekdays we do manual work,[1] according to the wise direction of our Holy Mother <Teresa of Avila> (for which I am very grateful). You have no idea how little it takes to make Carmel's children happy, and how munificent your package is for us. I would feel deeply embarrassed by such great love and goodness did I not know that it counts less for my person than for the holy vocation for which I have been chosen without deserving any of it, and which you appreciate so deeply. Therefore, every new token of love is a stimulus to collect all my powers in order to be a less unworthy *vas electionis* <chosen vessel>.

I know well that all I have written you is colorless. But in comparison with the fullness of grace that each day brings, a poor miserable human soul is so tiny. Yet, compared to what that soul can nevertheless comprehend, all words are inadequate. And when one has to write about this to so many people, one is afraid of making the sacred into something banal.

It would make me so very happy if you were able to come sometime. In the first place because I could then learn a bit more about your concerns than it is possible to put into writing, for you have not ceased to be *mea res* <my care>. And the more concrete a picture one has, the more one is impelled to come to the aid of our Sisters out there. I think, too, that it would do you good to spend some time with us. Of course, we have nothing great to offer you—no beautiful liturgy at all, or the like. Only our joyful poverty and our peace. These are so much more easily maintained by us than by those who have to go into battle daily and hourly. Therefore I am always glad when someone is able to derive some strength from it for the [ongoing] struggle.

The *Societas Religiosa* is under the protectorate of Cardinal Faulhaber; Maria Buczkowska[2] is my connection with it. I also know Venio House;[3] I stayed there the last time I visited Munich (at Easter 1932) and I was very happy to find the Benedictine spirit that is truly manifested there.

The Feast of the Purification was my Confirmation Day, so it still has particular significance for me. I will be happy if you remember me specially that day. But I ask urgently for prayers in the coming weeks, for I know I will have to earn the holy habit with some severe trials. They have already started in that my mother has begun with renewed vigor to oppose the forthcoming decision. It is so hard to witness the pain and the pangs of conscience of such a mother and to be unable to help with any human means.

In faithful remembrance, your grateful
Edith Stein

1. [Besides needlework, the Sisters brought to recreation whatever their ordinary work might require: preparing vegetables, mending clothing, packaging altar breads, making rope sandals.]
2. See Letter 121.
3. While a guest here, Edith met Fr. Erich Przywara, SJ, Fr. Aloys Mager, OSB, and Gertrud von le Fort.

166. Letter to Sr. Adelgundis Jaegerschmid OSB, Freiburg-Günterstal
Original in Convent Archive of Benedictine Sisters, St. Lioba, Freiburg-Günterstal

J.M.+J.T.

Pax Christi! Cologne-Lindenthal, February 22, 1934

Dear Sister Adelgundis,

In expectation of your kind visit, I do not need to write much. You will be most welcome here, even overnight if you like. But if so, do let us know so you will find the guestroom vacant for you. I'll write out our Lenten schedule so you can take it into account if necessary. From 6-7 o'clock in the morning, meditation; 7:30 A.M., Mass; before and after it, the Little Hours; 11 A.M., Vespers; 11:30 A.M., dinner followed by an hour of recreation. From 2-3 o'clock, the Litany of Loretto and spiritual reading. (Monday/Thursday, 3-3:30, Novitiate); 5-6 P.M., meditation, then the evening collation and recreation. At 7:30 P.M., Compline; 9 o'clock Matins and Lauds.[1] Best visiting hours are, therefore, 9-11 A.M., 3:30-5 P.M. plus, possibly, the recreation hours. Wednesday and Saturday are "turning out" days [*Kehrtage*]—(not days of recollection, but of sweeping the cells and halls!)—and so are less suitable [for visiting]. It is very easy to reach us: streetcar line 2 goes from the main rail station almost to our door.

I was very surprised by what you wrote about my dear old Master <Edmund Husserl>. He wrote so lovingly and with such understanding before my departure from Breslau that I brought the little card along and kept it. I will show it to you.

A very grace-filled Lent! To our joyous reunion! Your

Edith

[P.S.] Please give my best regards to Countess Bissingen. Sisters Marianne and Elisabeth are in Pawelwitz as foundresses of the Silesian Carmel,[2] so I will be able to comply with the request only when I have the opportunity to write.

1. This schedule for Lent has changed since then.
2. See Letter 155.

167. Letter to Sr. Adelgundis Jaegerschmid OSB, Freiburg-Günterstal
Original in Convent Archive of Benedictine Sisters, St. Lioba, Freiburg-Günterstal

J.M.+J.T.

Pax Christi! Cologne-Lindenthal, March 20, 1934

Dear Sister Adelgundis,

We have been so busy the past few days with celebrating that it was impossible to get to writing. I would have liked to do so even sooner, because it pained me so much to have to let you leave just as you had begun to speak about the most important matter, and I was unable to say anything to you about it. What I did hear was, after all, too little to enable me to make a clear judgment. But I believe I can say this: our effect on others will be blessed only as long as we do not surrender an inch of the firm foundation of our faith, and [as long as] we follow our conscience unerringly through all human considerations. Were this no longer possible at any point, I would say we would have to abandon the activity, no matter how much seems to depend on it. God always has other means and ways of helping souls. Naturally you are bound by obedience. But I am convinced that one would never oblige you to keep a position in which you can no longer remain within the declared boundaries. Probably you alone can judge when that point has been reached.

I cannot tell you how concerned I am to know you have such a heavy responsibility. Had our dear Mother Subprioress <Teresa Renata de Spiritu Sancto> been with us during our recent discussion, she would surely not have allowed us to break off at this point. But when I came away from the speakroom, I had no opportunity to explain the situation. And so I could do nothing more than to offer for you all that the rest of the day brought.

Only at night did I have time and quiet to think back upon your affairs; since then they have not let go of me; maybe in that way I am being allowed to share the weight of your burden.

In the meantime Fräulein Dr. Cosack[1] has informed me that you have been invited to come here for April 16. I am very happy.

To you and to good Sr. Placida, best cordial wishes for the end of Lent and for the Easter holidays.

In *caritate Christi,* your

Edith

1. Elisabeth Cosack, Ph.D (b. Cologne, 1885; d. Cologne, 1936), a friend of Edith Stein's, was a teacher in Cologne.

168. Letter to Mother Petra Brüning, OSU, Dorsten
Original in Convent Archive of Ursuline Sisters, Dorsten

J.M.+J.T.

Pax Christi! Cologne-Lindenthal, <Easter Week, 1934>

Reverend and dear Mother Petra,

Before I go into holy silence, I feel compelled to send you heartfelt thanks for the charming Easter package. Our dear Mother <M. Josefa>, Mother Subprioress <Teresa Renata> and I happily unpacked it together, and on Holy Saturday night, an Easter rabbit and an Easter candle were stationed in every cell of the novices. I received the beautiful wooden candlestick with the large Easter candle, although I surmise this large light was intended for the Novice Mistress <Teresa Renata>. It will burn for me now during my retreat, when I make my meditation in the solitude of my cell, away from the community. Our holy Father John of the Cross will be my guide: the Ascent of Mount Carmel.

Probably I will be allowed to begin early on Friday. I would like most of all to remain in solitude until the morning of the Clothing, but there is a possibility that I will be called out the day before at the request of guests from out of town. I look forward with so much joy to the silence. As much as I love the Divine Office and as loath as I am to be away from the choir even for the shortest of the Hours—the basis of our life, after all, is the two hours of meditation provided by our schedule. Only since I've been enjoying this privilege do I know how much I missed by not having it outside. Our Reverend Mother will surely be glad to send along [with this letter] the ritual for the Clothing ceremony. It will be so much better if you can read it before it takes place—even though you cannot be present yourself.

May I beg you, together with your community, to help us with a very important intention? On the 11th, the General Chapter of the Congregation of Beuron will begin in Gerleve. We know there are very important questions to solve. Will you join us in prayers to the Holy Spirit for a successful outcome? I am also a bit interested in it personally. If

Father Archabbot <Raphael Walzer> can close the Chapter on the 14th, he will be on time here to conduct the Clothing. But that, of course, is a small matter compared to all that is at stake there. I hardly need to say that I tell you this in confidence. I believe you will be happy to help because of your love for the Benedictine way of life.

Particular thanks for the Easter Prefaces: they are helping me celebrate the beautiful octave. And above all, thank you again for your love that I have in no way earned.

Always faithfully mindful of you, your grateful

Edith Stein

169. Letter to Peter Wust, Münster

Original in Convent Archive of Franciscan Fathers, Münster

J.M.+J.T.

Pax Christi! Cologne-Lindenthal, Holy Saturday, 1934

Dear Professor,

My reply to your dear letter comes with sincere Easter wishes for you and your family. It is good that you intend to come to my Clothing ceremony.[1] There may be hardly any opportunity for a personal conversation since so many people will be present. Perhaps later sometime, since you probably get to Cologne frequently.

I will gladly remember you in my prayers; I have done so for years. But I would also like to ask you, most sincerely, to have more confidence in yourself. I know that you have shown more courage at the lectern this past year than most of your colleagues. And it will not fail you should even more difficult things be demanded.

I commend myself to you for a remembrance during the next two weeks of preparation.

With a joyful Alleluia, your

Edith Stein

1. April 15, 1934.

Der Herr iſt mein Licht und mein Heil — wen ſollte ich fürchten?

(Ps. 26, 1)

Ich brachte euch in das Land des Karmel, daß ihr ſeine Früchte und ſeine beſten Güter genießet.

(Introitus d. Vigilmeſſe d. Karmelfeſtes)

Willſt Du dahin gelangen, alles zu ſein, verlange in nichts etwas zu ſein.

(Hl. Johannes vom Kreuz)

Zur Erinnerung an meine
hl. Einkleidung am 15. IV. 34
Teresia Benedicta a Cruce
C. D.
(Edith Stein)

Letter 170: A souvenir card for Edith Stein's Clothing Ceremony at the Carmel of Cologne-Lindenthal, on April 15, 1934.

170. Card to Dr. and Mrs. Fritz Kaufmann, Freiburg
Original in *Archivum Carmelitanum Edith Stein*

[Carbon copy on card without salutation]

Invitation to the Clothing Ceremony of our postulant, Edith Stein, which will take place on the 15th of April (Good Shepherd Sunday) in our monastery church at Cologne-Lindenthal, Durenerstr. 89
High Mass at 9 A.M., followed by Homily and Clothing Ceremony.
Carmel of Cologne-Lindenthal
[Lodging may be found in the League of Catholic Women's Center, Kaesenstr. 18.]

<Printed text of the souvenir card>
The Lord is my light and my salvation—whom shall I fear? (Ps. 26:1)
<Seal of the Order>
I brought you into the land of Carmel, that you may enjoy its fruits and its best goods. (Introit of the Vigil Mass of the Feast of Our Lady of Mount Carmel)
To arrive at being all, desire to be nothing. (St. John of the Cross)

<Handwritten addition on the souvenir card>
A remembrance of my Clothing Ceremony, April 15, 1934
Teresa Benedicta a Cruce OCD
(Edith Stein)

171. Letter to Mother Petra Brüning, OSU, Dorsten
Original in Convent Archive of Ursuline Sisters, Dorsten

J.M.+J.T.
Pax Christi! Cologne-Lindenthal, May 1, 1934
Dear Reverend Mother,

At last I come to thank you, from my heart, for your participation in my celebration. Since Emmy Schweitzer[1] was here, I take it for granted that she has written to you about what happened. I firmly believe that it was a day filled with great grace not only for me but for most of the others, too. Whenever something becomes reality that one has persistently prayed for for a long time, it seems to me almost more overwhelming than when it is granted immediately. And I continue to stand even now in amazement before this glorious fulfilment.

There were quite a few ladies here who were in Bendorf that time.[2] Gerta Krabbel[3] beamed for joy and said when she greeted me in my bridal attire before the High Mass: "I am so happy to be able to see you this way. This is just as it should be!"

I am sending you some holy cards for you, Mother M. Regina, and the other sisters who were with me in the Marianum. If there aren't enough, please write to tell me. Perhaps the snapshot our Father Provincial[4] took will please you also. For <the Benedictine Abbey at> Gerleve we prayed with good effect. Everything went smoothly and Father Archabbot <Raphael Walzer>[5] was able to be here by Saturday afternoon.

I would like to ask you right away for more help in prayer: tomorrow our youngest sister in the Novitiate will have a thyroid[6] operation. She is Sister Teresia Margareta,[7] only 23 years old, who comes from Westphalia. It is a serious matter. She was so brave and, to the last day, she did all her work here although everything was a very great effort for her. She writes very cheerfully from the hospital, but at the same time with a desire to go to heaven already, just like her patroness, our newest saint in the Order.[8] But, if possible, we would like very much to keep her among us.

Now I will write out our schedule for you. In summer:

4:30 A.M.	Rising
5:00–6:00 A.M.	Meditation
6:00–7:00 A.M.	Prime/None
7.00 A.M.	Mass
8:00 - 9:53 A.M.	Work Time
9:53 A.M.	Examination of Conscience
10:00 A.M.	Dinner, then 1 hour of Recreation
12:00 - 1:00 P.M.	Noonday Rest [Siesta]
1:00 - 2:00 P.M.	Work (for us, Novitiate at 1:30)
2:00 P.M.	Vespers, then spiritual reading
3:00 - 4:45 P.M.	Work, then the Stations of the Cross or spiritual reading
5:00 - 6:00 P.M.	Meditation
6:00 P.M.	Supper, then Recreation (now: 7:20 P.M., May devotions)
7:30 P.M.	Compline and Night Prayer
8:00 - 9:00 P.M.	Solitude in the cell
9:00 P.M.	Matins and Lauds, examination of conscience, preparation for morning meditation.[9]

In winter, we get up at 5:30 A.M., eat dinner at 11:00, and there is no siesta.

Always, in sincere gratitude and with a faithful remembrance *in Christo,* your humble Sister,

Teresa Benedicta a Cruce, OCD

1. Emmy Schweitzer (m. van Wersch), graduate of St. Ursula, Aachen, 1914. Studied and took the examination at the Social School for Women in Aachen. Secretary of the Catholic Society of German Women. [See Letter 188.]
2. See Letter 73.
3. Gerta Krabbel (b. Witten/Ruhr, 1881; d. Aachen, 1961), Ph.D., lived as private scholar and author in Aachen; president of the Catholic Society of German Women from 1926 on.
4. Georg Rauch, Fr. Theodor of St. Francis, OCD (b. Alteglofsheim, 1890; d. Regensburg, 1972); Provincial of the German Province of the Order of Discalced Carmelites from 1933 to 1936.
5. See Letter 55.
6. [Edith said the operation was for "Basedow." The German physician K. von Basedow (1799-1854) diagnosed thyroid gland hyperfunction from the symptoms of protruding eyeballs, growth of goiter and rapid heartbeat.]
7. Hedwig Drügemöller, Sr. Teresia Margareta of the Heart of Jesus, OCD (b. Vorhelm in Westphalia, 1910); companion of Edith Stein in the novitiate. The rapid conclusion of the written process for the cause of beatification of Edith Stein is due to her tireless labors. She is also the one who made this edition of the letters possible.
8. Anna Maria Redi, Sr. Teresa Margaret of the Sacred Heart of Jesus, OCD (b. Arezzo, Tuscany, 1747; d. Florence, 1770). She was canonized in 1934.
9. In the meantime, this schedule was changed in some instances.

172. Letter to Sr. Callista Kopf, OP and Sr. Agnella Stadtmüller, OP, Mannheim

Original in Convent Archive of Dominican Sisters, St. Magdalena's, Speyer

J.M.+J.T.

Pax Christi! Cologne-Lindenthal, May 3, 1934

Dear Sister Callista and Sister Agnella,[1]

You will surely be satisfied if I write one thank you letter to both of you. You can well imagine that I have even more letters to answer now than you remember from Christmas.

How happy I would have been to have you present on this great feast day. There were many faithful friends here, but I knew even more who could not come and who would have wished with all their heart to participate. What is of greatest importance is, of course, that you shared in the day's wealth of graces. I guess I may send you the booklet with the ceremonial for the Clothing. Then you can imagine everything more clearly. Father Archabbot <Raphael Walzer> had the Mass and gave the homily and, with mitre and staff and accompanied by all the assisting priests, came to conduct me into the church. Our kind Provincial <Theodor Rauch> presided at the Clothing ceremony. The photos will help to illustrate this a bit. The holy cards are for the two of you, then for the dear Mothers (Adelheid and Fidelia), for Srs. Amica, Ignatia, Domitilla and the other Sisters known to me, finally for Rev. Fr. Husse,[2] Anneliese Lichtenberger[3] (from whom I've heard nothing for many months) and Fräulein Perignon.[4] If there are not enough, please write to me.

My mother knows nothing of the Clothing ceremony. My siblings all wrote on the occasion; Rosa <Stein>[5] keenly regretted not being able to come. She gave me the silk for the bridal dress, which will now be made into a chasuble.[6]

In *caritate Christi,* your
Sister Teresa Benedicta a Cruce, OCD

[P.S.] Your dear Mother Prioress will be happy to hear that a niece of Canon Schwind[7] came to the ceremony.

1. Regarding Sr. Callista and Sr. Agnella, see Letters 44 and 40.
2. See Letter 78.
3. See Letter 79.
4. See Letter 339.
5. See Letters 24 and 290.
6. Despite the complete destruction of the Cologne-Lindenthal monastery during a bombing attack in October, 1944, this vestment was saved and is kept in the sacristy of the Cologne Carmel. [It was refashioned into the chasuble worn by Pope John Paul II for the Beatification Ceremony, May 1, 1987.]
7. See Letter 41.

173. Letter to Gertrud von le Fort,[1] Baierbrunn im Isartal
Original in the manuscript section of the German Literature Archive, Schiller-National Museum, Marbach a. N.

J.M.+J.T.

Pax Christi! Cologne-Lindenthal, May 4, 1934

Dear Gertrud von le Fort,

Since I heard nothing from you for so long, I thought to the very last day that perhaps you might come after all. It would have made me so happy. When I hear what an impression the ceremony made on such a great variety of persons, I have an idea what it would have meant to you particularly. But, after all, you will come some time and get to know the real Carmel.

Today I want to thank you sincerely for your dear words and send you a few souvenirs.

In the love of Christ, your sister
Teresa Benedicta a Cruce, OCD

1. See Letter 156.

174. Letter to Fritz Kaufmann, <presumably in Freiburg>
Original in *Archivum Carmelitanum Edith Stein*

Pax Christi! Cologne-Lindenthal, May 14, 1934

Dear Herr Kaufmann,

I am sorry that I could not thank you sooner for your dear letter. I have been writing thank-you letters for four weeks and am far from finished.

You were mistaken in thinking that you had to take leave of me. Naturally, our enclosure is strict: no one may leave or enter, and there is a double grate in the speakroom. But all my visitors who have been close to me have assured me that after a few minutes they are no longer aware of the grates because the spirit moves through them without hindrance. When you are in Cologne some time, you will also make the experiment, won't you? Whoever enters Carmel is not lost to his own, but is theirs fully for the first time; it is our vocation to stand before God for all.

Always with sincerest good wishes for you and yours, your sister

Teresa Benedicta a Cruce, OCD

175. Letter to Rose Magold,[1] <Speyer>

Original in Convent Archive of Cologne Carmel

Pax Christi! Cologne-Lindenthal, May 18, 1934

Dear Rose,

On my Clothing Day I learned from Fräulein von Bodman[2] that you are ill. I hope you have improved in the meantime. If you can and may, do write and tell me how you are.

The feast was beautiful. My children from Westphalia [Speyer] sent Elly Dursy[3] as representative, and Fräulein Nick was here in behalf of the teachers. When you are at home again, you will surely be told all about it.

I wish you a most blessed Feast of Pentecost and a quick, complete recovery. In the love of Christ, your sister

Teresa Benedicta a Cruce, OCD

1. See Letter 94.
2. See Letter 142.
3. See Letter 112.

176. Letter to Erna Biberstein,[1] Breslau

Original in private possession of Susanne Batzdorff, Santa Rosa, CA

Cologne-Lindenthal, May 4, 1934

My dear Erna,

I thank you and the children heartily for your dear letter. I was very happy that you wrote to me for my feast day, [*and that you passed the account from Frl. Dr. Gunther on to Rose (presumably Rose Guttmann). I immediately received a letter from her and I was, at first, completely amazed about the way she came to learn of my new name so quickly.*][2]

In the meantime, perhaps Professor Koch[3] has also called on you to tell you about the celebration. But, of course, no account can reproduce the beauty of the occasion. We continue to receive grateful letters from guests who went away very much impressed. I think you will be pleased at my sending you the snapshots that our Father Provincial <Theodor Rauch> took. [*There is even a better one that Hede Spiegel took (with the veil lowered as is actually proper) but for the time being we have only one print of it.*]

I told Prof. Koch that this is not the right time to visit Mama. I am always so sorry that you are again having a very difficult time. Mother has evidently revived her hopes for she is writing again—after a pause of many weeks—and each time it's a small attack. She must surely speak to you in the same vein, and then you are obliged to conceal what you know. It also makes me sad to see what caricatures she has thought up—not only about our faith and about life in our Order, but also about my personal motives—and to be unable to do anything about it. But I know every word would be useless and would only upset her without doing any good.

[*Please do recount to the two Stein families*[4] *what you hear from me; probably they do not get to see the letters and are not acquainted with the whole picture. I cannot possibly write to everyone. When you congratulate Frau Platau on her birthday, please take along many greetings and cordial best wishes from me. Whatever you tell her she will surely pass on to Lili.*[5] *I send her greetings, too, please.*] And when anything is particularly difficult for you, then use the quiet of your office hour in order to write to me. I am always so happy when I get mail.

You will gradually get used to my new name for the address (Teresia Benedicta a Cruce OCD—i.e., *Ordinis Carmelitarum Discalceatarum* [Order of Discalced Carmelites]). If you prefer to use the old one elsewhere, that will readily be understood and no offense will be taken. I trust you will not be cross with me if I now sign myself as my sisters here call me.

In heartfelt love, your sister
Benedicta

1. See Letter 24. [See also, her reminiscences in *Life,* pp. 14-18.]
2. [In three places, the German edition uses ellipses to indicate an omission. The original letter continues in each case with the text given here in italics.]
3. See Letter 95.
4. [This reference is to her brothers' families, Paul's and Arno's.]
5. [Frau Platau's daughter who married Paul Berg. See Letter 153, written at the time Erna took over Lili's medical practice. For more on Lili and Rose Guttman, see *Life,* pp. 111, 121, etc.]

177. Letter to Mother Petra Brüning, OSU, Dorsten
Original in Convent Archive of Ursuline Sisters, Dorsten

Pax Christi! Cologne-Lindenthal, June 26, 1934
Dear Reverend Mother,

My very best wishes for your beautiful name day feast and a faithful remembrance at the Holy Sacrifice and the Divine Office. Surely you have not forgotten that in my letter wishing you feast day blessings a year ago, I entrusted to you the secret of my vocation. And now I am already praying through the fourth volume of our beautiful breviary.

I have not heard anything from you for a long time and assume that much work and many cares do not allow you to write. I hope a worsening of your physical condition is not also responsible.

I believe in my last letter I commended our dear Sister Margareta to your prayers. The operation that time went very well; the wound healed quickly. By Pentecost, our little Sister was already able to celebrate with us. But soon thereafter she had to go away again for a lengthy convalescence, and she has not yet returned. From July 1st to the 3rd, we will be celebrating the canonization of her holy patroness Teresa Margaret. I was allowed to write the little biography of the new saint.[1]

In our novitiate, to whom you have already given so much love, some changes have been made in the meantime. My youngest sister novice, Fränzi Ernst, was clothed on June 17 and is now called Maria of God.[2] And our good Sr. Veronica,[3] a very dear lay sister, made her perpetual profession on the 21st and has left the novitiate. Perpetual profession (the temporary one, also) is celebrated privately here; the outside world notices nothing of it at all. But inside the house it is a feast of the first rank and is celebrated throughout the day. The entire community, wearing their mantles and carrying candles, goes to the cell of the bride at 5 A.M. to receive her and lead her to the choir. The rite of the ceremony is very much like the one at the Clothing, except that the *Veni Creator* is sung instead of the *Te Deum,* and the vows are made in the hands of our dear Mother <Prioress>. In the choir and the refectory, the bride takes her place beside our dear Mother, and at the processions she walks between Mother Prioress and Mother Subprioress. She wears a wreath of white roses, and at table a small [statue of the] Child Jesus, the Bridegroom, also wearing a crown, faces her. Everyone was especially happy this time because the poor little bride had just returned from the hospital at the beginning of her preparatory retreat, also after an operation, but a less serious one. Hers was the occupational illness of the Carmelites: an inflammation of the bursa of the knee. So far I have been spared that.

May I ask you, dear Reverend Mother, for prayers for two dear deceased members of my family?[4]

Again, my most sincere wishes for you and your entire religious family, your grateful

Sister Teresa Benedicta a Cruce, OCD

1. *St. Teresa Margaret of the Heart of Jesus.* Appeared in a publication of the Rita-Verlag, Würzburg, 1934. [The English translation is included in *The Hidden Life* (Washington, DC: ICS Publications, 1992), pp. 67ff.]
2. See Letter 233.
3. Agnes Keul, Sr. Maria Veronika a Ss. Vultu, OCD (b. Waldernbach/Westerwald, 1903; d. Cologne, 1973).
4. See Letter 178.

178. Letter to Mother Petra Brüning, OSU, Dorsten
Original in Convent Archive of Ursuline Sisters, Dorsten

J.M.+J.T.

Pax! Cologne-Lindenthal, July 23, 1934

Dear Reverend Mother,

Before your retreat begins, I would like to write that we will be remembering you and your religious family very particularly during these days. At the same time, thank you sincerely for your kind greetings on Carmel's principal feast and for the renewed proof of your kindness.

The translation I sent you is by our Sister Maria Angela <Schwalge>[1] who translates a great deal from the French. She was formerly in a Belgian monastery and was transferred here during the war.

Our dear Sister Margareta <Drügemöller> is back with us now. She is permitted to come to the refectory for meals; she takes part in the novitiate instruction periods and is with us for recreation. But she must still stay away from the choral office; and, for the time being, of her former duties (she had charge of the choir), only that of cutting flowers has been returned to her. I earnestly hope that her heart will regain its strength. You know how difficult it is to have to take it easy in the cloister, especially for so young a sister. She is very patient, and I have the impression that during the past few months she has gained years of maturity. At present, we are anxious about our dear Mother <M. Josefa>. She has had a cold for the past several weeks; now the doctor is afraid of pleurisy and had her taken to the hospital day before yesterday. Please help us to pray! Now Mother Subprioress <Sr. Teresa Renata>[2] has had to take over all the duties of the Prioress, so I am not certain whether she will find the time also to thank you herself, as she was planning to do.

My dear mother in Breslau is still very healthy, but she is constantly experiencing the death of persons who are very close to her. The two deceased for whom I asked your prayers were her favorite brother (12 years younger than she) and the mother of my brother-in-law <Hans Biberstein>[3] who lived with them [the Bibersteins] in our house for years.[4] I am very grateful that despite all the blows my mother remains so vigorous. We must pray for a great many things for her before she herself may go home. Now there is still much bitterness in her.

You asked about my name-patron. Of course it is holy Father Benedict. He adopted me and gave me the rights of home in his Order, even though I was not even an Oblate since I always had the Mount of Carmel before my eyes. Because of that my Carmelite Mother gave me the pleasure that yesterday—at the public celebration of our feast day [of St. Benedict]—we were allowed to sing a choral High Mass. That is something most extraordinary. Usually we remain very silent behind the grate, and visiting choirs sing the high Masses in our church.[5] But yesterday there was no choir to be had in all of Cologne. Eleven years ago, when that kind of dearth existed for a longer period, our Sisters learned [to sing] several high Masses under P. Ballman, OSB (Abbey of Maria Laach). So now the choral books were taken out; a very capable chaplain from St. George's helped with the practice and accompanied us; for support he brought six choir boys as cantors for the parts of the Common. Everyone was satisfied with the High Mass and the eight [Sister] singers were happy.

With sincere wishes and regards, your grateful Sister

Teresa Benedicta a Cruce

1. Martha Schwalge (Sr. Maria Angela of the Infant Jesus, OCD) (b. Kall/Eifel, 1880; d. Cologne, 1952). She entered the Carmel of Namur, Belgium, at the age of 19; she was deported as a German during WW II, and transferred to the Carmel in Cologne. For many years she was Subprioress there and developed a brisk activity as a writer.
2. See Letter 156.
3. See Letter 307.
4. Dorothea Biberstein, née Ledermann (b. Rawitsch/Posen, 1855; d. Breslau, 1934).
5. This custom, too, has been discontinued.

179. Plain postcard to Elisabeth Nicola, Düsseldorf
Original in Convent Archive of Cologne Carmel

Pax Christi! Cologne-Lindenthal, July 12,[1] 1934
Dear Fräulein Nicola,

If you come next Tuesday or Thursday (preferably between 3 and 5 o'clock) there should be no problem. I had already thought that you would come sometime after the examination. The public celebration of the Feast of [Our Lady of] Carmel will only be held on Sunday the 22nd, but there is more opportunity for a conversation on a work day.

You must have received my best wishes for the examination even though I did not get to express them in writing.

In sincere remembrance, your
Sister Teresa Benedicta a Cruce, OCD

1. [The date in the German edition is given as August 12, therefore this follows Letter 178. However, since the feast of Our Lady of Mt. Carmel is kept in July, in which month the 22nd was a Sunday in 1934, this letter should be #178, and the one to Mother Petra Brüning, July 23, #179.]

180. Letter to Elisabeth Nicola,[1] Düsseldorf
Original in Convent Archive of Cologne Carmel

J.M.+J.T.
Pax Christi! Cologne-Lindenthal, September 15, 1934
Dear Fräulein Nicola,

I was happy to hear from you again. Even more, that everything is going well and that you have found an advisor. Since you could not get away from home before Easter anyway, you might then still delay a bit before taking a decisive step. Perhaps it might be well to begin the preparations somewhat ahead of time, so that you can enter at Easter. Probably you could obtain your papers now: your baptismal and confirmation certificates, health certificate and letter of character reference from the priest. And when you come again for a visit, then you should take courage and speak to our dear Mother <Prioress>. True, at the moment there is no vacancy here, but it is not impossible that something could change in the next few months.

In any case, it would be good if our dear Mother could get to know you. In that event, the child would have to learn to speak a little: In order to make others understand that one has a call to Carmel, one ought to be able to talk a bit about how this came to be. Perhaps your discussion with your spiritual guide will be a kind of practice for you. Or would you prefer to try and write first? Sometimes people find that easier. One can apply by letter, too. But most of all, we will continue to pray that all will go right.

In *caritate Christi,* your sister
Teresa Benedicta a Cruce OCD

1. See Letter 150.

181. Letter to Ruth Kantorowitz, Hamburg[1]

Original in Convent Archive of Cologne Carmel

Pax Christi! Cologne-Lindenthal, October 4, 1934
Dear Fräulein Dr. Kantorowicz,

I was very happy with your kind letter with the good news, which was a surprise to me. I remember very well the little Ruth whom I got to know when she was a three-year-old child: a shy little girl who wanted nothing to do with anyone other than her parents and her aunt. Your good mother was very astounded when, at the Gordons,[2] you made no resistance to my taking you by the hand and leading you into another room. Through my sister <Else> and Ilse <my niece> I have been kept informed of external developments in your life, as you may have learned of mine.

That your becoming a Catholic gave your dear father joy is a very special grace for you and for him. This joy is, after all, a sign that he himself was very close to the Light and that he went into eternity in the friendship of God. Will you please help to pray for my mother, that her understanding, too, will be enlightened?

Now, to your questions. Before all else I would like to tell you to lay all care for the future, confidently, in God's hands, and allow yourself to be led by him entirely, as a child would. Then you can be sure not to lose your way. Just as the Lord brought you into his church, so he will lead you to the place in it that he wants you to have. Despite your 33 years, I would advise you to set aside, for the time being, the question of a religious vocation. God's will is not halted by any boundary of age. After all, I was accepted at 42 years of age, and many others even later. Naturally everything is easier when one enters while still young.

But that, after all, is no longer within our power. You would hardly find any monastery where you would be accepted immediately after conversion. Most of them require, for good reasons, several preliminary years spent learning to live in the Catholic world. And that seems to me most important for you at this time. If a religious vocation is genuine, it will endure such a waiting period. Should it be an illusion formed in the first fervor, it is better to recognize this outside rather than through a serious disappointment within the monastery.

What you write about your training and your inclinations seems to indicate much more an activity outside, such as the Caritas Union or the Borromaeus Society [under the patronage of St. Charles Borromeo]. But, obviously, after only one letter I am incapable of making a judgment about that. If you wished to enter an Order, you would have to give up every wish concerning the kind of occupation and, in holy obedience, allow your superiors to decide how your talents and knowledge were to be used. The daily schedule of Carmel allows very little time for scholarly work. That I should be permitted such work while still in the novitiate is an exception.

For the moment I would say: remain patiently at your job as long as you do not receive a definite hint from above to undertake something else. Use your free time to get to know and to love God and the church better: the doctrines of the faith, the liturgy, our saints; but also the religious institutions and Catholic life in the present time, along with its shadows, which will not remain concealed from you in the long run. If you lack personal contacts in Hamburg, I would be glad to help you to find some. You may always turn to me with questions—in writing or perhaps even verbally sometimes. The Gordons, of course, will not learn anything through me as long as you do not wish it.

With sincere best wishes for your further path, in the love of Christ, your sister

Teresa Benedicta a Cruce, OCD

1. See Letter 147. Ruth Kantorowicz would have liked to be a Carmelite nun. In 1936, she was received at the Carmel of Maastricht, Holland, as a postulant. However, she was not accepted into the novitiate. She found temporary lodging as a helper in the extern quarters of the Ursulines in Venlo (Holland). There, on August 2, 1942, she was arrested by the SS police, taken along with the Stein sisters to Westerbork, and on August 7, 1942 deported with them to Auschwitz, where she died in the gas chamber.
2. Family of Max and Else Gordon, Hamburg. See Letter 31.

182. Letter to Mother Petra Brüning, OSU, Dorsten
Original in Convent Archive of Ursuline Sisters, Dorsten

J.M.+J.T.

Pax Christi! Cologne-Lindenthal, October 17, 1934

Reverend and dear Mother,

Most cordial thanks for your greetings for the feast of the little St. Thérèse <of Lisieux>. We waited to write until now because we wished to express to you our mutual joy on the Feast of St. Ursula. After all, your patroness is especially celebrated in Cologne also.[1] One of our older Sisters is a native of Cologne and used to belong to the parish of St. Ursula. She received the religious name "Ursula of the holy Three Kings." This year on the 21st we will have, in addition, the Clothing of our lay postulant, so it will be a double feast.

I am allowed to send you the booklet on St. Teresa that I wrote for our dear Mother's name day and that has now appeared—although cruelly abridged.[2]

Of course, it will give us all great joy if you are able to come again soon. After all, I had been waiting a whole year to be able to welcome you here some time. I always had the certain hope that it would do you good. All the same, I am aware that you bring the best with you and that we have nothing to offer you for it except the "empty room." However, it is not entirely empty, for it is already filled with cordial love and gratitude. Unfortunately you were unable to see [what is on] the side of our Choir at the grate. As we go through the door, one's gaze is attracted first by the larger-than-lifesize painting of the Crucifix that hangs above the grate.

If you imagine me at my place in choir, then please without the white mantle that we wear only at Mass and at the Office on first class feasts. [See me] rather in the old brown habit, very small, [seated] on the floor. Just so, my meditations are not great flights of the spirit, but mostly very humble and simple. The best of it is the gratitude that I have been given this place as a home on earth and a step toward the eternal home. Now I have already begun my second year in the Order.

The feast of our Holy Mother <Teresa of Avila> is a joyous day and one for gratitude, for many reasons. In Speyer it was celebrated as my name day; then one room was not large enough to hold all the flowers and gifts. My greatest joy always came from the prayers and holy Communion of the many children and Sisters. I believe they did much to help me reach my goal. Here, besides [commemorating] our Holy Mother, we have a celebration for our dear Mother Subprioress <Sr. Teresa Renata> and for our eldest (80-year-old) Sr. Teresa. This time, therefore, we began already on Sunday.

I hope to see you again very soon. With most cordial wishes for you and your entire house, indeed for your whole Order, in *caritate Christi,* your grateful

Teresa Benedicta a Cruce OCD

1. St. Ursula is the patron of the City of Cologne; her feast is celebrated on October 21.
2. *Teresa of Jesus* (Constance: Kanisiuswerk, 1934). [Translated in *Hidden Life,* pp. 29-66.]

183. Letter to Gisela Naegeli,[1] Zurich

Original in Convent Archive of Cologne Carmel

Pax Christi! Cologne-Lindenthal, <Autumn, 1934>

Dear Fräulein Naegeli,

So that you need not worry unnecessarily about the fate of your mail, I want to notify you at once that it reached me today. The Cologne post office knows Carmel, and in Carmel my secular name is still known although I have been wearing the habit of the Order and [have had] a beautiful religious name for a good half-year.

Intentions such as yours are not out of the ordinary for us. Similar ones are brought daily to our door or come in the mail. After all, it is our profession to pray, and many people rely on that. We all pray in common, daily, for the intentions commended to us, and each one adds to that her own contribution for those who are especially under her care. To these, you and your protégés will now belong.

It is often a real source of embarrassment for us when people credit us with special effectiveness in prayer, or with holiness. We can detect nothing extraordinary about ourselves. Despite that it does seem that the Lord gladly helps those who turn to us. It is probably the reward of their confidence, perhaps also the return for our having given ourselves to him. But if the prayer is to be effective for you, then you have to do your part also; in other words, you have to be sensible and do whatever is necessary for your health. God is very pleased when one follows the directions of the doctor and the nurse as though they were his own, and when one uses the time for rest to rest completely, leaving all cares to him.

Should you meet Fräulein Dr. Borsinger[2] again, then please give her my best regards.

I am returning the picture of your lady friend. I will destroy all the letters.

With best wishes and regards in the love of Christ,
Your Sister Teresa Benedicta a Cruce, OCD

1. Gisela Naegeli (b. Rapperswil/St. Gallen, Switzerland, 1897) corresponded with Edith Stein. She was also a personal acquaintance of Sr. Adelgundis Jaegerschmid and Dr. Vérène Borsinger. Gisela Naegeli and Vérène Borsinger were very friendly with the Carmel of Le Pâquier. Together they endeavored, unfortunately without success, to make it possible for the Stein sisters to emigrate to Switzerland.
2. See Letter 331.

184. Letter to P. Laurentius Siemer,[1] OP, Cologne
Original in Provincial Archive of the Dominican Fathers, Cologne

J.M.J.T.

Pax Christi! Cologne-Lindenthal, November 4, 1934

Very Reverend Father Provincial,

Thank you very much for your kind letter and your frank appraisal [of the translation of Thomas Aquinas's *Quaestiones disputatae de veritate* (*Disputed Questions on Truth*[2]) from Latin into German]. You need not fear that your criticism has hurt me, or [if it did] it was only as much as it hurts when one touches an old wound. No one knows better than I how little versed I am in Thomism. When I undertook the translation, I was not fully aware of all that would be involved. Although in doing the work I realized some of the difficulties, it did get printed; therefore those experts to whom I submitted the manuscript and who were highly pleased with it share the responsibility with me. Of course, they were not specialists in Thomism. In recent years, it has cost me a great deal to become ever more aware that I lack the necessary equipment to undertake the tremendous intellectual tasks imposed on us by our times, which I am convinced I see very clearly.

Even more painful is the insight that it is too late to make up these deficiencies. I would be very happy not to have to do any more writing. But as long as my superiors are of the opinion that through my knowledge I may be able and obligated to be of use to others, I shall have to accept the fact that the shortcomings, so well known to me, will also become apparent to others.

I have one more question to ask you today. When correcting the unfortunate Index to the *Quaestiones de veritate,* I began to reflect that you might not be in full agreement with the foreword. I felt the need to mention, with thanks, your gracious assistance and I would be very happy if you would give me permission to do so. But I do want to inquire first whether for any reason whatsoever you find it unwelcome.[3]

In sincere gratitude *in Christo,* your humble, least[4]

Sr. Teresa Benedicta a Cruce, OCD

1. Siemer, Joseph (P. Laurentius, OP, Provincial) (b. Elisabetheim/Oldenburg, 1888; d. Cologne, 1956) significant Thomistic researcher. See *Edith Steins Werke,* Vol. IV.
2. [This work of St. Thomas Aquinas bears the title *Truth* in the English translation published by Henry Regnery Co. in 1952.]

3. [Presumably because of her Jewish descent. This was in 1934!]
4. [This form of signature was prescribed in Carmelite custom when writing to clerics and superiors.]

185. Letter to Ruth Kantorowicz, Hamburg
Original in Convent Archive of Cologne Carmel

J.M.+J.T.
Pax Christi! Cologne-Lindenthal, December 1, 1934
Dear Fräulein Ruth,

Before Advent begins I would like to send you a little greeting with best wishes for this holy season. Your first Advent in the Church, after all, must turn out to be particularly lovely. Do not allow yourself to be distracted by any outward unrest from living in the intense thought of the Advent liturgy. Then the Feast [of Christmas] will bring you an abundance of graces. In your last letter there was an echo of the rush of moving days; the earlier letters pleased me particularly by their calm and clarity. It would certainly be good if you were able to come here sometime; much more could be readily clarified in a thorough personal conversation. What kind of plans do you have for the days of Christmas? I would be very glad if you were able to spend them in genuine Catholic surroundings. With us, feast days are least suited for conversations [with visitors] because we have hardly any time then for the speakroom. Were you to think of Cologne, then, you would have to take care to be here not *only* for the feast days.

I have often asked myself why you are really keeping your conversion a secret. Is there someone you owe consideration? It is, after all, so much nicer when one can be completely open. My sister and her husband <Else and Max Gordon> would not understand it, but I doubt that you would have to fear any kind of attack; in any case, I have never been afflicted with any. In the case of Ilse <Gordon>, naturally her totally nonreligious upbringing has to be taken into account. You would find Anni <Gordon> warmly receptive. I am pleased that you sometimes go to the Gordons. One never knows whether, eventually, a tiny seed may take root.

With cordial wishes for blessings, your
Teresa Benedicta a Cruce, OCD

186. Letter to Ruth Kantorowicz, Hamburg
Original in Convent Archive of Cologne Carmel

J.M.+J.T.

Pax Christi! Cologne-Lindenthal, December 9, 1934

Dear Fräulein Ruth,

This time we consider it most important that you have a genuine Christmas. Therefore we propose that you spend the Holy Night with us. At Midnight, we have a High Mass (with Holy Communion), before that Matins and Lauds, after it the second and third Masses of Christmas, in silence. After that you could sleep in one of the guestrooms outside the enclosure, have breakfast here, and perhaps go to the Pontifical High Mass at the Cathedral. For the following days we would arrange to have you stay at a small convent near us where we often lodge guests, or in the Women's League house—the latter only if someone nice were to be there over Christmas, something we shall probably ascertain later today. Surely Cologne's beautiful ancient churches and great divine services would mean a great deal to you.

Until the 28th, my time will be extensively occupied by prayer and community Christmas observances. But at midday, from 1-2 o'clock, I would always be allowed to meet you in the speakroom, possibly also in the morning from 10 to 11 o'clock, if you do not prefer to be elsewhere at that time. Some things could be discussed during those times and the rest would be left for later. Will you please decide soon and let us know? But please, under no circumstances are you to stay in Hamburg over the holidays! If nothing else, go to Reinbek for sake of the good food.

You would have to make sure to arrive early enough during the day on the 24th so that I could instruct you somewhat in the use of the breviary; also, so you might rest a bit before the long night.

From the train station, the No. 2 streetcar[1] takes you almost to our house. Will you be telling the Gordons that you are coming here? They would surely like to send regards along with you. But, of course, your secret would then be semi-revealed.

With many good wishes for the next weeks, your Sister

Teresa Benedicta a Cruce, OCD

1. [In the margin here, Mother Teresa Renata wrote: Your stop: Essen, Kappelmann Street.]

187. Letter to Ruth Kantorowicz, Hamburg
Original in Convent Archive of Cologne Carmel

Pax Christi! Cologne-Lindenthal, December 14, 1934
Dear Fräulein Ruth,

You understood correctly: When you come to us from the train station (after all, no one can meet you), I will have just enough time to prepare you for all the events of the evening. Apparently you will make a reservation for the following days at the small convent of St. Anna, which is very near us. I am happy that you want to go to visit my relatives. Please take my best regards along. My sister <Else> will be a bit jealous.

In the hope that these days will be rich in graces for you, your Sister

Teresa Benedicta a Cruce, OCD

188. Letter to Mother Petra Brüning, OSU, Dorsten
Original in Convent Archive of Ursuline Sisters, Dorsten

J.M.+J.T.
Pax Christi! Cologne-Lindenthal, December 14, 1934
Dear Reverend Mother,

We are still in the midst of Advent, but I do have to get my Christmas greeting ready for you. Surely you often visit our choir in spirit now, because you know how well one can spend a silent Advent here, as secure as an unborn child waiting for the great day of new birth. Now, during the Octave of the Immaculate Conception, we have a small altar next to the grate in the choir. There stands, surrounded by pine branches and white blossoms, the Beuron "Mother of Life," Fräulein Schweitzer's[1] gift to us when I had my Clothing ceremony. Otherwise, we have her on a little baroque altar in the Novitiate. P. Desiderius[2] surely did not imagine her in such a setting (you have to add, mentally, two chubby faced cherubs above her to complete the picture—they did not get on the photo), but we are very happy with our altar and our Madonna. The other picture is something serious but, after all, the Passion does belong to the *Ecce venio* <Behold, I come> of Advent.

I did not know that you also have a title to your religious name. Where the custom began, I do not know. It must have been observed in Carmel even before the Reform, but perhaps not commonly carried out. When he was a Calced Carmelite, our holy Father John <of the Cross, Doctor of the Church> was known as John of St. Matthias; but our holy Mother <Teresa of Avila> kept her family name (de Ahumada) until she moved to the Monastery of St. Joseph. She herself considered that setting aside one's family name represented the renunciation of one's whole past. It was also intended to do away with every temptation to pride in noble ancestry and emphasis on social differences. But probably its deepest meaning is still that we have a personal vocation to live a particular mystery [of the faith]. Since all of them have an inner connection, each single one contains the entire fullness of God. Among us the Sacred Heart and the Blessed Sacrament are most frequently represented. Our youngest lay sister, who received the habit on the feast of St. Ursula, is called Anna of the Holy Family. I find "Christus Rex" <Christ the King> and "Christus Crucifixus" <Christ Crucified> beautiful titles, or "Mater gratiarum" <Mother of Grace>.

Gertrud von le Fort visited us during her lecture tour. She found great joy in getting to know Carmel.

Our novitiate lasts one year. Eight months of it have flown by. I already think frequently of my holy profession. It gives me great pleasure that by sharing in our life, you feel you are being helped in your difficult task. Together we will experience the feast of Christmas and the entire, beautiful holy time, won't we? Thank you, also, for the beautiful cross and the holy cards. [At the Divine Office] on the Holy Night, Sr. Maria <Ernst>[3] (my younger sister in the Novitiate) and I will be permitted to be chantresses. Then we will sing the "Christus natus est nobis" <Christ is born to us> for all who are united with us.

In grateful love, your least sister,
Teresa Benedicta a Cruce, OCD

1. See Letter 171.
2. Peter Lenz (P. Desiderius, OSB) (b. Haigerloch/Hohenzollern, 1832; d. Beuron Abbey, 1928) painter and monk, founder of the Beuron school of art.
3. [Edith spent her first Christmas as a Catholic, in 1922, as a guest in the Ernst home when Fränzi (Sr. Maria) was 18 years old.]

189. Letter to Hedwig Conrad-Martius, Bergzabern
Original in Convent Archive of Cologne Carmel; first published, *Kösel Verlag,* Munich 1960

Pax Christi! Cologne-Lindenthal, December 15, 1934
My dear Hatti,

Yesterday the pretty little basket arrived. We thank you sincerely, especially Autós <Theodor Conrad>[1] who surely wrapped the package. Our dear Mother <M. Josefa> and the "Sister Provisor"[2] (who comes from the Palatinate) were full of enthusiasm over the gorgeous fruit; I greeted each little apple lovingly and introduced him by name and am very peeved that you speak of "paltry fruit".

I am very grateful that you occupy yourself with *Akt und Potenz [Act and Potency]*.[3] I had just intended to ask you for that book in this letter. Mother Subprioress <Sr. Teresa Renata> is very eager for me to prepare it for publication. For the time being I still have several other things to do before I can get to it. But once I am ready for it, I would appreciate very much knowing whether you consider it worth publishing and spending as much time on it as revision would still require. In Münster, I myself filled a whole sheet listing passages I found in need of revision. You will probably find the debate with the *Metaphysical Discussions* impossible and will then, hopefully, put *Stufen des Seins [Steps of Being]* at my disposal. Nor do I know [your] book on plants.[4]

You are due to receive the second part of the Thomas review from me. The December issue [of the magazine] already contains the review of the 25th section (on the Incarnation).[5] Perhaps it will give Fräulein Käthi[6] pleasure if you give her the booklet on St. Teresa for Christmas.[7] Both of you will read it, of course. Unfortunately, I have nothing to send for Autós but my very best regards. Will he come to Cologne sometime?

I am delighted to hear that Hering[8] will visit you. I send him my best regards and consider his visit a substitute for mine. Remember me also to Erika <Gothe>[9] and her mother when you have a chance. Are they happy about my being in Carmel? My novitiate is now two-thirds completed; I joyfully anticipate making my profession in April. But it is a good thing that one need not be "finished" by that time, for I have a feeling that the actual novitiate began only recently, since I no longer expend so much energy in growing used to externals like ceremonies, customs, and so on.

We are having a beautiful Advent and happily look forward to an even more wonderful Christmas. For you also I wish the most beautiful and the best that the Feast can bring. Naturally I think of you every day, but I will do so especially during the Holy Night.

In love and gratitude, your
Sister Benedicta

1. See Letter 146.
2. [The "provisor" in Carmel has charge of purchasing, distributing and preserving food supplies.]
3. Edith's significant preparatory study for *Endliches und Ewiges Sein [Finite and Eternal Being]*. See *Edith Steins Werke*, Vol. II.
4. Studies and publications of Hedwig Conrad-Martius.
5. Appeared in *Die Christliche Frau [The Christian Woman]*, January 1935.
6. See Letter 120.
7. See Letter 182.
8. See Letter 16.
9. See Letter 11.

190. Letter to Ruth Kantorowicz, Hamburg
Original in Convent Archive of Cologne Carmel

Pax Christi! Cologne-Lindenthal, January 5, 1935
Dear Fräulein Ruth,

Just a brief thank-you note. The beautiful cake arrived right on time for *"U-Tag" [Unschuldigen-Tag* = Day of the Innocents],[1] just in time to be cut and served at the evening meal. I would also have told you about this feast had I not had so much other matter for conversation. On the 28th, you would even have gotten to see me as St. Francis.[2] I am so glad that you were able to make the Holy Hour on Thursday night and, generally, that the days were spent so happily.

Again, all the best! Your
Sister Benedicta

1. *"U-Tag"* was the novitiate's name for the Feast of the Holy Innocents, Dec. 28. [In Carmel, the custom was to observe this day as a holiday for those in the novitiate, i.e., the community's "holy innocents." The young sisters provided special entertainment, meals, etc.]
2. In a play presented by the Sisters in the novitiate, Sr. Teresa Benedicta was cast as St. Francis [of Assisi].

191. Letter to Gisela Naegeli,[1] Zurich
Original in Convent Archive of Cologne Carmel

Pax Christi! Cologne-Lindenthal, January 9, 1935
Dear Fräulein Naegeli,

You will be surprised at the speed with which your wish gets fulfilled. You timed it very well. I had just written down something about the spirit of our Order for another purpose, and needed only to change it a little and complete it. Permission to do so was granted with pleasure. But now our dear Reverend Mother has a request in return. Could you have several hundred copies printed for us? How much would 300 cost, and 500? And could the stipend for the article be applied to the expense?

Furthermore I would like to ask that the proofs be sent to me. Since the manuscript is handwritten, it will be necessary that I proofread it myself. If you consider it necessary to give my civil name, please add it in parentheses.

I continue my remembrance of you and those under your protection. With warmest wishes for the New Year, I am your

Sr. Teresa Benedicta a Cruce, OCD

1. See Letter 183.

192. Letter to Gertrud von le Fort, Baierbrunn im Isartal
Original in the manuscript section of the German Literature Archive, Schiller-National Museum, Marbach a. N.

J.M.+J.T.

Pax Christi! Cologne-Lindenthal, January 31, 1935
Dear Baroness,

Our retreat ended this morning. A retreat in Carmel—all that's lacking to make it heaven is one's own holiness. My spiritual reading those days was your new book. I could not get to it earlier. Now, at last, I can thank you for this beautiful Christmas gift. I would not like to think of this retreat, which has meant so much to me, without your book. It has a distinct place in it. And apart from this very personal aspect: I find that, actually, everything else that has been written about woman in the past decades is now superfluous. There is much written in your book that we already knew. But all that has now been taken back to its deepest roots and put into its place. And a line has been drawn under everything "problematic."

Thank you, too, for your kind letter. I have told you on earlier occasions that you need never feel distressed about not having time to write. Now, in Carmel, that is particularly valid. We too thought you would be coming back another time. After all, those were the assumptions that made your sudden departure acceptable. We will just leave it to the Lord whether he will lead you back here sometime. Or perhaps when you travel to Breslau you can visit our little Carmel "Mater Gratiarum" [Mother of Grace] in Breslau-Pawelwitz. I wish most earnestly that you could meet our dear Mother Marianne, the foundress of the Silesian Carmel.[1] When you see her, you will know why. You will always have part of your home with us here. The confidence that something of our peace and our silence flows out into the world, and supports those who are still on pilgrimage, is the only thing that can reassure me when I consider that I, rather than so many more worthy ones, have been called into this wonderful security. You cannot imagine how embarrassed I am when someone speaks of our life of "sacrifice." I led a life of sacrifice as long as I had to stay outside. Now practically all my burdens have been removed, and I have in fullness what formerly I lacked. Of course, there are Sisters among us who are called upon to make great sacrifices daily. And I do await the day when I shall be allowed to feel more of my vocation to the cross than I do now, since the Lord treats me once more as if I were a little child. For the time being, then, let us consider ourselves united in this way: you may at any and all times—at least in spirit—flee to us when a breathing spell is necessary. Perhaps, in the future, things may change.

I am writing this conclusion only today—February 1. We are having public Adoration [of the Blessed Sacrament] in our chapel, and I am now—shortly after 1:30 P.M.—in my cell for a few minutes, for the first time since 6 A.M. Soon I will be taking along your greetings to the Lord in the choir, which I had actually planned to show you.

In caritate Christi, your

Teresa Benedicta a Cruce, OCD

1. See Letter 156.

193. Letter to Paula-Maria Stolzenbach, (Frankfurt)[1]
Original in Convent Archive of Hainburg Carmel

J.M.J.T.

Pax Christi! Cologne-Lindenthal, February 3, 1935
Dear Fräulein Stolzenbach,

Only now, gradually, am I able to pay off my Christmas debts. And so please accept sincere thanks for the booklet on Purgatory that has enthusiastic friends in our house. Belated wishes for blessings in the New Year, also. In the meantime, you have had the days of retreat and hopefully have brought much that is beautiful away with you.

We, too, have just had our retreat—the first community one I have made in the monastery. It was given by P. Swidbert Soreth,[2] a Dominican who is very enthusiastic about our Order and who directed everything beautifully toward our goals. For me, it was already a very essential preparation for my profession [of vows] and I am very grateful for it. For the immediate preparation I will ask again, as I did for my Clothing, to have our holy Father John [of the Cross] as retreat master. Today I am already looking forward to that time. You will think of it also, won't you, that I am going forward to another great day of grace, and help me in the coming months especially by your prayers?

You never wrote anything about your experience of visiting the Carmel in Pützchen.[3] Did you receive the fine obituary published in the church bulletin by the pastor there?[4]

In faithful remembrance, your
Sister Teresa Benedicta a Cruce, OCD

1. Paula-Maria Stolzenbach (b. Frankfurt, 1892; d. Frankfurt, 1974) was a public school teacher and a longtime benefactress of Carmel.
2. See Letter 270.
3. She means a visit paid to the Carmel of St. Joseph in Bonn-Pützchen.
4. The foundress of the Carmel of St. Joseph in Bonn-Pützchen, Mother Maria ab Angelis, née Trost, died on September 27, 1934. Fr. Marten, pastor at Pützchen, wrote an obituary in the parish bulletin.

194. Letter to Rev. Konrad Schwind, Frankenthal/Mörsch[1]
Original in Convent Archive of Cologne Carmel

J.M.

Pax Christi! Cologne-Lindenthal, February 11, 1935
Dear Reverend Father,

We do not have our own publishing house; but having three "authoresses" in the house means we are selling a good number of publications on commission. So you will receive a sample shipment. Whatever you cannot use, of course you may just send back. The holy cards for the sick are being reprinted at this time. They sell for 3 pfennig apiece, 2.50 marks for 100.

Thank you so much for your kind letter; the very best wishes for the sick in your care, your pastoral ministry, and for the young graduate.[2] He will recall that, with his aunt, he visited me once at St. Magdalena's. I also remember his first Latin lessons with the [Very Rev.] Prelate.[3]

I will remember all your intentions. Please remember me, also, in the coming months; I hope to be allowed to make my first profession [of vows] in April. The question of whether I have accustomed myself to the solitude made me smile. For most of my life I have had much more solitude than I have here. I miss nothing that is outside, and have everything I lacked there; therefore I must be grateful for the entirely unmerited, immense grace of my vocation.

In *caritate Christi,* your Sister
Teresa Benedicta a Cruce, OCD

1. Konrad Schwind (b. Schifferstadt, 1898; d. Schifferstadt, 1976); for many years he was pastor and dean in Frankenthal.
2. Presumably a relative of Father Schwind.
3. Joseph Schwind, canon and vicar general of Speyer, uncle of this Father Schwind. See Letter 41.

195. Letter to Ruth Kantorowicz, Hamburg
Original in Convent Archive of Cologne Carmel

J.M.J.T.

Pax Christi! Cologne-Lindenthal, February 15, 1935

Dear Fräulein Ruth,

You had a few questions you wished me to answer. If my information is correct, there is a convent attached to St. Elizabeth's Church, where P. Joppen[1] offers Mass. The Sisters will surely know when the Jubilee is and what would please Father. So you would have to make connections with them. Were that to come to naught, you would probably be able to get the date from the Brother Porter at the Jesuit Residence. And in a diplomatic conversation with Father himself you could perhaps find out whether he has any wishes for books that you might fulfill. It is not out of the question that something by Gertrud von le Fort might be welcome. She herself considers the *Hymnen an die Kirche [Hymns to the Church]* as her most essential and fundamental work.

Has the question of your retreat been answered? We had a very fine retreat from January 22 to the 31st. And very soon now, I will be allowed to have another one entirely on my own, in preparation for my holy profession. Today I received the assurance that my dear superiors and Sisters want to accept me. Now two months remain for me to prepare myself for this great day of grace. Please help me to ask that I use them well, and to thank [God] for this great undeserved joy. You will understand this since you now know a little about our life.

I hope you have resolved the conflict in your business. On the 21st, my niece Eva <Stein>[2] will have her birthday. If you could send her birthday wishes for me, she would surely be very happy.

In faithful remembrance, your Sister
Teresa Benedicta a Cruce, OCD

1. [Karl Joppen, SJ (b. Strassburg, 1878; d. Cologne, 1938). From New Year, 1934, he was chaplain at St. Elizabeth's in Hamburg. His Silver Jubilee was held on October 16, 1935. From November 1, 1935, on he was superior of the Jesuits in Cologne.]
2. Eva Stein, the elder daughter of Arno Stein, the younger of Edith's two brothers. [See *Life*, pp. 103, 542.]

196. Letter to Mother Petra Brüning, OSU, Dorsten
Original in Convent Archive of Ursuline Sisters, Dorsten

J.M.+J.T.

Pax Christi! Cologne-Lindenthal, February 27, 1935

Very Reverend and dear Mother Petra,

I already owe you thanks for two dear letters since our Christmas letters crossed in the mail; I only received yours on the Holy Night. I thank you heartily for both, and for all the beautiful enclosures. I am very happy that you remembered my Candlemas Day[1] [anniversary]. Now you will be amazed what my next great celebration will be: I will be allowed to make my profession on Easter morning. Since we anticipate seeing you here even before then, we may perhaps be able to tell you in person just what will be happening. In case you cannot come, I will only mention that the celebration will be held early—about 5 A.M.—so that you can attend in spirit. I know how much you share my joy, and I commend myself to your prayers for the entire time of preparation.

Of course I think also about your worries. Just today I received word from Speyer about the great troubles of the Dominican Sisters at St. Magdalena's. In Bavaria, finally, the institutions for teacher training are being closed, and the Sisters are not to get the interdenominational intermediate school that is intended to replace them. For the convent there, this puts their existence in question. Since you are so familiar with this kind of worry, perhaps you and your community will help with your prayers.

I read Peterson's[2] article[3] in the B.M. <*Benedictinische Monatzeitschrift [Benedictine Monthly]*> with much pleasure. Peterson is an old acquaintance of mine, since Göttingen.

You have asked me twice, I believe, whether I have any connection to Gertrud von le Fort's Carmelite novella <*Die Letzte am Schafott*> [*The Song at the Scaffold,* trans. Olga Marx (New York, NY: Sheed & Ward, 1933)]. She hit upon the material without my having anything to do with it. However, soon thereafter she came to see me in Munich, and one afternoon we spoke about Carmel, from which she was spiritually still rather distant at that time. She only became engrossed in it through her work on the novella. Naturally she has also visited us when she was here [in Cologne], and was very happy to have the two hours at the grate.

Now I wish you and your whole community a very grace-filled Lent.
In caritate Christi, your grateful Sister
Teresa Benedicta a Cruce, OCD

1. Confirmation Day of Edith Stein.
2. Erik Peterson (b. Hamburg, 1890; d. Hamburg, 1960); originally a Protestant theologian and professor of New Testament and ancient church history in Bonn; became a convert in 1930; from 1934 on, professor at the Papal Institute for Christian Archaeology in Rome.
3. [*"Himmlische und irdische Liturgie"* ("Heavenly and Earthly Liturgy"), in periodical *Benediktinischen Monatzeitschrift* 16 (1934): 39-47.]

197. Letter to Ruth Kantorowicz, <Hamburg>
Original in Convent Archive of Cologne Carmel

J.M.

Pax Christi! Cologne-Lindenthal, April 25, 1935
Dear Fräulein Ruth,

Heartfelt thanks for your kind wishes and the beautiful book. A little while ago I spoke to our Reverend Mother about your visit. Of course you may come. But it would be well if you can manage it before April 30, or only in the second week of May. On the 30th we expect another guest whom many of the Sisters will have to talk to. And now that, after the long pause of Lent, visitors come more frequently than usual, it could happen that our two speakrooms would not suffice. You know what a small house we have.

So you will have to decide on the best way. Then we will discuss all your questions. And if there is enough time, you will get to hear something about the beautiful profession celebration. For the time being, [I enclose] a small branch of myrtle[1] as a remembrance.

With most heartfelt remembrance, your
Sr. Teresa Benedicta a Cruce, OCD

1. As was customary, myrtle was used in the wreath for her profession ceremony [on Easter Sunday, April 21, 1935].

198. Letter to Mother Petra Brüning, OSU, Dorsten
Original in Convent Archive of Ursuline Sisters, Dorsten

J.M.+J.T.

Pax Christi! Cologne-Lindenthal, April 25, 1935

Very Reverend and dear Mother Petra,

The Bridegroom sends you the little wreath[1] of myrtle with which your love decorated him, him as well as the bridal candle, the candles on the table, the napkin, cutlery, etc. The Bride wore a wreath of white roses. I was very happy to hear where the adornments came from. Heartfelt thanks for them. We have not yet finished discussing what else I am to receive from you. I thought of an emblem and lining for a vestment since the silk of the bridal dress has not yet been used and has been waiting for the necessary accessories since the Clothing Day. But perhaps our dear Mother <M. Josepha> will think of something more urgent.

When you visit us again—after all, we've been anticipating it with joy all winter—we will recount everything that happened from the first hours of the morning until night on this beautiful Easter Sunday. One cannot write about it in such detail. The Veiling ceremony will come only three years from now, after perpetual profession. For us, the preparation consists primarily of a ten day retreat made in total silence and solitude. During that time we are allowed to live like hermits. I will tell you about the daily schedule when I see you.

For my meditation I had our holy Father John <of the Cross>'s *Dark Night* and the Gospel of John. Usually, on the day before Profession, before dinner, one makes a public admission of one's faults.[2] I was allowed to do that at noon on the Wednesday of Holy Week so that it would not interrupt the silence of the Holy Triduum. I found it especially good [to comply to that custom] before the first of the Tenebrae offices—once they begin one wants to leave off all occupation with oneself. On Saturday evening I was called [to come for a few minutes to see the community] during recreation time; I received from each Sister the promise of a spiritual bouquet and a commendation of intentions.[3] Richly laden I then returned to the choir. Of course, out of the great riches of grace on this Easter day I let all those have a share who have given me something of their heart to take along into Carmel.

Once more, sincere thanks for all your goodness and love. In *caritate Christi,* your Sister

Teresa Benedicta a Cruce, OCD

1. Edith sent the small wreath that had been used on the statue to Mother Petra, who had provided it and all the flowers and decorations for the celebration. See the explanation in Letter177.
2. [This involved an admission of one's failures in observance of the regulations and customs of the Order, and was one of the forms of mortification or penance practiced in community by Carmelites at that time as a means of making up for failures in leading the common life in community. It entailed making a review of one's compliance with the daily schedule, and house rules and customs.]
3. [This is a figurative bouquet of a stated number of prayers offered for the Sister. Each donor determined her own contribution. In return, the recipient's prayers were requested for the many intentions entrusted to her at this visit.]

199. Letter to Hedwig Dülberg,[1] Marburg

Original in Convent Archive of Benedictine Sisters, St. Lioba, Freiburg-Günterstal

J.M.

Pax Christi! Cologne-Lindenthal, White Sunday, April 28, 1935

Dear Frau Dülberg,

Sincere thanks for your kind remembrance for my Profession Day, and for sending the beautiful photos. Despite the many reasons you give for your opinion that my verdict is to be taken into account, I want to reveal to you that it is a very inexpert verdict. I am neither an artist nor a connoisseur, not even—in the usual sense—an art lover. Certainly I have seen many a beautiful piece, and there are works I really like. But I have always been too much occupied with other matters to study art *ex professo* <professionally>. Therefore if I say anything about your tapestry, it is only to satisfy your wish.

Most important, probably, is that it is a real Pietà—Good Friday evening at the Cross. The pain of the Mother of God is as great as the ocean; she is immersed in it. But it is a totally restrained pain: she lays her hand firmly upon her heart so it may not burst. The dropped jaw of the Savior is an almost frightening symbol that he is really dead. But his head is, almost comfortingly, turned toward his Mother. And the cross is very light: the *lignum Crucis* <wood of the cross> becomes the *lumen Christi* <the light of Christ>.

When you come here you must tell me about the colors; they are obviously an integral part of it. In return I will then tell you all about my beautiful Easter morning, and everything else you would like to know about Carmel.

I am happy with you that you accomplished such a large project this winter. But I am also happy about your new activity. It is probably something that, by nature, suits you a great deal, and I think that will clarify many questions for you.

Everything else when we meet. In faithful remembrance, your sister

Teresa Benedicta a Cruce, OCD

1. Hedwig Dülberg (Sr. Simone, OSB) (b. Münchhausen, 1903); entered the Congregation of Benedictines at St. Lioba's Convent, Freiburg-Günterstal.

200. Letter to Elizabeth Nicola, Düsseldorf
Original in Convent Archive of Cologne Carmel

J.M.

Pax Christi! Cologne-Lindenthal, May 13, 1935
Dear Fräulein Nicola,

Only gradually am I reducing my letter-debts. Thank you sincerely for the beautiful book. I hope its turn will come soon for reading at table. Then all the sisters will enjoy it, and that surely will please you. I am also grateful that you join me in prayer and praise. For that, one needs lots of auxiliary troops. When you come again, I will tell you all about the beautiful day. A whole series of similar feasts lie ahead this summer: on Corpus Christi, June 20,[1] Sr. Maria <née Ernst> is to make her Profession; on July 7, our postulant Maria[2] will receive the habit; on the Feast [of Our Lady of] Mount Carmel, our Sr. Monika[3] will make her Perpetual Profession and on July 28, have her Veiling, again a big public feast. Surely you will want to participate in all of them in spirit.

Of course, I think of you daily. I am glad that you have found inner peace and resignation to God's holy will. That is what I beg for you and all your companions in suffering, out there.

By now your first school experiences are behind you. There will be many difficulties connected with [your work]. But surely you will be able to effect much good also. That will require more wisdom and prudence than would be needed in a parochial school,[4] but there is always a way. Above all, pray for the guidance of the Holy Spirit. In this lovely time between Easter and Pentecost one must persevere in asking for a generous outpouring. Then it will surely come. And the Mother of God is the best patron for the education of girls. The less you are permitted to talk about [a spiritual orientation], the more you must carry [it], in your heart, into every school period.

All good wishes and best regards to Fräulein Lieb[5] as well, when you have an opportunity to pass them on.

In caritate Christi, your Sister
Teresa Benedicta a Cruce, OCD

1. [The German version has June 30 here but the Feast of Corpus Christi in 1935 was on June 20.]
2. Maria Pohl, Sr. Maria Baptista de Spiritu Sancto OCD (b. Cologne, 1905). [Maria Pohl attended Edith's Clothing ceremony while she was waiting to enter Carmel.]
3. Maria Hemmes, Sr. Maria Monika a Divino Amore OCD (b. Koblenz, 1905).
4. [Because of Nazi regulations that restricted teachers greatly.]
5. See Letter 150.

201. Letter to Hedwig Conrad-Martius, Bergzabern

Original in Convent Archive of Cologne Carmel; first published, *Kösel Verlag,* Munich 1960

Pax Christi! Cologne-Lindenthal, May 21, 1935

My dear Hatti,

Although I am afraid you are not feeling better yet, I must come to you today to ask a favor. For the past few days our Father Provincial <Theodor Rauch> was here with us and he has given me the task of preparing *Akt und Potenz [Act and Potency]*[1] for publication. Of course, I took it out at once and have begun to review it. At first I found little that needed to be changed. But I know well that the final portions will need much revision. Above all—as I have always told you—the discussion of your *Metaphysische Gespräche [Metaphysical Discourses]* cannot remain as it is. At the time [I wrote it] I had no choice but to leave it as is, since there was nothing else available from you concerning these questions. Now I would have to use *Seinsstufen [Degrees of Being]* and the book on plants as a basis. I would be most grateful if you could send me both as soon as possible. Obviously your opinion would be most valuable. But I do not want to bother you with that now that you are not feeling well. Surely Autós <Theodor Conrad> will send the package as a favor to you and me.

Have I actually already sent you the review of the 25th [section of the] Thomas volume? In the meantime, those of the 2nd and 5th[2] have also appeared but I have no copies of them for distribution as yet.

With cordial wishes and greetings, your sister
Benedicta

1. See Letter 189.
2. Appeared in *Die Christliche Frau [The Christian Woman]*, Münster, 1934-1935.

202. Letter to Elly Dursy,[1] Hallgarten
Original in Convent Archive of Waldfrieden Carmel

J.M.

Pax Christi! Cologne-Lindenthal, June 14, 1935
Dear Elly,

Sincere thanks for many good wishes: for my name day, at Easter and at Pentecost. Yes, I have allowed a lot to accumulate. Despite that, the first thing I have to do is give you a lecture for having "simple" thoughts—in truth they are probably due to too little simplicity. Don't you have any idea what Carmel is like? I have never been forbidden to write to you. But I have been given the general directive to limit myself to what is most necessary. That is according to our holy Rule and the Constitutions of our holy Mother <Teresa of Avila>. Besides that, it is practically impossible to answer all the letters that come to me. That is why I was so happy that I could let you know so much through Kläre <Grass>.[2]

Now, first, concerning the question about the test. My advice to repeat it rested on the assumption that its result was decisive for getting the job. If that is not the case, forget it. You can spend the time more beneficially than in this useless studying. However, you should personally inquire, perhaps from the Speyer government officials, how significant the test results are. Otherwise the next school superintendent will tell you something else again. That candidates rarely repeat the exam is no reason against doing so. According to all I've heard so far, it is a far from rare occurrence. If you consider it a humiliation—then, for a candidate for the religious life—that ought to argue for, not against it.

Now, to the animal soul. The spirit-soul relationship is most difficult. I wrote a long article about it (in the fifth volume of Husserl's *Jahrbuch)*, but in no way did it offer a solution for all the difficulties. Here I can give you only a brief indication about the scholastic conception—in conjunction with Aristotle. The soul is the life principle, differing in plant, animal and human being. The higher souls perform all the functions that the lower ones carry out, plus their own individual ones. Therefore the human spirit-soul is at the same time the principle of the vegetative, animal and spiritual life. There are beautiful things about this contained in Hedwig Conrad-Martius's *Metaphysische Gespräche [Metaphysical Discourses,* published in] (Halle, 1921). Besides that, last year she wrote a small book about the plant soul (published by Borgmeyer, Breslau). A lower form of the act of understanding is probably to be ascribed to the animal—but not a real act of thinking, which, like the will, is free. But in no way can you deny them feeling, though naturally in a muted form, but even so an almost frightening mirror of ours. (N.B. Such questions I can probably answer for you sometime, but since information about them can be found elsewhere, of themselves, they are not a sufficient reason for a letter.)

When you associate with your young [male] colleague, do you think of the experiences in your last job before [you joined] the FAD *[Freiwilliger Arbeitsdienst]*?[3]

You told me very little about your inner life. I believe, if you are calm and satisfied, it cannot be in a bad way. It will probably be much easier on both parties to talk about such matters in person. You need not fear that I might leave here soon. Our Most Rev. Father Provincial <Theodore Rauch> is little inclined to send me to [the Carmel in] Silesia because he is eager to have me do some scholarly work, and it would be very difficult to arrange for it there. Besides, the house there is not ready as yet.

Now, if you go to Neuburg or write there, I would like to ask you, please, to thank good P. Peter <Jans, OSB>[4] most cordially for his greetings and the beautiful holy cards. His kindness meant a great deal to me. The intentions he commended to me belonged, even before his request, to my most urgent ones. I ask him to pray for Herr and Frau Dr. Spiegel[5] very specially now. You, too, please help along a bit. Besides that I ask anew for prayers for my relatives. My dear mother lost two brothers during the past year. It is always one blow after another.

In sincere remembrance, your

Sister Teresa Benedicta a Cruce, OCD

1. Elly Dursy (later Sr. Maria Elizabeth a Div. Providentia, OCD) (b. Lambrecht/Pfalz, 1910) was a student of Edith Stein's at the teachers college of St. Magdalena, Speyer. In 1938, she entered the Carmel of Kordel, which later moved to Waldfrieden/Auderath. See Letter 112. [The first paragraph's "lecture you" fails to express in English the same affectionate yet serious rebuke of the German *"muss ich Dir jetzt gleich den Kopf waschen,"* which literally would be "I have to give you a shampoo."]
2. Kläre Grass, a student of Edith Stein's at St. Magdalena's, the Dominican Sisters' teachers college in Speyer.
3. [The FAD *(Freiwilliger Arbeitsdienst)* [Volunteer Labor Force] was created by the Nazis, who made it obligatory for all youths between the ages of 18 to 25 to serve for six months; it was also the pre-military training program. Despite its name, there was nothing voluntary about the service.]
4. See Letter 104.
5. See Letter 151. Dr. Siegfried Spiegel, jurist (b. Tauberbischofsheim, 1897; d. Cologne, 1965) also converted to Catholicism in his later years.

203. Letter to Ruth Kantorowicz (Hamburg)

Original in Convent Archive of Cologne Carmel

J.M.

Pax Christi! Cologne-Lindenthal, June 21, 1935

Dear Fräulein Ruth,

In order to relieve the Hamburg book famine I have asked our dear Mother <Prioress> for permission to lend you (Matthias Scheeben's) *Mysterien des Christentums [Mysteries of Christianity].* You can take your time working your way through it. Should I need it, against all expectations, before you return it on your own, I would let you know. If you have finished the novel on St. Francis you might try to get the *Little*

Flowers of St. Francis of Assisi. That *has* to be available even now, surely in the Borromaeus Library, but possibly also in the public libraries since it is a "Pearl of World Literature" and has been printed by different non-Catholic publishing firms. Perhaps P. Joppen would lend you Meschler's *Das Kirchenjahr [The Church Year]* as a preparation for your Confirmation. It contains a very beautiful meditation for Pentecost on the Holy Spirit, a brief extract from the big book. And, speaking of Confirmation, I wanted to tell you that that is another opportunity for taking a new name. Since you missed doing so at your baptism, how about choosing "Maria"?

You will not mind if I enclose a small parcel for my sister <Else Gordon> in your package, and ask you please to bring it to her for the 29th (her birthday). I thought you would prefer me to do it this way rather than the other way around. And, for the sake of holy poverty, one has to avoid double postage. When you have a chance, you can bring us the tin foil. But I believe you could also find use for it with the Sisters in Hamburg. Most convents collect it for the missions. Stamps, as well—in fact, all of them, even the "ordinary" ones because there are always other countries where they are extraordinary.

What has happened to your aunt? Did they risk an operation?

Anni <Gordon> wrote to say she wants to rest up at home in autumn. Then you must try, unobtrusively, to talk to her alone sometime. You would find an entirely different understanding in her than in Ilse <Gordon, Anni's sister>. I believe she [Anni] yearns for something of a religious nature. I would like to write to her sometime, but there is never enough time to do so.

All the best for the future! In the love of Christ, your

Sister Teresa Benedicta a Cruce, OCD

204. Letter to Mother Petra Brüning, OSU, Dorsten

Original in Convent Archive of Ursuline Sisters, Dorsten

J.M.

Pax Christi! Cologne-Lindenthal, June 23, 1935

Very Reverend and dear Mother Petra,

We are preparing for the Feast of St. John [the Baptist, June 24] but I am already thinking of your beautiful big Feast Day [St. Peter, June 29] and would like to anticipate and send my greetings and warmest wishes today since I can write in greater peace on Sunday than during the week. We will be celebrating with you in great love and gratitude and will remember all your intentions. The burden is surely particularly heavy at this time, and only faith as strong as a rock is capable of carrying it. For the first time, in the past months I have been using the Acts of the Apostles for meditation, and now I am at the Epistles. Therefore I will be celebrating this double feast with a particular love for the two firm pillars of our holy Church. What an immeasurable treasure trove we have in Holy Scripture.

On the 30th we will have another special feast: the Clothing of our postulant Maria (Pohl). She will be called Maria Baptista of the Holy Spirit. Her vocation grew out of great suffering, and, more, she had to undergo a particular trial during her postulancy. Perhaps I can tell you about that some time. Please help with some prayers.

I also ask for your prayerful help for myself. For some weeks I have returned to philosophical work and have a big task ahead for which I lack much, very much, of what is necessary to accomplish it.[1] Were I not able to trust in the blessing of holy obedience and in the knowledge that the Lord can accomplish something through a totally weak and incapable tool when he wishes to do so, I would have to give up the race. So now I do what I can, and allow myself to recoup courage before the tabernacle when it has been crushed by the erudition of other people.

In the past weeks I have had the examination schedule of your little daughter Bernardine[2] before me on my desk, since she called on me as a helper in distress. Hopefully, she made it all right.

Again, all cordial wishes for you and your large family. In grateful love, your least Sister

Teresa Benedicta a Cruce, OCD

1. See Letters 189 and 201.
2. [Bernardine Westup (b. May 22, 1899; d. Dorsten, November 11, 1969) member of the Ursuline Community in Dorsten.]

205. Letter to Hedwig Conrad-Martius, Bergzabern
Original in Convent Archive of Cologne Carmel; first published, *Kösel Verlag,* Munich 1960

J.M.

Pax Christi! Cologne-Lindenthal, July 9, 1935
Dear Hatti,

I have kept postponing my thanks for your dear card and for the book on plants because I have been unable so far to study it. I was stuck in the first part of my manuscript[1] and, to get on with it, I urgently needed to consult other sources, particularly Aristotle and Thomas. The bibliography, however, made me aware that I have never seen the article on substance and soul that you wrote for *Recherches,*[2] and I need it badly. I did not want to bother you a second time and therefore I inquired first from Koyré.[3] He was going to see whether he still had the manuscript, but evidently he has not found it so far. He did send me other things that are most useful. Would you have another copy to give out, even if only on loan?

Probably very little of my manuscript will remain, for I now find it completely inadequate. So your not reading it saved you time. I hope I will succeed in producing something better in its place. In my case also, care has to be taken that Brother Ass[4] does not prematurely withhold further service. You still do not know what is wrong with you? I hope Dr. Sieben[5] is making every effort to find the trouble. Has your goiter operation helped at all?

Were you to come to our speakroom now, there would be plenty to talk about. Do you still remember how we sat together on the sofa in Speyer, having been told to discuss some financial matters, and instead, we got involved in philosophizing? And we were reprimanded by Autós <Theodor Conrad>. It appears he wants to have nothing to do with Sister Benedicta. But she refuses to let that keep her from thinking of him.

Again, with cordial thanks, many good wishes, and a faithful remembrance, your

Benedicta

1. See Letters 189 and 201.
2. The article *L'existence, la substantialité et l'âme* in *Recherches Philosophiques* (Paris, 1932-33).
3. See footnote to Letter 116.

4. ["Brother Ass" is the name given in Franciscan writings to the body that balks at times, through fatigue, for example, at tasks the soul undertakes. Here Edith makes an indirect reference to her own health.]
5. Family doctor of the Conrad-Martiuses.

206. Letter to Mother Petra Brüning, OSU, Dorsten

Original in Convent Archive of the Ursulines, Dorsten

[Pax Christi!] Cologne-Lindenthal, July 16, 1935

Dear Reverend Mother,

I have used the Feast Day[1] to write down these sparse words for you.[2] During the week such a thing is no longer possible. Work demands every available bit of time.

Cordial thanks for your kind letter and the generous feast-day gift. Mother Sub-Prioress <Teresia Renata> will surely inform you how it was used. I must correct a slight error: I will receive the black veil only three years from now. The photograph I enclosed in the last letter was of Rembrandt's Sibyl. You do understand, don't you, why I write so briefly today and that I prefer taking your intentions to the Choir for a while?

Yours with faithful remembrance always
Sr. Teresa Benedicta a Cruce, OCD

Reflections on the Mass and Divine Office

The two belong together, inseparably. The holy sacrifice of the Mass is one sacrifice in which all earlier sacrifices, which prefigured it, are fulfilled, made present and effective. It is the sacrifice for sins that sinful humanity offers through its High Priest, in order to obtain absolution and admission before the Face of God. It is the sacrifice of peace in which the forgiven ones are invited to the sacrificial banquet. It is the complete sacrifice in which Christ as head of humanity and king of creation surrenders himself and all that is created to the Divinity and highest Sovereignty.

That is the *rite* of the offering. The *songs* of offering give it expression and accompany it. The *psalms,* insofar as they are a cry from the depths, speak of petition for forgiveness. The *hymns* and jubilant psalms are songs of joy at the Wedding Feast. The *Sanctus* and, above all, the *Te Deum* are the adoration, the combined heavenly and earthly liturgy in praise and homage of the Most Holy by the entire creation.

Many thoughts are inspired by Erik Peterson's[3] book on the angels, which probably contains what is most decisive and profound on the subject.

1. [July 16 is the Feast of Our Lady of Mount Carmel.]
2. In answer to Mother Petra's request for some reflections on the Sacrifice of the Mass and on the Divine Office.
3. See Letter 196.

207. Letter to Ruth Kantorowicz, Hamburg

Original in Convent Archive of Cologne Carmel

J.M.

Pax Christi! Cologne-Lindenthal, August 6, 1935

Dear Fräulein Ruth,

For a long time it has been impossible for me to answer you. Meanwhile, your plan to come to Cologne has solidified. God's blessing on it. I too believe it will mean a great deal to you to live in Catholic surroundings. And since you already feel so much at home in Cologne, it is, after all, the most obvious choice. But it will certainly be difficult to find a job here. However, I think it probable that the ladies in the Women's League will sometimes be able to recommend you for occasional work. That would provide for small extra earnings so that your capital would not be used up too quickly. Just remain ever happy in the certain belief that God is already busily at work, building your nest for you. I no longer consider it likely that it will be with [the Sisters] at Nonnenwerth.[1] One gets the impression that the intimate bond has been broken. Perhaps what was so attractive to you a few months ago no longer finds the same receptive response in you because, in the meantime, some things have changed within you. It is good to allow things to take their course.

For the feast of Mount Carmel we have not only a proper festive Mass, but a vigil Mass as well. The proper Masses for the Carmelite Order have been published by the *Scapulier Verlag* of Linz [Austria] as a supplement to the missal.

August 7—If you visited the Gordons <family of Else Gordon> lately, you may have heard that I am busy again with philosophical work.

Therefore, I have hardly any time to write letters. So I ask you to have patience and indulgence if I write briefly and make you wait. Best regards to my relatives when you see them. But don't make a special visit!

All the best to you, your
Sister Teresa Benedicta a Cruce, OCD

1. [The reference here is to Franciscan Sisters whose motherhouse was at Nonnenwerth, an island in the Rhine.]

208. Letter to Karl and Katharina Lichtenberger,[1] Ludwigshafen
Original in Convent Archive of Cologne Carmel

J.M.

Pax Christi! Cologne-Lindenthal, August 7, 1935

Dear Frau and Herr Lichtenberger,

Yesterday I received the memorial [card] of our dear Anneliese, forwarded by Sister Agnella <Stadtmüller>. Thank you for it! It is such a dear and true picture. I received the announcement of her death a good while ago from St. Magdalena's. I must say that it was a comfort for me to know that your beloved child was released from her lengthy suffering and is now in the peace of the Lord. Of course it is very hard for both of you, but surely it was even harder to watch her suffering. I have been remembering Anneliese daily at Mass for years and will not forget her now. But I am confident that she hardly needs the help of our prayers any longer. You know well how much I always valued the purity of her convictions. What might have seemed a deficiency in human eyes—her reserve and her excessive anxiety—surely weighed very little in God's sight.

Kläre Grass, who visited me in March, was the last one who told me about Anneliese, and she probably brought her my greetings after the visit. Kläre thought that [Anneliese] stopped writing letters because she was afraid they might spread the germs of her disease. Now she is with God, and it is far more beautiful there than in her own native forest for which she always was so homesick. And she will ask for her beloved parents the grace to be happy with her.[2]

In sincere remembrance, your
Sister Teresa Benedicta a Cruce, OCD

1. Karl Lichtenberger (b. Germersheim, 1880; d. Ludwigshafen, 1956); Katharina Lichtenberger (b. Germersheim, 1880; d. Germersheim, 1964); parents of Anneliese Lichtenberger [See Letter 79, the first, and 148, the last from Edith to Anneliese.]
2. Edith Stein enclosed in this letter a holy card from Beuron showing an angel, and bearing the inscription *Pax aeterna* [Eternal Peace]. On the back, she wrote: "The souls of the just are in the hands of God. In the eyes of the foolish, they seem to have died, but they are in peace. E. St."

209. Letter to Gisela Naegeli, Zurich

Original in Convent Archive of Cologne Carmel

J.M.

Pax Christi! Cologne-Lindenthal, August 9, 1935

Dear Fräulein Naegeli,

Sincere thanks for the gift that was sent to us yesterday from Aachen. The article appeared on Laetare Sunday in the Saturday supplement of the *Augsburger Postzeitung.*[1] Unfortunately we received so few copies that it was impossible for me to send you one. But it will probably be printed, together with another article about Carmel, as a separate booklet. Then we will have more of those at our disposal.

In the meantime I have not forgotten you and your problem children. Again, sincere thanks and all good wishes from your

Sr. Teresa Benedicta a Cruce, OCD

1. The article printed in the *Augsburg Post* newspaper was *"Über Geschichte und Geist des Karmel"* ["On the History and Spirit of Carmel"] in the supplement, *Zu neuen Ufern [To New Shores]*, No. 13, March 31, 1935. [For an English translation, see *Hidden Life*, pp. 1-6.]

210. Letter to Gertrud von le Fort, Baierbrunn im Isartal

Original in the manuscript section of the German Literature Archive, Schiller-National Museum, Marbach a. N.

[Pax Christi!] Cologne-Lindenthal, <presumably late summer>, 1935

Dear Gertrud von le Fort,

When I received your dear letter of Ascension Day,[1] I would have been so glad to send you this photo[2] right away, since it is actually the first true bridal picture. But we had no copy of it at the time.

I hope you have not been waiting for a reply for Hedwig Michel. So far I have heard nothing from her. I know her through several articles. Naturally I would be delighted to have her visit. Besides, very close by is a friend of mine, also a convert from Judaism, who knows her family and would like very much to get to know her personally.

Is it true that you intend, again, to give a lecture in Breslau? My sister Rosa wrote to me about it and would surely be very happy to have a few words with you at that time. Will you please let me know where you would be staying in Breslau? You will no doubt remember our address (Michaelisstrasse 38). I hardly dare to make the request that you look up my mother since, at the present, she is most unwilling to talk about me. A dear acquaintance of mine from Münster[3] who recently took greetings from me to my relatives was very unhappy afterward because she was afraid she had done something wrong. My mother received her in a most friendly way, but absolutely refused to hear anything about Cologne. I would not want to expose you to such [a reception].

May I ask whether the *sponsa Christi* will appear in your major work for the sake of which you have long wanted to come to the Rhineland? Or is it to be something else entirely? This is now the third autumn that we've hoped would bring us together. Perhaps you will be able to come for the feast of either the great or the little Teresa. Only you would have to make sure that you could also spend at least one quiet working day. Otherwise, you would not have a true picture [of the Carmelite day].

In *caritate Christi,* your
Teresa Benedicta a Cruce, OCD

1. [The Feast of the Ascension was on May 30 in 1935.]
2. [It was a photograph of Edith on her First Profession Day.]
3. [Margaret Günther.]

211. Letter to Ruth Kantorowicz, Cologne

Original in Convent Archive of Cologne Carmel

Pax Christi! Cologne-Lindenthal, September 12, 1935

Dear Fräulein Ruth,

Here comes some work! It's not the whole of it—a little more than thirty pages will follow. Please make two carbon copies. (Also) please omit what you find in square brackets. The beginning is at the pencil line on the first pages. After the pencil mark on page 580 there is a lengthy omission that can probably be indicated by a series of dashes.[1]

In advance, heartfelt thanks and many good wishes, your

Sr. Teresa Benedicta a Cruce, OCD

[P.S.] Early Saturday <on September 14, the Feast of the Exaltation of the Cross> we will have our Renewal of Vows in common (and excluding the public).

1. See Letter 181. A supplementary remark: Ruth Kantorowicz continued to type, in grateful love, with extraordinary understanding, thousands of pages of manuscript for Edith Stein to the very last days. She was familiar with Edith Stein's handwriting and the often unclear phrasing of the text because of insertions, footnotes, etc. Beyond the grave that has no gravestone, the thanks of all of us go out to Ruth Kantorowicz, this quiet, frail, highly gifted friend of Edith Stein's. Her copies often made possible the reconstruction of destroyed, damaged, or incomplete manuscripts and proved to be an indispensable help in deciphering blurred or yellowed manuscript pages. [See *Life,* p. 12.]

212. Letter to Sr. Adelgundis Jaegerschmidt OSB, Freiburg-Günterstal

Original in Convent Archive of Benedictine Sisters, St. Lioba, Freiburg-Günterstal

J.M.

Pax Christi! Cologne-Lindenthal, November 2, 1935

Dear Sister Adelgundis,

In all haste, we are doing our best to fulfill your wish. We cannot recall any quotation of our Holy Mother (St. Teresa of Avila) in which she literally directs one to read Holy Scripture. She refers one to the Gospels only in Chapter 22 of her *Life,* in which she states that occupying oneself with the Humanity of Christ is the means to reach the most sublime contemplation, and earnestly warns one never to abandon it.[1] And her *Meditations on the Love of God* [2] are an exposition of the Song of Songs. Our Holy Father John [of the Cross] on the other hand, educates us to read the Scriptures. He is said to have had, at the end, only the New Testament in his cell.

You can see the fruits in the quotations we copied out for you from [the writings of] the two saintly Carmelite nuns.[3] These two alone would give rich material for your essay, for their entire life in the Order was a translation of Sacred Scripture into life. But surely you will not want to allow Carmel to have the only word. It would be a good idea to take the books along as reading material on your trip. You get an entirely different impression (from reading them) than from a few passages copied out for you.

We could have added much more. But, first, we assume you prefer not to have too much from which to choose, and, second, we have had to steal time from our work.

Without the advice and assistance of a generous Sister here, I probably would have been unable to help you. Philosophy is taking almost all my time outside of prayer. Sister Maria Angela <Schwalge> is also sending you the booklet she translated. She was in a Belgian Carmel for 15 years, and translates a great deal from the French.

To you, to Sister Placida <Laubhardt>,[4] to Reverend Mother Prioress and to Countess Bissingen,[5] in great haste, sincere greetings and blessings for all your work. Your Sister

Teresa Benedicta a Cruce, OCD

1. In fact, St. Teresa of Avila constantly refers to Sacred Scripture in her writings. [Nevertheless, it would have been extraordinary for Teresa to tell the nuns to *read Scripture* directly, when vernacular editions were forbidden and neither Teresa nor most of her nuns could read Latin. Despite that, Teresa had a deep knowledge and love of Scripture, drawn primarily from spiritual books, sermons and conferences in which quotations from the Gospels, etc., were cited.]
2. [This is the title given to Teresa's *Meditations* in Volume IV of the German edition published by Pustet. It appears as *Meditations on the Song of Songs* in *The Collected Works of St. Teresa of Avila,* trans. Kieran Kavanaugh and Otilio Rodriguez, vol. 2 (Washington, DC: ICS Publications, 1980).
3. [This description is eminently applicable to St. Thérèse of Lisieux and Saint Teresa Margaret Redi, about whom the Cologne Carmel distributed literature.]
4. See Letter 51.
5. See Letters 57 and 166.

213. Letter to Hedwig Conrad-Martius, Bergzabern

Original in Convent Archive of Cologne Carmel; first published, *Kösel Verlag,* Munich 1960

Pax Christi! Cologne-Lindenthal, November 17, 1935

My dear Hatti,

A letter has been intended for you for a long time. Now it will be finished, after all, before Advent. It was a wonderful gift for my feast day [October 15] to learn that you are well again, or at least significantly better.

When you wrote, I had just demanded the return of the book on plants from Paris: Koyré, the rascal, had smuggled it away! Did you know that he and Do <his wife> were here in August? I was very happy about it and got a lot of benefit from it; I gave him the first chapter of the big opus[1] to read, and he encouraged me to continue the work. That was really necessary since this kind of project is not easy to fit into the frame of our life and demands many a sacrifice, not only from me but also from my dear Sisters in the community. And that is something you don't want to take advantage of if it is not warranted.

I worked through both your manuscript and the plant book[2] a long while ago, each at the time when I had to struggle with similar questions in my work. We are very close on the subject. On the whole, though, I seem to be more Platonic and more Augustinian than you, perhaps precisely because I proceed from Aristotle-Thomas. What I say about substance resulted from a tough wrestling to understand the Aristotelian *ousia* [substance]. Essentially I owe the whole breakthrough from the first draft to the second to my work with Aristotle.

Your anthropology will of course be very important for me, too.[3] Were it possible, I would advise you not to divide it into "popular" texts, nor to add reference notes as in the plant book, but to structure all of it as one entity. Hopefully they will allow you enough space to do that.

I believe you would be pleased to read Gertrud von le Fort's book, *Die ewige Frau [The Eternal Woman]* (Kösel, 1934, surely available through the state library). It has three sections: *Die Ewige Frau, Die Frau der Zeit, Die Zeitlose Frau* [The Eternal Woman, Woman in Time, The Timeless Woman]. The final [section] is [on] the mother. And you would make Gertrud von le Fort very happy were you to send her the plant book; you will notice yourself how much the two belong together. After all, at my very first meeting with Gertrud von le Fort I found a strong affinity with you. It would be wonderful if the two of you got in touch. She lives in Baierbrunn in the Isar Valley, Haus Konradshöhe.

For me, it would be a gift from heaven if you were able to come here sometime. There would be so much to discuss. When the time comes for that, the Lord will surely arrange it as he does everything. Autós <Theodor Conrad> also seems to be thinking of a visit. That made me very happy. Probably he would be more displeased with the grate than you, but he would soon become accustomed to it.

Please pray for my loved ones at home. Difficulties are constantly increasing for them. Three nephews have already gone to America; one is getting ready to go to Palestine. That leaves only the youngest, who is thirteen[4]; he is to have his Bar Mitzvah on the 23rd: that means that as a "Son of the Law" he takes his place in the community.

In Christ's love, your Sister
Benedicta

1. Edith's philosophical work, *Endliches und Ewiges Sein [Finite and Eternal Being].*
2. See Letter 201.
3. Three lectures—*Der Mensch in der heutigen Naturwissenschaft und Philosophie* [Man in Today's Natural Science and Philosophy]—appeared in *Schildgenossen* (Rothenfels, 1935-1936).
4. Ernst Ludwig Biberstein, b. 1922.

214. Letter to Elizabeth Nicola and Helene Lieb, Düsseldorf[1]
Original in Convent Archive of Cologne Carmel

J.M.

[Pax Christi!] Cologne-Lindenthal, December 20, 1935

Dear Fräulein Nicola, dear Fräulein Lieb,

Our dear Mother has commissioned me to express to the two Carmelite children in exile our most sincere good wishes for a blessed Christmas, and at the same time our thanks for your greetings on the Feast of Holy Mother[2] and for the beginning of Advent.

A Christmas letter is hardly suitable for answering Fräulein Nicola's shop-talk questions. But that's the way it must be, and so I will take care of them right at the start. Catholic psychology and pedagogy is, after all, the unfinished business of the Münster Institute.[3] They have little to offer so far. However, there is the Institute's large *Lexikon der Pädagogik [Lexicon of Pedagogy];* I think that will be available to you at the Catholic School Organization at Reichsstrasse 20 if nowhere else. The same holds for those volumes of the *Handbuch der Erziehungswissenschaft [Handbook of Pedagogy]* that have appeared so far. In the *Lexikon* you will find a short reference and bibliographic data on every individual question. Of the *Handbuch* I would recommend particularly Volume 1 *(Jugendbildung*

[Education of Youth] by Eggersdorffer). It is a true attempt to build on a Cath-olic foundation and from that basis to evaluate modern trends without bias. For psychology you might want, as an introduction, Alois Fischer's[4] *Entwicklung, Gegenwartsstand und pädagogische Bedeutung der psychologischen Jugendforschung [Development, Present Status, and Pedagogical Significance of Psychological Research Concerning Youth]*. It was published by the *Zentralinstitut fur Erziehung und Unterricht* [Central Institute for Education and Instruction], 1926. For pedagogy, the writings of Otto Will-mann. Then, I found the Montessori literature very significant and, in any case, suitable for a Catholic application. (For you, the most important: *Montessori Education for School Children.)* The Catholic School Organization will surely be glad to give you personal information. You might introduce yourself to Pater Schröteler, SJ, by conveying my greetings to him.

Now enough of that. We would be very happy were you to manage to come here sometime after Christmas. Then you would probably gain renewed courage to endure the trial of your patience imposed by the long wait. For us, it is not convenient until after the 28th because we have the feastday schedule for four days and, so, little time for the speak-room. But those are days when you too will have to be with your families.

If you should still see Frau Dülberg, please give her cordial Christmas greetings also. We will do better to talk about that subject in person.

Two of our Sisters, unfortunately, will not be able to celebrate Christmas with us. I commend them, specially, to your prayers. Sr. Ursula [Klefisch] had an operation several months ago and then had to go away to recuperate. Our dear oldest Sister <Theresa> [of St. Joseph] has had the grippe for two weeks and is bedridden at home, so it will be a while before she can come to choir again.

Now, once more, I wish you so much grace at Christmas that even a Carmelite Christmas could not bring you more. After all, the Savior is everywhere with his love and his inexhaustible riches.

In that love, greetings from your Sister
Teresa Benedicta a Cruce, OCD

[P.S.] The new Carmel in Breslau-Pawelwitz was dedicated on December 8.[5]

1. See Letter 150.
2. The feast of St. Teresa of Avila on October 15.
3. *Deutsches Institut für wissenschaftliche Pädagogik* [The German Institute for Scientific Pedagogy], Münster.
4. [Alois Fischer (b. Furth/Bavaria, 1880; d. Munich, 1937) philosopher and pedagogue. From 1914 on he was professor in Munich. He developed a far-reaching theory of education and formation by including psychology and sociology.]
5. [This Carmel did not remain in Breslau long. The Nazis confiscated the monastery on June 4, 1941, and the nuns were forced to seek refuge in other Carmels. In 1952 they were able to lay the cornerstone for their own monastery in Witten, Diocese of Paderborn. It is noteworthy that in the Carmel of Witten are six nuns who are natives of Breslau, five of them professed after 1947.]

215. Postcard (Christmas-relief from Maria Laach) to Karl and Katharina Lichtenberger, Ludwigshafen
Original in Convent Archive of Cologne Carmel

Pax Christi! Cologne-Lindenthal, Christmas, 1935

With cordial gratitude I return all your dear greetings and wishes for the Feast. I remain united with you in the remembrance of your beloved Anneliese.

In Christ's love, your
Sr. Teresa Benedicta a Cruce, OCD

216. Letter to Prelate Martin Grabmann,[1] Eichstätt
Original in Convent Archive of Cologne Carmel

J.M.
Pax Christi! Cologne-Lindenthal, February 2, 1936
Very Reverend Prelate,

Because of the enclosed card,[2] our dear Reverend Mother Prioress (that is, since January 10, the former Subprioress <Teresa Renata de Spiritu Sancto>) has requested me to "give you a friendly reminder" of your promise to write a preface to her book <*Die siebenfache Gabe*> *[The Sevenfold Gift]*. We would be most grateful if you could steal some time from your other work to write it.

For me, this task is a welcome opportunity to ask you once more for your prayers and your blessing. Six months ago I began working on the new draft of *Akt und Potenz [Act and Potency]* and am still at it. It is a complete revision. Its new name is to be *Endliches und Ewiges Sein [Finite and Eternal Being]*. The book is to appear in Pustet's series *Christliches Denken [Christian Thought]*.[3] But a great deal of support from the Holy Spirit is needed to bring it to completion.

I remember your work and your intentions faithfully. The young student (a Fräulein von Stein) who visits me from time to time told me once of the difficulties you have teaching.

With respectful greetings, humbly yours *in Christo,*
Sister Teresa Benedicta a Cruce OCD

1. Martin Grabmann (b. Winterzhofen/Bavaria, 1875; d. Eichstätt/Bavaria, 1949) Prelate, professor of Christian philosophy in Vienna and Munich. [In February 1931, Prelate Grabmann wrote a six-page introduction for Edith's translation of Thomas Aquinas, published as Vol. III in *Edith Steins Werke*.]
2. [The card mentioned is not identified. It could be acceptance of the Prioress's manuscript by a publisher.]
3. Although Edith Stein completed the work it was not published in her lifetime. [Pustet did not follow through because of the ban on works by persons with Jewish ancestry.] It was finally published as Vol. II of *Edith Steins Werke* in 1950. See also Letters 248 and 257.

217. Letter to Helene Lieb and Elizabeth Nicola, Düsseldorf
Original in Convent Archive of Cologne Carmel

J.M.

Pax Christi! Cologne-Lindenthal, February 24, 1936

Dear little Sisters in exile,

Actually this is an answer to Fräulein Nicola, but I would not wish to raise another big fuss with it. Therefore it will go to Fräulein Lieb and she will have a slight profit from it.

We wish you both a most blessed Lent and great Easter joy. Consider Holy Mass in the morning, with its beautiful Lenten liturgy, as the highlight of the day, and the rest of it as a daily small sacrifice of thanksgiving. Then the time will pass well and quickly.

It would be good if, after Easter, you could come here once in a while. I believe Fräulein Lieb was here before our elections. Then you do not yet know of the changes in Carmel. Mother Teresa Renata is now our Prioress. Mother Josepha is her successor as Novice Mistress and is at the same time turn-Sister,[1] since the former turn-Sister Aloysia[2] became Subprioress. Your letters, however, reach their goal just the same.

With a plea for your prayers for me and mine, and for our entire Carmelite family, in faithful remembrance, your Sister

Teresa Benedicta a Cruce, OCD

1. [This office in Carmel meant having charge of the "turn," where the extern Sister delivered messages and donations received from visitors to the monastery. The turn sister also accompanied workmen on their assignments within the cloister.]
2. Angela Linke (Sr. Maria Aloysia a Ss. Sacramento, OCD) (b. Schlabitz/Silesia, 1893; d. Cologne, 1967) was elected Subprioress in 1936.

218. Letter to Elly Dursy, Hallgarten
Original in Convent Archive of Waldfrieden Carmel

J.M.

Pax Christi! Cologne-Lindenthal, February 26, 1936
Ash Wednesday

Dear Elly,

You can probably put this eternal question to rest only by way of obedience. So, write down, once more, all the pros and cons for P.P. <presumably, Pater Peter Jans, OSB>. I would include among the cons your stronger attraction to an interior life, and ask him to answer yes or no. And when you have that, then say *Deo gratias!* and give no more thought to the matter.

I am in no hurry for the books. I am satisfied that they are on the way. They would still be on time if you brought them along at Pentecost.

More than this, you won't get in this Lenten letter—so that *"servare ordinem"* <keep the Rule> does not merely hang on the wall.[1]

Cordial wishes for many blessings during the entire holy season to you and to Ännchen <Dursy>.[2] Please pray particularly for my relatives; at present they are especially in need of it.

In *caritate Christi,* your
Sister Teresa Benedicta a Cruce, OCD

1. [In many Carmelite monasteries, plaques bearing such mottoes are hung in corridors or stairwells.]
2. Ännchen Dursy (b. Lambrecht/Pfalz, 1912) catechist; younger sister of Elly Dursy (Sr. Mary Elizabeth of Divine Providence, OCD). See Letter 202.

219. Letter to Mother Petra Brüning, OSU, Dorsten
Original in Convent Archive of Ursuline Sisters, Dorsten

J.M.

Pax Christi! Cologne-Lindenthal, March 24, 1936

Dear Reverend Mother,

We do not want to delay our thanks for all the goodness you have again shown us. I am always moved anew when I am allowed to unpack the beautiful parcels with our dear Mother <Teresa Renata>. They are put together with so much care that one would never believe you have such a large religious family of your own as well as a whole series of institutions to provide for. But in a truly maternal heart there is room for any number of adopted children. That I experienced already at home. Now I always have the feeling that you are doing for me what my own mother would do, had she an understanding of our life. For the present we are just very grateful that she has come far enough to write "Greetings to all."

On the vigil of the Feast of St. Joseph we congratulated Mother Josepha, and on the lovely little baroque altar in the novitiate we piled up all the gifts, which naturally included the delicious little masterpieces of your kitchen-artiste. Belatedly, we celebrated the name day with an afternoon coffee on Laetare Sunday—also in the novitiate. Each of the six guests found one of those little masterpieces at her place and took it happily along [when they left]. The guests were our four mothers and the two eldest of the Sisters. We do actually have four mothers[1] now: "Reverend" Mother <the Prioress>, Mother Subprioress (who is not now Mother Josepha),[2] Mother Josepha, and Mother Gabriele[3] who has returned home from Kordel [Carmel] because she now has a young successor as prioress there.

Many thanks also for the generous provision of dramatic literature. We want to put on part of *Metanoeite* for the profession of our Sister Baptista,[4] probably on the [feast of] the Visitation. She has a great devotion to [John] the Baptizer, so at the end of the play she will receive the book itself. I just copied a suitable part out of *Mutter der Himmel [Mother of Heaven]* for our Sister Margareta[5] who will make her final profession tomorrow. That is the young Westphalian who had the serious Basedow [thyroid] operation. She is much, much better now. She is the oldest of fourteen siblings and her youngest little sister is to receive her First Communion on Sister's Veiling Day (on Easter Tuesday).

How long may we keep the loaned books?

I gave P. Bonaventura's[6] lectures to Mother Josepha first, because she will soon begin the second half of her retreat (the first half preceded the feast). I will then follow on April 1, and will be allowed to spend all of Holy Week in silence. I commend both of us to your prayers and will, naturally, take you with me into these holy days. If the Lord wanted to give me a big gift, he would send P. Bonaventura to hear my confession at the end of the retreat. But during Holy Week that can hardly be expected. There will surely be other gifts instead.

With the wish that Holy Week and the Easter holidays be filled with graces for you and all for whom you care, I am, in grateful love, your

Sister Teresa Benedicta a Cruce, OCD

1. [In Carmel, before Vatican II, any Sister who held the office of Prioress was addressed as Mother from then on, even after her term as superior expired.]
2. See Letter 217.
3. Katharina Leuffen, Mother Maria Gabriele ab Annuntiatione, OCD (b. Rheydt/Rhineland, 1860; d. Cologne, 1936) entered the Carmel of Maastricht (Holland) in 1886. She participated in the refounding of the monasteries of Aachen (1894) and Cologne (1896). [The nuns of these Carmels had chosen expatriation and exile during the *Kulturkampf* (1875) under Bismarck in preference to secularization.] From 1923 to 1936, Mother Gabriele was Prioress in the Carmel of Kordel near Trier (now Waldfrieden near Auderath). Shortly before her death in 1936, she returned to the Carmel of Cologne.
4. See Letter 204.
5. See Letter 171.
6. Presumably Alois Rebstock, P. Bonaventura, OSB (b. Stuttgart, 1876; d. Gerleve Abbey, 1958).

220. Letter to Sr. Adelgundis Jaegerschmidt, OSB, Freiburg-Günterstal

Original in Convent Archive of Benedictine Sisters, St.Lioba, Freiburg-Günterstal

J.M.

Pax Christi! Cologne-Lindenthal, April 29, 1936

Dear Sister Adelgundis,

Thank you so much for the beautiful [edition] of the Epistle. We would be grateful if we could have several copies of it. Sister Maria Angela <Schwalge> is especially pleased with it and, in gratitude, will be glad to send you a few more of her translations.

When I received your kind letter you were probably already in Rapallo.[1] So now I know no other way than to write to you in care of St. Lioba's. I want so much to have my greetings reach the dear "Master" soon. We will support you with our prayers. I have great expectations for these coming weeks.

As far as not wearing a veil in the speakroom is concerned: when my visitors are "good Catholics" I always wear the veil because they are the ones who, I presume, are most apt to have an understanding of our life. And from whom should we expect assistance in keeping our Rule and Constitutions unmitigated if not from our "fellow Sisters" in religious life? For that reason I cannot support your request to my dear superiors. But that does not take away your right to address yourself directly to our dear Mother <Prioress>.[2]

In caritate Christi, your
Sister Benedicta

1. Edmund Husserl (see Letter 1), accompanied by his wife Malvine (see Letter 19) and Sr. Adelgundis, spent several weeks here recuperating from his first serious illness.
2. Until Vatican Council II, it was prescribed in Carmel to keep the veil lowered over the face [when receiving visitors other than immediate family] in the speakroom.

221. Letter to Mother Petra Brüning, OSU, Dorsten

Original in Convent Archive of Ursuline Sisters, Dorsten

J.M.

Pax Christi! Cologne-Lindenthal, Vigil of St. John the Baptist, 1936

Dear Reverend Mother,

At the beginning of this feast, my heartfelt wishes for your beautiful feast day! May it be one blessed with the fullness of the Holy Spirit and the love of the Heart of Jesus. It is such a grace-filled time. Yet at home, in the midst of this time, the Lord has knocked at my dear, good mother's door in order to prepare her for the journey into eternity. A few weeks ago she had a gallbladder attack, but apparently minor. Since then her powers have diminished rapidly. There were repeated attacks of weakness that finally caused real alarm. Today my sisters wrote that she is somewhat better. She can rest outdoors, and medication to strengthen her heart seems to be taking hold. But still we must consider that every day is a special gift. Only eight days ago, she herself wrote in a most loving way. She was always full of life and untiringly active. That's why the inability to do anything is worst for her. But my sister <Rosa> writes that she is cheerful, patient and very lively. I am very happy about that. It was my big intention for her that all the harshness and bitterness of the past years should disappear, and that peace might come.

I saved up the little book on virginity for your name day. I followed it through *in statu nascendi* (its state of inception) since Sister Maria Angela <Schwalge> often asked my advice about her choice of passages and I always thought, even then, that you would be particularly pleased with it.

Of the books we borrowed, we are able to return at least some with heartfelt thanks. *König David* [*King David*] is something very marvelous but, for us, very difficult to utilize. The first part of *Metanoeite* will be put on in celebration of Sister Maria Baptista <Pohl>'s First Profession, which will take place on the Feast of the Visitation. She will then receive the little book as a gift, and it will please her very much. She is now in retreat; I commend her to your prayers. Likewise, our postulant Annemarie, who will become Sister Isabella of the Holy Spirit on July 26.

I do not know whether Ruth Kantorowicz wrote you that she went to Maastricht and has been accepted by our Sisters as a postulant. She is to enter on the feast of the Transverberation of the Heart of our Holy Mo-ther (August 27). She went to M<aastricht> with very little hope, so the successful outcome has made us all the happier. We must now all continue to pray that her strength will hold up. There is no lack of good will and courage for sacrifice.

All your intentions and the great intentions of the church, which are common to us all, will be commended to the hearts of the great Apostles on their feast.

Always in grateful love, your least Sister,
Teresa Benedicta a Cruce, OCD

222. Letter to Mother Petra Brüning, OSU, Dorsten
Original in Convent Archive of Ursuline Sisters, Dorsten

J.M.

Pax Christi! Cologne-Lindenthal, July 19, 1936
Dear Reverend Mother,

Since we will be sending you a live greeting next week, I want to give [her] a few lines to take along as thanks for your loving wishes for the feast and the great kindness you are showing us through your gracious hospitality. The day before yesterday, Sister Maria Angela <Schwalge> took me along to the speakroom that I might tell her niece something about Dorsten. She is anticipating her vacation with much joy. I want to share with you some wishes she divulged to us, for you will surely be glad to know how you can keep the little one occupied. She would very much like to go swimming, and after meals she would like to rest, perhaps in the garden if that is possible. I know you will be glad to give her some books from your library. For everything else, I advised her to turn in all confidence to you.

My dear mother's condition has improved somewhat; that is, her heart has become stronger and therefore there is no acute danger, but we are pretty certain that there must be some internal illness present. There will be no radical examination as that would be unnecessary torture; an operation is no longer feasible. We must foresee a lengthy time of suffering. That is so hard. You write, dear Mother, that the Lord will credit to her her belief in the Messiah. If only she had it! Faith in the Messiah has nearly disappeared among today's Jews, even the believing ones. And, almost as much, the belief in eternal life. For that reason I was never able to make Mother comprehend either my conversion or my entrance into the Order. And so, once more, she is suffering greatly because of our separation, and I am unable to say anything that will comfort her. I have to write to her, but I can't say anything significant. I can only build on the childlike confidence she has had in God all her life long, and on the fact that it was a life of sacrifice. And perhaps precisely this separation from her youngest child, whom she has always loved especially, and the small indications that I dare to make sometimes, will bring about some debate in the depth of her soul of which nothing surfaces. *Spem suam Deo committere* <"Let him place his trust in God" (*Benedictine Rule* 4:41)>, says holy Father St. Benedict.

Today we are having the external celebration of the Feast of Carmel (with thirteen hours of prayer in our church), and soon we shall be singing the first Vespers of our Father Elijah.

Always in faithful thought and grateful love, your
Sister Teresa Benedicta

223. Letter to Sr. Agnella Stadtmüller, OP, Landstuhl

Original in Convent Archive of Dominican Sisters, St. Magdalena's, Speyer

J.M.

Pax Christi! Cologne-Lindenthal, August 9, 1936

Dear Sister Agnella,

I kept the little letter in which, exactly a year ago, you told me about Anneliese Lichtenberger's death because I always intended to reply. Now, I thank you at the same time for the new letter.

Obviously, the Lichtenberger parents remember me faithfully. I received Christmas and Easter greetings from them. I am unable to reply to such mail. But I would be glad if you have an occasion to let them know that such greetings make me happy and that I remain united with the parents in prayers for their child.

So far, Fräulein Neumann[1] has not announced her visit. Of course I will do my best if she comes. I knew nothing at all, before this, about your being ill. You should not trouble yourself to give me more detail about it. I am not surprised when anyone who has a responsible activity today suffers a nervous breakdown. ...And in your case, you already had to contend with the history of nervous problems in your family. There is no need, in these circumstances, to seek any further explanations. But of course something like that is a tool in God's hands, and if we understand it that way, it is a grace.

May I ask you to offer some of your suffering for my poor mother? She has been ill now for three months. At first it seemed to be something harmless and temporary, but then it proved to be an incurable illness. For many weeks now she has been bedridden and can eat hardly anything; that I cannot be with her is, of course, very painful, and she cannot be made to understand it.

Our monastic family has also been visited with suffering in the past weeks. On the octave day of the Feast of Our Lady of Mount Carmel we had a sudden death (Mother Gabriele, former prioress of Kordel Carmel near Trier, who was to celebrate her Golden Jubilee on September 15) and right after that, several of the Sisters fell ill. Since that day I have been fully occupied with caring for the sick, and exactly on the Feast of St. Dominic I was able, for the first time, to go to Matins again.

I have sent memorial cards to Speyer and Ludwigshafen. Sisters Bernarda and Raymunda sent loving letters acknowledging them. When you have an opportunity, will you please thank them sincerely for me? I am so glad that *Die siebenfache Gabe [The Sevenfold Gift]* <by Sr. Teresa Renata de Spiritu Sancto> brought joy. I got to know everyone of these gifts immediately after it was born. The author was our Novice Mistress while the book was being written; since January she has been our Reverend Mother <Prioress>.

Now I want to add a suggestion: the next time you are sent to Gemünd, be sure not to bypass Cologne again. It is so much easier, in a personal meeting, to reach an understanding on many things that cannot be touched on in writing. That would surely do you a great deal of good now, as it did earlier.

Best wishes to good Sister Callista <Kopf> and to all in St. Dominic's <Dominican convent in Ludwigshafen>, at Sacred Heart of Jesus <the rectory of Father Husse> and St. Magdalena's <Speyer> and to your relatives. To you, most sincere wishes!

In caritate Christi, your faithful Sister
Teresa Benedicta a Cruce, OCD

1. E. Neumann, a young woman from Bonn with leanings toward the religious life, presumably a student in one of the institutions of higher education run by the Dominican Sisters. See Letters 243 and 249.

224. Letter to Hedwig Conrad-Martius, Bergzabern
Original in Convent Archive of Cologne Carmel; first published, *Kösel Verlag,* Munich 1960

Pax Christi! Cologne-Lindenthal, August 20, 1936
My dear Hatti,

When a long time passes without hearing from you, I think that you must be having as much difficulty finding time to write as I am, and also that you are probably having other difficulties besides. But I never imagined things could be the way they are now. I understand very well how difficult it was for you to go away and how glad you will be when the lectures are over.[1]

I have been wanting to write to you for a long time to beg your prayers for my dear mother, who has been ill since before Pentecost. At first it appeared to be something that would blow over, but then it turned out to be persistent. Now she does not even want to get out of bed, even though lying causes her so much pain. Taking nourishment is also a serious problem. The assumption is that she has a tumor, but there is no wish to plague her with a radical examination since an operation, after all, would no longer be possible.

During the early weeks, my sisters wrote to say she was cheerful and patient. But now she is very depressed most of the time. She refuses visits except from her nearest relatives. And she is constantly brooding, wondering why her youngest has "forsaken" her. What I tried so often to tell her, she refused to hear. As it is, when I write I must take care to be completely "harmless." And one longs so much to give her a little light on her dark journey. I can only pray that the Lord himself will enlighten her. And, from my heart, I am grateful to all who help me with this prayer.

Four weeks ago today, we had a sudden death. Our dear Mother Gabriele died after having a stroke. She was very cheerful and participated with zeal in the common life until the day before. We wanted to celebrate her golden Jubilee on September 15. Then afterward several of the Sisters became ill at the same time, and I was their nurse.

Now I have been able to resume work on the endless opus.[2] For several weeks I have been plaguing myself with an appendix on Heideggers' *Philosophy of Being.*[3] And, because I had to plow through all his works to do so, I could not even read your reprints. I thank you for them sincerely, and I hope I will soon have some time to spare for them. Professor Dempf[4] read the manuscript, without this appendix, shortly after Pentecost and was satisfied with it. It was a great relief to me that he found the treatment of scholastic matters very exact. I continue to feel very much like a dilettante; that is precisely why I was so eager to have the judgment of an expert.

I gave a great deal of joy to our youngest member [Sister Isabella of the Holy Spirit] by presenting her with your work on *Zeit [Time].*[5] She studied mathematics and was a student teacher. She likes to ruminate on philosophical and theological questions, but is unable to attain clarity without assistance.

We would have so much to tell one another if you were able to come to the grate again sometime. The main thing, though, is that we remain united in prayer and that someday we will find one another together in eternal light. The longing for it grows, the more one sees others preceding.

In the love of Christ, your
Benedicta

1. These lectures were given at Rothenfels on the theme: "Natural Creation—History and Creation." They appeared later in revised form in the book *Ursprung und Aufbau des Kosmos [Origin and Structure of the Cosmos].*
2. *Endliches und Ewiges Sein [Finite and Eternal Being,* in *Edith Steins Werke,* Vol. II.
3. See Volume VI of *Edith Steins Werke.*
4. See footnote to Letter 121. [At the time of this letter he was at the University of Bonn.]
5. Appeared in *Philosophischer Anzeiger,* Bonn, 1927.

225. Letter to Mother Petra Bruning, OSU, Dorsten
Original in Convent Archive of Ursuline Sisters, Dorsten

Pax Christi! Cologne-Lindenthal, September 13, 1936
Dear Reverend Mother Petra,

Your kind words did me a lot of good. I know what faithful sisterly love lies behind them. Every bulletin from Breslau reports a worsening.

I must be prepared to hear the worst any day. The *"Scimus, quoniam diligentibus Deum..."* <"We know that, for those who love him, God turns everything to the good" (Rom 8:28)> will surely apply to my dear mother too, since she truly loved "her" God (as she often said with emphasis). And, with confidence in him, she bore much that was painful and did much that was good. I also think these last months when her life was constantly in peril were particularly grace-filled days—above all, the days since she no longer troubles herself about anything in her external life. And no one but the Lord himself knows what is happening in her soul.

That phrase I quoted from the Letter to the Romans afforded me the greatest comfort and joy during the summer of 1933, in Münster, when my future was still shrouded in total darkness. Never have I prayed the Divine Office of the Martyrs, which recurs so frequently during the Easter cycle, with greater fervor than I did at that time.[1] Now it must be my support again. My mother was the strong bond that cemented the family together—four generations by now—for the common concern about her keeps us all bound to her, even the grandsons who are in far-off corners of the world. What will follow will be all the more difficult for those she will leave behind. For my whole life long I shall have to substitute for her [before God], together with my sister Rosa, who is one with me in faith.

You assumed correctly that the fate of my second home <Beuron> concerns me no less [than my mother's]. What you wrote about it, I already knew: even a bit more, but it is still possible that you are better informed than I.[2] But these are certainly things one cannot write about. I am in touch with V.E.[3] <Father Archabbot Raphael Walzer>. My letters travel a roundabout route and it takes a long time before they reach their goal. But once they arrive there, an answer comes at once. Naturally, there also much has to remain unsaid. These are but signs that physical separation cannot keep us apart if we are united in God. And after all, that would still be the case even if these signs also had to cease.

Concerning the book, much remains to be proofread and improved.[4] But I have not given up the hope that I can send it to the publisher by Easter. However, that depends on many unpredictable circumstances and so cannot at all be forecast with certainty.

On the 15th, Ruth Kantorowicz wants to go to Maastricht. Since she cannot take any money with her from here, the Sisters have asked

Rome for a dispensation from the dowry. Until word comes, she will have to stay in the extern quarters. Please help to pray that the enclosure will be opened for her soon, and forever.

In the love of Christ, your grateful
Sister Teresa Benedicta a Cruce, OCD

1. From the time of her baptism, Edith Stein prayed the full hours of the Roman Breviary daily.
2. The Archabbey of Beuron suffered severe damage under the Nazi regime.
3. [The initials stand for *"Vater Erzabt,"* Father Archabbot.] Archabbot Raphael Walzer was in Algeria at this time, having founded a Benedictine monastery there.
4. Her *Endliches und Ewiges Sein (Finite and Eternal Being)* [did not appear in print until 1950.] See *Edith Steins Werke,* Vol. II.

226. Letter to Mother Petra Bruning, OSU, Dorsten[1]
Original in Convent Archive of Ursuline Sisters, Dorsten

Pax Christi! Cologne-Lindenthal, October 3, 1936
Dear Reverend Mother,

Heartfelt thanks for your good, compassionate words.[2] I was so happy to hear that you have gone to Breslau. It seems to me as though you went there in my place, and that is why I have asked my sisters to visit you. You will surely be glad to have them tell you some more about my mother, and you will console them somewhat even though you surely have many demands made on you. You might like to know a little more about the situation [at home]. My sister Rosa (the only one besides me who never married) has been longing for Baptism for years but, out of concern for my mother, she renounced it so far. But she will soon be taking the preliminary steps, although without the knowledge of our brothers and sisters for the time being, to spare them additional pain. It will certainly mean a great deal to her if she can speak to you alone for a little while, but I thought it more appropriate to urge her and my other sister <Elfriede Tworoger[3]> with whom she lives, to visit you together. My mother wished the two to continue to keep our house open as a home for the entire family, and the important thing now is to create a strong bond between the two, despite their religious differences. I have advised them to telephone you first to determine a mutually convenient time, but I will give you the address just the same: Michaelisstrasse 38.

I would like to send another friend of mine to you; she is very close to me and shared in my conversion experience very deeply although she herself has remained a Jewess (Frau Professor Kuznitzky).[4] The last few years have been very hard for her. But I do not know whether you would have time for [another visitor]. If so, then a meeting with her could be arranged through my sister Rosa.

Across from the Ursuline convent—at Ritterplatz 1—stands the house in which I spent ten school years. (When I was a *Primanerin* [senior] we moved into a new school building.) At the 10 o'clock recess we always strolled on the open square in front of the convent. I only became acquainted with its interior when our dear Mother Marianne lived there while she was preparing for the foundation in Pawelwitz.[5]

Of course, I think constantly of my dear mother. But the severe pain of the first days was soon calmed because I can hope with complete confidence that God took her to himself very quickly, and that today she is able to celebrate her 87th birthday with our dear Sister Thérèse.[6] We have been celebrating since September 30, and surely a rich portion of the rain of graces will be flowing to the true friends of Carmel. May it be a benefit in all your deliberations also.

In faithful remembrance and grateful love, your least sister,

Teresa Benedicta a Cruce, OCD

[P.S.] Ruth K. (Kantorowicz) is in the extern quarters in Maastricht awaiting Rome's permission to enter the cloister. She no longer got to go to Heidelberg.

1. [The letter was probably mailed to Dorsten to be forwarded to Mother Petra who was in Breslau at this time.]
2. Condolences on the death of Edith's mother [who died on September 14, 1936].
3. Elfriede Tworoger, née Stein (b. Lublinitz, 1881; d. in Theresienstadt concentration camp, 1942) Edith's sister. Frieda had one daughter, Erika Tworoger. [See *Life,* p. 49.]
4. Trude [Elkes] Kuznitzky [later Koebner] (b. Posen, 1889; d. London, 1976) was divorced from her first husband, Prof. Kuznitzky, not long before this letter was written. See Letter 139.
5. See Letter 99.
6. The Feast of St. Thérèse of Lisieux (now October 1) was celebrated on October 3 in 1936. [September 30 is the anniversary of Thérèse's death. Frau Stein's birthdate was October 4.]

227. Letter to Sr. Callista Kopf, OP, Speyer

Original in Convent Archive of Dominican Sisters, St. Magdalena's, Speyer

J.M.

Pax Christi! Cologne-Lindenthal, October 4, 1936

Dear Sister Callista,

There is so much to write at this time that it was impossible for me to tell you sooner that we are remembering your dear sister who has gone to her [eternal] home. Death notices go into a little box in our choir so that those who have died have a share in all of our prayers.

At the same time, I thank you sincerely for your dear compassionate letter. My mother fell ill for the first time a short while before Pentecost, recovered a little once more; but since the end of June we've known it was incurable. There was a tumor in the stomach, probably cancerous. These summer months were very hard for her, for all at home, and also for me. The news of her conversion was a totally unfounded rumor. I have no idea who made it up. My mother held to her faith to the very last. The faith and firm confidence she had in her God from her earliest childhood until her 87th year remained steadfast, and were the last things that stayed alive in her during the final difficult agony. Therefore, I have the firm belief that she found a very merciful judge and is now my most faithful helper on my way, so that I, too, may reach my goal.

Rosa <Stein> is not alone. My sister Frieda <Tworoger>, my mother's faithful support in the business, also lived at home with them and, according to my mother's will, the two of them are to keep the house at Michaelisstrasse 38 as a homestead for all the brothers and sisters. They will certainly try to do that for as long as present circumstances allow.

Sincere thanks and greetings to your dear Mother Prioress and the other sisters. Whenever you have the opportunity, please, give them to Sr. Agnella <Stadtmüller>, too.

Most cordial greetings on your name day! In faithful remembrance, your

Sister Teresa Benedicta

228. Letter to Hedwig Conrad-Martius, Bergzabern
Original in Convent Archive of Cologne Carmel; first published, *Kösel Verlag,* Munich, 1960

Pax Christi! Cologne-Lindenthal, October 10, 1936
Dear Hatti,

Sincere thanks to you and Fräulein Käthi for your dear words. I have had to write so much during the past weeks that now I would prefer not to say anything at all any more. It is easier for me now than during the months when I always had to think that my mother, in her suffering, was waiting in vain for me. Now she is at peace and understands everything.

Please pray for my brothers and sisters. My mother's last great sorrow was that my brother Arno[1] (who had always worked as her associate) had decided to sell the business, intending to go to America. His wife and two of their children are already there, and it is understandable that he would like to have his family united again. But it is most unlikely that he will be able to make a living over there, and the business is not his alone; according to my mother's will my sister Frieda <Tworoger> is to take [mother's] place [at the lumberyard], and Rosa is to continue to keep house for them at Michaelisstrasse 38. As yet there is no way of knowing what will develop from all this.

You must not speak of a "great ontology" of mine.[2] It is only a small attempt, although at the same time it is unabashedly comprehensive. I continue to hope that by Easter I can finish the final proofs and give the manuscript to the publisher. The manuscript is to be published by Anton Pustet, Salzburg, in the series *Christliches Denken [Christian Thought],* which is being edited by the Abbey of Seckau (Steiermark) [Austria].

Your ontology is eminently ahead of mine, even if it is not written; it stands behind everything you have said and written in the past years. Recently I read the lectures on the human being,[3] and previous to that, once more, your work on time, and I have just taken out the *Realontologie* <Halle, 1932>. If my work deserves the right to exist beside yours at all, it is because it is connected to the tradition. It is an attempt to build bridges [by coupling phenomenology with tradition], and as such it may become useful to some people. I read in some reviews that you have written something on <Heidegger's> *Sein und Zeit* [*Being and Time,* 1927] that I have never seen, also that there is a book on the soul by Pfänder.[4] I would be most grateful for the loan of both when you can spare them.

Besides that I would like *very* much to have an introductory presentation of the latest on atomic theory, if you have anything on that.

There is as much truth to the rumors of Husserl's conversion as there is to those that keep popping up about you. At the time when one supposed him to be in Rome, he was in Kappel in the Black Forest. I know positively that he has no thought of making a change,[5] but in the past years his position on the church and religious life has been very positive. Should he ever come to such a decision, surely he would let me know about it.

Kaufmann has informed us he will be here on Friday, the second time he has come en route to London. Should Hering be at your place, or if you are expecting him, give him my very best regards. It is a very long time since I heard anything from him.

To all of you, most cordial greetings, and to Fräulein Käthi the assurance of my special regards.

In the love of Christ, your
Benedicta

1. Arno Stein (b. Gleiwitz, 1879; d. San Francisco, CA, 1948) second oldest brother of Edith Stein; his wife Martha Stein, née Kaminski: his children, Wolfgang, Helmut, and Lotte emigrated to America. [Another daughter, Eva, was denied an immigration visa to enter the United States, and remained with her relatives in Breslau. With them, she was a victim of the Nazis at Theresienstadt, where she died in 1943.]
2. *Endliches und Ewiges Sein [Finite and Eternal Being]*. See *Edith Steins Werke,* Vol. II. See also Letter 144.
3. See Letter 224.
4. *Die Seele des Menschen [The Human Soul]* (Halle, 1933). See Letter 22.
5. [Husserl and his wife had converted from Judaism to Protestantism many years earlier, so these rumors were concerning a change from Lutheran to Catholic affiliation. As Edith states, Husserl never made such a move; Frau Husserl became a Catholic before she died.]

229. Letter to Sr. Agnella Stadtmüller, OP, Landstuhl
Original in Convent Archive of Dominican Sisters, St. Magdalena's, Speyer

J.M.

Cologne-Lindenthal, November 15, 1936

My dear Sister Agnella,

Before Advent begins, I would like to send you sincere greetings and many good wishes for a grace-filled Advent and Christmas season, thanking you at the same time for your dear letter of September 19 and the help of your prayers. I am confident that you will continue to remember my mother faithfully and, besides, I ask especially that you continue to remember in your prayers my brothers and sisters, who still have to go through much that is very difficult. I hope to have my sister Rosa here before Christmas.

If you really come here sometime, I will be glad to give you details. Nowadays that is not easy to do in writing. I have had to write too much in the past months and this will continue for a while. Since I have heard nothing to the contrary, I presume you are still in Landstuhl. I am sending the letter there, and will include a little card for Sr. Ancilla <a former student>.

Would it not be good if at least your Reverend Mother were given the same insight as the doctor and the confessor? When decisions have to be made all concerned must have the same basis [for their judgment], otherwise it is probably understandable if the conclusions drawn will also be different. I have never heard anything more from Fräulein N.[1]

Yesterday we had the feast of All Saints of our Order, and today we begin the Novena in preparation for the feast of our Holy Father St. John [of the Cross]. These are always days of particular gratitude for the undeserved grace of a vocation in this elect family of God.

In sincere remembrance, your faithful
Sister Teresa Benedicta a Cruce, OCD

1. Presumably Fräulein E. Neumann, see Letters [223], 243 and 249.

230. Letter to Elly Dursy, Hallgarten
Original in Convent Archive of Waldfrieden Carmel

J.M.

Pax Christi! Cologne-Lindenthal, November 25, 1936
Dear Elly,

Once again, you've so cunningly written at the eleventh hour [this was Wednesday before Advent] that I have to answer promptly. I don't know which of us has expressed herself so badly as to be unintelligible. When one reads your letter, one might suppose I had advised you to do everything else rather than pray. Of course, all I meant to say was that you should not be disturbed if your professional duties do not permit you to arrange for as many regular hours of prayer as a monastic schedule would provide.

Obviously I am happy with you about all the free time you can find for your interior life, and would consider it wrong indeed to waste it on unnecessary things. After your expression of delight about the present circumstances that leave you such freedom, the thought of exchanging these for others, without any real necessity, surprised me. On closer reflection, are the "stimuli" you expect from being close to a larger city not rather distractions? Every change in the external circumstances of life is already apt to disturb one's inner peace. Therefore one should never seek [such a change] unless God provides it. Were it truly to ease things for your parents, one might take that into consideration. But I would suggest that you consider whether your savings in travel expenses might not be offset by increased costs for clothing and the like. But according to your own account this is at present not the issue. Whether you would get better children [as pupils] in exchange is very questionable. Usually one gets a heavier cross when one attempts to get rid of an old one. And, finally, those parishes are greatly to be pitied in which pastors and teachers stay only as long as it takes for something "better" to come along.[1]

1. The conclusion to the letter has been lost.

231. Letter to Hedwig Conrad-Martius, Bergzabern
Original in Convent Archive of Cologne Carmel; first published, *Kösel Verlag,* Munich 1960

Pax Christi! Cologne-Lindenthal, January 13, 1937
My dear Hatti,

At present, I've owed you thanks for Pfänder's book and the manuscript on being and time for ever so long.[1]

What can have happened in the meantime regarding the mysterious undertakings you alluded to? And how is Fräulein Käthi? And I have to express, belatedly, my heartfelt wishes for Christmas and New Year's.

This time we had a most extraordinary feast. My sister Rosa was here from December 16 to the 29th. As you know, she has always accompanied me, interiorly, on my way and suffered for many years because consideration for my mother would not allow her to do more than that. Now, on the afternoon of the 24th at four o'clock, she was baptized and received her First Holy Communion at [Mass] that Holy Night. When she arrived she was still numb from all the hardship she had experienced this past year. But here she soon thawed out and was happier than ever in her life. Now she is back home and all goes well, although things were very stormy at first, when she told the family about her intentions a few months ago. My sister Frieda <Tworoger> was particularly unhappy in the beginning, believing it would prove impossible for them to continue to live together. In accord with my mother's wishes, [Frieda] is replacing her in the business and at home, and that has probably made her feel a responsibility to preserve a Jewish point of view as strongly as possible. Erika (Frieda's daughter)[2] and my sister Erna <Biberstein>[3] were the intermediaries and now all is going along peacefully.

My brother <Arno> was in America during December, arranging for permission to emigrate, but he did not have all the necessary papers. As things now stand he has to wait another six months. The question is: Will he succeed then? And perhaps what awaits him, if he does succeed, will be worse than his present situation.

Immediately before Rosa's arrival—it's exactly a month today (the 14th), I had a little accident: I fell down the steps and broke my left hand and left foot. I was in the hospital until the 23rd, and my sister visited me there daily. I was allowed to celebrate Christmas at home. Now my hand is quite free, but still a bit stiff and weak. The foot is still in a cast, but I can walk fairly well.

As my first work after the pause demanded by the holidays, the visit, and the accident, I have taken up the Pfänder [book]. It touches me almost more as a personal document than in the factual content. After all, it is like the finale of a life and as such, despite all the good there is in it, somewhat sad. Are you still in touch [with him] personally? At some of the high-spirited exclamation points I would have liked to know whether they originated from Autós <Theodor Conrad>.

For my opus[4] I have now gathered everything necessary for a first volume; it has only to be typed and submitted for Father Provincial's <Theodor Rauch's> *Imprimatur.* Then it can be printed.

When you have time, let me hear from you how things are. Best regards to all, your

Sister Teresa Benedicta

1. See Letter 228.
2. See Letter 74.
3. See Letter 24.
4. *Endliches und Ewiges Sein [Finite and Eternal Being].* Cf. *Edith Steins Werke,* Vol. II.

232. Letter to Hedwig Conrad-Martius, Bergzabern

Original in Convent Archive of Cologne Carmel; first published, *Kösel Verlag,* Munich 1960

Pax Christi! Cologne-Lindenthal, January 20, 1937

Dear Hatti,

Our Sister Maria (formerly Fränzi Ernst, Frankfurt-am-Main) was in England for the last year (1932-1933) before her entrance and she has written down for me various addresses that may be useful to you. For the present I am only giving you one that seems to me rich in prospects for the research fellowship:

Women's International League
Miss Mary Sheepshanks, Hon. Secretary
International House, 55 Gower Street
London W.C. 1

A further [name that] belongs with this is: Dr. Hilda Clark, Hon. Foreign Relations Secretary, 44 Uper [sic] Park Road, N.W. 3.

From the second lady Sister Maria received a very friendly and interested letter in reply to her inquiry to the League. I believe this is one place where your attempt would be supported.

How about the lectures in Cologne? Time passed so quickly the other day.

With best regards to all, your
Sister Teresa Benedicta a Cruce

233. Letter (note) to Sr. Maria Ernst, OCD,[1] Cologne
Original in Convent Archive of Cologne Carmel

<Cologne-Lindenthal, presumably beginning of 1937>

Dear Sister Maria,

I just received this Ambrosian text, which I am translating for Your Charity:[2] "God does all things at the right time. Whatever he does is not outside of time but rather at the most opportune moment and comes at the right time for me." (To Psalm 118)

1. Fränzi Ernst (Sr. Maria de Deo, OCD) (b. Metz/Lorraine, 1904; d. Cologne, 1977) was a member of the Cologne community at this time. Erich Przywara, SJ, introduced Edith Stein to the family of Dr. Wilhelm Ernst in Frankfurt. She spent Christmas 1922, her first as a Catholic, with the Ernsts.
2. At that time, it was the Carmelite custom to address another sister as "Your Charity" instead of as the usual "you."

234. Letter to Hedwig Conrad-Martius, Bergzabern
Original in Convent Archive of Cologne Carmel; first published, *Kösel Verlag*, Munich 1960

Pax Christi! Cologne-Lindenthal, January 26, 1937
My dear Hatti,

Next time you will probably allow "the egg to be more clever than the hen"[1] and telephone the Rev. Monsignor first. I surely know that one can never count on him with certainty. I hope something will be done soon about the lectures.

Sister Maria has no close acquaintance with Miss Clark; at that time she merely received a very friendly and interested reply, plus an introduction to circles that were useful to her. I believe such ladies in the women's movement are always very happy to find a woman who is really achieving something and are then glad to be of help. I believe it would be best if you were to write a bit about yourself, enclose copies of your grandiose letters of recommendation, tell them you are trying to get the fellowship and ask them to support you in that.[2] I take "Hon. secretary" to mean "honorary." Sr. Maria <Ernst> has that included in several of her addresses but does not know what it signifies.[3]

On Monday the 18th, with the doctor's permission, we worked hard to free the foot from the cast. Then I had to spend two days in bed again—I was carried downstairs only for Mass—and [then had to] learn, once more, how to walk. I am already very good at it by this time, although the joint is still very stiff. By now I only need the cane for going down the stairs. Since Sunday I've been observing the full schedule again. However, in the hours outside of the choir and the refectory, I still live on the recliner with my foot propped up high.

I wonder whether Fräulein Käthi can soon return to you? In any case, it is good if the root of the trouble is determined. I think often of you and your intentions. On February 1st, we will have Perpetual Devotions in our church (that is Adoration [of the Blessed Sacrament] which is held in turn in all the churches of the diocese, so that, in general, it never ceases.) At night we take turns. And on the 2nd, Candlemas Day, we also have a quiet day of prayer. [On such days] one can commend intentions even more than usual.

Sister Teresa Benedicta a Cruce, OCD

1. [An idiomatic expression usually used to point out that a young person may have a better solution to a problem than someone older.]
2. [In the version of this letter published by Hedwig Conrad-Martius in 1960, there is an exclamation point here, seeming to indicate that this sentence and the extraordinary "grandiose" are teasing remarks on Edith's part.]
3. [Since the "Hon." is part of the official address, it can be assumed that it means "Honorable" rather than "honorary."]

235. Letter to Sr. Adelgundis Jaegerschmid, OSB, Freiburg-Günterstal
Original in Convent Archive of Benedictine Sisters, St. Lioba, Freiburg-Günterstal

J.M.

Pax Christi! Cologne-Lindenthal, January 28, 1937

Dear Sister Adelgundis,

I saved up the thanks for your dear Christmas greetings until your name day. To you and to Sister Placida <Laubhardt> (who will hardly receive another letter before her name day), especially sincere thanks for sharing the joy of the great gift of grace—that Holy Night.

I suggested to my sister <Rosa> that she answer Sister Placida herself, but do not know whether she has already done so. She found a lot of work awaiting her on her return home and also had a lot of correspondence to catch up with. Perhaps only someone who has personally experienced what it means to wait for years and to have the pressure of living in an environment totally differing in its value system from one's own can appreciate what the days here meant for her. She completely blossomed here. An understanding of our life is totally natural for her—just as she has grown into the world of faith without any struggles or difficulties, with the simplicity and readiness of a child. I am always filled with renewed gratitude when I think of the wonderful and mysterious providence of God in our lives.

When Fräulein Baring[1] visited her brother's house, she also experienced God's goodness so vividly that it will probably be a lasting help to her. I am very happy about that since her position is very difficult and she needs a very firm interior anchor.

Please remember me to the Husserls. Taking leave of both children[2] will be very difficult for them.

From my heart, I wish you the peace of Christ that exceeds all our understanding as the best protection in all your journeying.

To you, and to your Reverend Mother Prioress, to Sr. Placida, and all the Sisters I know, cordial greetings from your faithful

Sister Teresa Benedicta a Cruce, OCD

[P.S.] I commend to you our retreat, which begins on February 21.

1. Nina Baring (b. Leipzig, 1899; d. Eutin, 1972) Ph. D., studied under Heidegger. She held a position in social service, converted to Catholicism from the Reformed Evangelical

Church. She became acquainted with Edith Stein in Freiburg, visited her often then and also later, when Edith was in the Cologne Carmel.
2. Their daughter and one of their sons emigrated to the United States. See Letter 19.

236. Letter to Elly Dursy, Hallgarten

Original in Convent Archive of Waldfrieden Carmel

Pax Christi! Cologne-Lindenthal, February 17, 1937

Dear Elly,

Your question is a difficult one to answer. If I look at the matter without taking the family into consideration, everything seems to point in favor of remaining in Hallgarten: loyalty to the community, the possibility of leading a quiet and recollected life. You would soon see the proximity of Lambrecht[1] and the duty of going there daily as a severe distraction and would once more become nervous. What is decisive is whether your mother and Ännchen <Dursy> are really so much in need of your help that all these contrary factors carry no weight. But I must say that I do not trust myself to judge this since I do not know the circumstances from personal observation and have no clear picture of the situation. I believe Ännchen is the one most capable of informing you about the matter. She knows you and your situation and understands it; on the other hand, she knows what she and your parents need. Therefore I consider it best that you get her to make the decision in this case. Should there be no opportunity any more for a discussion or an exchange of letters, you might perhaps send your application to her, signed and sealed, and leave it to her whether she wants to forward it to the proper authorities. I hope I am not expecting too much from her in this matter.

I must confess that I do not know whether I have thanked you for your Christmas gift. I mean, I cannot remember writing to you, but your letter is no longer at hand and I usually keep what has not yet been taken care of. In any case, I say thank you again, most sincerely. We already owned that book, but I welcomed it very much as a gift I could pass on, not to my sister <Rosa> but with her agreement to a convert,[2] someone very close to me who took part in the celebration of the Baptism and showed us numerous kindnesses. Sometime I will tell you in person about all the pre- and post-events that accompanied this beautiful celebration.

Besides, another urgent matter is on my mind that I would like to discuss with you sometime. It concerns the position of the Catholic women teachers in the Palatinate. I have heard things that make me worry. I would like most of all to have you talk to Fräulein Clara Barth[3] sometime. She is the former regional president of the Women Teachers' Association and a delegate to the Provincial Assembly. When she visited me here a good while ago she still had her home in Ludwigshafen, but a teaching position in Landau. St. Magdalena's would surely know where she is now. But probably such a meeting with her would only be meaningful if the two of us could first discuss this matter.

Beginning on Monday, the 22nd, we will have a ten-day retreat. Please remember us. A grace-filled Quadragesima [Lent]. Your sister

Teresa Benedicta a Cruce

1. Hometown of Elly Dursy's parents.
2. [Possibly Dr. Nina Baring, mentioned in the previous letter.]
3. Clara Barth (b. Durmersheim/Saar, 1888; d. Landau, 1940).

237. Letter to Maria Mayer, Beuron[1]
Original in private possession of Mayer family

J.M.

Pax Christi! Cologne-Lindenthal, April 22, 1937

Dear Fräulein Mayer,

My sincere sympathy was awakened by the news of your mother's death. I was unable to write to you earlier because I was in retreat until early this morning. I join my prayers to yours. May I ask you to express my sympathy to Mother Cäcilia[2] when you have an opportunity to do so?

How lonely it will be for you in the dear little house next to the wooden bridge! But you will stay there, won't you? Perhaps someone has told you that I, too, lost my mother this past year. She was nearly 87 years old and, until her final year, remarkably hale and hearty. But then she suffered a great deal for several months.

Sincere thanks for the beautiful book you sent me. I was very surprised to receive such a gift.

You can well imagine that I have not forgotten Beuron. But I have no homesickness. That ceases when one has landed in one's true home.

In Christ's love, your
Sister Teresa Benedicta a Cruce, OCD

1. See Letter 46.
2. Mother Cäcilia was a nun in St. Gabriel's, Bertholdstein, Austria.

238. Letter to Sister Callista Kopf, OP, Ludwigshafen
Original in Convent Archive of Dominican Sisters, St. Magdalena's, Speyer

J.M.

Pax Christi! Cologne-Lindenthal, May 7, 1937
Dear Sister Callista,

I already knew what lies ahead for you, although not in every detail.[1] Since your companions are all younger, I assume you will be superior of the foundation. It is a great and difficult task for which we must earnestly beg the Holy Spirit's support. But I can also imagine that you perceive it as a release, getting away from the pressure of confining regulations and being allowed to build something new.[2]

It is good for us to hear something like this once in a while. So far we still live in deep peace, entirely unmolested within our cloister walls. But the fate of our Spanish sisters[3] tells us, all the same, what we must be prepared for. And when such profound upheaval takes place in such close proximity, it is a salutary warning. In any case it is our duty to support with our prayers those who have to perform such pioneer labors. It will be very difficult for your dear mother to take leave of you. Is your sister in Speyer?

Recently I received a very long letter from Sister Anna, and it made me very happy. Her illness gave her the time to write. I feel sure I may include here a note for her. Could you pass it on to Speyer when you have a chance? Of course, I have a lively interest in everything that happens at St. Magdalena's and in the entire Palatinate. Several teachers continue to write to me, and come here once in a while.

My sister <Rosa> will be confirmed on Pentecost Monday.[4] Surely you will want to be with us in spirit. She depends on the inner connection with those who are geographically distant from her. That she feels estranged from her immediate surroundings is very difficult for her. But still we must be very glad that they live together so peacefully. It is also beautiful that she draws all her strength and joy from her participation in the life of the church. We do everything possible from here to maintain for her a sense of belonging. While she was here she was received as one fully belonging to our small Carmelite family. Obviously that helps her a great deal, even more so since they are all very intimidated out there, for they can never really know whom they might still expect to associate with them.

To your dear Reverend Mother Prioress and all your dear companion Sisters in Mannheim and Ludwigshafen, the very best wishes in sisterly union when you have an opportunity to pass them on. To you, the fullness of the Holy Spirit as armor for your mission. Your

Sister Teresa Benedicta a Cruce, OCD

1. There were plans to transfer Sr. Callista to the Dominican Sisters' missions in Brazil.
2. The Dominicans' educational institutions suffered much from the repressive rules of the Nazi government. However, because of an illness Sr. Callista was unable to take part in the foundation in Brazil.
3. [On July 24, 1936, at Guadalajara, Spain, three Discalced Carmelite nuns were killed for their fidelity to the faith. The three were beatified by Pope John Paul II on March 29, 1987, 33 days before he beatified Edith Stein.]
4. On May 17, 1937, Rosa was confirmed in Breslau by Auxiliary Bishop Valentin Woszіech, D.Theol. [in the crypt of Holy Cross Church.]

239. Letter to Paula Stolzenbach, Frankfurt

Original in Convent Archive of Hainburg Carmel

J.M.

Pax Christi! Cologne-Lindenthal, May 18, 1937

Dear Sister Paula-Maria,

The feast of Pentecost, at last, brings you the greetings I had intended to send you for such a long time. Your last letter was written on August 13, 1936. On September 14, my dear mother died at the exact hour in which we had our festive renovation of vows here, as is customary on the Feast of the Exaltation of the Cross. In December, for the very first time, I had one of my siblings here, my sister Rosa, who had belonged to us in her heart,for such a long time. On the vigil of Christmas she was baptized, and received her first Holy Communion at the High Mass here on that Holy Night; yesterday she received Confirmation in Breslau. You will readily understand that she left her heart behind in Carmel, and it is very difficult for her to live in the family while she is interiorly all alone. We hope to see one another again at the Veiling Ceremony.[1]

The Cologne Carmel is celebrating its 300-year Jubilee. The foundation days are only in November, but the public celebration is to be joined to the Triduum in honor of St. Thérèse of the Child Jesus. Our dear Mother is writing the history of this foundation as a Jubilee publication. This will make you happy and you will be glad to help us pray that the celebration will bring rich blessings to our house and to as many persons as possible outside. Mother Isabella of the Holy Spirit,[2] about whom a small booklet is enclosed for you, was the second Prioress of the old monastery in the Schnurgasse. She was Spanish and entered in Antwerp shortly after the death of Mother Anne of St. Bartholomew.[3]

Belatedly, sincere thanks for the surplus you sent that time with your payment for the little books. With a faithful remembrance, your

Sister Teresa Benedicta a Cruce, OCD

1. [Edith received the black (final profession) veil May 1, 1938.]
2. Charlotte von Urquine (b. Brussels, 1606; d. Cologne, 1675) co-foundress (1637) and longtime prioress of the Cologne Carmel.
3. Daughter of Ferdinand Garcia and Maria Manzanas (b. Navall Morcueda near Avila, 1549; d. Antwerp, 1626) companion of St. Teresa of Avila from 1567 to 1582. She founded several monasteries in France and the Netherlands.

240. Letter to Sr. Agnella Stadtmüller, OP, <Gemund>

Original in Convent Archive of Dominican Sisters, St. Magdalena's, Speyer

J.M.J.T.

Pax Christi! Cologne-Lindenthal, August 12, 1937

My dear Sister Agnella,

This is a big surprise—that we may count on a visit from you so soon. I had given up all hope of it after Fräulein Pérignon's last information. You must not make such a serious and difficult thing of it. It is, after all, only a little Carmelite novice whom you are going to visit, not a physician and not a spiritual director. She does not claim to be able to cure your nervous condition, nor does she think to interfere in your interior life. If you do not want to, you do not have to say anything to me. I only thought that people who are "down" need to have a bit of relaxation during the [school] vacation—that's what the Lord made vacations for, after all—and I thought it would do you good to let yourself bask in the sunshine of Mount Carmel and breathe in its fresh air a bit more freely than elsewhere. During the hours when we can go to the speakroom, I would be at your disposal if you wish; and I would have enough to recount that might give you pleasure. Were you to prefer entertaining yourself in our Chapel with the Queen of Peace and our dear Saints of the Order, I would be just as satisfied.

Now we will simply await dear Reverend Mother's decision. If she grants permission, take it as a gift from God and tell him a nice, grateful "Yes, Father!" Please give my sincere good wishes to all the Sisters I know in Gemünd, especially Sister Donata. I knew nothing of her illness nor of Sr. Callista <Kopf>'s. Please will you give her, also, my regards when you have an opportunity; is she laid up in Mannheim?

Happily looking forward to the blessing of seeing you again, I am your

Sister Teresa Benedicta a Cruce

241. Letter to Hedwig Dülberg, Marburg

Original in Convent Archive of Benedictine Sisters, St. Lioba, Freiburg-Günterstal

J.M.J.T.

Pax Christi! Cologne-Lindenthal, August 18, 1937

Dear Frau Dülberg,

Today we had a letter from Mother Magdalena, the novice mistress in Maastricht, who was very distressed. They could not arrive at the majority of votes in the Chapter [required] to receive Ruth <Kantorowicz> into the novitiate. She [Mother Magdalena] herself, and the Mother Prioress who is seriously ill, deplore it very much. But they are unable to change it. Ruth wanted me to let you know. For quite a while, when she learned how slim the prospects were for her, she thought of calling on you for help. At the time I advised her to wait until after the votation. But now you would be badly needed there, if you are able to take a few days off. You can well imagine how perplexed and helpless the poor creature must be over there. Mother Magdalena writes that, should you be able to come, both of you could remain together for a while in the extern quarters. First one has to find out, clearly, what Ruth wants to do. I am to investigate the possibility of a return to Germany. I shall learn about that very soon from a well-informed source and then write to Maastricht accordingly. Were you able to go there you would surely go via Cologne, and we could have a preliminary consultation.

You have had a hard time since we last spoke together. I heard about it only much later through St. Lioba's, but only the bare facts. Naturally I would like very much to be able to find out for myself how things are with you. But in the meantime I have not forgotten you.

From September 30 to October 3 we will celebrate the 300-Year Jubilee of the Cologne Carmel. I am sending you the announcement about our commemorative booklet.[1] We are very grateful for all friendly assistance in its distribution since we had to publish it on our own.

In the love of Christ, your
Sister Teresa Benedicta a Cruce, OCD

1. See Letter 244.

242. Letter to Gisela Naegeli, Zurich
Original in Convent Archive of Cologne Carmel

J.M.
Pax Christi! Cologne-Lindenthal, August 29, 1937
Dear Fräulein Naegeli,

From September 30 to October 3 we will celebrate the 300-Year Jubilee of the Cologne Carmel. May I ask you, please, to help us a bit with the distribution of the commemorative booklet? It will appear in September.[1] Perhaps it would be possible for you to insert a brief notice in your publication?

I would like to take this opportunity to thank you again sincerely for the kind gifts you sent us some time ago from Frankfurt-am-Main. At that time I sent a thank you card at once to Frankfurt, care of general delivery. It was returned with the notation "not called for." Then I asked Sister Adelgundis to express our gratitude. But of course I cannot know whether she had an opportunity to do so or whether, under the pressure of her many duties, she forgot.

I still faithfully remember you and those in your care. I hope it will bear fruit sometime. With cordial best wishes and regards, yours *in Christo,*

Sister Teresa Benedicta a Cruce, OCD

1. See Letter 244.

243. Letter to Sr. Agnella Stadtmüller, OP, <Gemünd>

Original in Convent Archive of Dominican Sisters, St. Magdalena's, Speyer

J.M.J.T.

Pax Christi! Cologne-Lindenthal, August 31, 1937

My dear Sister Agnella,

Yesterday I thought of you a great deal. After we had your letter, we were especially sorry that you were unable to come. But that is from the human perspective. Surely there was a good purpose for it. I believe you already benefitted from the unabashed joy of the anticipated visit. Then this sacrifice was added to all the others you offer daily, and will bear its fruit. When I think of the serious intentions you wrote about, and of so much else I know from earlier times, then I believe I understand why a greater sacrifice is necessary. I will gladly take all of it before the tabernacle.

But with regard to the frustrated plan, I would like to make a suggestion. Should it turn out—as happened four years ago—that only the express permission did not materialize, but the readiness to give it was not lacking, then ask, in advance, for permission [to come] at the next opportunity. Should concrete objections present themselves, we will have to do without a reunion *in via* [in this life] and look forward with all the greater joy to the *visio beata* <the beatific vision>.[1]

May I ask you for Fräulein Neumann's address in Bonn? I had intended to ask you for it [in person]. I promised her at the last visit to send her an invitation to our Jubilee. She should receive it now.

Sincere greetings to Sister Callista. Will the others go without her?[2] Recently a little Frater[3] (of the Holy Family) visited us. He is to be professed on September 8th and will then go immediately to Brazil. I have a good number of budding priestly and religious vocations to care for. There can hardly be a more urgent cause at this time.

Greetings to all the dear Sisters. *In caritate Christi,* your

Sister Teresa Benedicta a Cruce, OCD

1. [Seeing one another in heaven.]
2. Sr. Callista was unable to go to the new foundation in Brazil because of illness. See Letter 238.
3. [P. Heinrich Hennes, of the Congregation of Missionaries of the Holy Family, of Biesdorf. His small stature—1.56 m.—won him exemption from military service and he went to the missions in Brazil instead.]

244. Letter to Mother Petra Bruning, OSU, Dorsten

Original in Convent Archive of Ursuline Sisters, Dorsten

J.M.

Pax Christi! Cologne-Lindenthal, September 4, 1937

Dear Reverend Mother,

Thank you very much for your dear letter. First of all, I want to tell you that the mother of our dear Mother Prioress[1] died this morning. We kindly ask your prayers. It was not a surprise; we expected the news to come any day. It was a very peaceful going home. This good mother had the heart of a child. She was happy to live, but also accepted death happily. Her husband preceded her by many years; and her only son died just fifteen years ago today. She was able to receive the commemorative booklet just before she died.[2] Although unable to read any of it anymore, she placed it over her heart.

We ask you to accept the book[3] as a small token in exchange for all your goodness to us. We enclose the announcement because we appreciate any help we receive with the distribution. Perhaps you could use a few more announcements to pass on to others? Orders are best sent here since Bachem would only forward them to us.

Your generous offer of a donation on the occasion of the Jubilee is accepted with sincere thanks. Our Reverend Mother will be very grateful for whatever you wish to give toward covering the expenses the feast demands. You will, of course, receive an invitation and the program for the celebration as soon as they are ready. If you are unable to come, you will [at least] be able to be with us in spirit.

Surely it would mean a great <deal> to my sister Rosa if you were to come to Breslau. After all, she is very much alone. Tomorrow evening the Jewish New Year begins. My mother was buried on that day last year.

You asked about our retreats. We have one in common every two years, besides which each one has an individual ten day retreat, privately, every year. The ones in common are good for the stimulus they give and for building a community spirit. The private ones, however, are—for me at least, and probably for most of the others—more effective. We take them when it is most convenient for each one. When possible, I take Holy Week. This year it was impossible because the Feast of St. Joseph would have been included. So I started shortly after Easter and closed with my profession day (April 21).

Ruth <Kantorowicz> left in deepest sadness. They let her wait ten months for a decision, and then she was not accepted. The Mother Prioress, who is terminally ill, and the Mistress of Novices were very much in favor of taking her, but the majority of the nuns were against it. Now she is unable to return to Germany.[4] The Sisters are still taking care of her, and she continues to hope that she will attain her goal somewhere else. I commend her, very much, to your prayers, as well as the poor sick Mother <Prioress> who is to celebrate her fortieth Jubilee in the Order on September 8. Finally, too, [pray for] our good Sister Clara,[5] the oldest lay sister in our house. A short time ago she became my patient. The doctors have not yet found anything, but her stomach is no longer functioning as it should and one must fear that something is seriously wrong.

Always in faithful remembrance and with grateful greetings to all, in the love of Christ from your least Sister,

Teresa Benedicta a Cruce, OCD

1. Frau Posselt, mother of the prioress, Sister Teresa Renata de Spiritu Sancto.
2. The commemorative booklet *Unter dem Zepter der Friedenskönigin [Under the Scepter of the Queen of Peace],* written by the prioress for the celebration of the Carmel's 300th year of existence.
3. [This gift may be another book. The abridged second edition of the commemorative essay has only 27 pages, and as Edith continually refers to the original as *Büchlein,* the publication has been referred to as a booklet.]

4. [Government restrictions had made it very difficult to leave Germany and, now, impossible to return because of her Jewish descent.]
5. Sr. Maria Clara of the Precious Blood, OCD, née Hustege (b. Frintrop, 1871; d. Cologne, 1938).

245. Letter to Mother Petra Bruning, OSU, Dorsten

Original in Convent Archive of Ursuline Sisters, Dorsten

J.M.J.T.

Pax Christi! Cologne-Lindenthal, September 24, 1937

Dear Reverend Mother,

Our Feast[1] must not begin before at least a short note of thanks goes to you. God reward you for everything: the interior participation in our whole life and the generous donation. We are convinced that, in your heart, you will be with us, and naturally we include you just as sincerely in everything. Surely you will be particularly pleased when you read the parts in the book that mention the hospitality of the Ursuline Sisters. Many thanks, also, for the beautiful yearbook. On Sunday we will immerse ourselves in it at recreation. There is no time for that on work days when, even at recreation, we are "to go about our ordinary manual labor" and, of course, right now there is much for skilled and even unskilled hands to do.

Since Tuesday we have had a novena in preparation, a brief devotion with Benediction in church every evening at 8 o'clock. Since the night before last a priest—popularly known as the *Kunstpastor* [artist-pastor]—is at work preparing the high altar for the reception of the [statue of the] Queen of Peace. She will be coming next Tuesday. Then we will receive her at the enclosure door, carry her to the Choir and sing the Vespers and Matins of the holy Archangel Michael in her presence. On Wednesday she will be moved into the church. We want to carry our dear invalid, too, into the Choir. Other times she is easily able to follow everything that goes on in the church from her bed [in the infirmary].

You will surely find joy in the Litany to the Queen of Peace, and in her Hours of the Liturgy. More after the feast. Today, in great haste, only many cordial and grateful greetings from us all.

In caritate Christi, your least
Sister Teresa Benedicta a Cruce

1. The 300-year jubilee of the Carmel of Cologne.

246. Letter to Sr. Callista Kopf, OP, <Donnersberg [a sanatorium]>
Original in Convent Archive of Dominican Sisters, St. Magdalena's, Speyer

J.M.J.T.

Pax Christi! Cologne-Lindenthal, October 15, 1937

Dear Sister Callista,

It is the evening hour of silence before Matins. I always save many things to do in this brief interval. Today I would like to use the close of this beautiful feast day [St. Teresa of Avila] at least to make a start on a letter to you. How much I have wished to write it earlier, ever since I heard that you had become ill and were unable to travel.[1] But I did not get to do so, nor could I express my good wishes for the 14th [feast of St. Callistus]. But I thought of you so much. The Lord has certainly asked a big sacrifice of you. But perhaps through this sacrifice you will bring about more blessings for the missionary work over there than [you would] through practical participation. I think of Pater Libermann[2] who founded a missionary order and always had to remain at home.

I imagine your TB must be a result of the acute illness and will heal completely at Donnersberg. In any case, you will accept the silence and solitude with deep gratitude after the years that are behind you. And who knows for what purpose you must now build up strength.

We celebrated our Jubilee from September 30 to October 3. The miraculous image of the Queen of Peace from our old monastery church—Mary of Peace—was present as our principal guest of honor. It was displayed on the beautifully decorated high altar; every morning we had a pontifical Mass, a high Mass and several other Masses; three times daily a sermon and a large crowd of people. One has to be grateful that something like this is still possible.

My sister <Rosa> continues to live peacefully within the family; of course, interiorly she is very lonesome. Every morning at five o'clock she goes to the first Mass in the Cathedral. That strengthens her. She seldom can take time to visit the Silesian Carmel. At heart she is always with us here.

Now I thank you most sincerely for your good wishes. Please thank your good mother for the Holy Sacrifice [of the Mass], which was again her gift to me. You wrote nothing about your father this time. Surely your illness is a harder cross for your mother than for you yourself. I include all your intentions in our prayers.

In caritate Christi, your
Sister Teresa Benedicta a Cruce

1. See Letters 238 and 243.
2. Pater Libermann, Jewish by birth, converted to Catholicism, became a priest and founded the Missionary Congregation of the Holy Ghost Fathers. [Jacob Libermann received the name of Francis when he became a Catholic. After his ordination to the priesthood, he first founded a missionary congregation under the patronage of the Heart of Mary. He and his companions later joined the Congregation of the Holy Ghost Fathers (CSSp) of which he is considered re-founder.].

247. Letter to Mother Paula Diez,[1] OP, Speyer
Original in Convent Archive of the Dominican Sisters in Speyer

Cologne-Lindenthal, October 17, 1937

Dear Reverend Mother Paula,

The letter to Sister Callista took me three evenings to write. Always, only a few minutes remain at my disposal for that purpose. Now I would like to add a few words for you. Most cordial thanks for your kind note and for the remembrance in your prayers. I am always touched anew when I see how faithfully you remember me. Several letters came from Speyer for the 15th. Is Sr. Teresa sacristan at St. Magdalena's or at your place? In any case, that is the most beautiful assignment for her, and I am very happy she received it.

What has become of your great-niece Anni? With all good wishes and best regards, your grateful

Sr. Teresa Benedicta a Cruce, OCD

1. Maria Diez (Mother Paula, OP) (b. Ballingshausen, 1877; d. Speyer, 1956) Prioress of the convent at St. Magdalena, Speyer.

248. Letter to Mother Petra Brüning, OSU, Dorsten
Original in Convent Archive of Ursuline Sisters, Dorsten

J.M.J.T.

Pax Christi! Cologne-Lindenthal, November 9, 1937

Dear Reverend Mother,

Sincere thanks for your kind letter. Of course we are happy to send you books for distribution. I thought you would read it with great pleasure. Only you may not draw conclusions about us from [the accounts of] those who went before us. That embarrassed us already during the Jubilee days to listen to so much undeserved praise. But it is always good to be told clearly what is expected of us. I do ask most sincerely that you help us to pray for the spirit of our foundresses, especially for me now in the time of preparation for perpetual profession.

I am surprised that we have never sent you photographs of little St. Thérèse. Naturally, they are entirely different from the pictures that are circulated from Lisieux. I have not read many books at all about little Thérèse. Petitot is always highly praised. In Lisieux they are distressed about Ghéon, but we were happy to read it at table. Of course there are things no outsider can understand. I believe what the saint herself has written is still the best. Other than her life, Lisieux has put out another book: *L'Esprit de Thérèse de l'Enfant Jésus [The Spirit of Thérèse of the Child Jesus]*, composed from notes and quotations. I found that very beautiful.

It will give my sister Rosa great joy to have you come to Breslau. Because of her previous experiences, she has become very intimidated in dealing with people of a different background, and also very reticent, even when that is not warranted.

May I also ask for a memento for my unlucky opus?[1] Pustet cannot print it now. Jakob Hegner in Vienna is not averse to accepting it. I have asked [the people in] Salzburg to return the manuscript. I hope everything will go smoothly. In any case, these are difficulties that have no place in Carmel. I need the time so sorely for things other than business correspondence.

My consolation is that the Lord will take care of the book, if it can be of use to him. Otherwise it may as well remain unprinted.

In the love of Christ, your grateful
Sister Teresa Benedicta

1. *Endliches und Ewiges Sein [Finite and Eternal Being]*; see *Edith Steins Werke,* Vol. II.

249. Letter to Sr. Agnella Stadtmüller, OP, <Presumably in Gemünd>
Original in Convent Archive of Dominican Sisters, St. Magdalena's, Speyer

J.M.

Pax Christi! Cologne-Lindenthal, November 14, 1937
(All Saints of our Order)

My dear Sister Agnella,

Before Advent begins, I would like to send you greetings. E. Neumann will have told you that she celebrated part of our Jubilee with us. She will probably make another appointment after her test is behind her. She is not certain yet about her career. I am advising her, of course, not to take any concrete steps until she has clarified this problem interiorly. I understand very well that the great apostolic tasks that need to be carried out today urge one to effective action. That is necessary, of course, even though the final decisions are reached elsewhere.

I return to everyone the greetings you passed along. Should you be writing soon to Donnersberg, then please tell Sister Callista <Kopf> that I am happy to include all her family's intentions in my prayers. I do hope that before Advent begins I can send a greeting to her. To be sure, it is going to be difficult to reduce the stack of letters awaiting answers by then.

Since early September I have been taking care of a sick fellow-sister. With our schedule, there is little time left over for other tasks. Please say a little prayer for our invalid and for her nurse. According to the doctors' judgment, there is no hope of healing. But now that she has been resting for a long time, her condition is substantially improved, and so Sister Clara continues to hope for recovery. She is our oldest lay sister, who has accomplished a great deal for our house, and she is a model for all of us in her penitential fervor and mortification. Now all intentions are brought to her and commended to her prayer and suffering.

What news do you have of your brother R.? I have not heard from your cousin A.P. <Auguste Pérignon> for ages. She is also among those who are awaiting something from me for a long time. Did she perhaps bring you our commemorative booklet?[1] Surely it will make you happy to get such a vivid insight into our life.

Now I wish you, all your Sister companions, and all who are entrusted to you the richest blessing of graces in the holy season.

In caritate Christi, your Sister
Teresa Benedicta a Cruce, OCD

1. See Letter 244.

250. Letter to Uta von Bodman,[1] Speyer
Original in Convent Archive of Cologne Carmel

Pax Christi! Cologne-Lindenthal, November 16, 1937
Dear Fräulein von Bodman,

The martyrology reminded me again of [Saint] Otmar's[2] day. So I was able to remember you with best wishes. A few months ago the *Benediktinische Monatschrift [Benedictine Monthly Magazine]* (issue 7/8, 1937) carried a picture of a beautiful wooden sculpture of St. Otmar and several details about him. Perhaps you can look up that magazine in the library sometime.

My broken arm and leg can soon celebrate the "year's mind."[3] I no longer need to take them into consideration. For nearly three months my duties have been in the infirmary again, and that means, principally, making many trips between the sickroom, the kitchen and the cellar, also to the garden for the past few weeks since our patient is happiest to lie outside, wrapped up in many warm blankets.

My sister Rosa is living wholly on faith. Each morning at 5 o'clock she goes to the first Mass in the cathedral in order to get nourishment for the day. All is peaceful in the family, but interiorly she is completely alone. I do not yet know how she will spend Christmas. Naturally she would like, most of all, to be here. But that will not do since she would like to come to my Veiling Ceremony after Easter. She cannot easily be spared at home, you see.

How nice that you have been able to find employment at the Municipal Teachers College. Surely you are glad that you can continue to have your home at the convent. Have you heard what has happened to Miss Muthmann? And does Sister Gonzaga hear from Frau Weber once in a while? She wrote to me once here (probably for my Clothing), but never again since then. I am very grateful to your Portress-Sisters for their greetings for October 15 (that also includes Sister Cornelia). Sister Bonaventura told me when she visited that good Sister Anna had sent her. Will you please convey my sincere thanks to Sister Anna, and to Mother Jordana, too, for their kind notes and their remembrance, and Sister Chrysostoma, likewise; I would like to tell the latter also that no one is thinking of transferring me to the Silesian Carmel. If her brothers and sisters want to see me again, they would have to visit me in Cologne. You will probably be able to convey, in person, my greetings and thanks to Sisters Bernarda, Raymunda, Amata and Reginalda.

To you and to all the named and unnamed, my sincerest wishes for a blessed, holy, Advent- and Christmas-time, your

Sister Teresa Benedicta a Cruce

1. See Letter 142.
2. [Uta is a feminine derivative from the masculine, Otmar.]
3. [The expression is similar in German and English folk usage. Month's mind or year's mind is the term for remembering an occasion one month or one year after it happens. For instance, the anniversary of a death is commemorated by a "year's mind Mass".]

251. Letter to Sr. Callista Kopf, OP, <Donnersberg>

Original in Convent Archive of Dominican Sisters, St. Magdalena's, Speyer

J.M.

Pax Christi! Cologne-Lindenthal, November 16, 1937

Dear Sister Callista,

It had not yet been possible for me to answer your last dear letter, and now the latest news has come—not unexpected, almost hoped for, since it is after all the best solution for your dear father, and for your mother also. But of course that does not lessen the sorrow. And I can also imagine that your mother will find it very hard to be removed once more from her own home such a short time before death. But greater than all is still the peace of eternity in which all fetters and veils are removed. Please convey my condolences to your loved ones. I put up your little card at our choir door immediately. When the Sisters go to meditation later, your dear father will receive a memento from each one of them.

I rejoice to think of the little Carmelite family at Donnersberg. I have often thought here about dear Sister Canisia who told me one time of her early attraction to Carmel. And I always remember Sister Irmgard very well, and can imagine how meditatively she must be living in the silence up there.

I wish all of you the grace of a most blessed Advent and a joyful Christmas season.

In caritate Christi, your
Sister Teresa Benedicta a Cruce, OCD

252. Letter to Hedwig Dülberg, Marburg

Original in Convent Archive of Benedictine Sisters, St. Lioba, Freiburg-Günterstal

J.M.

Pax Christi! Cologne-Lindenthal, December 4, 1937

Dear Frau Dülberg,

Actually I wanted to write to you before Advent began, but then came a verbal message from Ruth <Kantorowicz> that I should inform you about several things, but only after I got further directions. After that I received a letter that sounded as though I had better not inform you [at all]. Now I feel compelled to tell you on my own how I see the situation, for I still see you as the person most likely to be of help. You must know that Ruth is leaving the extern quarters of Carmel one of these days and is going to the Ursulines in Venlo. The Sisters at Maastricht will pay her board until she finds something.

I have repeatedly advised her to look around for work, to learn to speak Dutch in order to have better chances, etc. In answer I always get reasons why this would not work, for instance, that there are only job possibilities for which she is unsuited. I have the impression that she wants nothing other than to wait to see whether perhaps some Carmel will accept her after all. At New Year's she wants to apply once more with a recommendation from her Mother Magdalena (I surmise it will be in Austria, since Mother Magdalena comes from Vienna). So far, she has clung so closely, physically, to Mother Magdalena and interiorly to the Carmelite lifestyle that I do not know whether it would still be possible for her to fit into another Order anymore.

You already found her fearfully helpless, and I am afraid she is even more so now. I believe someone would have to take her by the hand now and help her to get a foothold in the world again. I wrote her in my last letter that she would most likely have better prospects as a postulant if she stood on her own two feet, than in the present situation where the suspicion arises that she is only seeking a refuge. But one cannot expect a little rabbit to behave like a lion.

Perhaps it may be easier for you now than in August to arrange some free time and to look in on her. I believe you would find it easier with her in Venlo than in Maastricht.

It is Advent and I would not like to write more than is necessary. Therefore I will only add the most sincere wishes for this holy time. In faithful remembrance, your

Sister Teresa Benedicta a Cruce

253. Plain Postcard to Hedwig Dülberg, Marburg
Original in Convent Archive of Cologne Carmel

Pax Christi! Cologne-Lindenthal, December 7, 1937
Dear Frau Dülberg,

As I was very happy to have your dear letter, I want to assure you at once that you can have the amount you named. Let me know before you come, please, so it can be ready for you. It will be all right even if you cannot make the trip until after New Year's.[1] I am so glad that an opportunity exists at all. We will be able to talk about the matter before then, won't we? I believe we will be completely in accord. When your plan is finalized will you send it to Ruth <Kantorowicz>? I believe it would be a bright star in her beclouded Christmas. Perhaps together, then, you will be able to celebrate Epiphany.

The bells of the cathedral have just finished their beautiful ringing in of the Feast of the Immaculata. We shall be praying Matins soon! *In caritate Christi,* your

Teresa Benedicta a Cruce

1. [Evidently Frau Dülberg planned to go to Holland to see Ruth K. There is no explanation of the source of the "ready" funds, but see Letter 270 for a reference to Ruth's financial situation.]

254. Letter to Mother Petra Brüning, OSU, Dorsten
Original in Convent Archive of Ursuline Sisters, Dorsten

J.M.J.T.

Pax Christi! Cologne-Lindenthal, Gaudete Sunday, 1937

Dear Reverend Mother,

I could not send you my Christmas greetings on a better day: I wish you the holy joy of today's Divine Office for the whole Advent of our lives. May the peace of Christ be jubilantly in your heart and the hearts of your daughters throughout all the sufferings of this age.

In your last letter you sent me the beautiful picture of the Holy Face from [the] Turin [shroud]. I took it to be a gift from the Lord and thought it one of the means of his grace by which he is preparing me for my holy Profession. So I placed it on the small table in my cell in order to be able to see it often. (Of course I do not get to sit there often since taking care of the sick is an ambulatory occupation). Now I have written a little something about it and send it to you as my thanks.[1]

My sister <Rosa> will probably be in Breslau over Christmas. I believe that gratitude for what the past year has brought her is so great that, in comparison, the adversity of the prevailing circumstances does not weigh all too heavily. The Lord will not allow a shortage of new gifts. The prospect of seeing you again is also a great Christmas joy for her.

The day after tomorrow is the anniversary of my fall down the stairs. I believe you did not know at all that I was just hurrying to get something for your Christmas package when it happened. Perhaps this year also someone will return home from [the hospital in] Hohenlind[2] this Holy Night. Have I written you already that our Mother Subprioress has been there for weeks? (That is not, as you sometimes take it, Mother Josepha, but Mother Aloysia whom you do not know personally.) She had a boil on her lip. Now the danger has passed. But because she had already been so worn out (largely the after-effects of the Jubilee) she was unable to regain her strength in a hurry. Sister Clara, my patient, is at present making a retreat. She is a venerable old oak, able to hold her own with unbelievable tenacity. She puts up a stiff battle every time her illness demands that she sacrifice some strict observance.

Today our Father Provincial <Heribert a S. Maria> is with us on his return trip from America. Last evening at recreation, he told us a great deal. He had been over there since September and was very painfully missed here since there was so much to be discussed with him. After all, Carmel is one large family, and the Province a smaller one. You do not know at all how it feels to have a Father to whom one owes obedience and who shares all our cares and responsibilities.

In all tranquility and friendship I have now requested from Pustet the return of the manuscript of my first volume[3]—and have received it. A copy has gone to Hegner in Vienna. Were he to accept it, that would be a wonderful Christmas present. I do not know if I can ever write anything major again. For the present, entirely different tasks seem to await me. I take what comes and ask only that I be granted the necessary abilities to accomplish whatever is required of me. In any case, it is a good school of humility when you are constantly required to perform tasks that, in spite of great effort, you accomplish only in a very imperfect manner.

Again, most sincere wishes and a faithful remembrance. In grateful love, your

Sister Teresa Benedicta a Cruce, OCD[4]

1. It has unfortunately been lost.
2. St. Elizabeth's hospital in Cologne-Hohenlind. [In 1936 Edith was the one to return from St. Elizabeth's. After her fall she was admitted to Trinity Hospital, but later was transferred to St. Elizabeth's where Rosa was baptized.]
3. See Letter 248.
4. [In the margin of this letter there is a handwritten Christmas greeting from Mother Josepha to Mother Petra. Mother Josepha was Mistress of Novices at this time and, as Edith was still under her direction, the letter to Mother Petra went first to Mother Josepha. It is evident that Edith was willing to write about her intimate feelings although she knew that M. Josepha would be reading the letter.]

255. Letter to Elizabeth Nicola, Kevelaer
Original in Convent Archive of Cologne Carmel

J.M.

Pax Christi! Cologne-Lindenthal, Vigil of the Epiphany, 1938

Dear Fräulein Nicola,

Cordial thanks for your dear Christmas greetings and the beautiful book you sent us. Very belated congratulations to you and Fräulein Lieb on passing the examination, and heartfelt wishes for blessings in the New Year from all of us.

The holy Three Kings are bringing us a new little sister, a lay-postulant, Maria Sommer.[1] After all, our dear Sister Clara has been unable to do any work for more than four months and she grows weaker constantly. I am not caring for her anymore since I was given the charge of portress several weeks ago. Our Mother Subprioress has also been ill for several weeks. Please pray for them and also for a poor deceased woman in Breslau who was released from prolonged suffering shortly after Christmas. If you write to Fräulein Hillen,[2] please greet her (for me).

In caritate Christi, your
Sr. Teresa Benedicta a Cruce

1. See Letter 309. [It appears, since Edith adds the reference to Sr. Clara's incapacity, that this postulant was accepted to replace her even though the Carmel had its quota of lay Sisters.]
2. Emma Hillen (b. Düsseldorf, 1907) *Oberstudienrätin* [senior high school teacher] in Düsseldorf, a friend and fellow-student of Elizabeth Nicola and Helene Lieb, all of whom Edith Stein met in the Collegium Marianum in Münster.

256. Letter to Elly Dursy, Hallgarten
Original in Convent Archive of Waldfrieden Carmel

J.M.

Pax Christi! Cologne-Lindenthal, January 8, 1938

Dear Elly,

I am returning your Christmas greetings with many thanks for the beautiful book. Actually you should not have done something like that since you are supposed to be saving your money. Make a note of that for the next occasion.

With all my heart I wish you a genuine Carmelite Christmas for next year. It is good that an understanding with [the Carmel of] Kordel was reached so easily. I expect that you will soon take a trip there since it is now your home.

The Three Kings brought us a new little Sister—a young lay postulant. We will be together in the novitiate for a little while yet. Actually I no longer really belong in it anymore since for the past few weeks I have had the position of portress. Then one usually has duties to perform even at recreation time. My predecessor has now taken over the care of our patient, Sister Clara, whose strength is declining noticeably. I probably wrote you that our Mother Subprioress has also been ill for many weeks. The danger that existed at first has passed, but she is having a very difficult recuperation.

Other than our invalids, I would like to commend to you another poor soul who is very close to my heart. My sister was able to spend Christmas Eve with her. A few days later the poor creature was relieved from many years of severe bodily and mental suffering.[1]

Fond greetings to Herta [Nenninger] and Ännchen <Dursy>. Wishing you a "Year of Grace," I am your

Sister Teresa Benedicta a Cruce, OCD

1. [Helene Hartig, a Catholic friend of the Stein family in Breslau.]

257. Letter to Hedwig Conrad-Martius, Munich

Original in Convent Archive of Cologne Carmel; first published, *Kösel Verlag,* Munich 1960

J.M.

Pax Christi! Cologne-Lindenthal, January 17, 1938

Dear Hatti,

Getting a detailed letter from you was an unexpected delight. Thank you very much for it. It is impossible for me to imagine that the orchard and Eisbrünnel-House no longer exist.[1] Maybe someone will take pictures of your home in Munich sometime so I can better visualize you in it.

Otto Müller, with whom you have such good business dealings, has been bad luck for my opus.[2] He acknowledged the arrival of my manuscript at the publisher's, A. Pustet. A few days later he left the firm, and as a result the publisher suffered such a crisis that he is not in a position to publish [anything] in the foreseeable future. I asked for the return of the manuscript and sent it to Hegner (Vienna), who seemed inclined to take it. Now I have been waiting weeks for his decision. If it fails there I probably will also have to tie in with O. Müller. In some ways it would be practical since I already have the *Imprimatur* from [the diocese of] Salzburg. Will you please give me his address just in case?

For a long while now I have hardly been able to do any work. From the beginning of September until the middle of December, I took care of our good, eldest lay sister, Sr. Clara (cancer of the liver, as far as the doctors can tell). Then I got the office of turn-sister [portress], which means being a contact between the cloister and the outside world. You can imagine that for this one needs a serviceable walking apparatus. I hope to be allowed to make my perpetual profession on April 21. Soon thereafter follows the Veiling Ceremony. That is, again, a big public celebration that the beloved baptismal sponsor [Hedwig Conrad-Martius] should not miss. Hopefully the League of Academics will again cover the cost of travel. We celebrated the 300th Jubilee Year of the Cologne Carmel for four days at the end of September/beginning of October. Our dear Mother <Teresa Renata> wrote a beautiful commemorative booklet for the occasion. I believe you will receive it as a gift when you next visit us.

Do you know that Husserl's health is very poor? This summer he suffered a severe recurrence of pleurisy and is not recovering well from it. Would you write to him sometime perhaps? They now live in Freiburg-Herdern, at Schöneck 6.

Your new living arrangement would seem satisfactory to me if you were not so terribly overloaded. But I do not know what to advise; I can only help to pray that you will have the necessary strength. Many cordial greetings to you, Autós <Theodor Conrad>, Fräulein Käthi, Wolfgang, and if you have an opportunity, to Erika <Gothe> also.

In the love of Christ, your
Benedicta

1. The Conrad-Martiuses had sold their property at Bergzabern, including the orchard, and lived from that time on in Munich.
2. See Letter 248.

258. Letter to Hedwig Dülberg, Marburg

Original in Convent Archive of Benedictine Sisters, St. Lioba, Freiburg-Günterstal

J.M.

Pax Christi! Cologne-Lindenthal, January 21, 1938

Dear Frau Dülberg,

When I received your kind letter of December 23, I was very sad about the unhappy little rabbit <Ruth Kantorowicz> who barred herself from receiving the help she needed so much. Now she herself is pleading most urgently for your visit: today a new cry for help was raised because in M. <Maastricht> it has been decided that her rent will be paid for only three more months. She should have found work by then. I hope it will be possible for you to make the trip now. Then I will tell you, orally, everything I know.

I am not worried about your profession. I have the firmest conviction that you will do, without hesitation, what the Lord asks of you. That is the *unum necessarium* <one thing necessary>. But I do not neglect to remember you [in prayer].

In caritate Christi, your
Sister Teresa Benedicta a Cruce, OCD

259. Letter to Sr. Adelgundis Jaegerschmid, OSB, Freiburg-Günterstal
Original in Convent Archive of Benedictine Sisters, St. Lioba, Freiburg-Günterstal

Pax Christi! Cologne-Lindenthal, March 23, 1938
Dear Sister Adelgundis,

Our greetings go from one death-bed to the other. Our Sister Clara departed today for eternity, very gently, after a year of suffering. I commended our dear Master (Edmund Husserl) to her often, and will do so again tonight at the wake. I believe one is well taken care of in her company. She was our eldest lay sister, tireless in the lowliest of tasks, but a strong and manly character who had grasped and lived the Carmelite ideal with complete determination. So faith turned it into a completely spiritual life. I am not at all worried about my dear Master. It has always been far from me to think that God's mercy allows itself to be circumscribed by the visible church's boundaries. God is truth. All who seek truth seek God, whether this is clear to them or not. I am most grateful to you for every [bit of] news. April 21 will be my perpetual profession; on May 1, my Veiling.

After your letter of the 21st, I was able to ask the Sisters, as a community, to offer their Holy Communion for H. <Husserl> as a name day gift.[1]

Most cordially, your
Teresa Benedicta a Cruce

1. [March 21 is the feast of St. Benedict and the memento for Husserl was a name day gift for Sr. Benedicta.]

260. Letter to Emil Vierneisel,[1] Heidelberg

Original in Convent Archive of Cologne Carmel

Pax Christi! Cologne-Lindenthal, May 6, 1938

Dear Professor,

Cordial thanks for your good wishes and your remembrance. In addition to the holy card of 1934 another is enclosed (one each for you and your dear wife). It hopes to find a place [as a reminder on each future] April 21 or May 1.[2] I commend myself as well for all future deployment. I remember so well your two eldest. They were introduced to me, asleep in their little beds, as a future Jesuit and Benedictine. What do you think of that today? Can our Order possibly have expectations of any of your offspring?

Did the newspapers in Baden publish anything about Husserl's death <April 27, 1938>? Today someone sent me a short notice that appeared in the *Hamburger Fremdenblatt* [a Hamburg newspaper]—it is frighteningly icy.[3] That cannot harm the Master. He was detached from all that is mundane by the time he went home. But against the world he left, one might almost wish to levy the strong language Goethe used against those who denounced Hans Sachs. I will be glad when you find the way to Lindenthal sometime.

With cordial greetings and the hope of many blessings for your whole family, your

Sister Teresa Benedicta a Cruce, OCD

1. See Letter 66.
2. Edith Stein's holy cards were souvenirs of her Clothing Ceremony in 1934, her perpetual profession on April 21, 1938, and the Veiling Ceremony on May 1, 1938. Verses were printed on the back. [See Letter 170.]
3. Husserl, as a "non-Aryan," had been harrassed by the Nazis, but his international reputation prevented more serious mistreatment.

261. Letter to Katharina Schreier, Munich[1]
Original in Convent Archive of Cologne Carmel

J.M.

Pax Christi! Cologne-Lindendenthal, May 13, 1938
Dear Fräulein Schreier,

Sincere thanks for your kind wishes for my Profession. Fräulein Pérignon brought more greetings from you to the Veiling Ceremony and gave me the prospect of a visit from you this summer. Were we able to speak to one another I would also be better able to convince myself whether things are really as bad for you as you wish to make me believe.

Surely Fräulein Pérignon will be glad to tell you about the beautiful celebration. She was very happy to be able to attend. There were a few other guests here from the Palatinate.

External ties with Munich have pretty well stopped, but I forget no one. I know that things are difficult for you, and remember all those with whom I worked in former times.

With sincere wishes for the blessings of a grace-filled Pentecost, your

Sister Teresa Benedicta a Cruce, OCD

1. See Letter 50.

262. Letter to Sr. Adelgundis Jaegerschmid, OSB, Freiburg-Günterstal
Original in Convent Archive of Benedictine Sisters, St. Lioba, Freiburg-Günterstal

J.M.

Pax Christi! Cologne-Lindenthal, May 15, 1938
Dear Sister Adelgundis,

Forgive me for thanking you at such a late date for all the love you showed me by [sending me] your reports. I take it for granted that you read the letters that arrived at Schöneckstrasse,[1] and I have so many letters to answer that it is impossible to foresee when I will finish all of them. The day after my profession I received a card from Frau Husserl, in which she shared with me what he said on Holy Thursday.[2]

I took even those words as a very great gift for my Profession. I always anticipated that the release would come around this time. You see, I considered that it would be a coincidence similar to the one that occurred when my mother died at the hour we made our renewal of vows. You will not think of me as being so confident of the efficacy of my prayers, or even of "merits." No, I am merely convinced that God calls no one for one's own sake alone. Also, that he is prodigal in demonstrating his Love when he accepts a soul.

For my Veiling, Maria Offenberg[3] brought me a copy of your letter to her. I showed both[4] and the beautiful obituary to Nina Baring. She was very grateful for that. The poor thing could not come for the Veiling Ceremony because she had the flu. She had looked forward to it with such joy.

May 16. One of her first ventures outdoors was to come here. Yesterday a thank-you note arrived from Frau Husserl. I imagine you will get to visit her before I am able to write to her, or at least [you] will be inquiring about her by telephone. Would you please tell her I would be most grateful if she could send me some photos taken during these last years. I could return them. Our Sisters would like to see some, and I have only one from 1918 and left that one back in Breslau. I hope you can give me more details when time permits. I know nothing at all about the funeral. There was nothing about it in the obituary notice. I wonder how the university acted? How did Heidegger react?[5] Did Dr. Fink[6] come to the house often, right to the end, and did the turn toward religion make an impression on him? As far as I know, his family background is Catholic.

Please remember me to Reverend Mother Prioress and Sr. Placida <Laubhardt> most cordially and give them two of the holy cards. I ask Sr. Placida to be satisfied with hers, for the time being, as my thank-you for her dear letter. I just cannot write any more now.

I commend to you several serious intentions of our house, and also our dear Sister Maria <Ernst> who will follow me in making her perpetual profession on June 20, and with her Veiling on the 26th.

In caritate Jesu et Mariae, your
Sister Teresa Benedicta a Cruce, OCD

1. See Letter 257. Sr. Adelgundis was the spiritual companion of Edmund Husserl in his final months and at his death bed; at the same time, she helped his wife faithfully in giving him nursing care. After his death she continued to be of assistance to the widow.
2. Edmund Husserl died on April 27, 1938.

3. Maria Offenberg (b. Düsseldorf, 1888; d. Aachen, 1972) Ph.D., senior high school teacher in Aachen; for many years principal of the *Sozialen Frauenschule* [Social School for Women] in Aachen and a coworker in the League for Catholic German Women.
4. [Frau Husserl's note is meant in addition.]
5. See Letter 85.
6. Eugen Fink (b. Constance, 1905; d. Freiburg, 1975) professor of philosophy in Freiburg/Brsg.; Edmund Husserl's assistant for several years.

263. Letter to Sr. Callista Kopf, OP <Donnersberg>

Original in Convent Archive of Dominican Sisters, St. Magdalena's, Speyer

J.M.

Pax Christi! Cologne-Lindenthal, May 19, 1938

Dear Sister Callista,

Sincere thanks to you and the other dear sisters for all the good wishes and prayers, especially for the Holy Sacrifice of the Mass. It was [offered] about the time that Auxiliary Bishop Stockums[1] gave his beautiful homily about the *Sponsa Christi* [Spouse of Christ].

Fräulein Pérignon took along holy card souvenirs of the Profession for all at Donnersberg. You have probably received them. Should Sister Agnella <Stadtmüller> no longer be there, I beg you to forward the letter and two pictures of the Queen of Peace to her. The third one is for you.

Hopefully you will soon be able to take on some work again. Surely the prospect of it already makes you happy and grateful. How is your dear mother? I will surely be happy if someone brings me personal greetings and news from you.

Forgive me for being so brief. I have frightfully many letters to write after the celebration and very little time for it. To you and to the dear Sisters who think of me so faithfully, I commend a very serious intention for our house.

With all sincere wishes for blessings in the grace-filled coming Ember-[2] and Feast-Days, your faithful

Sister Teresa Benedicta a Cruce, OCD

1. [Auxiliary Bishop Wilhelm Stockums gave the black veil to Sr. Teresa Benedicta on April 21.]
2. [At that time, the "Ember Days" were days of obligatory fast and prayer, Wednesday, Friday and Saturday of one week near the beginning of each of the four seasons.]

264. Letter to Katharina Lichtenberger, Ludwigshafen
Original in Convent Archive of Cologne Carmel

J.M.

Pax Christi! Cologne-Lindenthal, May 23, 1938
Dear Frau Lichtenberger,

Sincere thanks to you and your dear husband for the beautiful gift, for your kind letter and especially for your coming. It was a special joy for me that you took part in the celebration. Surely your husband will also find his way here sometime. I don't know whether it is possible for you to travel together. When one has a business that is always difficult, of course. It must be a loss for you that Sr. Agnella <Stadtmüller> is no longer in Ludwigshafen. Perhaps you will get together with Fräulein Pérignon sometime instead.

I suspect that in the great bustle recently you did not get any remembrance other than the little profession cards, so I'm enclosing something more today.

With the most sincere wishes for many blessings on the coming beautiful Feasts,[1] I greet you in the love of Jesus and Mary, your grateful
Sr. Teresa Benedicta a Cruce, OCD

1. These were, in 1938: Ascension Day, May 26; Pentecost, June 5-6; Corpus Christi, June 16.

265. Letter to Katharina Schreier, Munich
Original in Convent Archive of Cologne Carmel

J.M.

Pax Christi! Cologne-Lindenthal, May 23, 1938
Dear Fräulein Schreier,

I must follow with a further expression of gratitude the thanks I sent recently: Fräulein Pérignon sent me a beautiful present in your name. She begged me urgently to write down the names of several books that would give me pleasure. I listed a number of Church Fathers because I feel that there is no healthier nor more nourishing spiritual fare than the Sacred Scriptures and the Fathers. And since we are still pretty poor in that line, I like to use every favorable opportunity to fill in the gaps. You have enriched us with one volume of Basil's. For that we thank you most sincerely.

We are in the Rogation Days[1] now and have such great days of grace ahead of us. We will unite in [praying for] all of our intentions, won't we? I particularly commend to you something that is a very great worry to our house.

Wishing you the richest graces and blessings of the Holy Spirit, your grateful

Sr. Teresa Benedicta a Cruce, OCD

1. The Rogation Days were three days of prayer for a good harvest: Monday, Tuesday and Wednesday before Ascension Day.

266. Scenic Postcard to Hedwig Dülberg, Marburg
Original in Convent Archive of Cologne Carmel

J.M.

Pax Christi! Cologne-Lindenthal, May 28, 1938
Dear Frau Dülberg,

Sincere thanks for your kind wishes. I remember faithfully you and all those in your care. Your Carmelite candidate will probably have entered in Kordel near Trier where our dear Mother <Teresa Renata de Spiritu Sancto> was novice mistress for nine years. However, we have had no word from there about it [her entrance]. Please put Venlo[1] on your program for the first possible date. I believe it to be urgently necessary. On the way you will surely stop here for a thorough preliminary discussion.

Wishing you all the gifts of the Holy Spirit, your
Sr. Teresa Benedicta a Cruce, OCD

1. To the Ursuline Convent, Venlo (Dutch Limburg) in which Ruth Kantorowicz had found lodging through the mediation of Mother Petra Brüning, OSU, Dorsten.

267. Letter to Walter Warnach,[1] Cologne
Original in Convent Archive of Cologne Carmel

Pax Christi! Cologne-Lindenthal, Pentecost Monday, June 6, 1938
Dear Herr Warnach,

The Holy Spirit urges me to write a few words about your poems. I read them for the first time as soon as they arrived. At that time I expected to be able to talk to you about them when you come to visit, but perhaps you are waiting for my comments.

I understand well that it is essentially part of your life to express yourself in this form and to seek clarity thereby. Your verses require no apology for being either too harsh or too gloomy. It is probably a sign of your great sensibility that you yourself consider them that way. Of course, they are not easily accessible. I can't say that even I can understand every word. But I believe I can understand something of the spiritual wanderer's frame of mind out of which they were composed. And I believe the closer he comes to the summit the better able he will be to make himself understood. In places, he is already managing it. Perfect poetry is—I believe—like perfect wisdom and sanctity, unpretentious and transparently clear.

With reference to the poem *Gebet um Trost* ["Prayer for Consolation"] I would like to break a lance for the angels [i.e., champion their cause]. They do not stand like a barrier between us and God. The ray of illumination that (according to Dionysius) descends on us after having passed through all nine Choirs [of angels] connects the entire grace-inundated spirit world; the Trinity is personally present on every level; even in the lowest choir of angels it is he himself whom we meet. It is not his unapproachable majesty that God communicates to us through his messengers, but rather his overflowing love. It is their bliss, just as it will be ours (and already is to some extent), to be allowed to cooperate in God's dispensing of graces. Consider yourself fortunate indeed if these hunters have picked up your scent, and allow them to drive you into the arms of the Spirit of love and of truth.

In caritate Eius [in his love], your
Sister Teresa Benedicta a Cruce, OCD

1. Walter Warnach (b. Metz/Lorraine, 1910) Ph.D., reader for Schwann and Patmos Publishers. Professor of philosophy at the *Staatlichen Kunstakademie* [State Academy for the Arts], Düsseldorf; first met Edith Stein presumably in autumn, 1937, at the request of the French Dominican, Pere R. L. Bruckberger (editor in chief of the *Revue Thomiste*). Prof. Warnach read and forwarded the galley proofs of the manuscript of *Finite and Eternal Being,* which was being set in print by Borgmeyer. He maintained a constant exchange of ideas in philosophy with Edith Stein. He is currently [1991] living in Cologne.

268. Letter to Anni Greven,[1] Krefeld
Original in private possession of Anni Greven

J.M.

Pax Christi! Cologne-Lindenthal, June 14, 1938

Since Sunday suits you best, our dear Reverend Mother will keep some time free for you this coming Sunday. We would be grateful if you could arrange [to come] between 9 and 10 A.M. or between 3 and 5 in the afternoon. These hours are free from community exercises. The Holy Masses on Sundays are at 7 and 8:15 A.M.

With friendly greetings from our dear Reverend Mother also, in the love of Christ, your

Sr. Teresa Benedicta a Cruce, OCD

1. Anni Greven (b. Krefeld, 1896) maintained friendly contact with Edith Stein until the latter's death.

269. Letter to Anni Greven, Krefeld
Original in private possession of Anni Greven

J.M.

Pax Christi! Cologne-Lindenthal, June 21, 1938
Dear Fräulein Greven,

Enclosed is the membership certificate for Rev. Sr. Marciana.[1] She will be able to gain a plenary indulgence already on the Feast of the Sacred Heart.

I am happy that you found Carmel so pleasant. I will also be happy to greet Sr. Marciana if a visit is possible for her. We do have to mete out our time in the speakroom as briefly as possible, but when anyone has an intention we are allowed to listen in all patience. One is then better able to commend things to the Lord. Obviously I will always answer questions as well as I can. Surely you will not be coming before the 26th. A Veiling Ceremony always brings many guests and therefore also work. After that, I shall be more available again.

I wish you a speedy recovery and strength for your difficult profession, and the same for Sister Marciana. With sincere greetings in the love of Jesus and Mary, your

Sr. Teresa Benedicta a Cruce, OCD

1. This acquaintance of Anni Greven's belonged to a society of Sisters [whose origin connects them to the Beguines of the Middle Ages. Their rule was based on that of St. Augustine. Their title, "Cellitines," was derived from the name of the monastic cell in which they lived. Their house on Kupfergasse in Cologne, where Sr. Marciana was stationed, was destroyed during WWII.] In this letter Edith Stein enclosed Sr. Marciana's membership certificate for the Theresian Fraternity.

270. Letter to P. Swidbert Soreth, OP,[1] Cologne
Original in Convent Archive of Cologne Carmel

J.M.

Pax Christi! Cologne-Lindenthal, July 21, 1938

Very Reverend Father Subprior,

Last evening I was still[2] able to talk to our Reverend Mother about R's <Ruth Kantorowicz> affairs and heard something then that I had not known. Namely, there is no longer a bank account in R's name but rather everything has been transferred to Dr. Str. <Strerath>.[3] That changes the situation completely and cancels everything I said yesterday. I believe it would be very good if your Reverence were to speak to Dr. Strerath and Dr. Reeb[4] before the negotiations with L. are begun so as to be completely clear about all the circumstances and the practical possibilities.

May I ask you for a memento to our holy Father (St.) Elijah of the intentions I commended to you yesterday?

To my great joy, he is my patron this month[5] and I have a lot of confidence in him, especially in this matter.

Asking for your blessing and in faithful remembrance of your Reverence *in Christo,* I am, with grateful respect, your

Sr. Teresa Benedicta a Cruce, OCD

1. Fr. Paul Soreth (P. Swidbert, OP) (b. Düsseldorf, 1890; d. Düsseldorf, 1975) author and translator but principally retreat master for many years (especially for religious women).
2. [This "still" means that Edith Stein was able to speak to the Prioress before the beginning of "grand silence," that is, between P. Swidbert's visit and Compline. Once the silence had begun it was the custom to write out messages rather than to speak.]
3. See Letter 290.
4. Attorney Dr. Otto Reeb of Cologne, at that time in Maastricht [Holland].
5. [The Carmelites had a devotional practice of drawing the names of Carmelite saints at the beginning of each month.]

271. Letter to Paula Stolzenbach, Frankfurt

Original in Convent Archive of Waldfrieden Carmel

Pax Christi! Cologne-Lindenthal, July 21, 1938

Dear Sister Paula-Maria,

I am allowed to send you this little book in gratitude for the French *Consummata* volumes with which you equipped me for Carmel. Those volumes helped a great deal in the preparation of this book and furnished the majority of the pictures. Our Sister Angela[1] is the author. Until the war began she was in a Belgian Carmel, and she reads and translates a great deal from the French. You will surely be glad to help us, again, to publicize the book.

How are your dear ones? I would like to commend my relatives to you. The situation gets more and more difficult for them. Perhaps in Frankfurt you get to hear many things about that subject, too.

Always with a sincere remembrance and with all good wishes, your

Sister Teresa Benedicta a Cruce

1. Martha Schwalge (Sr. Maria Angela of the Child Jesus, OCD) *Ein Leben der Liebe, Marie Antoinette de Geuser [A Life of Love, M.A. de G.],* Laumann, (Dülmen, 1938).

272. Letter to Rudolf Allers,[1] Washington, DC

Original in private possession of Mrs. Christel Allers,[2] Washington, DC

J.M.

Pax Christi! Cologne-Lindenthal, July 23, 1938

Dear Dr. Allers,

A few months ago I sent an invitation to my Veiling ceremony to your Dittesgasse address <in Vienna, Austria>. It came back marked "Moved!" In the meantime I have learned where you are, so I am sending you the souvenir cards of my profession as a sign that I have not forgotten you, and with them comes a plea to keep me and my relatives in mind. All of my brothers and sisters are still in Germany, but one sister-in-law and two nephews and a niece[3] are in the United States, and others will probably follow them soon.

You will have learned from the newspapers that Husserl died on April 27 after a long illness. You probably have not heard, however, that during his final weeks he detached himself from all earthly concerns and had but one longing, to be united with God.

With all best wishes *in caritate Christi,* your
Sister Teresa Benedicta a Cruce, OCD

1. Rudolf Allers (b. Vienna, 1883; d. Washington, DC, c. 1960) emigrated to the United States in 1938. From 1938, he was professor of psychology and philosophy in Washington; he made a synthesis of the Viennese school of psychology with Catholic anthropology.
2. Wife of Dr. Ulrich Stephan Allers, daughter-in-law of Rudolf. Ulrich Allers (b. Vienna, 1920; d. Washington, DC, 1974); professor of sociology and political science.
3. Arno Stein's wife, Martha, née Kaminski, his son Helmut, and daughter Lotte; and Else Gordon (née Stein)'s son, Werner.

273. Letter to Sr. Callista Kopf, OP <Speyer>

Original in Convent Archive of Dominican Sisters, St. Magdalena's, Speyer

J.M.

Pax Christi! Cologne-Lindenthal, August 1, 1938

Dear Sister Callista,

It is surely a great joy for you to be back in your old convent-home, even though perhaps the joy is tinged with sadness. Please remember me to your dear relatives. I hope you found everything well with them. Surely the family must find consolation in having you nearby for a while. Everyone out there in the world is having such a difficult time now.

I would like to send a picture of our youngest, Susel and Ernst Ludwig <Biberstein>[1] for you to see. They are now in their 16th and 17th years, both in the *Unterprima.*[2] My sister and brother-in-law, <Hans and Erna Biberstein>[3] wanted to stay in Germany as long as possible, and to keep their children with them. But now they have to admit that it cannot go on any longer. They have a possibility of shelter for the children in England. The two are bound by a deep love for one another and would like to stay together if they have to be separated from their parents. I hope for that also, since I believe his sister is a good support for the boy.

In sincere union in the Heart of Jesus, your

Sister Teresa Benedicta a Cruce, OCD

1. See Letter 24.
2. Corresponds to final years in high school, approximately.
3. See Letters 24 and 307.

274. Letter to Maria Mayer, Beuron

Original in private possession of the Mayer family[1]

J.M.

Pax Christi! Cologne-Lindenthal, August 12, 1938

Dear Fräulein Mayer,

With all my heart I remember you and your dear sister who has gone to her [eternal] home. It must have been a great blow for you even though you have long been prepared for [her death]. Still you have the consolation that all your loved ones are now in eternal peace. My brothers and sisters and their children, on the other hand, are in great trouble. I must pray that they find a home on earth as well as in eternity. Will you please help me in this?

In the love of Jesus and Mary, your

Sister Teresa Benedicta a Cruce, OCD

1. When Edith Stein used to go to the Benedictine Abbey in Beuron, she stayed in the Mayer's guest house.

275. Letter to Elly Dursy, <Kordel>
Original in Convent Archive of Waldfrieden Carmel

J.M.

Pax Christi! Cologne-Lindenthal, September 18, 1938

Dear Little Sister,

Deo gratias ex toto corde [Thank God with all my heart] for your landing in port! Our Father Provincial told me a week ago that Your Charity was expected in Kordel on the 17th. I thought of it yesterday morning even before the latest news arrived from Hallgarten, but I was glad to receive confirmation.

How well I can share your feelings, when I think back to the time five years ago: the difficulty of the farewell, and the deep sense of security, as soon as[1]

1. The text ends here in the original. The conclusion of the letter was lost.

276. Letter to Anni Greven, <Krefeld>
Original in private possession of Anni Greven

J.M.

Pax Christi! Cologne-Lindenthal, October 6, 1938

Dear Fräulein Greven,

Thank you sincerely for the beautiful little roses and the picture. We will celebrate the feast of our holy Mother [St.] Teresa on Sunday, October 16. Low Masses will be offered at 7, 8:15, and 10 o'clock, and a High Mass at 9:15 that morning. In the afternoon, we will have a sermon, Compline and Benediction at 5 o'clock.

It would be wonderful if you could come. However, I cannot promise you that a speakroom will be free on that day. We have only two and on feasts of the Order they are much in demand. If you seek the silence of the cloister, a workday or a quiet Sunday is more suitable [for a visit]. But perhaps this time you would like to share in the Feast and come some other time for a quiet visit.

With all good wishes, I greet you in the love of Christ, your

Sister Teresa Benedicta a Cruce, OCD

277. Letter to Sr. Callista Kopf, OP <Speyer>
Original in Convent Archive of Dominican Sisters, St. Magdalena's, Speyer

J.M.

Pax Christi! Cologne-Lindenthal, October 20, 1938

Dear Sister Callista,

Thank you very much for your dear wishes for the Feast of our holy Mother and for the Mass. One could not wish for a more wonderful "pension."[1] My sincere sympathy to all of you in your convent at the going-home of dear, good Mother Jordana. Today, more than ever, one does not begrudge anyone eternal rest and is grateful for all who have escaped the sufferings of these times. Sincere thanks to Sister Bernarda for her communication, to the dear Sister-Portresses and to Fräulein von Bodman for her good wishes.

[You ask] whether the life of mystical graces is reserved for a few? Your brother [Dominican], Garrigou-Lagrange, has attempted to show with great emphasis (and many have concurred in his opinion) that it is but the unfolding of the three theological virtues and that all Christians are called to what is the *essential* [element] of it, namely, to union with God. This [union] is not extraordinary, but only the ecstasies, visions and the like that accompany it in some cases. The obstacles people put up account for the fact that only a few actually attain to that [union]. Our holy parents in the Order are not completely of that opinion. In any case, for the consolation of those not mystically graced, both emphasize that what is decisive is union with God in the will, that is, conformity to the divine Will. But our Holy Mother saw a vocation to Carmel as synonymous with a vocation to contemplation. That surely holds for every "contemplative" Order. Anyway, I think there is more security in doing all one can to become an empty vessel for divine grace. "Tear your heart away from all things. Seek God, and you will find him." (Maxim of our Holy Mother.)

What is our life like? Early in the morning, just about three hours in the choir: one hour of meditation, the Little Hours <Liturgy of the Hours>, Mass. Then just about two hours <...>[2] of work. This working time is filled differently by each one, but it has to be used well by all of us. For several years I was allowed to use it mostly for intellectual work. I used to send most of the short writings to you (together with Sister Agnella <Stadtmüller>). The big opus *Endliches und Ewiges Sein [Finite and Eternal Being]* is now being printed (by Borgmeyer in Breslau). A few weeks ago one of my articles appeared in a collection *(Die in Deinem Hause wohnen [Those Who Live in Your House],* edited by P. Eugen Lense, OCist, published by Benziger, Einsiedeln). [It is] the biography of Mother Franziska Esser who founded the second Cologne Carmel.[3]

Since December of last year, I've had charge of the turn, that is, I carry on all the business with the outside world with the help of the Portresses we have outside the enclosure. I also take care of the telephone. No one else except Reverend Mother and Mother Subprioress may use the telephone. In addition, the turn is always kept locked, and I carry the key at my cincture. I have to guard the enclosure at both points. Therefore I am usually on the move since I have this office, and there is very little time to spend at my desk. Every letter is written in many segments. It is a pretty unusual way of life, but a post that has great meaning in a house with strict enclosure, and I am grateful that it has been entrusted to me.

On October 14, my brother <Arno> came to say goodbye before setting out for America, perhaps forever. His wife has been over there for some time, as well as two of his children; the two eldest still remain in Germany. My brother-in-law <Hans Biberstein> (the father of our two youngest) is also over there looking for a livelihood for his family since his medical license was taken away here. That was a few months ago. After that the children were also taken out of school. They were both in *Unterprima,* one and a half years from *Abitur* [graduation]. Susel has to work hard as a mother's helper in a family they have known for some time. Ernst Ludwig went to a [training] farm in order to learn agriculture. My older nephew Wolfgang <Arno Stein's son> (now 26 years old) has been there for several years and will probably be emigrating from there to Argentina with some companions soon.[4]

I am very grateful to you for your assistance in prayer. Best regards to all your dear Sisters and relatives.

In the love of Jesus and Mary, your
Sister Teresa Benedicta a Cruce, OCD

1. A Mass was offered for Edith Stein and her intentions every year on October 15. (A note from Sr. Callista Kopf, OP.) See Letter 182. [Edith calls this a pension because of her past employment as a teacher in Speyer.]
2. See Letter 171 [for rest of schedule].

3. *Eine deutsche Frau und grosse Karmelitin, Mutter Franziska von den Verdiensten Jesu Christ, OCD (Katharina Esser),* 1804-1866; in E. Lense, *Die in Deinem Hause Wohnen* (Einsiedeln: Benziger), Vol. 1.
4. Niece and nephews of Edith Stein. See *Edith Steins Werke,* Vol. VII, or, in English, *Life.*

278. Letter to Sr. Agnella Stadtmüller, OP, <Ludwigshafen>
Original in Convent Archive of Dominican Sisters, St. Magdalena's, Speyer

J.M.

Pax Christi! Cologne-Lindenthal, October 20, 1938

Dear Sister Agnella,

I have wanted to answer your kind letter for ever so long, but there was so much else to do that for a long time I had to let all the letters wait. Now, in a short breathing pause, I can reduce the mountain a bit. Among the variety [of things to do during] the past weeks there was a heap of proofreading.[1] Now things are at a standstill again. Because everything is so irregular, it is impossible to judge when the opus will appear. Actually, Volume I ought to be finished by Christmas. Perhaps Fräulein Pérignon might be able to inquire at Borgmeyer's (Sandkirche 3, Breslau I) when the book will appear. I believe that [an inquiry] always gives a slight impetus to go ahead with publication. The subsidy we paid toward the printing costs is to be repaid in the form of copies of the book, and we will then have to see how we will store them.

Yesterday, greetings from you were passed on to me in a letter from the Lichtenbergers. I hope you have settled in somewhat in the meantime.[2] Certainly it is difficult to live outside the convent and without [having] the Blessed Sacrament [reserved in the house]. But God is within us after all, the entire Blessed Trinity, if we can but understand how to build within ourselves a well-locked cell and withdraw there as often as possible, then we will lack nothing anywhere in the world. That, after all, is how the priests and religious in prison must help themselves. For those who grasp this it becomes a time of great grace. We have already heard this of some people [in such a situation].

The best edition of the writings of our Holy Mother is the new one from Kösel, Pustet. The *Leben [Life]* appeared in 1933. The *Klosterstiftungen [Book of Foundations],* the first volume of the *Briefe [Letters],* and *Die Seelenburg [The Interior Castle]* followed. There are two more volumes to come.

Last Friday my brother <Arno> came to say goodbye before setting out for America. It was exactly the fifth anniversary of my entrance, and the first time we saw one another since then. Perhaps now it will be forever. Everything is disintegrating and changing. Please help with your prayers.

A little while ago, Sr. Bonaventura came here from Bonn again and told us about St. Magdalena's. Sr. Bernarda, the faithful chronicler, informed me about Mother Jordana's death. [The latter] had sent an acknowledgment of my congratulations on her Jubilee. Our "Jubilee-bride" is still very cheerful and vivacious.

Most cordial greeting to all the dear Sisters in Ludwigshafen, to Fräulein Pérignon and the good Lichtenbergers. In Jesus's love, your

Sister Teresa Benedicta, OCD

1. See Letter 277.
2. During the rule of the Nazis, all schools operated by religious orders were closed. Sr. Agnella stayed in Ludwigshafen with several other Sisters. They lived in a small private dwelling and Sr. Agnella occupied herself with private tutoring.

279. Letter to Walter Warnach, <Cologne>
Original in Convent Archive of Cologne Carmel

J.M.

Pax Christi! Cologne-Lindenthal, October 25, 1938

Dear Herr Warnach,

Here are the missing pages (they had slipped into another pile; please forgive the disorder) plus the continuation, p. 105-137, and 1-5 (a comment for the last chapter).[1]

Would you have the kindness, perhaps, to send your duplicates at your convenience?

With sincere greetings, yours *in Christo,*

Sr. Teresa Benedicta a Cruce, OCD

1. See Letter 267.

280. Letter to Hedwig Dülberg, Marburg

Original in Convent Archive of Benedictine Sisters, St. Lioba, Freiburg-Günterstal

J.M.

Pax Christi! Cologne-Lindenthal, October 31, 1938

Dear Frau Dülberg,

When your kind letter of September 29 arrived, everyone was bustling about: Triduum for the little St. Thérèse and a 60-Year Jubilee. Then right afterward the feast of our Holy Mother, which is at the same time Reverend Mother's name day. In addition, large piles of proofreading since the big book is actually being printed. So I could not satisfy your request for a sign of life before now.

On August 1, we accepted an extern postulant, a very good child but unfortunately not suited for the position; on Saturday she left, again with a heavy heart. For two weeks now we've had another one who makes a very good impression, but we would dearly love to have a third. Josephine is to receive the habit on Gaudete Sunday; she really should make her novitiate inside the enclosure, but that will be impossible as long as we do not have two other reliable ones outside.

Ruth <Kantorowicz> is still *"Mädchen für alles"* ["maid for all jobs"] at the Ursulines in V. <Venlo, Holland>. Various expectations that surfaced always sank into oblivion again. She asked about you, too, recently. It is always a good deed when you write to her. It would be even better if you were able to visit her again.

Sister Placida <Laubhardt> stopped by once for 20 minutes on her way to Namur; she has been transferred there. She is just as she always has been. For a long time there has been no news from Countess Bissingen; perhaps her asthma is giving her trouble again. On the 26th, Pater Przywara[1] gave a lecture here to the *Akademiker-Verband* [League of Academicians] and visited us for the first time the following morning.

In Carmel the usual autumn colds are making the rounds. Two Sisters have been dispensed for a longer period, and so the rest have more to do. You just cannot believe how active our contemplative life is. But we had a day of recollection yesterday and were really able to spend it contemplatively, at the feet of the [Eucharistic] King.

On the 14th[2] my brother <Arno> said goodbye to me before his departure for America. On All Souls Day we will both remember our mother. This remembrance is always very comforting for me. I have the firm conviction that my mother now has the power to help her children in these great afflictions.

I wish you great progress in the Carmel of the divine Will. *In caritate Christi,* your

Sister Teresa Benedicta a Cruce

1. See Letter 59.
2. [This corrects a misprint of "October 24" in the German edition.]

281. Letter to Mother Petra Brüning, OSU, Dorsten
Original in Convent Archive of Ursuline Sisters, Dorsten

J.M.

Pax Christi! Cologne-Lindenthal, October 31, 1938

Dear Reverend Mother,

Thank you so much for your kind account about Breslau. It was surely a big sacrifice for my sister <Rosa> that she could not come to see you a second time. It would have been good for her to have a chance to talk at greater length. I already know from her letters that she is very depressed and worn out because of the constant agitation.[1] I am allowed to write to her frequently, but it is a poor substitute for being together in person. If at all possible we would like to have her here for Christmas. I wrote about that in one of my letters to the family recently, so that the others would adjust to it. There is no longer any sense to saving [money] since they have to turn everything in when they emigrate. If only they knew where to go! But I trust that, from eternity, Mother will take care of them. And [I also trust] in the Lord's having accepted my life for all of them. I keep having to think of Queen Esther[2] who was taken from among her people precisely that she might represent them before the king. I am a very poor and powerless little Esther, but the King who chose me is infinitely great and merciful. That is such a great comfort.

We shall soon be singing First Vespers of All Saints. I have to give the letter to Reverend Mother.

In grateful love, your least
Sister Teresa Benedicta a Cruce, OCD

1. [The harassment by the Nazis increased daily.]
2. [Edith's identification with Queen Esther caused the pertinent section of the Book of Esther to be used as a first reading during the Beatification Ceremony on May 1, 1987.]

282. Letter to Peter Wery,[1] Grossbüllesheim
Original in private possession of the Wery family, Grossbullesheim

J.M.

Pax Christi! Cologne-Lindenthal, November 4, 1938

Dear Herr Wery,

Pardon me for taking so long to thank you for the lovely poem.[2] There is surprisingly much to do in our contemplative life, and the turn-sister[3] may not, outwardly, resemble a well-rooted lily.[4] But then it is all the more necessary that in her active existence she have her roots deep in God. That is why I thank you not only for the poem and the trouble you took in copying it, but also and especially for every friendly remembrance in prayer that will help me to reach the goal. I may surely also commend my relatives to you. At this time they are all very worried.

Now I wish you and your loved ones a truly grace-filled Advent and a joyous Feast, for I will hardly be able to send another greeting before that.

Surely I may enclose another little letter for Frater Koronowski <Kronenberg>.[5]

In caritate Christi, your
Sister Teresa Benedicta a Cruce, OCD

1. Peter Wery, cousin of the former Prioress, Mother Maria Josepha a Ss. Sacrament, née Wery. Old "Uncle Peter" founded a so-called Teresian Flower Garden in honor of St. Thérèse of Lisieux. It was a matter of a private arrangement that gave the elderly gentleman great joy and, at his advanced age, a big prayer-obligation. In this Theresian garden, Edith had been designated as the lily.
2. The poem mentioned has not been preserved.
3. [The duty of the "turn-sister" in Carmel was to handle all contacts with the world outside the enclosure.]
4. A reference to Edith Stein. [Her floral designation in Uncle Peter's Teresian garden.
5. Pater Dr. Karl Kronenberg, formerly Koronowski (1914 Bochum), Congregation of the Missionaries of the Holy Family, Biesdorf. Unlike his classmate P. Hennes [see Letter 243], P. Kronenberg was not sent to Brazil since he was drafted into the army in 1937. Resulting from his service in WWII, he spent a long time in the United States as a prisoner of war. He was director of students in Biesdorf after his return to Germany.

283. Letter to Anni Greven, Krefeld
Original in private possession of Anni Greven

J.M.

Pax Christi! Cologne-Lindenthal, November 5, 1938

Dear Fräulein Greven,

Today is my first opportunity to thank you, most sincerely, for the various rose-greetings. I trust that [celebrating] the feast of Teresa in Carmel was good for you.

On October 23, we began the "big Advent," that is, the nine weeks before Christmas. When the Church's Advent begins we stop writing letters (except about business matters that cannot be postponed) and also stop going to the speakroom. That is why we already have to think of wishing a grace-filled time for our dear ones outside. Therefore I am sending you very cordial wishes for blessings for Advent and Christmas as well. If we prepare our hearts in these beautiful weeks of preparation, then surely the Divine Child will not fail to give us rich graces.

I am happy to include you, dear Fräulein Greven, and Sister Marciana in our liturgy for the holy season of Advent and in all of our prayers. In the love of Christ, your

Sr. Teresa Benedicta a Cruce, OCD

284. Picture postcard to Karl and Katharina Lichtenberger, Ludwigshafen
Original in Convent Archive of Cologne Carmel.

J.M.

Pax Christi! Cologne-Lindenthal, November 9, 1938

Sincerest thanks for your dear greetings for the Feast of our Holy Mother. I am very glad that you have dear Sr. Agnella <Stadtmüller> in your vicinity again and that you can visit her sometimes.

With most cordial wishes for the blessings of a grace-filled Advent and Christmas season, your

Sister Teresa Benedicta a Cruce

285. Letter to Katharina Schreier, Munich
Original in Convent Archive of Cologne Carmel

J.M.

Pax Christi! Cologne-Lindenthal, November 10, 1938
Dear Fräulein Schreier,

Before Advent begins I would like to send you greetings and to wish you from my heart an Advent rich in graces. You might want to adopt the custom of the big children in Carmel who at the beginning of the Advent season receive a small crib to keep in their cell, into which they lay a piece of straw for every small sacrifice? I have no idea what the weakness you reproach yourself for might be, nor would I expect you to be more specific. But are you not tempted to make the struggle against this weakness your Advent preparation and so make ready the way for the Lord? He will not allow you to outdo him in generosity, and if only you stretch out your arms toward him, he will lift you up and over all the debris that lies in your path. I will gladly think of you along these lines, and will be very happy if I receive a joyous Christmas greeting.

You can well imagine that now I am very worried about my relatives. Will you please help me, so that for them also a great light will illumine the darkness?

Greetings to you in the love of Christ, your
Sister Teresa Benedicta a Cruce, OCD

286. Letter to Walter Warnach, Cologne
Original in Convent Archive of Cologne Carmel

J.M.

Pax Christi! Cologne-Lindenthal, December 1, 1938
Dear Herr Warnach,

Cordial congratulations on having passed the examination. I am very happy that you are now free from this pressure. At the time, the page proofs 185-203 arrived late from the printer. I put them aside for you, and with them the conclusion of Volume I and the beginning of II.[1]

Should you be traveling for an extended time, I would ask you kindly to drop off all the pages here before you leave. One cannot exclude the possibility that they might be needed again.

This is so brief only because it is Advent. With most sincere good wishes *in Christo*, your

Sister Teresa Benedicta a Cruce, OCD

1. See Letters 267 and 279.

287. Letter to Mother Petra Brüning, OSU, Dorsten
Original in Convent Archive of Ursuline Sisters, Dorsten

J.M.

Pax Christi! Cologne-Lindenthal, December 9, 1938

Dear Reverend Mother,

Many thanks for your loving letter of November 23. I must tell you that I already brought my religious name with me into the house as a postulant. I received it exactly as I requested it. By the cross I understood the destiny of God's people which, even at that time, began to announce itself. I thought that those who recognized it as the cross of Christ had to take it upon themselves in the name of all. Certainly, today I know more of what it means to be wedded to the Lord in the sign of the Cross. Of course, one can never comprehend it, for it is a mystery.

My brother <Arno> left for the United States on October 14, just in the nick of time. His oldest son <Wolfgang> was in a [concentration] camp until a few days ago, but now will probably be able to follow [his father] soon. My brother-in-law <Hans Biberstein> has been over there [in the U.S.] for several months seeking information [concerning job opportunities]; he has now received permission to remain there and to have his wife and children join him immediately. He has already obtained a teaching position at a university.[1] The Hamburg relatives <the Gordons> are getting ready for their departure to join their son in Colombia [South America]; one daughter is going to Norway. My sisters in Breslau are the worst off. My hope is that the Bibersteins (that is, my brother-in-law and my sister Erna) will soon be able to get permission for them to follow.

B. <Borgmeyer> continues to print the second volume now, but everything is still in galleys. I do not yet know what will happen about the publication. Should it become possible, after all, it would be my farewell gift to Germany. Our Reverend Mother has asked our sisters in Echt (Holland)[2] to receive me. Today their loving acceptance arrived. If it is possible to get all the necessary papers together in time, we would like to make the transfer even before December 31. These are the facts.

And now I would like to wish you a very grace-filled Christmas feast. As the atmosphere around us grows steadily darker, all the more must we open our hearts for the light from above. Most cordial thanks once more for all the love you have shown me in these five years in the Order. Since your way sometimes leads to Holland, I may even have the hope of seeing you again. I commend myself to your prayers for the next weeks and months.

In caritate Regis qui venturus est <in the love of the King who is to come>, your grateful

Sister Teresa Benedicta a Cruce

1. [at the post-graduate medical school at Columbia University.]
2. [Echt was actually in the province of Limburg, the Netherlands (not Holland).]

288. Christmas card to Walter Warnach, Cologne
Original in Convent Archive of Cologne Carmel

J.M.

Pax Christi! Cologne-Lindenthal, December 16, 1938

Dear Herr Warnach,

Unfortunately I must ask you to bring back the galley proofs before Christmas. I am about to be transferred to Echt (Holland) and would very much like to leave a complete and thoroughly corrected copy [of the manuscript] behind. Until then I could put the final galleys (23-117) at your disposal.[1] But you surely will not have any more time for them.

With most cordial wishes for blessings on the Feast and for the New Year, *in Christo,* yours respectfully,

Sister Teresa Benedicta a Cruce, OCD

1. See Letter 267 and the following letters to Walter Warnach.

289. Letter to Elly Dursy, <Kordel>[1]
Original in Convent Archive of Waldfrieden Carmel

J.M.

Pax Christi! Cologne-Lindenthal, December 16, 1938
My dear Elly,

Surely the eyes of the little child of Carmel will open wide at the marvels of the Holy Night! May it bring Your Charity[2] the fullness of grace. No, I am not surprised that all is going well. After all, I had long been convinced that the time had come. And then the Lord does his part.

I have already written to your Reverend Mother that my transfer to Echt is imminent. Your Charity will surely help to pray especially for that and for everything connected with it.

Please, will Your Charity also extend my cordial Christmas wishes to Ännchen <Dursy> and my thanks for her dear letters. I will no longer get to write to her now. In Jesus' love, your least sister,

Teresa Benedicta a Cruce

1. Elly (Elizabeth) Dursy had just entered the Carmel at Kordel as a postulant. At her Clothing ceremony, she received the name Sr. Elizabeth of Divine Providence. She made her first profession in 1940. In 1985, she was a member of the Carmel of Waldfrieden.
2. "Your Charity" was used in Carmel when speaking to another Sister; "Your Reverence" was used for a superior.

290. Letter to Mother Petra Brüning, OSU, Dorsten
Original in Convent Archive of Ursuline Sisters, Dorsten

J.M.

Pax Christi! Echt, January 3, 1939
Dear Reverend Mother,

Our Christmas letters and packages crossed in the mail. You will have received ours in time, and will have known [by Christmas] what lay ahead of us in Cologne. Despite everything, we celebrated with heartfelt joy. You wrote, dear Reverend Mother, [wondering] what one could say to me for consolation. Of course there is no human consolation, but he who lays the cross [on us] understands well how to make the burden light and sweet. During the octave of Christmas, all documents necessary for departure arrived with almost miraculous speed. A faithful friend of our house (that is, of the Cologne Carmel) drove me here on New Year's Eve.[1] The good Sisters here had done everything possible to speed up the granting of an entrance permit [to the Netherlands], and received me with heartfelt love. This is, after all, the old Carmel from Cologne,[2] as you may remember from our Jubilee brochure.

On our way here by car, I had permission to stop first in Schnurgasse[3] to seek the blessing of the Queen of Peace for the trip. I need not tell you how painful it was to take leave of my dear religious family in Lindenthal, especially from the kind Mothers [the Cologne superiors]. I do not know whether you have received a thank-you from [Cologne] already. If not, I express our gratitude again in Reverend Mother's name. I wrote thank-you notes for her even to the last days, for it is impossible for her to manage all of them, and she is always in need of some support.

Now everything here is all new again. Please help me to pray that I may be able to repay the great love with which all of them received me, and that I can make myself useful to the community. I was given the cell of Sister Gertrudis (Erzberger[4]). I once sent you a [memorial] prayer leaflet [about] her. We believe she had a bit of a hand in my coming here.

My sister Erna (the physician) will soon be going to America with her two children. She has just sent me word from Berlin that everything is finally ready. I do not yet know whether I shall see her. She had every intention of passing through Cologne, but they could come here only if they were traveling by a Dutch [steamship] line. Such a possibility remains uncertain.

Over there my brother-in-law awaits them with great longing and they are naturally happy about the coming reunion. But their leave-taking in Breslau will be very difficult, even more for those left behind. Rosa[5] is making attempts to come to Holland through the *Raphael Verein*. For her, of course, that would be the very best solution. Surely you will be glad also to pray for these intentions. Cordial thanks again for all your love and kindness.

In grateful love, your
Sister Teresa Benedicta a Cruce, OCD

1. Paul Strerath, M.D. (b. Leverkusen-Schlebusch, 1880; d. Elberfeld, 1945) safely transported Edith Stein across the border by car to the Carmel of Echt, in the Limburg sector of the Netherlands. [Dr. Strerath had already been helpful to Edith in her efforts to arrange for Ruth Kantorowicz to emigrate to the Netherlands five months earlier.]
2. More information will be given in Letter 293.
3. [Because they are cloistered, Carmelites were required to go by the shortest route when travelling, without making detours or stops. Edith requested and received permission for a detour to the Church of the Queen of Peace on Schnurgasse—the church in the original monastery of the Discalced Carmelite Nuns in Cologne. Letter 246 mentions that the small statue of the Queen of Peace was brought from Schnurgasse to Lindenthal for the celebration of the founding of Carmel in Cologne. When the city was being rebuilt, after being ravaged by 1000 hours of bombing in WWII, the Discalced Carmelite Nuns were invited by the Cardinal to return to the original site of Carmel, since the monastery in Lindenthal where Edith had lived was destroyed by an incendiary bomb. So this final visit to the church in Schnurgasse is now a consolation to the nuns who live there, because of its connection with Blessed Sr. Teresa Benedicta (Edith Stein), whose memorial shrine can be found in the crypt of this venerable church.]
4. Maria Edeltraud Erzberger (Sr. Gertrudis of Saint Agnes, OCD) (b. Stuttgart, 1902; d. Echt, 1937) was the daughter of Matthias Erzberger (b. Buttenhausen/Wurtt, 1875), German statesman and Minister of Finance. [He led the German delegation for the Armistice in November 1918]; in 1921, he was murdered at Griesbach in the Black Forest [by two Nationalist assassins].
5. See Letter 24.

291. Letter to Walter Warnach, Cologne

Original in Convent Archive of Cologne Carmel.

J.M.

Pax Christi! Echt, January 13, 1939

Dear Herr Warnach,

In haste, only the reassurance that I have a complete, fully corrected copy here. Nor was anything missing at the printer's.[1] You received the extras, unfortunately a little too much, in the rush of cleaning up. Please, for the time being store it away somewhere yourself, or it might cause confusion in the Cologne Carmel. I only received the conclusion of Volume II (columns 166/199) here, and will send it to you when I receive word that the corrections have arrived safely at the printer's.

With sincere best wishes and greetings (please, also to Fräulein Dr. Baring), yours respectfully *in Christo,*

Sister Teresa Benedicta a Cruce

1. Cf. Letters 267 and following to Walter Warnach.

292. Letter to Anni Greven, <Krefeld>
Original in private possession of Anni Greven

J.M.

Pax Christi! Echt, January 14, 1939
Dear Fräulein Greven,

Kindly forgive me for not thanking you before for your beautiful Christmas package. I had to use the Octave of Christmas to get ready for my departure, probably for the rest of my life. Early on December 31, I received the passport and I left that afternoon. I did want to write you soon afterward, but I did not have your address and had to ask for it first from Cologne. So, again, forgive me and accept belatedly my heartfelt thanks for everything, especially for the exquisite burse.[1] How much trouble you gave yourself when your professional duties are so difficult! For the new year, which is already two weeks old, my heartfelt wishes for many blessings; please,[pass them on to] Sister Marciana, too.

I began my [life] in the circle of my new monastic family before the Most Blessed Sacrament. You can imagine how very painful it was to leave Cologne. But I am again in Carmel, surrounded by cordial maternal and sisterly love. The house here was founded by the Cologne Carmelite Nuns who were exiled in 1875 and had to leave the monastery near St. Gereon's.[2] I have been given the cell of a Sister (Sr. Gertrudis Erzberger) who died the year before last with a reputation of sanctity. I shall ask our dear Reverend Mother to enclose a picture of her.

Again, thanks and sincere best wishes and best regards. Yours *in Christo,*

Sister Teresa Benedicta a Cruce, OCD

1. [A burse is a pocket made of two square cloth-covered cards joined on three sides, often tastefully hand-embroidered, used to hold the folded, starched corporal prescribed for Mass and Benediction. In the revised norms for the liturgy, its use is no longer obligatory.]
2. [One of the many Catholic parish churches of Cologne. Most of the city's ancient churches were restored for their historic value after being bombed in WW II.]

293. Letter to Baroness Uta von Bodman, Speyer
Original in Convent Archive of Cologne Carmel

J.M.

Pax Christi! Echt, January 22, 1939
Dear Fräulein von Bodman,

Your New Year's greeting just reached me immediately before I left Cologne. I arrived here on New Year's Eve. Parting was a very hard decision to make for all of us in Cologne. But I was firmly convinced that to do so was God's will and that thereby something much worse could be prevented. No pressure from outside had been exerted yet. I have been received here with the greatest love. The good mothers and sisters had done their utmost to obtain the entry permit and paved the way for me by their prayers.

This house was founded by Carmelites from Cologne when they were exiled in 1875. The cemetery is within the enclosure, so I have been able to greet the erstwhile Cologne Sisters who are buried here. There are still Sisters alive now who knew them. I received the cell of Sister Maria Gertrudis who died the year before last (1937) with a reputation for sanctity. At present, the majority here are German Sisters, several from Bavaria since the monastery formerly belonged to the Bavarian province of the Order.[1]

We are trying to find a place here for my sister Rosa. For the time being she is still in Breslau. My sister in Hamburg <Else Gordon>, whom you know, is going with her husband and her elder daughter to [join] her son in Colombia (South America). The younger daughter went to Norway (on December 31) [the same day I left Germany]; faithful friends have obtained prospects of a job and an entry permit for her there. The family is scattered all over the world, but God knows the good of that.

Sincerest greetings to all in St. Magdalena, and to your sister and (if possible) to Fräulein Ost. All the best to you; I remembered you on the 13th also. Your

Sister Teresa Benedicta a Cruce

1. [Friars from the Bavarian Province had founded a monastery at Holy Hill, near Milwaukee, WI, and still had jurisdiction over it at the time Edith Stein went to the Netherlands. Holy Hill later became part of the Washington province of Discalced Carmelites.]

294. Letter to Mother Petra Brüning, OSU, Dorsten
Original in Convent Archive of Ursuline Sisters, Dorsten

J.M.

Pax Christi! Echt, February 17, 1939
Dear Reverend Mother,

I would have liked to thank you long ago for your dear letter of January but there was always too much else [to do]. In the meantime you have been to Cologne and learned some of the news. But before Lent, I want to send you a greeting and heartfelt wishes for many blessings. When I stood for the first time at the grave of Mother Paula here, I recalled your connections with her even before you wrote about them. The Sisters still speak often and with much love about her. If you are able to send me personal greetings I will be very happy, and even more if you yourself could visit sometime.

My sisters and brother cannot visit me here. Erna sailed from Bremerhaven to the United States yesterday with her children; she could say farewell only by letter. Only persons who permanently immigrate to Holland or use a Dutch steamship line have the possibility [to enter the country]. But entering Holland as an immigrant is not easy. We have made all kinds of efforts on Rosa's behalf; so far, all to no avail. Please help us to pray. She does not know at all what is to become of her. She would gladly come here; nothing else appeals to her.

At every moment available for work now I am occupied proofreading and making the index;[1] both consume more time than one has in Carmel. If you want to do me a favor: I would be grateful, with all my heart, were you able to help the Cologne Carmel somewhat to meet the cost of printing the book and, when it finally appears, to help publicize it. Our dear Mother in K. <Cologne> (on the 14th she was re-elected) has surely discussed this with you. And then, in addition, perhaps a Mass for my relatives, living and deceased? For my mother, of course, I am wholly confident. But lately I found my soul very burdened at the thought that I have done so very little for my father.[2] He died when I was not quite two years old; I have no memory of my own about him, although my mother always tried her best to evoke memories [in me].

How are your dear invalids, especially the one with the stomach ailment? How is Sister Maria Regina? Does she still think of me?

I have experienced a great deal that is good here, and I am heartily grateful for it. Surely it is God's will that has led me here. And that is the most secure port of peace. Now the three great days of prayer are coming.[3] We will pray together for all the great general and personal intentions, won't we? I would like to write more but soon the bell will ring for Matins. Again, a grace-filled Quadragesima![4] *Praestolamini silentio salutem Dei!* <Await in silence the salvation by God!> In grateful love, always, your faithful Sister,

Teresa Benedicta a Cruce, OCD

1. This was for *Finite and Eternal Being;* when it was published as Vol. II of *Edith Steins Werke* it had no index, since Edith's death prevented her from completing it.
2. Siegfried Stein (b. Langendorf, Kreis Tost, 1843; d. near Frauenwaldau and Goschütz, 1893), father of Edith Stein. He died [apparently] of a heat stroke on a business trip. [See *Life*, pp. 38-41, etc.]
3. [She refers here to Sunday, Monday and Shrove-Tuesday, special days of prayer observed while most people were revelling at Carnivals or Mardi-Gras.]
4. [Latin for Lent, but it was used in German interchangeably with the German *Fastenzeit* (time for fasting).]

295. Letter to Sr. Maria Mechtildis Welter, OCD,[1] Cologne

Original in Convent Archive of Cologne Carmel

J.M.

Pax Christi! Echt, February 21, 1939

Dear Sister Mechtildis,

Before the door closes[2] I would like to write a greeting for Your Charity's name day. The holy card from Beuron arrived just in time. Our Lady of Grace must tell Your Charity everything I have given her to do for Y.C.[3]

We received a wonderful gift for the beginning of Lent. Last Saturday a tabernacle was built into our choir grate. Now the Blessed Sacrament is as visible to us as it is to you. And for me its location is even more favorable: since the large altar is in the center, the tabernacle had to be placed on the right—above the communion window.[4] I kneel on that side and I can look directly at it. Besides, it can be seen from everywhere since no candles obstruct the view. For the time being everything is still rather primitive, so the Blessed Sacrament has been replaced in the tabernacle on the altar every evening. However, during these three prayer days we have had it in Exposition from 6 in the morning until 6 at night.

How is P. N. Heribert?[5] I hope he was able to return home in good health. There has already been some mention in the papers about the matter he was so worried about.

On the 19th, Sister Theresia was 71, and the 18th was the 50th anniversary of her entrance. Nobody thought of it. She wants to have her jubilee next year on her profession day. But Sister Maria will have a golden jubilee of profession already this year (on Father Elijah's feast).[6] Four sisters in the house are 71 years old; other than the two already named, they are Sister Josepha and Sister Magdalena. Sister Theresia and Sister Josepha continue regularly to be bell-ringer and server at table, etc., as though it could not be otherwise.[7]

Again, a blessed Lent and heartfelt greetings to all, Y.C.'s least
Sister Teresa Benedicta

[P.S.] Sister Josepha would like to have the Office of Brother Konrad of Parzham. Perhaps you have an extra copy: you will need them for April 21.

1. Helene Welter (Sr. Maria Mechtildis a Matre Dolorosa, OCD, (b. Cologne, 1885; d. Cologne, 1957).
2. [No letters were written during Lent; on this Shrove Tuesday evidently the time limit for letters was the usual time when the portress locked the turn-room door, since outgoing mail was to be deposited there.]
3. [These explanations will be pertinent to all the letters written to Carmelites. In her letters wherever one would say "you" she uses the abbreviation E.L., for *Euer Lieb,* in English "Your Charity" or, as here, Y.C. That was the customary way in which Sisters addressed one another. Superiors and former Prioresses were addressed as "Your Reverence"—E.E. in Edith's letters, and Y.R. in the translation. The ease with which the abbreviated form was used indicates that within the community constant use had made this form of address as familiar and unstilted as "you" would have been. For that reason the abbreviations are kept, since "Your Charity" and "Your Reverence" would make the reader assume more formality in these letters than Edith intended.]
4. [The communion window was an opening cut into the wrought iron or other metal grilles (called grates in Carmel) customary because of the law of enclosure. This small window was always kept locked except during Mass, when it was opened to allow the celebrant to give the host at Communion to the Sisters who knelt, in turn, at the window.]
5. [His title was "Pater Noster" or "our Father" since] P. Heribert a St. Maria, OCD, was at the time provincial of the Bavarian Discalced Province of the Holy Cross. [The German Discalced Carmelite Nuns were under the jurisdiction of the Fathers and the provincial was their major superior.] Father Heribert became ill during a stopover in Cologne on one of his pastoral journeys within his province.
6. [The feast of the prophet and proto-Carmelite Elijah (or Elias) is observed in Carmel on July 20.

7. [At that time, the customs of the nuns provided that once a sister was 70 she need no longer take a turn at ringing the bells or serving at table or other duties assigned weekly on the "board of offices." In most monasteries today that custom is no longer observed and duties are shared by all, regardless of the sister's age, unless a physical disability makes the duty difficult.]

296. Letter to Mother Ottilia Thannisch,[1] OCD, Echt

Original in Convent Archive of Beek Carmel

<Echt> Passion Sunday, March 26, 1939

+ Dear Mother: please, will Y.R.[2] allow me to offer myself to the heart of Jesus as a sacrifice of propitiation for true peace, that the dominion of the Antichrist may collapse, if possible, without a new world war, and that a new order may be established? I would like it [my request] granted this very day because it is the twelfth hour. I know that I am a nothing, but Jesus desires it, and surely he will call many others to do likewise in these days.

1. Maria Margaret Thannisch (Sr. Ottilia a Jesu Crucifixo, OCD) (b. Wickrath, 1878: d. Echt Carmel, Dutch Limburg, 1958) Prioress of the Carmel of Echt at that time .
2. See footnote 3 to Letter 295.

297. Letter to Mother Johanna van Weersth, OCD[1] Beek

Original in Convent Archive of Beek[2] Carmel

J.M.

Pax Christi! Echt, April 10, 1939

Dear Reverend Mother Johanna,

To Y.R. and all the dear Sisters, cordial thanks for the name day greetings and especially for the spiritual bouquet that is so welcome. Please continue the prayers; my relatives are still very much in need of them. At the same time I wish you all the richest blessings and graces of the Easter season. For your amusement I may enclose the illustrated broadside from Cologne's prankster Mechtildis.

In the love of the Risen Savior, greetings to Y.R. and the entire Carmel of Beek, Y.R.'s grateful, humble,[3]

Sister Teresa Benedicta a Cruce, OCD

1. Ida Josefa van Weersth (Sr. Johanna a Cruce, OCD) ((b. Hauset, Belgium, 1901; d. Echt Carmel, 1971). At the time of this letter, she was the prioress of the newly founded Carmel of Beek, Dutch Limburg. She did not know Edith Stein personally but kept up a lively, friendly correspondence with her. After Mother Johanna returned to the Carmel of Echt in 1946 [before the fate of Edith Stein was known], she collected all the available writings of Edith Stein. Thanks to her interest, the documents were preserved. Cf. Foreword of German editors in Vol. I of *Edith Steins Werke.*
2. See footnote, Letter 305.
3. [This form of closing is again a of the time. Instead of "sincerely" the nuns signed "your humble" in English, and in German, "the least" before their name. Like Y.C. or Y.R., constant use made it so familiar that it hardly served its original purpose anymore.]

298. Letter to Anni Greven, Krefeld
Original in private possession of Anni Greven

J.M.

Pax Christi! Echt, April 12, 1939
Dear Fräulein Greven,

Cordial thanks for the friendly greetings in February, for the fine purificators,[1] and your good wishes for Easter, but above all else, thank you and Rev. Sister Marciana for your prayers. I beg you earnestly to continue them; I always need them urgently for my dear relatives and for many intentions. I wish both of you, from my heart, the richest blessings and graces of the Risen Savior. Is your health better now than in the past year? You will certainly be in great need of an extended vacation to recuperate.

When you get to Cologne again and visit my beloved former monastery-home, take along many greetings from me, and to the Queen of Peace in the [church in] Schnurgasse also. Did I tell you I was allowed to go get her blessing before I came here? The car that brought me here took me there first. I was upstairs in the old choir[2] for the nuns, so I could go up close to the miraculous statue; then I also went to the crypt where the Carmelites of old are buried. The sisters who came here from St. Gereon's in 1875 to found Carmel in Echt are here in the cemetery, which is on the monastery grounds; we visit them every Sunday and holiday. The altar in our choir and many other [items] were brought along from Cologne. But, above all, there is the true spirit of Carmel here. That is most wonderful.

In the love of Christ, greetings from your
Sister Teresa Benedicta a Cruce, OCD

1. [A purificator, hand sewn in this case, is a small, rectangular linen cloth used by the priest to dry the chalice he rinses out (i.e., purified) after Communion.]
2. [The rule of enclosure formerly required the Carmelite nuns to have a room in which they attended daily Mass, unseen [and unseeing!]. The room was usually behind the main altar of the public chapel of the monastery. This room was called the nuns' "choir" because it was used for the Divine Office, and the nuns were seated in opposing choirs for the alternate recitation of the Psalms. This former choir is still in existence, as is the crypt, where a plaque commemorating Blessed Edith Stein has been mounted.]

299. Letter to Walter Warnach, Cologne

Original in Convent Archive of Cologne Carmel

Pax Christi! Echt, April 14, 1939

Dear Herr Warnach,

Many thanks for your dear good wishes for my name day. Holy Father Benedict was my patron of the month for March, and in February it was St. Scholastica. Since the slips of paper are drawn blindfolded, I took it as a friendly sign that the two want to keep their adopted child in Carmel under their particular protection. As patron for the year, on the first day of my presence here,[1] I drew St. (Mary) Magdalen de Pazzi who was my patron last year also. She has a great deal to teach [us], and evidently in one year I had not yet learned enough from her. It is good to think about our having our citizenship in Heaven[2] and the saints of Heaven as our fellow citizens and housemates. Then it is easier to bear the things *quae sunt super terram* <which are on earth>.

I wonder whether you have found any kind of employment? The Lord probably wants you for himself, and one day it will be apparent at which place and in what service. Until then it means having patience and tarrying in the darkness.

After Epiphany, the last galleys of Volume II and the page proofs of [Vol.] I arrived, one right after the other. So I was able to begin with the index and have gone through Volume I for that purpose.[3] But now all of it has come to a halt, and it looks once more as though it just does not want to come to a conclusion. So I too have to practice patience. I had intended to send you the final galleys when I got the page proofs of Volume II. Since you have not got that far, at least I have not delayed anything.

Now I must wish you, with all my heart, all the graces and blessings of the Easter season. These days between Easter and Pentecost are, after all, extremely beautiful and consoling. Please, cordial greetings to Fräulein Dr. Baring, should you see her.

In faithful remembrance,
your Sister Teresa Benedicta a Cruce, OCD

1. [She left Cologne on December 31, 1938 and arrived during the night, so New Year's, the day patrons are drawn in this Carmelite custom, was her first in the monastery of Echt.]
2. [Phil 3:20]
3. See Letter 294.

300. Letter to Mother Petra Brüning, OSU, Dorsten
Original in Convent Archive of Ursuline Sisters, Dorsten

J.M.

Pax Christi! Echt, April 16, 1939
Dear Reverend Mother,

For your very kind letter for my name day you should have received thanks at Easter. But I was only waiting for a reply from the Carmel in Cologne regarding a matter I would eventually have had to write you about. Now it is no longer necessary. In the meantime I laid my wishes before the Lord. Everything that concerns you is, after all, always included in my prayers. All the blessings and graces of the Easter Season, dear Mother Petra. All peace and consolation of which the wonderful liturgy between Easter and Pentecost speaks!

I would rejoice with all my heart if you were able to come here sometime. You would come to love the Carmel of Echt as quickly as you did the one in Cologne. And the Sisters would be happy to tell you about Mother Paula, who is said to have been such a holy little Mother. I am allowed to send you the photos as a small Easter treat. Thanks from the heart for the holy Mass and for the generous donation to Cologne. The printing is again stopped, and everything is in question once more.[1] Naturally I am in touch with my brothers and sisters; there are prospects of Rosa's getting to Belgium, to a Tertiary of our Order.[2] All this, however, I would rather tell you in person.

With V.E.R.[3] I now have easy and speedy connections, and need no longer go on a detour through B. <Beuron> or Rome. Judging by his brief greetings, he is at peace and is satisfied, lives as a simple monk, makes himself useful wherever he can, and therefore has a lot of work. In G. <Gerleve> apparently they know very little about him; the same holds for B. <Beuron>.

My basic attitude since I've been here is one of gratitude—grateful that I may be here and that the house is as it is. At the same time I always have a lively awareness that we do not have a lasting city here.[4] I have no other desire than that God's will be done in me and through me. It is up to him how long he leaves me here and what is to come then. *In manibus tuis sortes meae.* <My days are in your hands. (Ps 31:15)> There everything is well cared for. I need not worry about anything. But much prayer is necessary in order to remain faithful in all situations. Especially [must we pray] for those who have heavier burdens to carry than I have, and who are not so rooted in the Eternal. Therefore I am sincerely grateful to all who help.

I knew Helene Lieb very well. After all, we were together the whole time in the Marianum. She came to my Clothing and Veiling Ceremony and often, otherwise, for brief visits; and she applied a long time ago. Our dear Reverend Mother in Cologne had her come to take leave of me a short while before my departure. At that time we impressed on her that she should enter soon. I have had news that she arrived on Easter Tuesday.[5] So she is my successor.

With all sincere wishes in the love of the Risen One, your grateful

Sister Teresa Benedicta a Cruce, OCD

1. See Letters 294 and 299. [It may be that Edith had counted on Mother Petra's help with financing the printing. Now that the project was again at a standstill "it is no longer necessary."]
2. [This is a lay person, woman or man, who belongs to the "Third" Order of Carmel. Today Tertiaries are known more appropriately as Secular Carmelites. Edith here says "tertiary" in good faith. However, the woman was an impostor who defrauded Rosa of all her personal belongings in Belgium. Edith's sister finally got to Echt but had nothing left of the things she had managed to take out of Germay with her.]
3. This is Father Archabbot Raphael Walzer, OSB, [at the time in Algeria] (cf. Letter 225). [He kept little contact with his archabbey in Beuron because it would have caused even more harassment from the Nazis. Gerleve was another foundation of his. It is evident from Edith's letter here that she had to be circumspect since letters even at this time were randomly opened by German censors and she did not wish to incriminate others.]
4. [Heb 13:14]
5. [On April 11, 1939, Helene Lieb entered the Cologne Carmel. She received the name Sister Carmela of the Blessed Trinity and then made her profession on October 27, 1940. She died in Cologne Carmel on July 4, 1991.]

301. Picture postcard to Karl and Katharina Lichtenberger, Ludwigshafen
Original in Convent Archive of Cologne Carmel

J.M.

Pax Christi! Echt, April 21, 1939

Your dear Easter wishes are hereby returned most sincerely. Will you please deliver cordial greetings to Sister A. <Agnella Stadtmüller> and tell her all is going very well with me here. Surely you, dear Frau Lichtenberger, will be thinking of the journey you made on the Rhine in the past year. My sister <Rosa> is making preparations to move to Belgium.

With sincere remembrances, your
Sister Teresa Benedicta a Cruce

P.S. The Carmel in Beek was founded from Echt.[1]

1. The postcard carried a sketch of the monastery at Beek.

302. Letter to Peter Wust, Münster[1]
Original in Convent Archive of the Franciscans, Münster

J.M.

Pax Christi! Echt, August 28, 1939

Dear Herr Professor,

Rev. Msgr. Donders is good enough to give us news about you sometimes so we may join our prayers to those of the many friends who are concerned about you. So we heard yesterday about your most recent operation, and this time with special understanding because, during the past months, we have had to witness one of our dear fellow sisters being ravaged by the torment of cancer. Immediately before the Octave of Our Lady of Mount Carmel ended, in the night between July 23 and 24, she was called home. Despite painful bodily suffering until the end, her going home was extremely peaceful. Our dear patient knew from the start what was wrong with her and that there were no prospects of a cure. She offered everything for the great intentions of this time. I believe that will be your great consolation also.

I was deeply moved that the suffering involves for you the very organs with which so many sins are committed today. It seems to me like a call to make a particular kind of reparation. Such a call is an extraordinary grace. I believe that such suffering, when it is accepted with a willing heart and carried to the end, is reckoned before God as a true martyrdom. It is in this sense that I remember you before the Lord. I beg him for strength also for your dear relatives for whom the sacrifice is surely even harder than for you yourself.

In caritate sacratissimi Cordis Jesu, your
Sister Teresa Benedicta a Cruce, OCD

1. See Letter 67. Professor Wust died in 1940.

303. Letter to Rev. Ludwig Husse, Ludwigshafen[1]
Original in private possession of Father Husse, Ludwigshaven

J.M.

Pax Christi! Echt, September 6, 1939
Dear Reverend Father,

By this time you will probably be home from Lake Constance. I am deeply grateful to you for permitting me to take part, even though belatedly, in your great days of grace. I read your letter just before Matins and could then lay my good wishes for blessings into the Divine Office at once. 1914-1939:[2] what impact is conveyed by these dates. In such a coincidence I see no pure accident. Now you will have an extra call on prayers from Carmel. We feel called upon by the current events to take our vocation most seriously.

For your *memento ad altare* [remembrance at the altar] sincerest thanks! May I beg you to include my relatives in it (the family is now very scattered, but in our hearts all the more closely united) and that holds too for the two monastic families of Cologne and Echt, in which I now have the rights of home.

All most cordial greetings and wishes to your sister also, yours sincerely *in Corde Jesu,*

Sister Teresa Benedicta a Cruce, OCD

1. See Letter 78.
2. Father Husse celebrated his Silver Jubilee of Ordination in 1939. Edith refers to two coincidental events in Europe: the beginning of WW I in 1914, and of WW II in 1939.

304. Letter to Anni Greven, Krefeld
Original in private possession of Anni Greven

J.M.

Pax Christi! Echt, September 29, 1939
Dear Fräulein Greven,

Sincere thanks for the faithful remembrance and the practical gift. If you had also sent along the time to write, I would answer with a letter. But we always have so much to do. Therefore I beg you to be satisfied with these few words and a heartfelt memento to our holy Mother and Sister Thérèse.[1]

With all good wishes for you and Sister Marciana, your grateful
Sister Teresa Benedicta a Cruce, OCD

1. A reference to the feasts of St. Thérèse of Lisieux, Oct. 3, and St. Teresa of Avila, Oct. 15.

305. Letter to Sister Aloysia Smeets, OCD,[1] Beek
Original in Convent Archive of Beek Carmel[2]

Pax Christi! Echt, October 18, 1939
Dear Sister Aloysia,

With all my heart I offer my sympathy at the death of your dear father. I know since my own good mother died what it means not to be able to be at home at such a time. Rosa <Stein>[3] saw Y.C.'s father after he died and told us how nice he looked and how peacefully he lay there. There one could see the majesty of death. She also went to the funeral, and other than that has been to Y.C.'s parental home several times. Last Sunday she told Sister Margareta and me about it in the speakroom.

United with Y.C. in prayer for your good father, Y.C.'s least sister,
Teresa Benedicta a Cruce, OCD

1. Maria Petronella Smeets (Sr. Aloysia a SS. Corde Jesu, OCD) was born in Echt, 1908.
2. The Sisters of Echt Carmel, including some who had lived with Edith before her arrest, merged with the Carmel of Beek, which had been founded from Echt. The merger also meant combining the archival properties, now all at Beek.
3. By this time Edith's sister Rosa had arrived in Echt, where she lived in the extern quar-

ters of the monastery and served the community as an extern helper. Representing them at family funerals and visiting sick relatives would be part of her duties.

306. Letter to Sr. Agnella Stadtmüller, OP <presumably Ludwigshafen>
Original in Convent Archive of Dominican Sisters, St. Magdalena's, Speyer

J.M.

Pax Christi! <Echt>, in Sol. Christi Regis, October 29, 1939

Dear Rev. Sr. Agnella,

On the evening of the Feast of Christ the King, my sincerest thanks for your kind letter for the feast of our holy Mother St. Teresa[1] and also the one of June 11. I did not write sooner because I did not get to it—nor did I even get to check to whom I still owe urgent answers.

At that time you wanted to hear something about balancing, harmoniously, Christian freedom and the fulfilling of monastic prescriptions. I think the balance lies in the *"Fiat voluntas tua"* <Thy will be done>. Our holy Rule and Constitutions are for us the expression of the Divine will. To sacrifice personal inclinations for their sake is to participate in the sacrifice of Christ. To conform as well to the unwritten laws, the customs of the house, and the preference of the community is demanded by love. If we do all this in order to give the Heart of Jesus joy, it is not a restriction but the highest activity of freedom, a free gift of bridal love. If we have this basic attitude—to seek everywhere for ways to please Jesus—then we will also discover in which cases it is permitted, indeed commanded, to dispense oneself from a rule or prescription, etc. Through that attitude, also, one's personal uniqueness will come into its own without having to seek for its rights. I believe that you yourself have already found an answer in your "being a root"—an image to be understood *cum grano salis* [with a grain of salt] because, after all, we are not a grapevine, but simply branches. Our roots are in the heart of Jesus. In the eyes of the ordinary human being this is a dark terrain. For the eyes of faith it is the clear eternal light.

Where is Sr. Callista <Kopf>? For the first time I did not receive a greeting from her for October 15. Before she left, Sr. Immolata sent me a farewell greeting through Fräulein von Bodman. I never hear anything from her missions. The connection with Sr. Reinhildis stopped when she was in Munich recently.

The big opus is resting.[2] The first months I was here I received the last corrections of the galley proofs for volume II, and the first page proofs of volume I. Then it went no further because the publisher lost courage. All efforts have failed. I do not know what more to do, other than to leave the whole thing up to the Lord. After I finished with the proofreading I asked for work in the house. It was very much needed: we are only 18 (we lost one dear Sister in July through a painful cancer); only a few are young and fully able to work and so they are overburdened. Since the middle of June, I've been second portress and have charge of the refectory. Added to that are common labors in this large, rural household (big laundry days, harvesting fruit—an overabundance of it this year—and preserving it, cleaning the house, etc.). After our seven hours of prayer, then, there is little time left to spend at the desk.

During the past months, I have completed a small biography of the Carmelite Marie-Aimée de Jesus (of the Paris Carmel) for a collection that P. Eugen Lense is editing for Benziger.[3] The first volume *(Die in Deinem Hause wohnen) [Those Who Live in Your House]* appeared last year. For that I contributed a biography of the foundress of the second Carmel of Cologne (Mother Franziska, née Katharina Esser).[4]

You will now understand why I must let letters lie unanswered for such a long time. In my prayer I am always sincerely united to everyone. With all cordial wishes for a grace-filled Advent and Christmas Season, *in Corde Jesu,* your faithful

Sister Teresa Benedicta a Cruce

1. October 15, feast of St. Teresa of Avila.
2. See Letters 294, 299 and 300.
3. *Ein auserwahltes Gefass der gottlichen Weisheit. A Chosen Vessel of Divine Wisdom Sr. Marie-Aimee de Jesus, Carmel of Avenue de Saxe in Paris,* 1839-1874 Echt, 1939. [It is included in *Hidden Life,* pp. 76-90.]
4. See Letter 277.

307. Letter to Hans Biberstein,[1] New York

Original in private possession of the Batzdorff-Biberstein family

Echt, November 17, 1939

Dear Hans,[2]

Although we don't know whether and when this note will reach you, we don't want to leave the attempt unmade to appear for your 50th birthday. What a celebration that would have been in Breslau! Even so you will probably be surrounded by quite a lot of people. There is, after all, quite a large circle of relatives and friends there. I have often had to think of you during the last months. You must find as I do that all the old war memories arise and one feels so strongly the contrast between now and then. And today it is not possible for us to follow the events with undivided heart. You know that I wish you and all our dear ones well with all my heart. The two of us will spend the day with you in spirit. Most especially I wish that Erna may soon regain her health and effectiveness. I know well how much it depresses you when she is not up to par. You will surely recall the time of your engagement, when she had to go to the mountains to recuperate; our walks together from the *Stadtgraben* (where I was then staying with Aunt Bianca) to Max Street or from there to Michaelis Street. It is amazing how long ago all that happened. In those days there were no little Bibersteins in existence yet, and today they are already such grownup people and cannot imagine at all that we were once as young as they. For them, the decisive years are now coming. I am glad the pressure has been taken from them that burdened them for so long. And yet I would not want them to become totally alienated from their homeland. But you will take care of that, I am sure.

Nowadays I always feel transported into Napoleonic times, and I can imagine in what tension people lived then everywhere in Europe. I wonder: will we live to see the events of our days become "history"? I have a great desire to see all this sometime in the light of eternity. For one realizes ever more clearly how blind we are toward everything. One marvels at how mistakenly one viewed a lot of things before, and yet the very next moment one commits the blunder again of forming an opinion without having the necessary basis for it.

Perhaps these aphorisms may spur you on to let me in on some of your own thoughts. I would be happy, but if you cannot find the time I understand. Again, all my good wishes and regards for you and all dear ones.

Your,
B.

1. Hans Biberstein (b. Breslau, 1889; d. New York, 1965) M.D., medical chief of the dermatology clinic at the University of Breslau; after emigration he was professor in Columbia University Post-Graduate Medical School, then NYU-Bellevue Medical Center, Gradu-

ate Division. A friend of the two youngest Stein sisters from their university days, he married Edith's sister Erna. [See *Life,* pp. 117-238, etc.]
2. [Susanne Batzdorff, daughter of Hans and Erna, niece of Edith Stein, supplied the full text of this letter in her translation, since it reveals so much of Edith's relationship with her family. The letter begins speaking as "we," meaning Edith and her sister Rosa, who wish to greet their brother-in-law on his birthday, but Edith quickly reverts to "I" as she recalls the past.]

308. Letter to Elizabeth Nicola, Düsseldorf
Original in private possession of Elizabeth Nicola, Siegburg

J.M.

Pax Christi! Echt, December 29, 1939
Please forward!
Dear Elizabeth,

Sincere thanks for your kind Christmas greeting and the beautiful little book. All blessings and graces for the Christmas season and the New Year.

So far I have not received any photos of the Clothing Ceremony. Naturally I too am very happy that Sr. Carmela[1] has settled in so well. Do your parents know about it?

In faithful remembrance, your
Sister Teresa Benedicta a Cruce

1. Helene Lieb (Sr. Maria Carmela a Ss. Trinitate, OCD) had entered the Carmel of Cologne. Edith called Sr. Carmela her "replacement" in Cologne; cf. Letter 300.

309. Letter to Sr. Maria Electa Sommer, OCD[1] Cologne
Original in Convent Archive of Cologne Carmel

J.M.

Pax Christi! Echt, January 24, 1940
My dear little Sister,

With all my heart I join in the celebration of Y.C.'s big feast. Two years ago <February 11, 1938> Our Lady of Lourdes brought me acceptance for my perpetual profession. So it is a very special day to remember for me, too. We will unite our petitions and our thanks, won't we? It is a joy for heaven and earth when another soul gives herself completely to the Lord. May our dear Queen of Peace make Y.C. an angel of peace for the beloved Cologne Carmel and for all of troubled humanity.

I beg Y.C. for a particular memento for my sister Erna, who is a medical doctor in New York. She will have her 50th birthday on Y.C.'s profession day and she is greatly in need of prayers so that she can recover from the great difficulties she has passed through, and catch up on all her duties as wife and mother. Please commend her to the Mother of God, that she may lead her to the sources of happiness and strength.

With Y.C., I also rejoice that another little Sister has arrived at her goal: the Good Shepherd. I wish Y.C. the richest of blessings for the whole family, the natural and the monastic, from all of us in the Carmel of Echt.

In the Hearts of Jesus and Mary, Y.C.'s least,
Sister Teresa Benedicta a Cruce, OCD

1. Maria Sommer (Sr. Maria Electa a Regina Pacis, OCD) (b. Mönchen-Gladbach, 1913; lives in Cologne Carmel). She made her first profession on February 11, 1940.

310. Memorial card[1] for Sr. Maria Electa Sommer, OCD, Cologne
Original in Convent Archive of Cologne Carmel

<Echt, January 24, 1940>

"My God and my all."

To her dear Sister M. Electa a Regina Pacis on the great day of grace of Holy Profession, Feb. 11, 1940.

Sister Teresa Benedicta a Cruce, OCD

1. Sr. Benedicta wrote the above on the back of a holy card. This card was enclosed with Letter 309.

311. Letter to Sr. Agnella Stadtmüller, OP, <Speyer>
Original in Convent Archive of Dominican Sisters, St. Magdalena's, Speyer

J.M.

Pax Christi! Echt, March 30, 1940

Dear Sr. Agnella,

To you and all my dear ones in St. Magdalena all the graces and blessings of the Easter season! Many thanks for all the news. Now I want to answer your questions at once.

"Pure love" for our holy Father John of the Cross means loving God for his own sake, with a heart that is free from all attachment to anything created: to itself and to other creatures, but also to all consolations and the like which God can grant the soul, to all particular forms of devotion, etc.; with a heart that wants nothing more than that God's will be done, that allows itself to be led by God without any resistance. What one can do oneself to attain this goal is treated in detail in the *Ascent of Mount Carmel.* How God purifies the soul, in the *Dark Night.* The result, in the *Living Flame* and the *Spiritual Canticle.*[1] (Basically, the whole way is to be found in each of the volumes, but each time one or other of the stages is predominant.)

(Dominica in Albis [Sunday after Easter]) But if you want the most essential points condensed in a brief summary, you will have to get the *Kleinen Schriften* [Short Works] (in the The-atiner edition, Vol. V). I think you will be able to find that in Speyer, perhaps through Rev. Dr. Lutz[2] (with best regards from me).

Should we strive for perfect love, you ask? Absolutely. For this we were created. [Perfect love] will be our eternal life, and here we have to seek to come as close to it as possible. Jesus became incarnate in order to be our way. What can we do? Try with all our might to be empty: the senses mortified; the memory as free as possible from all images of this world and, through hope, directed toward heaven; the understanding stripped of natural seeking and ruminating, directed to God in the straightforward gaze of faith; the will (as I have already said) surrendered to God in love.

This can be said very simply, but the work of an entire life would not attain the goal were God not to do the most essential. In the meantime we may be confident that he will not fail to give grace if we faithfully do the little we can do. The little—taken absolutely, is for us a great deal. And while we are about it, we have to be careful not to wish to judge for ourselves how far we have come. Only God knows that. That brings me to Psalm 18[3] (so simple, as I understand the phrase). What we recognize of ourselves, and of our faults and behavior, is only the illuminated surface. The depth they come out of is to a large extent hidden from ourselves. God knows that depth and can purify it. The *ab alienis*[4] can probably be understood in different ways. I think of it principally as what burdens us through unknown faults. But one could also think of that in which we are implicated by others. *Delictum maximum*[5] probably is not to be understood as anything definite. To me it seems to point far more to Divine Mercy's immensity and Salvation's almighty power, for to them nothing is too great.

Emissiones tuae paradisus <from the *Song of Songs*>. In oriental symbolic language it is probably a reference to the pleasing fragrance coming from the bride. Non-metaphorically: Mary is full of grace and virtue. They stream from her like a perfume that pleases God and enriches us.

It is good when you ask me questions. I think only in response to challenges. Otherwise my mind rests. But I am glad when it is given a nudge and can be useful to someone. During Lent, it was allowed to do something very nice: to compose a Mass and Office in honor of the Blessed Virgin Mary, *Regina Pacis* [Queen of Peace] for the Carmel of Cologne, which wishes to ask Rome for a First Class Feast, preferably for the whole Church, but at least for the whole Order. The Picpus Fathers and Sisters already have such a feast, so do our Fathers of the Flemish Province, whose Patroness is the *Regina Pacis;* but they use the Common of Our Lady for nearly everything. Now that we have all the parts proper except the Psalms and the hymns of the Little Hours, we have only to await Rome's reply.[6]

In turn, I have a request. I do not know who is in charge of the Auxiliary Sisters at present. Would you please ask her to write down for me something on the particular tasks of the Auxiliary Sisters in your order, the guidelines for their training, the scheduling of their work and prayer, and about their participation in the community exercises? I would like to have it to compare with our lay Sisters' legislation and would treat it in strict confidence. If something about that is available in print, I would be glad to see it, too. If the present directress cannot do it, perhaps Sister Adelheid would be able to help. Heartfelt thanks in advance.[7]

To you and all the dear Sisters and Fräulein von Bodman, many cordial greetings. *In Corde Jesu,* your least

Sister Teresa Benedicta a Cruce, OCD

1. [See *The Collected Works of St. John of the Cross,* trans. Kieran Kavanaugh and Otilio Rodriguez, 2d ed. (Washington, DC: ICS Publications, 1991).]
2. Otto Lutz (b. Linden, 1882; d. Speyer, 1952) S.T.D., dean of the priests' seminary, Speyer, professor of dogma and homiletics, for many years confessor to the Dominican Sisters at St. Magdalena's, Speyer.
3. [This would be Psalm 19 in most versions (18 in the Vulgate).]
4. "ab alienis" is concluded with "peccatis"—"from unknown faults" is the present translation of this ancient Latin term.
5. "Delictum maximum"—most grievous fault [a concept expressed, for instance, in the Latin "Confiteor" as "maxima culpa".]
6. [The Cologne archivist adds the note: "Of course, refused at that time."]
7. [Edith's interest in the status of the lay sisters two decades before the Second Vatican Council is worth noting.]

312. Letter to Mother Petra Brüning, OSU, Dorsten
Original in Convent Archive of Ursuline Sisters, Dorsten

J.M.

Pax Christi! Echt, April 26, 1940

Dear Reverend Mother,

Your dear letter of April 15 made me very happy. Of course the account of the long illness and all the pain was an unpleasant surprise; I had no idea of it. I assumed your long silence was caused by your being overburdened and by the pressure of circumstances, or I would certainly have inquired earlier. On top of that I was still somewhat depressed because, when you were kind enough to visit me, I was unable to spend as much time with you as you had set aside to give me; now I am happy that you were still able to use that time so fruitfully. Surely you understood readily that, even to honor the dearest guest, I did not want to be absent for too long from our communal work. As it is, I am all too weak a member of the work force for all we have to do here in the house. That you are able to keep up with all your multiple duties is really a marvel of providence.

I am still in contact with St. Magdalena's (Speyer) and was able to follow its gradual dissolution. I was informed from time to time through

Professor Donders[1] of Prof. Wust's illness, i.e., through his appeals for our prayers before every new operation. The obituary notice came to me via Cologne. I have not yet received the farewell letter, and would be most grateful for it. (And for something else also: the book about Frau Le Hanne that was written in your house—in case you have a copy left.[2] They are now reading it in the refectory in Cologne. We would like to read it too. A most cordial thank you in advance.)

I no longer had any direct communication from Professor Wust—I believe not for three years.[3] Yes, he was at my Clothing and later visited us sometimes. He was enchanted by our dear Mother Teresa Renata. He was always a little afraid of me—he assured us of that, often, orally and in writing—because I was a genuine student of Husserl while he (Wust) was self-taught. And for all the time I was in Münster he was noticeably reticent. Before he withdrew altogether, he sent us his latest book of that time and asked me urgently for an honest criticism. It was very painful for me; I would much rather have had him go on his way undisturbed. But since he insisted, I wrote down what comments I had. I had left the letter with Reverend Mother for mailing when Professor Wust came in person. She gave it to me to take to him in the speakroom and I handed it over, telling him a little of what it contained. I never had a reply to it, not by word of mouth or letter, and I never saw Peter Wust again. From here I wrote Wust a letter that I forwarded to Do. <Donders>, leaving it to him to deliver it.[4] Do.<Donders> thanked me sincerely, but I do not know the outcome. It makes me feel so sorry. I could only try to make amends by my prayers. Now the poor little man has overcome this, too. Probably no one can know how much he suffered from *"Mikos"*[5] <an inferiority complex> even in the years of his fame.

My best wishes and remembrances for your sick brother and for his family. We include him in our daily prayers for all the sick who have been commended to us.

During Lent I was allowed a beautiful task: to prepare a Mass and Office for a Feast of *Regina Pacis* [the Queen of Peace]. Cologne wants to apply for a First Class Feast for the entire Church (July 9). I can send you a carbon copy of the Mass text. I have no more copies of the Office, unfortunately. Perhaps Cologne will be typing it again. Then you could get a carbon copy of it there. That would make me very happy.

Now something about Rosa <Stein>. We had hoped that since she has at last been given a residence permit [in Holland] she could soon become an extern Sister. But our superiors (our dear Rev. Mother and the Father Provincial) think the time is not suitable for making such a change. They suggested Rosa become a Third Order member for the time being and that she wear the habit. It is a very painful disappointment for Rosa. She does not like the busy activity connected with being a portress, would much rather live inside the cloister, and hoped for at least a year inside in the novitiate since that is prescribed for extern Sisters. As consolation Reverend Mother promised her that I would be allowed to come to her every Sunday in order to introduce her to the spiritual life. Will your Reverence please help me to ask for the guidance of the Holy Spirit, that I may successfully transmit the true Carmelite spirit to her? After all, that is of prime importance.

I would like to ask for something else as well. From the first months of my being here in Echt, I have wanted to write something about the duties of the lay sisters in our Order. There is absolutely nothing available on that subject, and that has unfortunate consequences in practice. For comparison and stimulation, would you send me something from your Order, if possible, in written or printed form about the basic guidelines of your formation of the lay novices, and about the prayer and work schedules of your lay Sisters. It need be no more than a few key words that would enable me to get the picture. I would have liked to get started soon after Easter, but now there remains hardly any time, for all kinds of springtime jobs have to be performed and a great many correspondence debts are left over from Lent.

Our youngsters[6] in New York are getting acclimatized excellently. Suse was on the honor roll of her college, and her parents received an official letter of congratulations on her achievements; Ernst Ludwig had an "excellent" in all subjects and was awarded a medal. For the older generation, it is difficult. All of them are homesick for one another and worry about the ones who are still in Br. <Breslau>.

Wishing you and your entire natural and spiritual family the fullness of the Holy Spirit, I am your grateful

Sister Teresa Benedicta a Cruce

P.S. Best regards from Rosa.

1. Prelate Prof. Dr. Adolf Donders (b. Anholt/Westfalen, 1877; d. Münster, 1944) Provost of the Cathedral in Münster. He was a close friend of Edith Stein ever since she taught in Münster.
2. Mother Maria Victoria Hopmann, *Marie Le Hanne-Reichensperger, "Die Frau Bergrat," 1848-1921* (Mainz: Matthias Grünewald, 1939). Mother Le Hanne was a co-foundress of the third Carmel of Cologne (Lindenthal) after the *Kulturkampf.*
3. [Probably in 1937 when, on March 3, he gave a lecture in Cologne on "God and Man in the Confessions of St. Augustine," as announced in the February 28, 1937 Cologne diocesan newspaper.]
4. See Letter 302.
5. [Mikos, a contraction formed from the German *Minderwertigkeits komplexe,* inferiority complexes.]
6.The daughter and son of her sister, Erna Biberstein. [To one familiar with her own account of her school years, it is touching to see her emulating her older relatives who reported to one another her success in school.]

313. Letter to Ernest Marx, Sittard, Holland[1]

Original in private possession of Sofie Caroline Marx, née Wilsberg, Sittard

Echt, June 11, 1940

Dear Herr Marx,

I rejoice with all my heart that you are to receive the strengthening Sacrament of Confirmation at this time. We all will pray that the Holy Spirit may give you all his gifts and fruits—love, peace, joy, of which no one and nothing can rob us, and which make us independent of all external happenings.

As a courageous warrior of Christ you will surely be happy to carry with you a picture of the High Commander of His army.[1] I send it to you as a souvenir of your confirmation.

With cordial wishes and greetings to you and your wife, I am, *in Christo,* your

Sister Teresa Benedicta a Cruce, OCD

1. Ernest Marx (b. Kessenich-bei-Bonn, 1893; d. Sittard (Holland), 1967) was a convert to Catholicism and became acquainted with Edith Stein in Echt.
2. Edith Stein gave him a small crucifix.

314. Letter to Mother Johanna van Weersth, OCD, Beek
Original in Convent Archive of Beek Carmel

J.M.

Pax Christi! Echt, July 10, 1940
Dear Reverend Mother Johanna,

Our Reverend Mother gave me this gorgeous sheet of stationery[1] with the kind directive that I should use it to give you an account of something beautiful that happened here. Last evening after 8 o'clock there were two sharp rings at the turn[2] and soon thereafter the Sister Portresses recognized the vigorous voice of our Father Bishop.[3] A few minutes later the domestic bell[4] called all the Sisters together. Father Bishop most cordially greeted each one, individually, and exhorted us not to worry, to have great confidence, to sleep well, and to talk to one another more frequently since this would be good for us at a time like this. But above all else he urged us, of course, to untiring prayer and sacrifice and to fidelity to our vocation since we must now fight in the front line.

You do know that eight persons searched his house for hours. He told them off in no uncertain terms: one must, after all, tell those poor people the real truth for once. First Bolshevism had come from the east to fight against God, then National Socialism [Nazis] came with the fight against the Church. But neither would be victorious, because in the end Christ would conquer. All of us would at some time have to get on our knees. But first there would be a relentless battle between these philosophies of life. He continued: we had nothing against the people as individuals. But we have to be steadfast in our principles and may not surrender on any point. That was how Father Bishop had spoken to the people, and that was how we were to speak to them should they come to us. In conclusion he even gave them his pastoral letter of the previous year to take along; they should read it through thoroughly to understand his thinking.

Father Bishop wants to be in Maastricht on August 15 in order to dedicate the entire diocese anew to the Mother of God in the basilica *Sterre der Zee* [Star of the Sea]. Prior to that a triduum—[three days] of prayer and penance—is to be held in all the churches and chapels in the bishopric. Now we must pray that this plan does not prove impossible to carry out as happened currently with the Marian Congress. Father Bishop is, after all, prepared for a whole lot more. He will gladly accept being *episcopus et martyr* [bishop and martyr].

A while ago (between 1 and 2 o'clock) there were again two rings. Our Reverend Mother is now getting Rosa's report. All good wishes and cordial greetings to Your Reverence and all the dear sisters. *In caritate Jesu et Mariae,* your Reverence's least

Sister Teresa Benedicta a Cruce, OCD

1. [The paper was either a sample of stationery or an advertisement, blank on the reverse. The sisters customarily used such paper for correspondence.]
2. [The signal of two rings would have called the Prioress to go directly to the speakroom where the Bishop awaited her. The inside Portresses would not have had to serve as intermediaries. Later in this same letter, two rings are mentioned again, and the Prioress went directly to receive Rosa's report. Extern Sisters were accustomed to give an account every evening of all the events of the day.]
3. [The Most Rev. J.H.G. Lemmens, Bishop of Roermond, was one of four bishops who, with Dr. J. de Jong, Archbishop of Utrecht, on July 20, 1942, signed the pastoral letter of protest against the deportation of the Jews that so enraged the Nazis that the arrest of Catholic Jews, among them Blessed Edith Stein, followed on August 2; within a week of the arrest they were deported and killed in Auschwitz. Bishop Lemmens himself asked to be addressed and spoken of as "Father Bishop," says Maria Buchmüller, a German authority on Edith Stein. In an interview with Dr. Buchmüller on June 17, 1960, the Bishop reported how he had urged Blessed Edith and her sister Rosa to go into hiding and testified that they preferred to remain in the community at Echt. Bishop Lemmens died on July 22, 1960.]
4. [In monasteries, besides the church bells used at times of public services, there is a smaller bell, called the domestic bell, within the monastery to signal times when the community gathers for chapter meetings, concludes regular periods of recreation, or (as in this case), is unexpectedly wanted for an extraordinary event.]

315. Letter to Hedwig Conrad-Martius and Theodor Conrad, Munich[1]

Original in Convent Archive of Cologne Carmel; first published, *Kösel Verlag,* Munich 1960

Pax Christi! Echt, November 5, 1940

(No salutation given in letter)

Your dear letter of April 26 came such a short time before the gates were shut that I was no longer able to thank you.[2] For a long time we have been writing a card only in most urgent cases. But now I am permitted to go beyond that and give a sign of life in several directions where someone is worried about us.

We have been able to live our lives undisturbed. Rosa <Stein> continues to be a faithful portress, and since June she has belonged to our Third Order.

Will it ever be possible for you to send me the new book? Since September 29 we've had a new Mother <Prioress, Sr. Ambrosia Antonia Engelmann>[3] who would like me to write something again. So far I have done household chores almost exclusively since the printing of the book came to a standstill.[4]

I received news from Münster whenever Peter Wust was about to have another operation; then the obituary notice and his farewell letter to his students.[5] Now we are reading his memoirs at table.

Do you know where Anna Reinach is?[6] I know nothing about anyone. Hans L. (Lipps)[7] is surely going to be serving in the war for the duration. Where may his children be? And Ingarden[8] and his four sons?

This year we had a lot of yellow plums, and they were nice ones. We thank you, Hans <Theodor Conrad>, particularly for the professional advice.[9]

Most cordially, your
Benedicta

1. See Letters 23 and 146.
2. Edith's reference is to the invasion of Holland by the Nazis, May 10-19, approximately. Her last letter to Mother Petra in Germany has the same date as Hedwig's to Edith: April 26. Once the invasion began, mail service was disrupted.
3. See Letter 330.
4. See Letter 306.
5. See Letter 312.
6. See Letter 21.
7. See Letter 4.
8. See Letter 3.
9. Hedwig's husband had operated an orchard for many years.

316. Letter to Mother Johanna van Weersth, OCD, Beek
Original in Convent Archive of Cologne Carmel

J.M.

Pax Christi! Echt, November 17, 1940

Dear Reverend Mother Johanna,

For a long time I have been resolved that for your nameday I would make up for all I neglected to do during your long illness. Your Reverence will surely not have taken it as a lack of sympathy that I did not write at all. I was always wholeheartedly involved whenever we received anything from Your Reverence, and feel myself closely united with Your Reverence through the cross. Now for the feast of *our* holy Father, I am sending *my* holy Father[1] to bring Your Reverence the most cordial wishes for many blessings. May both of them bless you and implore all the blessings of the Cross on Your Reverence. After all, one cannot wish for a deliverance from the Cross when one bears the noble title "of the Cross."[2]

I am sending along for Your Reverence a short biography of Sr. Marie Aimée.[3] I wrote it more than a year ago for a collection of articles that should have come out about Easter. Now it cannot be printed before the war ends. In any case, Sr. M. Electa will be interested in it. Her translation, which we read at table, made me choose M. Aimée when I was asked for a portrait of a Carmelite nun.

Just now I am gathering material for a new work[4] since our Reverend Mother wishes me to do some scholarly work again, as far as this will be possible in our living situation and under the present circumstances. I am very grateful to be allowed once more to do something before my brain rusts completely.

For several weeks I have also been responsible for the subject matter for meditation and, in preparation for the feast, am now taking short excerpts from the *Ascent of Mount Carmel.* That was also my meditation material for my retreat before Clothing. Then each year I would go one step further—in the volumes of holy Father John [of the Cross], but that does not mean I kept up with it. I am still way down at the foot of the mount. Next Sunday [November 24, 1940] we will be united with the Holy Father in the prayer campaign.[5] We have already made a beginning of that today.

Once more, most cordial wishes for Y. R. and for the whole family, including the new addition.

In Corde Jesu, Y. R.'s least
Sister Teresa Benedicta a Cruce

1. [For the feast of St. John of the Cross, celebrated at that time on November 24, Edith sent either a holy card or a medal of St. Benedict to Mother Johanna.]
2. [Both Sisters had that title as part of their religious name.]
3. See Letter 306.
4. *Kreuzeswissenschaft [The Science of the Cross],* published as the first volume of *Edith Steins Werke.*

5. [The archivist in Cologne Carmel says this time "Holy Father" refers not to St. John of the Cross but to the Pope, Pius XII. It must have been a universal day of prayer for peace, but in Germany the Nazis may well have suppressed any word of it under the pretext of its being "subversive."]

317. Letter to Anni Greven, Krefeld
Original in private possession of Anni Greven

J.M.

Pax Christi! Echt, 2nd Day of Christmas, Dec. 26, 1940

Dear Fräulein Greven,

On Christmas night I received your kind letter with the beautiful poem and, today, the book. Everything does take a long time to get here. Many thanks to you and to Reverend Sister Marciana for all the gifts and all your faithful remembrances. But such means would not be necessary for me to remember you. I do not forget you.

On the Holy Night we had a High Mass at midnight and immediately following, two silent Masses as usual. Only this time there was no one in our Chapel except the priest at the altar and our three portresses. (Probably I have told you already that one of these is my natural sister.) We were ourselves the acolytes at the grate that was installed recently between the Chapel and the sacristy. Our choir is situated behind the high altar, so that from there we are unable to see the altar. Now we can attend Mass from the sacristy and follow all of it.

Now I wish you, with all my heart, the Christ Child's richest blessings for the Christmas season and the New Year.

In His love, your
Sister Teresa Benedicta a Cruce

318. Letter to Anni Greven, Krefeld
Original in private possession of Anni Greven

Pax Christi! Echt, May 1, 1941

Dear Fräulein Greven,

Cordial thanks for your kind Easter greeting. Unfortunately the poor flowers spent ten days en route. The present time is too raw for such tender attentions. In future I will be very glad to take the intention for the deed. We too are compelled now to forego much in the way of kindnesses that we otherwise could do for others.

Hopefully by this time your sister is feeling all well again. How is your own health? I wish you and Sister Marciana rich graces for the rest of Eastertide. Today is the third anniversary of my Veiling Ceremony, which, if I remember correctly, you celebrated with us.

In Corde Jesu, your
Sister Teresa Benedicta a Cruce

319. Letter to Sr. Agnella Stadtmüller, OP, <Speyer>
Original in Convent Archive of Dominican Sisters, St. Magdalena's, Speyer

J.M.

Pax Christi! Echt, May 14, 1941
Dear Sister Agnella,

I received your kind greetings of February 21 after the usual delay, so I was unable to reply before Lent began. On Easter Monday evening I went into retreat. So I am only now gradually getting my debts paid.

I felt Sister Bernarda's death deeply. For such a long time she was my faithful chronicler, as she was for the convent also. A most cordial greeting for Mother Subprioress Ignatia. I have her in fond remembrance. It was a happy surprise for me that Sr. Callista <Kopf> is doing so much better. Please, best wishes to Fräulein Pérignon, Fräulein von Bodman, the dear Sister Portresses, and all the others who still think of me at St. Magdalena's and elsewhere.

I am at work on a little piece about the *symbolic theology* of the Areopagite. It is intended as an article for a new phenomenological journal in America.[1] If I manage to finish it, it may also be possible to send it over there.

In expectatione Sancti Spiritus <In expectation of the Holy Spirit>, your

Teresa Benedicta a Cruce

1. *Wege der Gotteserkenntnis: Die "symbolische Theologie" des Areopagiten und ihre sächlichen Voraussetzungen* appeared in German in *Tijdschrift voor Philosophie,* Vol. 8, No. 1, Feb. 1946. See "Ways to know God: The 'symbolic theology' of Dionysius the Areopagite and its factual presuppositions, " trans. Rudolf Allers, *The Thomist* (July, 1946). Reprinted in pamphlet form by Edith Stein Guild (New York, NY: 1981).

320. Letter to Sr. Maria Ernst, OCD,[1] Carmel of Cologne
Original in Convent Archive of Cologne Carmel

J.M.

Pax Christi! Echt, May 16, 1941
Dear Sister Maria,

I received Y.C.'s letter today and am allowed to reply to Y.C. at once.[2] I believe it is very good for Y.C. to be working at something definite, for there is a strong creative talent there that needs to be directed into a definite channel. It also seems to me that a good beginning has been made. Surely these books did not come "accidentally" into Y.C.'s hands. Reverend Mother knows how things happened for me in this respect: how in an appropriate moment it would "occur" to me what I needed at the time, and then it would come to me from somewhere. Y.C. probably knows that there is still a fragment there by our Holy Mother St. Teresa on the *Song of Songs.* The *Spiritual Canticle* will also be very helpful to Y.C. And surely Y.C. would be glad to take St. Bernard to hand. But I do not know whether there is a translation. Were I there I would gladly translate everything for Y.C. A commentary by P. Athanasius Miller, OSB, can probably give you a bit of an insight into the present interpretation. Surely there are still Paters coming to the house (P.S.S.[3]) who could give information [on sources] and provide from somewhere what Y.C. needs. Aside from that, the help of the Holy Spirit is obviously most important. I am very happy to ask for that help with Y.C., and will also be very grateful if Y.C. does the same for me, for I am unable to count on anything else. I am going about my new task like a little child making its first attempts at walking.[4]

The Holy Spirit must help Y.C. not only at your work, but also in overcoming new crises that work may easily occasion. After all, no spiritual work comes into the world without severe labor pains. It tends to absorb the total person and that, of course, is something we may not permit. On principle, it is very good that the regular schedule and our daily duties bar the door to "letting oneself be consumed," but the way to achieve this balance cannot be found without our being aware of it. I would be very happy were we able to talk about all this sometime. But it surely is not accidental that such an opportunity has been taken from us. So we will be grateful that we are united in the kingdom that knows no boundaries or restraints, no separation and no distance.

Since we have a little postulant in the house again, I think often of our own young days in the Order and of the wonderful [providential] guidance that each one's way to Carmel signifies. Perhaps even more wonderful is the story of the souls *in* Carmel. They are hidden deep in the Divine Heart. And what we believe we understand about our own soul is, after all, only a fleeting reflection of what will remain God's secret until the day all will be made manifest. My great joy consists in the hope of that future clarity. Faith in the secret history must always strengthen us when what we actually perceive (about ourselves or about others) might discourage us. Today is the feast of St. Simon Stock. We sang his high Mass this morning and used "Flos Carmeli" as the hymn for our May devotion.[5] There are so many promises contained in it.

In Corde Jesu et Reginae Carmeli Y.C.'s faithful, least Sister
Benedicta

1. See Letter 233.
2. Sr. Maria's letter arrived on a Friday. Writing was usually postponed until free time on Sundays. The immediate reply meant the letter could be mailed before the weekend, and was a sign of the importance of the bond between Edith and the Carmel of Cologne.
3. Her reference here is to P. Swidbert Soreth, OP.
4. A reference to *Kreuzeswissenschaft [Science of the Cross],* published as Vol. I of *Edith Steins Werke.*
5. The Nuns honored Our Lady every day during "her" month of May in a short liturgical commemoration: a Marian hymn followed by a brief prayer. "Flos Carmeli" [Flower of Carmel] is a traditional hymn asking for Mary's protection for her daughters and sons in the Order of Carmel.

321. Letter to Mother Petra Brüning, OSU, Dorsten
Original in Convent Archive of Ursuline Sisters, Dorsten

J.M.

Pax Christi! Echt, June 13, 1941
Dear Reverend Mother,

Today we are having a feast day (our Reverend Mother's name day).[1] I took the occasion to ask leave to write you a real letter for your name day, and I am using a few free minutes right away in order to take advantage of the permission that was granted so kindly. Before all else, most cordial wishes for many blessings. I wish you and your whole family everything I attempted to express in the brief St.-Angela-Conversation;[2] I think of you often and keep you firmly included in everything. At the end of this month—probably on the 25th—Rosa will be permitted to make her Profession as a member of the Third Order.

Surely I already told you that our elderly portress, Paula,[3] withdrew several months ago to spend her remaining days in the little convent of the Sisters of St. Joseph and that Rosa has taken her place. She now has the lovely duties of the sacristan and is housekeeper in the portresses' lodge. A beautiful and enriching job, naturally rich also in effort.

Our eldest brother <Paul[4]> and our sister Frieda <Elfriede Tworoger> are still in Br. <Breslau>. The relatives in Am. <America> are all making efforts to get them there; so far nothing has been of any avail. Erna, the gynecologist, has passed the state board examinations there after a great deal of trouble and has begun a practice again. Things are excellent with the youngsters. My brother-in-law <Hans Biberstein> wrote that they are a source of joy in every respect; they always pass with distinction the tests that are so frequent over there. The daughter was able to begin college studies at once; the boy was still too young and had to go to high school (something similar to our *Gymnasium*) for one more year. Now, by his choice, he is attending an agricultural college. He was always highly gifted and kind-hearted, but also high-spirited and not as serious about his studies as his sister, but apparently he has matured through these difficult years.

My second brother's family <Arno's>[5] is totally scattered, unfortunately. Three of his children are in America but at different places, one daughter remains in Breslau, and his wife has a domestic position in a suburb of N.Y. <New York>; he is all on his own. My eldest sister in S.A. <Else Gordon in South America> probably suffers the most in this separation from all her siblings. News travels back and forth once in a while; usually it is very much outdated.

I do not know whether I wrote to you that as part of my new duties I am to write a short preliminary study as a contribution to the periodical *Philosophy and Phenomenological Research,* which has been published since last year by some Husserl disciples at the University of Buffalo, NY. This minor work ("Ways to Know God: The 'Symbolic Theology' of the Areopagite and Its Factual Presuppositions")[6] is at present being typed by Ruth K. (Kantorowicz).[7]

I will send it first to Valkenburg where there are two Dionysius scholars[8] in order to get an honest critique by experts before I dare to get it published and go on to further work. Should the decision be favorable I could probably send you a carbon copy of it as a supplementary name day gift. Unfortunately, at the moment I have nothing else on hand that I could enclose. The brief play on the Sacraments that opened the name day celebration on Thursday evening, I could not get typed because Ruth was busy with the other task. But I know, after all, that you count most on the prayers. There will be no lack of them.

In grateful love *in Corde Jesu,* your respectful, least

Sr. T. B. a C.

Reverend and dear Mother Petra!

At last I have caught an opportunity and am able to send along a few lines to Your Reverence. First of all, I want to send you very heartfelt wishes for blessings on Your Reverence's name day; on the day itself I will be sure to pray before the Tabernacle, especially, for your Reverence; I do that daily.

Sr. Benedicta will perhaps have told you in her letter how well off I am here, and that I am allowed to take care of the chapel and the sacristy; I do this with great joy and with much help from above.

I wonder how things are going where we first met;[9] I think often, and with sadness, of all the places where I frequently sought rest, peace and comfort, and also found them.

Let us pray for one another and together, for all. *In Corde Jesu* and with respectful greetings, your

Rosa Stein

1. [The letter was written on Mother Antonia's feast day (St. Anthony, June 13) and was intended for Mother Petra's on June 29.]
2. [The reference is to a dramatic piece Edith wrote for Mother Ottilia's name day in December 1939. It was an imaginary conversation between Mother Ursula and St. Angela Merici, foundress of the Ursulines. This piece can be found in *Hidden Life,* pp. 116-121.]
3. The portress named Paula was not a religious but a laywoman who had served the community for years as an "extern," answering the door, running errands, etc.
4. Paul Stein (b. Gleiwitz, 1872) was Edith's eldest brother. He and his wife Trude and his sister Elfrieda died in 1943 in Theresienstadt concentration camp. See also *Life,* pp. 40ff.
5. See Letter 228.
6. [See Letter 319, n. 1.]
7. See Letter 319.
8. [They were unnamed members of the Jesuit Community at Valkenburg, Limburg (The Netherlands).]
9. Breslau; see Letter 226.

322. Letter to Mother Johanna van Weersth, OCD, Beek
Original in Convent Archive of Cologne Carmel

J.M.

Pax Christi! Echt, July 23, 1941

Dear Reverend Mother Johanna,

I did *not* bring along the writings of our Order's parents in French. Only the book *about* our Holy Mother that Your Reverence has on loan there, and then *L'Esprit de Sainte Thérèse de L'Enfant Jésus,* three *Consummata* volumes and the life of *Mère Angélique.* But our Reverend Mother would be glad to acquire the writings of our Holy Father [St.] John [of the Cross] in French or Flemish, if Your Reverence could get them for us.

I would also be very grateful if I could have Baruzi's book on Holy Father John; Reverend Mother would like to buy that also. (Unfortunately, at the moment, I cannot say just what the exact title is; perhaps it is listed in the bibliography given in the book on Holy Mother that Your Reverence has there.)

I am sorry that Your Reverence did not bring back any better diagnosis from the examination.[1] But all of us will pray fervently. After all, much is possible for heaven that medical skill cannot achieve.

Particular greetings to dear Sr. M. Electa. Today is the anniversary of her twin's death. Even though death occurred only after midnight, we had awaited it this entire day. On Sunday I discovered the first begonia blossoms on her grave; all the others were not yet ready. When does Sr. Isabella celebrate her name day? I thought of it on July 8. Elizabeth of Portugal, after all, is the actual Isabella.

Most cordial greetings and wishes *in Corde Jesu* to all the dear ones in the Beek Carmel, especially your Reverence, from your least

Sister Teresa Benedicta a Cruce, OCD

1. Already at this time the first symptoms of a severe cancer of the tongue appeared; Mother Johanna was delivered from this suffering in 1971. [Mother Johanna visited the Cologne Carmel shortly before her death and gave the Cologne community originals of nine of the letters she received from Blessed Edith. The rest were kept in the Carmel of Beek, Netherlands. See also Letter 305, n. 2.]

323. Letter to Mother Johanna van Weersth, OCD, Beek
Original in Convent Archive of Cologne Carmel

J.M.

Pax Christi! Echt, October 8, 1941

Dear Reverend Mother Johanna,

Our dear Mother gave me permission to send Y.R., once more, the exact titles of the books I would like to have.

1. P. Bruno de J.-M., *Saint Jean de la Croix,* Paris, 1929 (522 p., 40 Fr.. The small book Your Reverence sent is a sort of digest. I am reading it now and am very grateful for it, but I still need the big one.)

2. Baruzi, *St. Jean de la Croix et le problème de l'expérience mystique,* Paris, 1924.

Besides, Reverend Mother would like three more copies of the book *Aimer souffrir,* which Y.R. sent recently. P. Antonius received the first one on September 30 for his 50th birthday.

On Monday morning Rosa and I went to the Police Commissioner in Maastricht to register according to regulations. In the meantime, the Sisters prayed here and all went very well.

Rosa reported that Y.R. is better. That made me very happy. Please, will Y.R. also pray a little to the Holy Spirit and to our Holy Father [St.] John for what I am now planning to write. It is to be something for our Holy Father's 400th Birthday (June 24, 1942), but all of it must come from above.[1] In the big book about St. John there is, among other things, a sketch he drew after having a vision of the Crucified.

From the bus recently, (when) I saw the little monastery in Beek and also the house where Sister Johanna lives, I sent greetings over to them. Best regards to all the dear Sisters, especially to Y.R.

In Corde Jesu, Y.R.'s least, grateful
Sister Teresa Benedicta a Cruce

1. *Kreuzeswissenschaft [Science of the Cross],* Vol. I of *Edith Steins Werke.*

324. Letter to Mother Johanna van Weersth, OCD, Beek
Original in Convent Archive of Cologne Carmel

J.M.

Pax Christi! Echt, October 13, 1941
Dear Reverend Mother Johanna,

Cordial thanks for Your Reverence's kind good wishes and already, in advance, for the announced collective letter.[1] I was not at all prepared for so much celebration! Just think, Your Reverence—I saw not only Abraham, but Enoch and Noah as well, Isaac and Jacob, Moses and Aaron, David, Elijah and Elisha. They all appeared just as they are described in the Book of Ecclesiasticus [Sirach 44-48]. Abraham was a most distinguished personage (Mother Subprioress). As for Moses, only his nose was impressive; the rest of him was small and quaint; the reverse of his Tablet of the Commandments was seen to be last week's kitchen list (Sister Agatha).

I asked for P. Bruno's big book a few weeks ago through P. Mauritius of Geleen, but he was unable to get it. It is not available in Valkenburg.[2] Now I have written again to Father Prior in Geleen to say I would very much like to have it if they are no longer using it. Father Provincial has promised me Baruzi in November. P. Amandus is supposed to be finished with his book, but the printing probably has not been completed.

I well know that Baruzi is an unbelieving[3] author, but I believe one cannot easily do without him if one wishes to write about Holy Father [St.] John [of the Cross]. There is surely much in his book that cannot be found elsewhere. He is always being cited by Catholic authors.

I have not yet read Mère Amabelle. There is not even enough time to read what I need to use. So I really have to let other things go.

Sincere thanks for everything. Greetings to all. In the love of the Divine Heart, Y.R.'s least

Sister Teresa Benedicta a Cruce

P.S. Particular greetings to Sister Johanna.

1. October 12, 1941, was Edith's 50th birthday. The Sisters in the Carmel of Echt celebrated it, and the Sisters from Beek sent greetings.
2. See Letter 321.
3. [Jean Baruzi, a French agnostic, published studies on St. John of the Cross in Paris between 1924 and 1935. Sanjuanist scholars today still consider his work of such importance that it cannot be ignored.]

325. Letter to Mother Johanna van Weersth, OCD, Beek
Original in Convent Archive of Cologne Carmel

J.M.

Pax Christi! Echt, October 21, 1941

Dear Reverend Mother Johanna,

Now I have the Baruzi from Valkenburg: a book of more than 700 closely printed pages, with all scholarly material. I have already seen from the foreword to the second edition where the main targets for criticism are. But it was produced with the greatest devotion and as a serious study it probably cannot be supplanted by anything else.

In Corde Jesu, Y.R.'s grateful

Sister Teresa Benedicta

326. Letter to Sr. Agnella Stadtmüller, OP, Speyer
Original in Convent Archive of the Dominican Sisters in Speyer

J.M.

Pax Christi! Echt, November 7, 1941

Dear Sister Agnella,

Sincere thanks for your kind greeting for October 12. I was surprised that you even thought of this "anniversary." Here it was celebrated by having Father Abraham appear accompanied by a whole crowd of the patriarchs as they are described in the Book of Ecclesiasticus <Sirach 44-45>. The stately procession was made possible because, by Carmelite standards, we have an unusually large novitiate right now. On October 30 the first of five postulants received the habit; the second is to follow on February 11; the other three only entered in October. So much young life in the house—that is an extraordinary grace for a small and hitherto very superannuated family. I am allowed to give the little ones Latin lessons and am glad, in this way, to get to know them.

I knew nothing of M. Hyacintha's death, for the chronicler herself has gone into eternity. R.I.P. [Rest in peace].

A brief article[1] went off in September to Buffalo where an American substitute for Husserl's *Jahrbuch* is published. Will it arrive? Now I am attempting something[2] for the 400th anniversary of the birth of our Holy Father [St.] John; I beg prayers for that.

With best regards and best wishes to all in St. Magdalena's and its auxiliaries, *in Corde Jesu,* your

Teresa Benedicta a Cruce

P.S. How is Fräulein von Bodman?

1. See Letter 319.
2. See Letter 323.

327. Letter to Mother Johanna van Weersth, OCD, Beek
Original in Convent Archive of Cologne Carmel

J.M.

Pax Christi! Echt, November 11, 1941

Dear Reverend Mother Johanna,

Now P. Mauritius has brought me P. Bruno's big book. I am very glad because Baruzi has astonishing gaps and needs to be supplemented. For instance, he is completely silent about the apparitions of the Mother of God. But despite being thus supplied I still have requests, if not for me personally, then for the community.

Y.R. was the first to call my attention to the articles in the *Rozengaarden.* I then tried to gather together all the issues, but I was unsuccessful: the March and April issues are missing. Could Y.R. lend us those? Then we would have something on hand to read at table for the feast. It would be very good for the children as an introduction.

But besides that, I would like to have something by *our Holy Father John, himself*[1] in Dutch (or Flemish) for meditation. Last year I was able to use the German edition but now we must take the Dutch children[2] into consideration. Could Y.R. help us out with something in that line? Had I more time, I would try to translate something from the French. But I cannot get to it.

Sincere thanks in advance! *In Corde Jesu,* Your Reverence's least

Sister Teresa Benedicta a Cruce

1. Edith probably underlined the words in italics here for emphasis.
2. "Children" here refers to the postulants.

328. Letter to Mother Johanna van Weersth, OCD, Beek

Original in Convent Archive of Cologne Carmel

J.M.

Pax Christi! Echt, November 18, 1941

Dear Reverend Mother Johanna,

To Y.R., to dear Sister Cäcilia and to little Sister Elizabeth all the best wishes for your name days, which I intend to celebrate with you in sincerest remembrance in my prayers. I tried to make a copy of the sketch our Holy Father John made on a piece of paper about 5 cm. in size, after the vision he had of the Crucified at the Monastery of the Incarnation. The reproduction of it in P. Bruno's book is not exactly sharp, and I am anything but an artist. But I made it with great reverence and love, and think that Your Reverence will get at least a little idea of it.

Because of the work I am doing[1] I live almost constantly immersed in thoughts about our Holy Father John. That is a great grace. May I ask Y.R. once more for prayers that I can produce something appropriate for his Jubilee?

I would also like to beg all the dear Sisters, sincerely, for a memento of a dear friend of mine from our student days <Hans Lipps> who was shot in the head at the Eastern Front. I received the obituary notice yesterday after it had made many detours. He leaves two daughters for whom he was father and mother, since his wife died very early on.

My brothers and sisters are also very much in need of prayers. The sister who remained in Breslau <Elfriede Tworoger> was transplanted to the country where, with eleven other ladies, she is housed in an attic room and obliged to an eight-hour work shift. She is assigned to a sewing room. My eldest brother <Paul> and his wife live with the expectation of a similar compulsory action. So far all the attempts made by our relatives in America to get them over there have been in vain. They report the facts without complaint.

Again, most cordial wishes for blessings and many greetings to all the dear Sisters, *in Corde Jesu,* your grateful, least

Sister Teresa Benedicta a Cruce

1. *Kreuzeswissenschaft [The Science of the Cross],* Vol. I of *Edith Steins Werke.*

329. Letter to Mother Johanna van Weersth, OCD, Beek
Original in Convent Archive of Cologne Carmel

J.M.

Pax Christi! Echt, November 20, 1941

Dear Reverend Mother Johanna,

In great haste, sincere thanks for the magazines you sent. Actually, we do have *Morgen- und Abendbrot*[1]—every Sister has her own copy. If need be, I will take it. But, to be honest, it is too dry for me. And I would much prefer to present Father John [of the Cross] to the dear Sisters in a more original manner. That is why I would be so grateful for the Minor Works or for Sister Hildegard's book. If it is no longer possible *before* the Feast, then eventually through Pater Mauritius, who is to preach here on the Feast. If the article on the poet "John of the Cross" is good, I would also like very much to read it.

A thousand thanks for everything, and again most cordial wishes! *In Corde Jesu,* Y.R.'s least, grateful

Sister Teresa Benedicta a Cruce

1. *Geistliches Morgen- und Abendbrot [Spiritual Breakfast and Supper]* a book of meditations by P. Gregor a S. Joseph, OCD (Druckerei Weiss, 1885); new edition by P. Aloysius Alkhofer (Paderborn, 1932).

330. Letter to Mother Ambrosia Antonia Engelmann, OCD,[1] Echt
Original in Convent Archive of Beek Carmel

<presumably December, 1941>

Dear Mother,

Once Y.R. has read the letter from P. Hi.[2] you will know his opinion. Now I would like to do nothing more at all about the matter of my stability.[3] I put it in Y.R.'s hands and leave it to Y.R. whether to call on the Sisters, Pater Provincial, or our Father Bishop for a decision. I am satisfied with everything. A *scientia crucis* <knowledge of the Cross> can be gained only when one comes to feel the Cross radically. I have been convinced of that from the first moment and have said, from my heart: *Ave, Crux, spes unica!* <Hail, Cross, our only hope!>

Y.R.'s grateful child,
Benedicta

1. Maria Theresia Engelmann (Sr. Ambrosia Antonia a Spiritu Sancto, OCD) (b. Eltville, 1875; d. Carmel of Echt/Dutch Limburg, 1972) was prioress at that time in Echt.
2. Pater Johannes Hirschmann, SJ, member of the Jesuit community at Valkenburg (Limburg, Netherlands).
3. Edith refers to her *stabilitas loci,* that is, her incorporation in the [chapter of the] monastery of the Nuns in Echt. [Unlike Benedictines, Carmelites do not take a vow of stability as such, but they are assigned conventuality to a particular monastery. Since efforts were already being made to have Edith go to another monastery outside the Netherlands, the involved canonical procedure of incorporation at Echt would have to be superseded by a subsequent one. If it were delayed at this point, the transfer could be effected directly from Cologne to the new Carmel.]

331. Letter to Hilde Vérène Borsinger,[1] Bern, Switzerland
Original in private possession of Dr. Hilde Vérène Borsinger

J.M.

Pax Christi! Echt, December 31, 1941
Dear Gibi,

May I come to you again after a long time and ask you for a great service of love? Today it is three years that I've been in the Carmel of Echt. A short time ago, both chapters decided that the transfer should be a permanent one. The decision must be made after three years and may not be taken up sooner.

Now, just in the days when this was being voted on, the Occupation Forces issued a decree that declared all non-Aryan Germans in the Netherlands as stateless and ordered them to report for emigration by December 15. We, i.e., my sister Rosa and I, complied because failing to do so would have incurred a severe penalty. But I immediately drafted a petition for us to be permitted to remain in the Carmel of Echt and to be taken off the list of emigrants; the petition is now being typed. But in case that fails we have to look for alternative possibilities.

More than anything else, our Reverend Mother would like to put us up with the Carmelites of the Divine Heart (the Sisters of Sittard) in one of their Swiss convents, until such time as a return will be possible(?). Their Mother General lives here in Limburg, and the petition to her convents in Switzerland could pass through her hands. From you, on the other hand, I would like to find out whether, provided we are accepted by a convent, we could obtain an entry permit and visa, and to whom we ought to apply for it. I do know that Switzerland is strictly closed to immigrants, but I could imagine that under these particular circumstances an exception would be made.

Any other country is practically out of the question. If we are unable to get out in this way, we will be deported by the authorities in any case. In that manner one of my sisters, the one who had remained in Breslau, was deported to a so-called "Jewish residential community" in Silesia.[2] There she lives, together with eleven other ladies of the best social circles of Breslau, in a large attic room and works an eight-hour shift daily, sewing or peeling potatoes. She has accepted this very bravely and, naturally, were that necessary, we would adjust to a similar lot.

But you do understand that our superiors would like to spare us that. And through my vows I am obliged to make every effort to be able to continue living according to our holy Rule. My sister, who was baptized in Cologne at Christmas 1936, has been here since the 1st of July 1939, and is well established as an extern and outside sacristan, so that she will be sorely missed; she is also a Tertiary of our Order (Sister Rosa Maria of Jesus).

Now I wish you the richest graces and blessings for the Christmas season and the New Year. I do not know where you live at present, but hope the letter will reach you; and I will be very happy to hear from you again sometime.

In Corde Jesu, your
Sister Teresa Benedicta a Cruce, OCD

1. Hilde Vérène Borsinger, (b. Baden/Aargau, Switzerland, 1897; [d. Luzern, Switzerland, January 21, 1986]) a jurist, completed her studies at the University of Zurich with a thesis on the Legal Status of Woman in the Catholic Church. This theme continued to be a lifelong concern of the author and is mentioned by Edith Stein in Letter 100. Dr. Borsinger, editor of *Schweizerin [The Swiss Woman],* (periodical of the League of Swiss Catholic Women), was foundress and head of an educational authority for youth (Problems with the Learning Disabled). She met Edith Stein in 1930 at Beuron through P. Erich Przywara, SJ. This first meeting led to a lifelong connection. The sisters Edith and Rosa Stein were indebted to her for her tireless efforts to gain them entry into Switzerland. Despite following every avenue of appeal, unfortunately Dr. Borsinger was unable to get the permission in time. Dr. Borsinger was called "Gibi" by her family, and the affectionate name was also given her by her closest friends.
2. See Letter 328.

332. Letter to Maria Delsing,[1] Echt
Original in *Archivum Carmelitanum Edith Stein*

J.M.

Pax Christi! Echt, January 22, 1942
Dear Maria,

As you requested, I have made a list of all the things that may be taken along[2] and that we do not currently have in our house. Whatever you cannot give, Reverend Mother will then take care of. Since all items must be listed in the questionnaire, with their value, I would ask you please to list the value in all instances; probably it does not need to be the store price.

Sincerest thanks for all your kindness. I beg the Lord to reward you with eternal goods.

In Corde Jesu, your grateful, least
Sister Teresa Benedicta a Cruce

1. Maria Delsing, (b. Echt (Dutch Limburg), 1890; [d. Echt, October 17, 1979]) resident of Echt; a close friend and benefactor of the Echt Carmel who, out of deep respect for Edith Stein, had formed a friendship with both sisters, Edith and Rosa.
2. This letter refers to the order of expulsion mentioned in Letter 331. It was a ruse of the Nazis to issue such lists of things persons were "permitted to take along" or allowed to ask for when they were in detention. What was delivered by anxious and loving relatives and friends was then confiscated, often immediately *before* the relatives were told the detainees had left the camp.

333. Letter to Mother Johanna van Weersth, OCD, Beek
Original in Convent Archive of Cologne Carmel

J.M.

Pax Christi! Echt, February 2, 1942
Dear Reverend Mother Johanna,

Sincere thanks to Your Reverence and dear Sister Electa for the very loving letters, and to all the Sisters for their sisterly sympathy and the efficacious help with prayers. Naturally we are very grateful that we are allowed to stay here at least until further notice. (As people see it, it should be called: not being sent away.) The "further notice" now depends totally on the development of the overall situation—a further reason to pray untiringly for the great common concerns. Surely we are united in doing this. Please consider, also, that we are expecting an invitation to Amsterdam, one we may not decline, that will not take us to the benevolent *Joodsen Raat* [Jewish Council] but to the S.S. But we will put up with that, also, if we will be left in peace afterward. We still have some hope they will be in no hurry about us, since our questionnaires make it evident there is nothing to be gained from us. In any case we put our trust for whatever is still to come in your prayers.

Yesterday, when I looked at a picture of the Infant of Prague, it suddenly occurred to me that he is wearing imperial coronation dress and surely it was not accidental that his efficacy should come to the fore precisely in Prague. After all, Prague has been the court of the old German or Roman Emperors, respectively, and the city makes such a majestic impression that no other city known to me can compare with it, not even Paris and Vienna. The Little Jesus came exactly when the political imperial grandeur came to an end in Prague. Is he not the secret Emperor who will someday put an end to all misery? After all, he holds the reins even though people believe they are the rulers.

A hearty welcome to Sister Aloysia <Smeets>! I hope she will make such a rapid recovery with us that you will be richly rewarded for your sacrifice in parting with her.

Most cordial greetings to you all! *In Corde Jesu,* Y.R.'s grateful, least
Sister Teresa Benedicta a Cruce OCD

334. Letter to Anni Greven, Krefeld
Original in private possession of Anni Greven

J.M.

Pax Christi! Echt, April 7, 1942
Dear Fräulein Greven,

Please forgive me for not having answered your kind Christmas greetings this time. It was only because I have to be so miserly with my time since I am working on a book that, if at all possible, should be finished this year—for the 400th birthday of our Holy Father [St.] John of the Cross.[1] So please accept my very belated thanks, together with cordial wishes for many blessings during the Easter season. Please extend my sincere greetings and best wishes also to Sister Marciana. I will be very grateful if you both continue to pray for us.

Do not be sad because you are no longer able to send anything. In these times that is self-evident. We must be grateful that so far heaven has always provided for us with the utmost love, and trust that this will continue. In grateful remembrance, your

Sister Teresa Benedicta a Cruce

1. See Letter 328.

335. Letter to Sr. Agnella Stadtmüller, OP, Speyer
Original in Convent Archive of the Dominican Sisters in Speyer

J.M.

Pax Christi! Echt, April 7, 1942
Dear Sister Agnella,

I return your kind pre-Lenten greeting with sincere wishes for many blessings for all at St. Magdalena's and the daughter-houses, especially to Sister Callista <Kopf>. Is she home again?

I had also heard from Valkenburg that P.P. <Pater Przywara, SJ> is not well. There they believe he is in Munich but do not know in which house of the Jesuits. If it is possible for you to send him my greetings I would be most grateful. Perhaps it would interest him that I am permitted to work on a *Kreuzeswissenschaft [Science of the Cross]* in honor of [St.]

John of the Cross and that in all my work I have been helped most effectively by [the Jesuits at] Valkenburg.

Humanly speaking, my sister Rosa and I are in a somewhat precarious situation. But as far as we know there will be no change before the end of the war. We are leaving everything confidently to Providence, and calmly go about our duties.

Could you find out, perhaps through Ännchen Dursy, what has happened to Sr. Elizabeth <Dursy> and her family? We heard months ago that they are no longer in their old home.[1]

Since yesterday, we too have a Sister Elizabeth (of the Blessed Trinity[2]); on the 15th and 19th we are to have two more Clothing Ceremonies. Then all five of our postulants will have been transformed into novices.

In Corde Jesu, your
Teresa Benedicta a Cruce

1. [Ännchen was Sr. Elizabeth's sister. Edith is trying to get information about the fate of the Carmel of Kordel, near Trier. A rumor had spread that Kordel had been seized by the Gestapo, but it proved to be false.]
2. She was Prioress of the Carmel of Echt for many years, and died in 1971.

336. Letter to Sr. Maria Ernst, OCD, Carmel of Cologne
Original in Convent Archive of Cologne Carmel

J.M.

Pax Christi! Echt, April 9, 1942
Dear Sister Maria,

Last evening I received your dear letter of Joseph's Day [March 19]. I was able to read it without too much trouble and it made me very happy.[1] Precisely because our ways have to be so diverse, both by nature and by development, it means so much to me when they at times meet at a temporary goal.

I have to produce everything with a great deal of effort. To be sure, the building plan is another gift bestowed on me, i.e., it unfolds little by little, but I have to quarry the stones by myself, and prepare them, and drag them into place. Besides, while working on this task[2] it often happened when I was greatly exhausted that I had the feeling I could not penetrate to what I wished to say and to grasp. I already thought that it would always remain so. But now I feel I have renewed vigor for creative effort. Holy Father John gave me renewed impetus for some remarks concerning symbols. When I finish this manuscript I would like to send a German copy to P. Heribert[3] to have it duplicated for the monasteries.

The only reason I write so little is that I need all the time for Father John. Y.C. will understand and take my essays as letters as I take Y.C.'s letters as essays. Our Reverend Mother would be very grateful if Y.C. would order for us the beautiful Scheeben[4] book, to be sent to us with the bill by the book store. Since Monday, we have a Sister Elizabeth of the Blessed Trinity.[5]

Most cordially, Y.C.'s least Sister
Benedicta

1. The reference is to Sr. Maria's nearly indecipherable handwriting.
2. *Kreuzeswissenschaft [The Science of the Cross]*, Vol. I of *Edith Steins Werke.*
3. He was at that time Provincial of the German monasteries. By inference, as she speaks of a *German* "copy," it would appear the work was intended to be published also in the Dutch language.
4. Matthias Scheeben (1835-1888) was an influential German theologian, and this seems a reference to one of his books.
5. See Letter 335.

337. Letter to Hilde Vérène Borsinger, Bern, Switzerland
Original in private possession of Dr. Hilde Vérène Borsinger

J.M.

Pax Christi! Echt, April 9, 1942

Dear Gibi,

Now that, after years, I am out to pay my correspondence debts, I would also like to thank you sincerely for your kind note of January 23. Since I have had no further word from you, I take it that you have received [in Bern] the same answer we had here from the Superior General of the Carmelite Sisters of the Divine Heart[1]: that entering Switzerland is impossible.

At the end of January we had to go to Maastricht about our affairs and to Amsterdam at the end of March. We were assured that there could be no thought of emigrating before the end of the war. And we cannot possibly prepare today for what is going to happen then. So we continue to lead our lives calmly and leave the future to him who alone knows anything about it.

In the questionnaire we had to fill out we gave the U.S.A. as our destination. In the meantime, I have also received a letter from a Spanish Carmel[2] urging me to come there, but that would also be impossible now.

I sent the information for our siblings and our Provincial in the U.S.A.[3] to an acquaintance in Canton Bern (because at that time I did not yet have your address) but received no reply, so I do not know whether the letter reached him or whether he forwarded it. Would you, perhaps, inquire about it sometime? The address is: Dr. Sieben, Lotzwil.[4]

Do you hear from P. Prz<ywara>? They say he is not well.[5]

Sincerest thanks for all your efforts and all the graces of the Easter season, your

Sister Teresa Benedicta a Cruce, OCD

1. [This is a congregation of active Sisters, not cloistered contemplative nuns. They were to provide a place for Rosa Stein while Sr. Teresa Benedicta was to go to the Carmel of Le Pâquier, Switzerland.]
2. [The Carmel in Spain has not been definitely identified. Since Edith's friend, Frau Anna Reinach, found refuge for a time in Spain, it is assumed that a Carmel she befriended is meant. Further inquiries will hopefully establish its identity.]
3. [This provincial was Fr. Cornelius Leunissen, OCD, who had become an American citizen when he was Master of Novices for the American communities of Discalced Carmelite friars founded from the Bavarian Province. See Letter 293, n. 1. The story of his escape is told in *Edith Stein: Philosopher and Mystic* (Collegeville, MN: Liturgical Press, 1990) pp. 169-170. Since his escape route took him through southern Europe, he might also have attempted to interest a Spanish Carmel in offering refuge to Edith.]
4. [See Letter 205. Dr. Sieben was Jewish and fled to Switzerland, probably before that country was so inundated by refugees that, as in Edith's case, entry was delayed or denied.]
5. [Erich Przywara was born October 12, 1889, in Kattowicz, Upper Silesia (now Katowice, Poland). When he was 18 he entered the Jesuit order in Holland. While at Valkenburg, often mentioned later by Edith, he became interested in the writings of John Henry Cardinal Newman. He was instrumental in having Edith translate Newman into German. P. Przywara helped to publish the magazine *Stimmen der Zeit (Voices of the Times)*, which drew strong opposition from the Nazis and was suppressed by them in 1941. Under great difficulties and danger, P. Przywara continued his ministry of preaching and writing in Munich and environs, but the stress undermined his health. His close friend Hans Urs von Balthasar was able to get P.P into Switzerland for medical attention. His illness was most severe from 1945 to 1951 and he retired to live and write in the country. Fr. Przywara was very ill in these years, but despite his precarious health he was very active in giving spiritual guidance, conferences (including radio addresses) and a steady stream of writings until he died in Germany on September 28, 1972.]

338. Letter in French to Mother Marie Agnes de Wolff, OCD,[1] Le Pâquier
Original in Convent Archive of Le Pâquier Carmel

Echt, July 24, 1942

My dear Reverend Mother,

Today we received your good letter. I thank you with all my heart for being willing to accept me as a member of your dear family—yours and that of all my dear sisters. I am unable to tell you how touched I am by your goodness and even more that of the Good God. You will understand it even better after you have heard the history of our lives and that of our family. We will now see if it is possible to get permission to leave the Netherlands. But it will probably take much time—months I suppose. I shall have to be content with such a promise.

Our dear Reverend Mother and my sister Rosa will add a few lines. Again, a thousand thanks, my dear Reverend Mother, and the expression of my respectful love in Jesus Christ.

Your very little and humble, unworthy,[2]
Sr. Teresa Benedicta a Cruce, OCD

[To Edith's French letter is appended a note in German from Rosa Stein:]

Dear Reverend Mother Prioress,

May God reward Your Reverence and the Reverend Mother Prioress of the Convent of the Tertiaries for the great love and goodness with which Your Reverence and the other Mother Prioress are ready to receive us.

With respectful greetings, in deep gratitude,
unworthy[2] Rosa Stein

1. Emma de Wolff (Sr. Marie Agnes de L'Immaculee Conception, OCD) (b. Switzerland, 1880; d. Le Pâquier/Fribourg, Switzerland, 1967). Foundress and longtime Prioress of the Carmel of Le Pâquier.
2. This form of closing the letter is given in the old custom books for letters from a nun to her Superior.

339. Letter to Auguste Pérignon,[1] Ludwigshafen
Original in private possession of Auguste Pérignon

J.M.

Pax Christi! Echt, July 29, 1942

Sincere thanks for your kind note. R.I.P. for your dear brother. You will be grateful that he has found release. Since you are informed about us, I need only tell you the latest: Switzerland wishes to open its doors to my sister Rosa and myself, since the only cloistered monastery of our Order in that country—Le Pâquier in the Canton Fribourg—will receive me, and a Convent of the Third Order Carmelites an hour away [from the Carmel], my sister. The two houses have certified, to the aliens' office of the police, that they will provide for us for our lifetimes. The big question remains: will we be given permission here [by the Nazi occupation forces] to leave [the country]. In any case, it will probably take a long time. I would not be sad if it did not come. After all, it is no slight matter to leave a beloved monastic family the second time. But I will accept whatever God arranges. Will you please tell them in Speyer and Kordel about this and ask for prayers?

To you and all who continue to think of me, cordial greetings. *In Corde Jesu,* your

Teresa Benedicta a Cruce

1. Auguste Pérignon (b. Landstuhl, 1886; d. Speyer, 1971) teacher; colleague of Edith Stein at the Dominican college in Speyer; a relative of Sr. Agnella Stadtmüller, OP.

340. Letter to Mother Ambrosia Antonia Engelmann, OCD, Echt
Original in Convent Archive of Beek Carmel

Drente-Westerbork, Barracks 36, August 4, 1942

Dear Mother and Sisters,

During the past night we left the transit-station A. <Amersfoort> and landed here early this morning. We were given a very friendly reception here. They intend to do everything possible to enable us to be freed or at least that we may remain here.+

<In the margin [near +] is written> Aug. 5: Is no longer possible.

All the Catholics are together and in our dormitory we have all the nuns (two Trappistines, one Dominican),[1] Ruth <Kantorowicz>, Alice <Reis>, Dr. [Lisamaria] Meirowsky, and others are here. Two Trappist Fathers from T.[2] are also with us. In any case, it will be necessary for you to send us our personal credentials, our ID cards, and our ration cards. So far we have lived entirely on the generosity of the others. We hope you have found the address of the Consul and have been in touch with him. We have asked many people to relay news to you. The two dear children from Koningsbosch <Annemarie and Elfriede Goldschmidt>[3] are with us. We are very calm and cheerful. Of course, so far there has been no Mass and Communion; maybe that will come later. Now we have a chance to experience a little how to live purely from within. Sincerest greetings to all. We will probably write again soon.

In Corde Jesu, your

B.

When you write, please do not mention that you got this.

[From Rosa:]

Sincere greetings to all. We are very sorry not to have seen Mother Ottilia any more. In this brief time we have experienced a great deal; one lives together with the others and everywhere people help each other. We have slept very little, but have had a lot of good air and much traveling. Many greetings to Sophie, Maria <Delsing> too, and to everyone; they were so upset; we not at all.

In Corde Jesu we all find ourselves in gratitude.

Rosa

<Edith Stein enclosed in this letter the following message written by herself on a separate piece of paper>:

Carmelite Monastery Echt
Bovenstestraat 48

Sister Teresia Benedicta a Cruce (Edith Stein)
Rosa Stein,
Swiss Consulate, Amsterdam C., Heerengracht 545,
Enable us as soon as possible to cross the border. Our monastery will take care of travel expenses.

1. [These were the religious women besides Edith and Rosa.]

2. [The two Trappists were from Tilburg, Holland and were blood brothers of the two Trappistine sisters already mentioned.]
3. [They were only 20 and 19 years old. As none of those mentioned in Edith's note survived their journey to Auschwitz, it is presumed that all those collected in this specific roundup in Holland on August 2 died together on the following Sunday upon arrival at Auschwitz. Their stories and those of the Lob family (the Trappist priests and nuns) are told in *Als Een Brandende Toorts,* published in 1967 by friends of Edith Stein in Holland.]

341. Letter to Mother Ambrosia Antonia Engelmann, OCD, Echt
Original in Convent Archive of Beek Carmel

<Drente-Westerbork, Barracks 36>, August 5 <1942>

My dear Ones,

A R. C. nurse from A.[1] intends to speak today with the Consul. Here, every petition [on behalf] of fully Jewish Catholics has been forbidden since yesterday. Outside [the camp] an attempt can still be made, but with extremely little prospect. According to plans, a transport will leave on Friday. Could you possibly write to Mère Claire in Venlo, Kaldenkerkeweg 185 [the Ursuline Convent] to ask for our [my] manuscript[2] if they have not already sent it. We count on your prayers. There are so many persons here who need some consolation and they expect it from the Sisters.

In Corde Jesu, your grateful
B.

1. A Red Cross nurse from Amsterdam.
2. Completed portions of the unfinished manuscript *Kreuzeswissenschaft [The Science of the Cross]*; they were in the care of Ruth Kantorowicz for typing when she was arrested at the Convent of the Ursulines in Venlo. [A laywoman, Ruth was in the same transport as Edith and presumably died the same way on the same day as Edith and Rosa, and the others mentioned in the previous letter.] The manuscript was published as Vol. I in *Edith Steins Werke.*

342. Letter to Mother Ambrosia Antonia Engelmann, OCD, Echt
Original in Convent Archive of Beek Carmel

J.M.

Drente-Westerbork, Barracks 36, August 6, 1942[1]

Dear Mother,

A Mother Superior from one of the convents arrived last evening with suitcases for her child and now offers to take some short letters along. Early tomorrow a transport leaves (Silesia or Czechoslovakia??).

What is most necessary: woolen stockings, two blankets. For Rosa all the warm underwear and whatever was in the laundry; for us both towels and wash cloths. Rosa also has no toothbrush, no Cross and no rosary. I would like the next volume of the breviary (so far I have been able to pray gloriously). Our identity cards, registration cards [as Jews], and ration cards.

A thousand thanks, greetings to all, Y.R.'s grateful child,

B.

<P.S.> 1 habit and aprons, 1 small veil[2]

1. Edith wrote the numbers of the date in error as 6.IV.1942 (which would have been April) instead of the correct date 6.VIII.1942. Likewise on the envelope she gave as return address Barrack 16, but on the letter itself the correct 36.
2. [Every Sister had three types of veil as part of her religious clothing: 1) the small veil, black, with gathers above the forehead where pins attach it to the unstarched, white-linen headpiece known as the toque; 2) the Communion veil, without gathers, but the same measurements as the small veil, over which it was worn for the recitation of the Divine Office in choir, and with the white mantle, at Mass. Then, 3) the large, or "grate" (not great) veil worn over one or both of the others, usually turned down to conceal the face whenever the Sisters had contact with or could be observed by persons outside the enclosure, especially at the grate or grille. In the best known portrait of Sr. Teresa Benedicta she wears the grate veil turned back, as it was her passport photo.]

[Number 342 is the final letter. From the transport as it stopped in the Schifferstadt railway station, early on August 7, a woman in "dark clothing" identified herself as Edith Stein (she had acquaintances in that city) and left a message either orally or perhaps in writing: "We are travelling east."]

The last photo of Edith Stein (Sr. Teresa Benedicta), taken in the spring or summer of 1942.

Thematic Index

An alphabetical listing of addressees and persons mentioned in the letters may be found in the Editors' Foreword (pp. xv-xx). The following supplementary index is based upon the editors' list of major themes (pp. xii-xiii). References in both places are given according to the letter (not page) number.

I. CHARACTERISTICS OF EDITH STEIN

II. FAMILY AND PERSONAL LIFE

III. RELATIONSHIPS OUTSIDE FAMILY

IV. PROFESSIONAL LIFE AND RELATIONSHIPS

V. RELIGIOUS LIFE AND RELATIONSHIPS

The Institute of Carmelite Studies promotes research and publication in the field of Carmelite spirituality. Its members are Discalced Carmelites, part of a Roman Catholic community—friars, nuns and laity—who are heirs to the teaching and way of life of Teresa of Jesus and John of the Cross, men and women dedicated to contemplation and to ministry in the Church and the world. Information concerning their way of life is available through local diocesan Vocation Offices, or from the Vocation Director's Office, 1525 Carmel Road, Hubertus, WI 53033.